Schools and Delinquency

Schools and Delinquency provides a comprehensive review of the current research about the causes of delinquency, substance abuse, dropout and truancy, and the role of the school in preventing delinquent behavior patterns. Examining school-based prevention programs and practices for grades kindergarten through 12, Denise Gottfredson identifies a broad array of effective strategies geared toward improving the school environment as well as some that specifically target youths at risk for developing problem behaviors. She also explains why several popular school-based prevention strategies are ineffective and should be abandoned. Gottfredson analyzes, within the larger context of the community, the special challenges to effective programming that arise in disorganized settings, identifying ways to overcome these obstacles and make the most troubled schools safer and more productive environments.

In the wake of highly publicized incidents of violence in American schools, this book offers a timely focus on school safety. It transcends the boundaries of psychology, sociology, and criminology to develop a broad understanding of the causes and prevention of delinquency in schools, from the earliest school ages through the teen years. In addition to scholars and researchers (in criminology, sociology, and psychology), educators, education policy makers and analysts, and social workers will find this invaluable reading. Gottfredson challenges many of our assumptions about the role of schools in fostering and preventing problem behavior.

Denise C. Gottfredson is Professor of Criminology at the University of Maryland and Vice President of Gottfredson Associates, Inc. She is coauthor of *Closing Institutions for Juvenile Offenders: The Maryland Experience* (1997) and *Victimization in Schools* (1985). Her articles have appeared in *American Sociological Review, Criminology, Journal of Research in Crime and Delinquency, Journal of Quantitative Criminology, American Educational Research Journal, Journal of Personality and Social Psychology,* and *Journal of Consulting and Clinical Psychology* and other such publications.

Cambridge Criminology Series

Editors
Alfred Blumstein, *The John Heinz School of Public Policy and Management,*
Carnegie Mellon University
David Farrington, *Institute of Criminology, University of Cambridge*

The Cambridge Criminology Series aims to publish the highest quality research on criminology and criminal justice topics. Typical volumes report major quantitative, qualitative, and ethnographic research, or make a substantial theoretical contribution. There is a particular emphasis on research monographs, but edited collections may also be published if they make an unusually distinctive offering to the literature. All relevant areas of criminology and criminal justice are to be included, for example, the causes of offending, juvenile justice, the development of offenders, measurement and analysis of crime, victimization research, policing, crime prevention, sentencing, imprisonment, probation, parole, and more. The series is global in outlook, with an emphasis on work that is comparative or holds significant implications for theory or policy.

Other books in the series:

Life in the Gang: Family, Friends, and Violence, by Scott H. Decker and Barrik Van Winkle
Delinquency and Crime: Current Theories, edited by J. David Hawkins
Recriminalizing Delinquency: Violent Juvenile Crime and Juvenile Justice Reform, by Simon I. Singer
Mean Streets: Youth, Crime, and Homelessness, by John Hagan and Bill McCarthy
Criminality and Violence among the Mentally Disordered, by Sheilagh Hodgins and Karl-Gunnar Janson
The Framework of Judicial Sentencing: A Study in Legal Decision Making, by Austin Lovegrove
The Criminal Recidivism Process, by Edward Zamble and Vernon L. Quinsey
Judicial Policy Making and the Modern State: How the Courts Reformed America's Prisons, by Malcolm M. Feeley and Edward L. Rubin

Schools and Delinquency

Denise C. Gottfredson

University of Maryland

CAMBRIDGE
UNIVERSITY PRESS

PUBLISHED BY THE PRESS SYNDICATE OF THE UNIVERSITY OF CAMBRIDGE
The Pitt Building, Trumpington Street, Cambridge, United Kingdom

CAMBRIDGE UNIVERSITY PRESS
The Edinburgh Building, Cambridge CB2 2RU, UK
40 West 20th Street, New York, NY 10011-4211, USA
10 Stamford Road, Oakleigh, VIC 3166, Australia
Ruiz de Alarcón 13, 28014 Madrid, Spain
Dock House, The Waterfront, Cape Town 8001, South Africa

http://cambridge.org

First published 2001

Printed in the United States of America

Typeface New Baskerville 10/13 pt.   *System* QuarkXPress [BTS]

A catalog record for this book is available from the British Library.

Library of Congress Cataloging in Publication data

Gottfredson, Denise C.
    Schools and delinquency / Denise C. Gottfredson.
    p.   cm. – (Cambridge criminology series)
    Includes bibliographical references (p.   ) and index (p.   ).
    ISBN 0-521-62324-3 (hard). – ISBN 0–521–62629-3 (pbk.)
    1. Juvenile delinquency – United States – Prevention.   2. Deviant behavior
– United States – Prevention.   3. Education and crime – United States.
4. Problem children – Education – United States.   5. Problem youth –
Education – United States.   I. Title.   II. Series.
HV9104.G63335   2000
364.36'0973 – dc21   99-42107
                                                                          CIP

ISBN   0 521 62324 3   hardback
ISBN   0 521 62629 3   paperback

B+T
NR/EN

To Gary, for your inspiration and support

Contents

Tables and Figure

Tables

Figure

Acknowledgments

I am indebted to Stacy Skroban, John (JT) Ridgely, and Todd Armstrong for major research assistance in the preparation of this book. I am also grateful for the constructive comments of my colleagues Gary Gottfredson, Ray Paternoster, Kathryn Russell, and David Wilson. Shannon Womer, Veronica Puryear, and Nicole Leeper provided library assistance and coding. Thanks also to the series editors, David Farrington and Alfred Blumstein, for support and to the staff at Cambridge University Press. Finally, I wish to acknowledge the financial support of the University of Maryland Graduate School and the moral support of all of my colleagues at the university. I express my most sincere thanks to all of these individuals. I also wish to acknowledge the National Institute of Justice for supporting work that contributed to the writing of this book.

School's Potential as a Location for Delinquency Prevention

The salutary effects of school experiences are ordinarily taken very much for granted by most parents, teachers, principals, and others. . . . In the case of the . . . delinquent sample of school children who were manifesting aggressive-delinquent behavior, however, much of the school data point to a multiplicity of unwholesome, unsatisfactory, unhappy, and frustrating situations in which the delinquents were enmeshed. These data suggest that the school may be full of predisposing stimuli which elicit aggression responses on the part of the maladjusted child. (Kvaraceus, 1945, p. 135)

One of the situations in which children of all social levels come together and compete for status in terms of the same set of middle-class criteria and in which working-class children are most likely to be found wanting is in the school. . . . To the degree to which [a boy] values middle-class status, either because he values the good opinion of middle-class persons or because he has to some degree internalized middle-class standards himself, he faces a problem of adjustment and is in the market for a "solution." The delinquent subculture, we suggest, is a way of dealing with the problems of adjustment we have just described. (Cohen, 1955, pp. 112, 119, 121)

If the adolescent male fails in school or drops out, or for other reasons finds school roles unsatisfactory or unplayable, he finds himself in an institutional void. . . . A high incidence of delinquent behavior indicates a breakdown of the machinery through which the needs of different segments of the population are met through conventional institutions. (Shaw and McKay, 1969, pp. 384, 385)

Schools may prevent delinquency if they successfully socialize people to fit into the society, yet the schools cause delinquency in those who reject that socialization. If the economy and society demand that most people engage in alienating labor and exhibit obedience to authority, the schools will try to prepare them for such a life. Those students who refuse the precast mold and react with anger, resistance, and rebellion become "delinquents." The very refusal to fit *is* delinquency. (Liazos, 1978, p. 368)

Even without parental support, in our view, the net effect of the school must be positive. As a result of the school experience, some students learn better to appreciate the advantages and opportunities associated with self-control and are thus effectively socialized regardless of their familial experiences. One of the major school correlates of crime has always been the mundane homework. Those who do it are by definition thinking about tomorrow. Those who do not do it have a shorter time frame. One mark of socialization is considering the consequences of today's activities for tomorrow. Homework thus indexes and perhaps contributes to socialization. (Gottfredson and Hirschi, 1990, p. 106)

MOST CRIMINOLOGICAL perspectives on the causes of delinquency have implicated schools. But criminologists disagree about the mechanism through which schools influence delinquency and even the direction of the influence.

Strain theorists (exemplified by Cohen, 1955) claim that delinquent behavior is a natural reaction to a system that judges all school students according to the same "middle-class measuring rod," despite differences in students' opportunities to achieve these standards. Youths whose behavior does not conform with teachers' expectations feel the strain associated with failure and rebel against middle-class norms. Schools are therefore an important part of the social mechanism that creates delinquent behavior. Reorganizing schools to increase the ratio of success to failure experiences and exposure to accepting adults (Gold, 1978) should reduce delinquency.

Marxist theorists (exemplified by Bowles and Gintis, 1976; Greenberg, 1977; and Liazos, 1978) see no possible solutions *in school* to the delinquency problem as long as schools must prepare students for alienated work. Schools in capitalist societies merely socialize youths for the lives and jobs to which they are destined. Schools succeed in teaching most youths from middle- and working-class backgrounds to be obedient and disciplined and to accept their fates. Those youths who refuse the "precast mold" become delinquents. The roots of crime are found in the economic system that determines the function of schools. A socialist society in which students prepare for meaningful work would experience less delinquency.

Social disorganization theorists (exemplified by Shaw and McKay, 1969) also place the social and economic system at the root of the crime problem. When cities grow, business and industry "invade" residential areas and cause a disintegration of the community as a unit of social control. A population shift occurs, as residents with resources move toward the outskirts of the city and new immigrant or other disadvantaged populations replace them. The rapid population shift diminishes the capacity of community organizations – including schools – to socialize the population effectively. Cultural and language barriers and relative anonymity prevent effective communication and community problem solving. According to this perspective, schools are only a part of a larger community disintegration process that allows delinquency to flourish.

Social control theorists (exemplified by Hirschi, 1969) assign schools a critical role in restraining delinquent behavior. Schools provide opportunities and incentives for youths to develop attachments to prosocial others and commitment to conventional pursuits. They provide instruction and reinforcement for the development of self-control. Although the family is the first and most important source of social control, the school provides an important backup system. When schools fail in their role as secondary socializing agents, youths are more likely to act on their natural impulses toward self-gratifying and delinquent behaviors.

Routine activity theorists (exemplified by Cohen and Felson, 1979; Felson and Cohen, 1980) see schools as a place where crime is likely to occur. According to this perspective, a crime is more likely to occur when a motivated offender is in the same place as an attractive target in the absence of a capable guardian. Because schools assemble large numbers of members of the most delinquent segment of the population (teenage boys) in a place in which other teenagers are displaying desirable goods (CDs, designer jackets, concert tickets, electronics, etc.), crime is likely to occur unless the place is protected by capable guardians – guards, watchful school staff, or managers.

These and other perspectives on the causes of delinquency suggest that the role of schools in the generation of delinquent behavior is complex. The schooling process might increase delinquency by alienating certain youths from sources of reward and satisfaction and decrease delinquency by providing additional sources of social control. A particular school might increase delinquency by bringing together motivated offenders in time and space without effective guardianship or decrease it by providing a watchful environment that effectively reinforces appropriate and punishes inappropriate behavior. At the very least, schools have potential as a control agent simply because they occupy large segments of time for teenagers. School environments can be structured to minimize opportunities for delinquent behavior during the school day. But schools also have the potential to influence delinquency that occurs outside of school by providing a convenient setting for prevention activities.

In this book I explain the mechanisms through which schools affect levels of delinquent behavior and suggest ways in which schools might be organized and managed to increase their potential to prevent delinquency. This chapter defines "delinquency," summarizes what is known about the association of these behaviors with gender and age, and examines evidence relating the status of being in school with delinquency.

Definition of Delinquency

Delinquency – broadly defined in this book as problem behavior displayed by a minor – includes such behaviors as cussing at a teacher, biting a classmate, shirking homework, being late to class, writing on school walls, cheating on tests, bullying classmates, lying, fighting, stealing, joyriding, drinking alcohol, having sex, selling drugs, assaulting or robbing others, setting fire to property, raping, and murdering. These behaviors have in common the inability or unwillingness to curb natural impulses to pursue pleasure or to relieve sources of irritation.

The narrower definition of delinquency commonly found in criminological work – behavior in violation of the law – fails to distinguish between the actual delinquent behavior and the sanction applied as a result of the behavior. Many acts are behaviorally analogous to crime in terms of their causation, and attempts to understand their causes are unnecessarily constrained when the dependent variable is restricted to illegal acts.

This perspective on the nature of delinquent behavior seems especially appropriate for the study of schooling and delinquency. In this book, I explore mechanisms through which schooling or exposure to particular school environments influences levels of problem behavior. Many of the behaviors of concern to schoolteachers and administrators are not criminal per se, but are disruptive and often harmful to the child who presents it as well as to other students. Limiting attention to school's effects on behavior specifically defined as criminal would overlook effects on younger children (whose defiance and disobedient behavior are most often not defined as criminal) and on other problematic but not necessarily illegal adolescent behaviors. In short, delinquency is defined here according to Gottfredson and Hirschi's (1990) definition of crime: behavior involving the use of force or fraud, acts of defiance and disobedience, and acts that deliberately cause harm to self or others.

Rates of Delinquency

All children engage in problem behavior, and most learn to limit the amount of such behavior they display as they mature. The selfish or harmful exploratory behavior displayed by very young children is usually not labeled delinquency by observers, of course. Behaviorally, however, a toddler's attempts to poke her parent's eyes with a pencil or her act of reaching out of a shopping cart in a grocery store to grab an apple and put it directly in her mouth are both clear examples of unrestrained problem behavior. Nearly all children learn to restrain themselves from displaying most of this kind of behavior rather quickly.

Most young people also engage in problem behavior that is more easily recognized as delinquent. Three-fourths of high school seniors report having drunk alcohol in the last year, and half have gotten drunk. More than half of high school students have had sex. A third of high school seniors have stolen property, and 40% have been involved in a physical fight. In fact, *most* young people report behavior that everyone considers criminal: in 1976, 76% and 52% of the nation's male and female eleven-through seventeen-year-olds reported being involved in some form of delinquent behavior (Elliott, Huizinga, and Menard, 1989).

Estimates of the level of delinquency are often obtained from official records (e.g., schools, police, courts) and youth self-reports, and somewhat less often from reports of parents or teachers about youth behavior. These methods complement one another and together form the scientific literature on the prevalence and incidence of delinquent behavior.

Arrest Rates

The Federal Bureau of Investigation's Uniform Crime Reports (UCR) show age-specific arrest rates for "index offenses" each year in the United States: serious violent index crimes include murder and nonnegligent manslaughter, forcible rape, aggravated assault, and robbery; serious property index crimes include burglary, larceny-theft, and motor vehicle theft. Another category of crimes reported by the FBI includes drug abuse violations, which include unlawful possession, sale, use, growing, and manufacturing of narcotic drugs. Uniform Crime Reports show that arrests for all types of crimes are much higher for males than for females, and that arrests increase from low rates for young children, peak between ages 16 and 18, and then decline (U.S. Department of Justice, 1993). The peak comes earlier for property crimes (age 16) than for violent and drug-related crimes (age 18).

The relation of crime as measured by official data to age and gender appears nearly universal and has led to speculation about age-related conditions or characteristics that might produce the association. Several factors have been hypothesized, the most credible of which are declining parental supervision and control and increasing peer influence during adolescence (Farrington, 1986a).[1] Participation in school is another age-related condition that has been linked with delinquency. Evidence pertaining to this association is examined later in this chapter.

---

[1] Hirschi and Gottfredson (1983) suggest that age has a direct effect on crime that transcends social explanations of crime. They argue that contemporary explanations for the age-crime curve are inadequate because they cannot possibly explain the similar age-crime association at other places and in other times (e.g., in England and Wales in the 1840s) when social conditions for adolescents were very different. Others (Farrington, 1986a; Steffensmeier, Allan, Harer, and Streifel, 1989) believe that subtle differences in the age-crime curve across time and space and for different types of crime are meaningful and encourage continued inquiry into age-related explanations for crime.

Juvenile arrests for serious crimes are relatively rare. Uniform Crime Reports for 1996 (Snyder, 1997) show that approximately 2,400 arrests for serious property crimes were made per 100,000 youths between ages 10 and 17, accounting for 35% of all such arrests. Approximately 465 arrests for serious violent crimes were made per 100,000 youths between ages 10 and 17, accounting for 19% of all such arrests. More than one-quarter of all juvenile arrests are for status offenses (e.g., liquor law violations, disorderly conduct, curfew violations, and running away). Offenses that result in the greatest number of juvenile arrests are larceny-theft, simple assaults, disorderly conduct, drug abuse violations, runaways, curfew violations, and liquor law violations. In 1996 these offenses accounted for 60% of all juvenile arrests.

The official crime statistics summarized so far tell us about neither the proportion of individuals at different ages who are engaged in crime nor the level of offending for those engaged in crime. These two dimensions have been separated in a comprehensive National Research Council study of criminal behavior (Blumstein, Cohen, Roth, and Visher, 1986). U.S. studies using official records to measure the prevalence of arrest in particular birth cohorts (e.g., a 1945 Philadelphia birth cohort of males or a 1955 birth cohort of residents in Racine, Wisconsin) indicate that the percentage of males having some kind of nontraffic arrest or police contact prior to their eighteenth birthday ranges from 25% to 47%. The comparable prevalence rate for arrests for the more serious "index" offenses, based only on data from Philadelphia residents, is about 15% for males and about 4% for females. Rates of arrest frequency are more difficult to obtain, but one estimate (also derived from the 1945 Philadelphia birth cohort) is that active male juvenile offenders are arrested at average annual frequencies of .23 for robbery, .13 for other violent index offenses, and .41 for property index offenses, with an overall frequency for all offenses of .84 arrests per year. Farrington (1986a) decomposed the age-crime curve into portions due to prevalence and incidence (defined as the rate of individual offending). He found that for both officially recorded and self-reported crime, the peak in crime during the teenage years is due primarily to an increase in the proportion of youths engaged in crime rather than an increase in the rate of offending for those engaged in crime.

Average frequency rates mask an important feature of offending: a small percentage of offenders is responsible for a disproportionate number of offenses. In the Philadelphia study 6% of the boys was responsible for 52% of the police contacts found for the entire study population (Wolfgang, Figlio, and Sellin, 1972). The distribution of self-reported crimes across individuals is also lopsided. Elliott, Huizinga, and Menard (1989) found, for example, that the 8.6% of the total sample identified as "serious" offenders was responsible for 62% of all general offenses reported and over 75% of the reported index offenses.

Self-Reports

A more complete understanding of the prevalence of delinquent behavior can be obtained from self-reports. One useful source is the survey of U.S. high school seniors, Monitoring the Future (MTF; Bachman, Johnston, and O'Malley, 1993), conducted annually by the Institute for Social Research at the University of Michigan. Table 1.1 shows the percentage of 1993 U.S. high school seniors admitting involvement in various delinquent activities during the preceding twelve months. As with the official records, the least-serious problem behaviors are the most prevalent: 88% of high school seniors fought with their parents in the past year, 32% engaged in minor theft; and 26% trespassed. More serious transgressions are relatively rare: fewer than 10% of youths reported that they engaged in arson (3%), hit an instructor or supervisor (4%), strong-armed a person (5%), or took a car without permission (6%); 18% of the youths engaged in serious fighting, with 13% admitting to hurting their victims badly; between 11% and 15% of youths reported crimes involving major theft and property damage; and only 10% reported being arrested. The self-reports also show males to be far more active than females in every form of delinquent behavior except arguing with parents.

Table 1.2 shows prevalence rates for alcohol and substance abuse by adolescents (Johnston, O'Malley, and Bachman, 1994). These data also come from MTF, but, unlike the delinquency data shown in Table 1.1 for students in grade 12, substance use data were also collected for students in grades 8 and 10. Table 1.2 shows that the use of all substances except heroin increases with age. Also, the more harmful and more addictive drugs are far less prevalent than alcohol and marijuana. Approximately the same percentage of females and males reported using alcohol, and only a slightly higher percentage of males reported using marijuana. Gender differences are noticeable for the more exotic substances but never reach the magnitude observed for other criminal behaviors.

Table 1.3 shows prevalence rates for several health-risk behaviors reported in a nationally representative sample of students in grades 9 through 12 in 1993 – the Youth Risk Behavior Surveillance System (YRBSS) Survey (Centers for Disease Control and Prevention, 1995). This survey shows that fighting is common among high school students (42% engaged in physical fighting in the preceding year), and that weapon *carrying* is higher than suggested in other surveys that asked only about weapon *use*: 22% of students reported carrying a dangerous weapon in the past thirty days, and 8% reported carrying a gun. Risky sexual behavior for adolescents is common: 53% reported they are sexually active, and 19% reported having had four or more sex partners in their lifetime. Only slightly more than half of sexually active students reported using a condom during their most recent sexual intercourse. Males engage in health risk behaviors more

Table 1.1. *Percentage of High School Seniors Reporting Involvement in Selected Delinquent Activities in Past 12 Months, Class of 1993*

Delinquent Activity	Males (N = 1,294)	Females (N = 1,321)	Total (N = 2,770)
Interpersonal			
Argued or had a fight with either of your parents	84.5	92.0	87.9
Hit an instructor or supervisor	5.7	1.7	3.8
Gotten into a serious fight in school or at work	21.6	13.0	17.7
Taken part in a fight where a group of your friends were against another group	29.0	14.5	22.2
Hurt someone badly enough to need bandages or a doctor	21.4	5.0	13.4
Used a knife or gun or some other thing (like a club) to get something from a person	8.1	1.0	4.6
Property			
Taken something not belonging to you worth under $50	40.1	23.5	32.1
Taken something not belonging to you worth over $50	17.5	4.4	11.3
Taken something from a store without paying for it	37.6	23.3	30.7
Taken a car that didn't belong to someone in your family without permission of the owner	8.8	3.8	6.4
Taken part of a car without permission of the owner	12.5	2.1	7.3
Gone into some house or building when you weren't supposed to be there	34.1	17.5	26.3
Set fire to someone's property on purpose	5.9	.9	3.4
Damaged school property on purpose	22.3	7.2	14.7
Damaged property at work on purpose	11.5	2.0	6.4
Other			
Been arrested and taken to a police station	14.5	4.5	9.6

Source: Bachman, Johnston, and O'Malley, 1993.

Table 1.2. *Percentage of Students Reporting Substance Use in Past 12 Months, by Gender and Grade, 1993*

| | Grade 8 | | | Grade 10 | | | Grade 12 | | |
| | M | F | T | M | F | T | M | F | T |
Substance	(N = 8,600)	(N = 9,200)	(N = 18,300)	(N = 7,300)	(N = 7,800)	(N = 15,300)	(N = 7,500)	(N = 8,200)	(N = 16,300)
Alcohol[a]	51.8	52.3	51.6	68.9	69.6	69.3	75.9	76.0	76.0
Been drunk[b]	17.8	18.8	18.2	38.6	36.9	37.8	53.4	46.1	49.6
Marijuana	10.5	8.0	9.2	21.2	16.9	19.2	29.0	22.4	26.0
Cocaine	1.9	1.5	1.7	2.5	1.6	2.1	4.0	2.3	3.3
Heroin	.8	.5	.7	.9	.4	.7	.7	.3	.5

Notes: The number of cases for each group appears at the head of each column. M = male, F = female, T = total.
[a]Data based on one of two questionnaire forms for eighth and tenth grades and on three of six forms for the twelfth grade. N is one-half of N indicated for all grades.
[b]Twelfth grade only: data based on five of six questionnaire forms. N is five-sixths of N indicated.
Source: Johnston, O'Malley, and Bachman, 1994.

Table 1.3. *Percentage of High School Students Reporting Involvement in Risk Behaviors in Past 12 Months,[a] 1993*

Health Risk Behavior	Males (N = 8,441)	Females (N = 7,855)	Total (N = 16,296)
Carried a weapon such as a gun, knife, or club in past 30 days	34.3	9.2	22.1
Carried a gun in past 30 days	13.7	1.8	7.9
In a physical fight at all	51.2	31.7	41.8
Injured in a physical fight	5.2	2.7	4.0
Had sexual intercourse ever in lifetime	55.6	50.2	53.0
Had four or more sex partners during lifetime	22.3	15.0	18.8
Condom use during last sexual intercourse, among sexually active students	59.2	46.0	52.8

[a] Unless otherwise indicated.
Source: Centers for Disease Control and Prevention, 1995.

than females do, but the differences for sexual behaviors, like those for alcohol and other drug use reported here, are not as great as for crimes against persons and property.

These surveys provide hints about how delinquent behaviors change with age. MTF shows sharp increases between grades 8 and 12 in all forms of substance use except heroin, which is extremely rare for all age groups. But the YRBSS shows decreases in fighting and weapon carrying between grades 9 and 12 (e.g., among ninth and twelfth graders 25.5% vs. 19.9% carried a weapon and 50.4% vs. 34.8% were in a physical fight). In cross-sectional studies of school populations such as these, differences in prevalence rates across age groups may be confounded with differences in absenteeism and dropout rates. They also fail to separate age effects from cohort effects.

The National Youth Survey (NYS; Elliott et al., 1989) is useful for separating these confounding effects.[2] This study initially surveyed a single cohort between ages 11 and 17 in 1976, then again in 1980 and 1983.

[2] Of course, age effects are confounded in this panel study with period effects. That is, changes in crime rates may be due to either the aging of the cohort or the influences specific to a particular time period. Farrington (1986a) examined crime rates as a function of age, period, and cohort and found that although period effects are clearly present (in England between 1961 and 1983), age effects are larger. Regardless of the period examined, crime rates increased from age 10 to 14.

Follow-up surveys were conducted with the entire cohort, regardless of the youths' dropout status. The percentage of youths who were age 11 in 1976 who reported involvement in general delinquency declined from 56.4% in 1976 to 46.7% in 1983, when they were age 17. Dramatic increases in annual prevalence were observed for alcohol use, other drug use, and public disorder offenses (including drunkenness and disorderly conduct). Felony theft and illegal services (e.g., drug selling and prostitution) also increased during this time, and minor theft increased only up to age 15. Decreases in annual prevalence were observed for crimes involving interpersonal aggression (assault and robbery). When the NYS data are used in this way to track prevalence for a specific aging cohort, they show that the annual prevalence of delinquency is already in decline at age 11 for assault and vandalism, and begins to decline at about age 15 for robbery and minor theft but not until age 17 for offenses involving drugs, alcohol, and illegal services. The behaviors that increase most rapidly during the period from ages 11 to 17 are those requiring access to alcohol or other drugs, motor vehicles (theft as measured in the NYS includes joyriding and auto theft), and sexual maturity. Offenses for which the opportunity does not increase in early adolescence such as minor assault (hitting others) and vandalism (damaging property) decline beginning in the junior high school years.

Parent and Teacher Reports

Epidemiological studies of antisocial behavior cover wider age ranges than typical self-report surveys. Although rare, these studies provide important information about the early development of delinquent behavior. The Ontario Child Health Study (OCHS; Offord, Boyle, and Racine, 1991) – a provincewide prevalence survey of emotional and behavioral problems in children ages 4–16 conducted in 1983 – obtained teacher and parent reports of child problem behavior, as well as self-reports for youths ages 12–16. Table 1.4 shows the percentage of youths in each of two broad age groups displaying a variety of conduct problems according to each type of rater. Several patterns are evident. Some behaviors are much more common than others. "Lies and cheats" and "gets in many fights" are far more prevalent than "vandalism," "sets fires," and "runs away from home." With few exceptions, and regardless of age of respondent, boys display more problem behavior than girls. The only notable exceptions are cutting school, for which older girls self-report higher rates than boys, and running away, for which older girls both self-report and are reported by their parents as having higher rates. Important for understanding the development of delinquent behavior, the symptoms reported by parents generally *do not change appreciably* from childhood to adolescence except in the case of truancy, which rises dramatically for the older group. Early reports from

Table 1.4. *Percentage of Children, Ages 4–11 and 12–16, Displaying Conduct Problems According to Parent, Teacher, and Self-Report, 1983*

Symptoms	Boys (4–11)		Girls (4–11)		Boys (12–16)		Girls (12–16)	
	P	T	P	T	P	S	P	S
Interpersonal								
Physically attacks people	7.2	18.1	4.5	4.4	6.9	12.3	2.9	7.1
Gets in many fights	22.4	30.9	8.5	9.8	19.7	29.5	9.6	21.0
Threatens to hurt people	4.9	13.1	4.1	4.0	8.1	28.8	5.1	18.1
Property								
Destroys things belonging to others	13.2	10.6	6.3	4.4	9.8	14.3	3.8	7.6
Vandalism	.3	2.9	.1	.6	1.8	9.2	.2	4.6
Sets fires	1.5	.8	.2	.1	1.6	6.4	.1	1.9
Steals things at home[a]	2.5	—	2.8	—	5.8	10.0	3.8	9.5
Steals from places outside of home[a]	2.1	—	1.2	—	3.0	8.9	3.1	4.3
Other								
Cuts classes or skips school	.6	2.1	.3	1.8	7.6	14.9	6.2	18.4
Lies or cheats	28.0	23.4	21.8	12.1	26.0	34.8	21.2	33.6
Runs away from home[a]	.8	—	1.1	—	1.9	3.3	2.4	4.3

Notes: Percentages are the percentage of respondents who reported the behavior was "sometimes or somewhat true" or "often or very true" about the target child. P = parent, T = teacher, S = self-report.
[a]These items were omitted from the teacher form.
Source: Offord, Boyle, and Racine, 1991.

another large-scale epidemiological survey in Canada, the National Longitudinal Study of Children and Youth (Offord and Lipman, 1996; Tremblay, Boulerice, Harden, McDuff, Pérusse, Pihl, and Zoccolillo, 1996), show that rates of physical aggression as well as hyperactivity (both predictors of later delinquent behavior) actually decline from early childhood (ages 4–7) to preadolescence (ages 8–11).

These data reveal for the most part a continuity of problem behavior over the childhood years. A general trend toward socialization occurs during this time. With respect to physical aggression, this downward trend continues through adolescence. Two things change as children move into adolescence, however: opportunities for engaging in problem behavior increase, and adults react differently to misbehavior. Alcohol, other drugs, and weapons become more available to youths, thus increasing the potential harm to self and others resulting from their antisocial behavior. Work becomes available, providing discretionary money with which to purchase illegal commodities. Parental supervision diminishes. Association with delinquent peers becomes easier. These increases in opportunities for problem behavior explain the increase observed in certain types of problem behavior during adolescence. Also, whereas delinquent acts in early and middle childhood are usually responded to informally by parents and teachers, delinquent preadolescents and adolescents are more at risk for official sanction by police and the courts. This shift in response creates the appearance of a rapid increase in antisocial behavior in early adolescence when only official records are examined. As Farrington (1986a) pointed out, most studies of age and crime based on self-reports show crime peaking earlier than do studies based on official reports. In fact, fewer adolescents engage in antisocial behaviors during the high school years than in the years leading up to high school.

These facts about problem behavior – that it appears early in some individuals, is relatively stable during the childhood years, and increases during adolescence as opportunities increase – have certain implications for the practice of school-based prevention. Prevention activities should begin early and continue through childhood and into adolescence. They should focus on accelerating the socialization process for children who are already displaying problem behaviors. They should also focus on reducing opportunities for engaging in problem behaviors as youths move into adolescence. Schools have a role in preventing problem behavior both in school and out. Their access to children for extended periods places schools in a unique position to try to alter youthful dispositions toward problem behavior as well as opportunities to engage in these behaviors. The following section begins the discussion of school's role in prevention by examining whether simply being in school rather than out of school has the potential to reduce problem behavior.

Delinquency and Being in School

Do school-age youths engage in different amounts of delinquent behavior when they are participating in school than when they are not? This question can be answered at different levels, using different indicators of participation. The level of youth participation in schools varies over time and across geographic locations. If being in school influences the level of delinquency, we should observe covariation between aggregate rates of juvenile crime and the percentage of the school-age population enrolled in school. At the individual level, we should see evidence that youths who persist in school longer are more or less delinquent than youths who drop out of school, holding constant characteristics that would cause both delinquency and dropout. The timing of crime should also be related to when students are in and out of school.

Aggregate Rates of School Participation and Juvenile Crime

Over-Time Comparisons within the United States. The percentage of school-age youths enrolled in school has increased drastically over the past century. During the 1889–1890 school year, only 5.6% of the nation's youth between ages 14 and 17 were enrolled in a public or private school. This figure rose to 72.6% by 1940, 83.4% by 1960, 90.3% by 1980, and 93.7% by 1990 (National Center for Education Statistics, 1994). G. Gottfredson (1981) summarized changes in youth experiences that accompanied this large shift in the school enrollment status of youth. More so today than earlier in the century, youths are estranged from adults in an age-segregated system of compulsory schooling and spend much larger amounts of time in school as opposed to work or preparation for work. Greenberg (1977) argued that alienating youths from productive activity through compulsory schooling increases juvenile crime. If true, we should see a huge increase in juvenile crime during the past century. Unfortunately, reliable estimates of juvenile crime are not available before 1940, when the largest increase in school enrollment occurred. But rough comparisons can be made for the years between 1940 and 1980. Steffensmeier, Allan, Harer, and Streifel (1989) used UCR data to show that the peak age for crime generally decreased and the shape of the age distribution became more skewed between 1940 and 1980, suggesting a higher concentration of crime among the young in the later years. This general trend is consistent with the hypothesis that being enrolled in school increases the likelihood of criminal offending among school-age youths. But a more fine-grained comparison of the two twenty-year periods does not support the same conclusion. Steffensmeier et al. found that the downward shift in the age of crime commission was more apparent for the 1960 through 1980 than for the 1940 through 1960 period. But the percentage of school-age youths enrolled in school increased more dramatically between 1940 and 1960 than between 1960 and 1980.

The trend in the age distribution of crime documented by Steffensmeier et al. is more consistent with a weakened family than with an increased schooling hypothesis. Divorce rates in the United States climbed sharply between 1960 and 1980, leading to large increases in the number of children living with one parent. Hernandez (1994) showed that the proportion of children living with a mother only hovered around 7% until 1960, and then nearly tripled by 1990. This major demographic shift is a more likely candidate for explaining the trend toward younger offenders, especially after 1960. Aggregate comparisons such as these, though provocative, remain inconclusive as to the association between school enrollment and crime.

State-Level Comparisons within the United States. States differ in their laws regarding the age at which students may voluntarily leave school. Toby (1980, 1983, 1995) has long argued that compelling unwilling youths to attend school promotes a climate of violence and fear in public schools, makes it difficult for adults in the school to maintain control over student behavior, and reduces the ability of public school to compete with private schools. He presented data on number of referrals to the police for *school crimes* per 1,000 enrolled students in 1974–1975, showing lower average rates (8.0) in states with compulsory school attendance through age 15 and higher average rates (20.1) in states with compulsory schooling through age 18. Referrals per 1,000 elementary students were also somewhat higher in states with higher compulsory attendance ages.

More pertinent for the discussion at hand is whether the age of compulsory school attendance is related to juvenile crime *in general* rather than to crime that occurs only in school. It may well be that schools can achieve lower levels of in-school crime by allowing (or requiring) crime-prone youths to leave. But does lowering the compulsory school-leaving age decrease crime? McKissack (1973) argued that being in school is conducive to a delinquent life-style and showed that property offending in New Zealand peaks in the year prior to the official school-leaving age.

UCR data from the United States allow for a more recent comparison of juvenile crime rates for states with differing school-leaving ages. In 1992, thirty-two states required youths to stay in school until age 16. For nine states, the age of compulsory school attendance was 17 and for ten it was 18 (National Center for Education Statistics, 1994). If requiring school attendance of unwilling youths increases crime, higher rates of juvenile crime should be observed in the states with the higher compulsory attendance ages. State-by-state arrest rates are available in the UCR data base for forty-four of the fifty-one states.[3] The number of arrests in 1992 per 100,000 juveniles ages 10 through 17 was 2,975 in the twenty-eight states with a school-leaving age of 16, 2,758 in the seven states with a school-leaving age of 17, and 3,943 in the nine states with a school-leaving age of 18. The arrest rate for states that compel those through age 17 to stay in school is higher (p = .05) than for the other states, but the rate in states that require those through age 16 to stay in school is lower than in states that allow them to leave. Furthermore, three states for whom arrest rates are available changed their compulsory attendance laws between 1992 and 1994. One state (California) that decreased the age of compulsory education from 18 to 16 experienced a decrease in juvenile crime. But two states (Arkansas and New Mexico) that increased the compulsory education age to 18 also experienced a decrease in juvenile crime. These patterns are inconsistent with the hypothesis that compulsory education increases crime.

Earlier G. Gottfredson (1979) examined the same data on which Toby (1995) based his observations and concluded that the cross-sectional examination of state-level data produces untrustworthy results. He recommended the examination of time-series data to learn what happens when attendance laws change. It would be useful to supplement the casual observations summarized here with more careful time-series investigation of the effects of changing attendance laws.

Dropout Studies

Delinquency is highly related to educational attainment. School dropouts have higher rates of delinquency than high school graduates, and high school graduates in turn have higher rates of these behaviors than youths who continue their schooling beyond grade 12 (Bachman, O'Malley, and Johnston, 1978). Researchers and social scientists have scrutinized this association to clarify the causal mechanism underlying it. Much attention has been focused on understanding the extent to which the dropout decision increases, decreases, or is inconsequential to the rate of future offending.

Social control theory (Hirschi, 1969) predicts an increase in crime after dropout to the extent that school acts as a source of social control. Strain theory (Cohen, 1955) predicts a decrease in crime after school dropout because a major source of failure experiences and alienation is removed. Problem behavior theory (Jessor and Jessor, 1977) predicts no clear consequence for crime as a result of the dropout decision because dropout and delinquency are both manifestations of a disposition to problem behavior. Adolescents who hold nonconforming attitudes and

[3] The District of Columbia is included as a state.

values are more likely to engage in various forms of deviant behavior, and the decision to abandon the role of student is simply one more instance of deviance.

Research on the effects of dropout is particularly thorny. The topic does not lend itself to experimental study, and it is difficult to control statistically for the many common antecedents shared by delinquency and dropout. Also, it is difficult to disentangle effects of dropout from effects of aging. Early research, most notably two studies by Delbert Elliott (Elliott, 1966; Elliott and Voss, 1974), showed that delinquency was highest for dropouts just prior to leaving school and declined sharply after leaving, which they interpreted in support of the strain theory hypothesis. But the studies suffered from short follow-up periods and did not adequately control for age. The sharp drops in crime for the dropouts after leaving school might be explained by the older age of the dropouts (who are more likely to have been retained for one or more grades) compared with that of the graduates.

More recent research rejects the strain notion and suggests rather that dropout increases crime. Thornberry, Moore, and Christenson (1985), analyzing a random sample of youths from the Philadelphia cohort study, showed that crime peaks at age 16 and then declines for dropouts as well as graduates, and that in two out of three age groups crime increased rather than decreased in the year following dropout. The study also showed that, controlling for the influence of age, dropout status had a significant positive effect on subsequent crime through age 25, regardless of the age of dropout. Interestingly, the effects of dropping out on subsequent crime were in part (but not wholly) mediated by employment status following dropout. If dropping out increases crime, it does so primarily because it reduces the likelihood of employment. The Thornberry et al. study, although clearly more rigorous than any study of delinquency and dropout before it, may have overestimated the effect of dropout on subsequent crime because it did not control for the general predisposition to problem behavior.

Farrington, Gallagher, Morley, St. Ledger, and West (1986) also found evidence that leaving school does not decrease crime. By comparing crime rates for the same individuals during periods of school enrollment, employment, and unemployment, they showed that the number of offenses per year was lowest when youths were enrolled in school, slightly higher (although not always significantly so) when they were employed full-time, and by far the highest when they were out of school and unemployed. This study did not directly examine the effect of dropping out of school on crime, but the results lend support to the conclusion that staying in school protects youths from crime somewhat more than working (perhaps because of the disposable money provided by working) and dropping out increases crime to the extent that it increases unproductive time (i.e., time not spent in work or school).

LeBlanc, Vallières, and McDuff (1993) reported results of a longitudinal study of Canadian boys between ages 14 and 16. Nearly one-quarter of the boys in the study dropped out of school. This study examined the influence of school experiences on current and subsequent offending. Predictors included measures of socioeconomic status, school performance, self-control, bonding to school, and graduation from high school. Although several of the measures of school performance predicted later offending behavior, graduation status did not.

Bachman et al. (1978) followed a sample of U.S. males from grade 10 (in 1966) to five years beyond high school (in 1974). They found that delinquency in 1974 was explained primarily by delinquency during high school. Educational attainment (a continuous variable ranging from dropout to graduate work in college) was not a good predictor of subsequent delinquency once earlier predisposition to delinquency was controlled. This finding accords with the results of earlier analyses of the same sample (Bachman, Green, and Wirtanen, 1971), which examined the specific effect of dropping out on delinquency (measured in 1970). They concluded, "the data do *not* square with the interpretation that dropping out is a *cause* of delinquency, and there is no basis in our findings to believe that keeping boys in school by one means or another would make much of a difference in their level of delinquent behavior" (p. 125). In fact, more evidence suggests that delinquency (Bachman et al., 1978) and substance use (Garnier, Stein, and Jacobs, 1997; Mensch and Kandel, 1988) lead to dropout than the other way around.

Jarjoura (1993) also studied dropping out and delinquency in a national longitudinal sample of American youth surveyed first in 1979 and then in 1980. Jarjoura statistically controlled for several factors likely to predict both dropout and delinquency (including gender, age, ethnicity, prior problem behavior, school performance, and curriculum track during high school). He found that the nature of the association differs depending on the reason for dropping out, but that overall dropouts are *not* more likely to engage in delinquency once prior predispositions are held constant.

Additional studies are needed to further explicate and generalize the findings of these studies. All but two of the studies included all-male samples, and all are based on samples of youths who were in high school prior to the 1980s. Labor market demands and expectations for high school completion have changed dramatically over the past thirty years, but the results to date permit us to reject the notion that leaving school reduces subsequent crime. It either has no effect or increases later crime.

In-School versus Out-of-School Crime

The question of whether schools are "criminogenic places" has been examined using both police records and victimization surveys. Roncek and

Lobosco (1983), examining crimes known to San Diego police, showed that more crimes occur in residential blocks adjacent to public high schools than on other residential blocks, even when other characteristics of the blocks were held constant. Adjacency effects were found for burglary, auto theft, robbery, and assault, but not for murder, rape, and grand theft. Interestingly, adjacency to public but not to private high schools increased crime. Roncek and Faggiani (1985) showed that the results generalize to Cleveland, where adjacency to public high schools had even larger effects on residential crime rates, and effects were found for all types of crimes. In the most recent study along these lines, LaGrange (1999) found that the presence or absence of public high schools (and shopping malls, where teenagers often "hang out") were robust predictors for three types of minor property crimes: mischief, damage to bus stops and shelters, and park vandalism. Proximity to Catholic schools and public junior high schools generally increased the likelihood of these property crimes, but the effects usually did not reach statistical significance. Presumably, blocks next to high schools are visited more often than other blocks and are visited more by the worst-behaved segment of the population – teenage boys.

Victimization surveys and youth reports of their own behaviors are helpful for learning about the experiences of students in and around schools. These sources are better suited for this purpose than police records because crimes occurring in school as opposed to on the street are much less likely to be reported to the police. According to the National Crime Victimization Survey (NCVS; Whitaker and Bastian, 1991), only 9% of violent crimes against teenagers occurring in school were reported to the police compared with 37% occurring on the streets.

Several sources of reports of crime and other health-risk behaviors in and out of school are available. Before summarizing results, I briefly describe these sources. The NCVS is a survey of nationally representative households conducted twice each year by the U.S. Department of Justice's Bureau of Justice Statistics. Household members age 12 and older are asked to report on their victimization experiences every six months for three years. Data reported here are primarily from NCVS surveys conducted between 1985 and 1988 and from special school crime supplements administered in 1995. In 1993, a special National Household Education Survey was conducted by Westat, Inc., for the U.S. Department of Education's Center for Education Statistics. This study collected information on victimization experiences from a nationally representative sample of students in grades 3 through 12, selected through random digit dialing methods. The U.S. Department of Health and Human Services' Centers for Disease Control and Prevention also conducts school-based surveys of students in grades 9 through 12 as part of its Youth Risk Behavior Surveillance System (YRBSS). This system, which includes a national survey as well as twenty-four state surveys and nine local surveys, asked youths in

1993 to report about their own health-risk behaviors and where these behaviors occur.

The NCVS (Whitaker and Bastian, 1991) showed that young persons are more likely than older persons to be crime victims. From 1985 through 1988, teens (ages 12–19) were two to three times more likely than adults to experience a violent crime or a crime involving theft. Crimes against teens frequently occurred at school, especially for the younger teen group (ages 12–15); 37% of crimes of violence and 81% of crimes of theft against young teens occurred in the school building or on school property; 17% of crimes of violence and 39% of crimes of theft against teens ages 16 through 19 occurred in these places. School crimes experienced by older teens are fewer not only because criminal behavior is on the decline for this age group, but also because a higher percentage of youths in this age group are no longer enrolled in school. Only a small percentage of older teens (ages 18 and 19) selected to participate in the NCVS were enrolled in school (Bastian and Taylor, 1991). Crimes occurring in schools were similar in severity to street crimes, except that violent street crimes were more likely to have been committed by an armed offender than were violent crimes in school buildings. But similar proportions of victims of violent crimes in school buildings and on the street were physically attacked and sustained injuries.

School victimization experiences have not changed substantially since these reports from the late 1980s. In fact, the percentages of twelfth graders who have been injured at school have not changed notably over the past twenty years. The patterns described here by age of student and by in-school versus out-of-school crimes also appear in the most recent reports of the NCVS for 1996 (Kaufman et al., 1998).

Although the percentages of crimes against teens occurring in schools as opposed to other places is high, the overall rates of serious criminal victimization in school are relatively low. Chandler, Chapman, Rand, and Taylor (1998) showed only 15% of students ages 12 through 19 in 1995 reported being the victim of at least one crime in and around their school over a six-month period: 4% reported experiencing one or more violent crimes, and 12% reported at least one property crime. Violent crimes were largely composed of simple attacks without weapons resulting in minor injuries such as cuts or bruises.

The National Household Education Survey (Nolin, Davies, and Chandler, 1995) found 4% of students in grades 6 through 12 were physically attacked, 8% were bullied, and only 1% robbed at school or on the way to or from school during the 1992–1993 school year. In this study, physical attack included students getting into fights at school, and bullying included repeated threats of harm.

These findings accord with those of the National Institute of Education's Safe School Study (SSS) and a recent report on school-associated violent deaths in the United States. Based on the SSS data, a national sample of schools collected two decades ago, Gottfredson and Gottfredson (1985, p. 5) found that "the typical student or teacher experience of personal victimization in schools is of a minor incident. Serious victimizations are rare." The study concluded that the high frequency of minor victimizations and indignities (e.g., swearing, obscene gestures), as opposed to more serious victimizations, constituted a major problem of school disorder.

An analysis of violent deaths among children ages 5 to 19 (Kachur et al., 1996) found that fewer than 1% of the homicides and suicides among school-age children occurred while the victim was at school or in transit to or from school or a school event.

Self-reports of health-risk behaviors occurring in schools from the 1993 YRBSS (Centers for Disease Control and Prevention, 1995) suggest somewhat higher prevalence rates, probably because of differences in the wording of the questions. These data from surveys administered to a nationally representative sample of students in grades 9 through 12 show that 7% of students reported being threatened or injured with a weapon and 33% reported that property had been stolen or deliberately damaged on school property in the last year. Certain questions were asked with respect to both general behavior and behavior that occurred in schools: 22% of students reported that they had carried a weapon at all in the past thirty days, and 12% reported doing so on school property; 42% reported being in a physical fight in the past year, and 16% reported fighting on school property.

These comparisons of in-school and out-of-school delinquency can be better understood by taking into account the relative amounts of time spent in school and in other places by students. A National Institute of Education report (1978) estimated the typical student spends 25% of his or her waking hours in school. This estimate assumed a six-hour school day and did not account for absenteeism. A more precise estimate is available from a Timmer, Eccles, and O'Brien (1985) study, which asked children and adolescents to keep time diaries. Children ages 12 through 17 reported spending an average of 5.47 hours in school on weekdays, and no time on weekends. Using figures from the same study on the amount of sleeping time, I estimate that students spend 18% of their waking hours in school.

But we have seen that more than 18% of the crimes experienced by teens occurred in school. The NCVS showed that among crimes experienced by teens ages 12 through 15, 37% of violent crimes and 81% of thefts occurred on school property. The YRBSS showed more than half of the people carrying weapons do so on school property, and nearly 40% of the fighters fight on school property. The amount of crime victimization experienced and delinquent behavior committed by youths in and around schools is disproportionately high.

Data on the timing of criminal events tend to support the hypothesis that crime is lowest during times when youth are typically in school. The number of incidents per month for most types of crime peaks during the summer months (Rand, Klaus, and Taylor, 1983). But this trend is as likely due to the tendency of people to spend more time outdoors (making themselves more vulnerable to crime) and to leave their homes unattended as it is to youths being out of school. Perhaps more compelling is the finding that one in five violent juvenile crimes occur in the four-hour period following school closing on school days (Sickmund, Snyder, and Poe-Yamagata, 1997). The same pattern was found in juvenile crime data sixty years earlier for the state of New Jersey: Kvaraceus (1945) reported that more juvenile crime occurred on weekdays than on weekends, and that the peak time for juvenile crime to occur was in the midafternoon, following the close of school.

As we have seen, the number of crimes occurring during the school day are drastically underestimated in official records because school crimes are less likely to be reported to the authorities. This caution aside, the higher rates of officially recorded crime during the after-school hours may be explained by the lower levels of supervision experienced by youth during these hours. Students are more likely to be unsupervised during the hours between school dismissal and dinnertime, when parents return from work. The data on the timing of offenses accord with studies that have shown that children who are not supervised by an adult for extended periods of time are at especially elevated risk for engaging in problem behavior.

Richardson et al. (1989) showed that eighth grade children who care for themselves for eleven or more hours per week without an adult present are twice as likely to abuse substances as those who are always supervised. The researchers found that this was true even when factors that might explain the relationship – for example, socioeconomic status, living with a single parent – were held constant. They also showed that the higher level of drug use among the unsupervised teens was explained in large part by their greater association with delinquent peers. Clearly, school provides beneficial supervision for delinquency-prone youths. If the alternative is no supervision, being in school reduces the likelihood of youth crime.

Conclusion

Does participation in school influence crime? We have seen on the one hand that the amount of crime and victimization experienced by school-age youths is disproportionately high when they are in school. Schools concentrate large numbers of teenagers in one place for long periods of time, and the concentration of delinquency-prone students in schools has increased as the proportion of teenagers enrolled in school has grown. It is likely that some schools are more effective than others at controlling youth crime during the school hours (Gottfredson and Gottfredson, 1985), and that their effectiveness somehow interacts with the burden placed on them by the communities they serve. But even the less competent schools probably offer some level of control and supervision. When these controls are removed at dismissal time, youths are more likely to engage in delinquent activities until they come again under the watchful eye of an adult.

The implication is that relaxing school participation requirements will not be sensible crime prevention policy unless we can find a suitable alternative that prepares youths for work and provides supervision. While the amount of crime that occurs in the school building can certainly be reduced by expelling troublemakers or by allowing them to drop out of school, crime in the community is likely to increase. State-level data fail to show a consistent pattern of lower crime rates when smaller percentages of the school-age population are in school, and studies suggest that dropping out does not reduce crime. Rather, it may increase crime by increasing the amount of unproductive, unsupervised time for persons who remain unemployed after leaving school. The cost of increasing school enrollments as we have throughout the twentieth century is an increase in the proportion of youth crime occurring in and around school buildings. But the alternative, setting youths afloat in a society that does not offer them other opportunities for productive engagement, is likely to produce more crime. Because this crime will not occur in schools, schools will be more orderly, however. Setting youths afloat to improve schools for those who remain can be expected not to reduce crime among the floaters but rather to change their locus operandi.

The challenge is to understand how schools can better control student behavior both in and out of school. What characterizes schools that are able to control problem behavior in school – to provide environments that provide less opportunity for crime and other forms of misbehavior? And what can schools do to reduce enduring youth dispositions to engage in misbehavior both in and out of school?

Overview of the Book

The next chapter summarizes a large literature on the links between individual delinquency and school-related characteristics, attitudes, and experiences. It discusses attachment and commitment to school, school performance, prolonged exposure to negative peers, conduct problems, social competency skills, and attitudes and beliefs regarding deviant behavior. It summarizes what is known about the causal connection between these individual motivational characteristics and delinquency and draws attention to developmental differences in these correlations. The issue of stability and change in problem behavior is addressed, and implications for the timing and sequencing of prevention activities are discussed.

Chapter 3 distinguishes between characteristics of schools related to delinquency and individual attitudes, beliefs, and behaviors related to delinquency. It presents evidence from school-level and multilevel studies about environmental characteristics of schools (e.g., clarity of rules, staff morale, communal organization) related to levels of delinquency and draws conclusions about the potential malleability of these characteristics.

Chapters 4 though 6 examine what works in school-based delinquency prevention. Chapter 4 provides an overview of the studies and describes the methodology used for locating and coding the studies. Chapter 5 summarizes the studies of changes to environmental features of the school, and Chapter 6 summarizes studies of interventions aimed at changing individual characteristics, attitudes, beliefs, and behaviors. Chapters 5 and 6 are organized by grade level in order to highlight any developmental differences in the effectiveness of prevention practices that might emerge. These chapters conclude that some types of prevention do work to reduce problem behavior, but the results of the research are not highly generalizeable to natural school settings.

Chapter 7 explores the gap between research and practice. It summarizes data describing the level of program implementation and relating implementation integrity to program outcomes. It shows that certain characteristics of programs, schools, and communities are related to the level of implementation of school-based prevention strategies and, by extension, their effectiveness. It highlights problems faced by urban schools and discusses ways to strengthen programs in these more troubled areas.

Chapter 8 concludes the book by outlining the most promising programs, practices, and policies discussed in earlier chapters as well as implications for improving the translation of research-based knowledge into practice. It includes recommendations for legislators, funding-agency personnel, and educational policy makers and practitioners. Finally, recommendations for further basic and applied research are provided.

School-Related Individual Characteristics, Attitudes, and Experiences

WHAT TYPE of student engages in problem behavior? How does the school encourage or discourage the development of these characteristics, if at all? This chapter examines evidence from a variety of research traditions on individual-level correlates of problem behavior and attempts to identify which of the many correlates of problem behavior are also causes. It summarizes contributions from personality research and criminological theory on the stability of these individual factors over the life course, and constructs a model of the development of problem behavior during the schooling years. The chapter ends by discussing school's potential role in increasing or decreasing problem behavior.

Correlates and Antecedents of Problem Behavior

Persons who engage in one form of problem behavior are highly likely to engage in others: 59% of youths who have committed serious crimes have also used multiple drugs, compared with 19% among youths who had not committed these crimes (Elliott et al., 1989); school dropouts have four times as many police contacts as high school graduates (Elliott and Voss, 1974); among males who had used marijuana by their senior year, 44% had also had sexual intercourse compared with 17% for males who had not used marijuana (Jessor and Jessor, 1977). Risky sexual behavior is also highly correlated with antisocial behavior, smoking, alcohol use, and illicit drug use (Biglan et al., 1990). This "comorbidity" of problem behaviors is well established.

Furthermore, the antecedents of the various forms of problem behavior are mostly the same. Dryfoos (1990) summarized correlates of delinquency, substance abuse, pregnancy, school failure, and dropout. She found many more common than uncommon antecedents. Early initiation of any of the problem behaviors – poor academic performance and low expectations for educational success, general misbehavior (e.g., acting out, truancy, antisocial behavior, and other conduct disorders), negative peer influence, poor parenting (e.g., insufficient parental monitoring, supervision, guidance, and communication, and low attachment to parents), and residence in a low-income, urban area – all predict each of the problem behaviors. Risk factors that predict one and not another problem behavior tend to be related to the opportunity to engage in the specific type of misbehavior: easy availability of drugs predicts drug use and gun ownership predicts violent crime, for example. Similarly, low socioeconomic status increases the risk for dropout and delinquency, but it lowers the risk for substance use – presumably because disposable money is needed to purchase drugs.

During the 1990s, many persons associated with the prevention field adopted a "risk and protective factor" approach to prevention (Institute of Medicine, 1994), which relies on the knowledge that different problem behaviors are highly related and share common antecedents. Asserting that the common antecedents are the risk and protective factors identified in research as correlates of problem behavior (e.g., as summarized in reviews such as Hawkins, Catalano, and Miller, 1992), it reasons that prevention efforts aimed directly at these risk and protective factors will reduce problem behavior. This "risk and protective factor" framework for prevention is described here.

Risk Factors for Problem Behavior

Risk factors are characteristics of individuals and their environments that, when present, signal an increased likelihood that individuals will develop a disorder or disease (Garmezy, 1983). Protective factors are individual or social characteristics that, when present, signal a reduced likelihood of a disorder. They are thought to mediate or mitigate the negative effects of risk factors. Protective factors may directly reduce a dysfunction, reduce the effect of the risk factor, disrupt the mediational chain through which the risk factor operates to cause a dysfunction, or prevent the initial occurrence of the risk factor (Coie et al., 1993).

Considerable research has been conducted to identify risk factors for problem behavior. Research on protective factors as distinct from risk factors has not been as abundant. Three broad categories of factors that seem to protect against problem behaviors are resilient temperament; cohesion, warmth, or bonding during childhood; and norms, beliefs, or behavioral standards inconsistent with problem behaviors (Hawkins, Arthur, and Catalano, 1995). But because these same factors – when reflected or labeled to emphasize the negative end of their measurement scales – have been identified as risk factors, the incremental utility of the protective factor idea is not clear. Farrington (1995) recently reviewed the scant research on protective factors and concluded that "more effort should be made to identify factors that protect vulnerable children from developing into antisocial teenagers" (p. 120). Protective factors are given short shrift in this chapter because there is little consensus about what they are or how they operate to reduce problem behavior.

Several excellent reviews of risk factors are available (e.g., Farrington, 1995; Gottfredson, Harmon, Gottfredson, Jones, and Celestin, 1996; Hawkins et al., 1992; Loeber and Dishion, 1983; McCord, 1979). Most reviews of factors related to delinquency and drug abuse include school and community contextual factors as well as family, peer, and individual factors. School and community factors are discussed at length in Chapter 3. Family risk factors – among the strongest correlates of problem behavior – include family history of criminality, alcoholism, or drug use; parental attitudes favorable to drug use; poor family management practices; low family support or attachment to family; and family conflict. These factors affect the characteristics of students entering school and require school action to cope with their results; however, because intervention to reduce these family risk factors is beyond the practical scope of most schools, they are not discussed any further here. Also, some reviews (e.g., Hawkins et al., 1992) identify genetic markers and biochemical factors as specific risk factors for alcohol abuse, but these specific factors are also not included in our discussion. The next three sections present the remaining risk factors for problem behavior.

Individual Traits or Attitudes

A large body of research supports a connection between certain characteristics of individuals and a variety of problem behaviors. Because several readily available reviews summarize this research in detail, only a few of the strongest studies that form the core of the evidence are discussed here.

Early Aggression and Conduct Problems, Early Initiation of Delinquency and Drug Use. In the nomenclature used in clinical psychology, the term "conduct disorder" (DSM IV; American Psychiatric Association, 1994) subsumes a variety of antisocial and aggressive behaviors: defiance, disrespect, rebelliousness, hitting, stealing, lying, fighting, talking back to persons in authority. These and similar behaviors are usually chronic, and individuals differ in the levels they display – maintaining their rank order in a relatively stable manner over time. This stability makes early displays of conduct problems useful predictors of later problem behaviors of diverse kinds.

Several prospective longitudinal studies have demonstrated that such early conduct problems predict later delinquent behavior and drug use. These studies generally rely on teacher or parent ratings of the child's early childhood behavior to predict self-report or official measures of delinquency and drug use during adolescence. Taken together, they provide indisputable evidence that conduct problems and aggressiveness measured at nursery school age (Block, Block, and Keyes, 1988), kindergarten (Spivak and Cianci, 1987), first grade (Kellam, Ensminger, and Simon 1980; Tremblay, LeBlanc, and Schwartzman, 1988), early elementary school (Brook, Whiteman, Finch, and Cohen, 1996; Farrington, 1991; Feldhusen, Thurston, and Benning, 1973), and upper elementary and middle school (Feldhusen et al., 1973; Shedler and Block, 1990) predict later delinquency and drug use. In studies of older children and adolescents, the predictive value of earlier problem behavior (including earlier drug use and delinquency) for later problem behavior and drug use is well established, with a number of large sample studies finding strong associations (Bachman, 1975; Elliott, Huizinga, and Ageton, 1985). The association has been found for males and females, persons of different racial and ethnic backgrounds and from different countries, using data from different sources (e.g., self-report and official). Loeber and Dishion (1983) and Loeber and Stouthamer-Loeber (1987) provide detailed summaries of the evidence relating early conduct problems and later delinquency, showing consistent evidence from dozens of longitudinal studies that conduct problems in childhood and adolescence predict later delinquency. Farrington (1991) shows a remarkable continuity in aggression and violence spanning nearly a quarter of a century: teacher ratings of aggressiveness at ages 8 and 10 predict criminal behavior at age 32. Hawkins et al. (1995) summarize the evidence relating early problem behaviors to later substance use.

Impulsiveness and Low Self-Control. Impulsiveness and low levels of self-control are strongly associated with conduct problems. A few studies, some of which also measured early conduct problems, have demonstrated that early impulsive and undercontrolled behavior predict later problem behavior. Block et al. (1988) studied children ages 3 to 4 from Berkeley, California, following them until they were age 14. They showed that teacher ratings of a child's social behaviors during nursery school predicted drug use at age 14. Among the specific teacher ratings that predicted later drug use for both genders were: teases other children, is aggressive, and behaves in a dominating manner – indicators of the early conduct problems discussed already. Other correlates of later drug use included indicators of what the authors named "ego under control" or low self-control. These items included rapid shifts in mood, easily irritated or angered, reacts and moves quickly, and unable to delay gratification. The under-control scale correlated .48 and .33 with later marijuana and hard drug use for girls, and

.69 and .65 for boys. A follow-up study of the same sample (Shedler and Block, 1990) showed that psychologists' ratings of the same children made at ages 7 and 11 predicted drug use at age 18. Ratings of low ego-control (e.g., unable to delay gratification, unpredictable and changeable behavior, self-indulgent) predicted more drug use at age 18.

Farrington (1995) summarized additional literature linking impulsiveness to later delinquency. He noted the difficulty of separating this personality construct from conduct disorder, but cited one study from the Cambridge Study in Delinquent Development (Farrington, Loeber, and Van Kammen, 1990) that showed impulsiveness (or, more precisely, a construct called "hyperactivity-impulsivity-attention deficit") at ages 8 to 10 predicted convictions through age 25 independently of measures of conduct disorder.

Smith and Fogg (1978) showed that a related but broader set of personality measures predicted lower levels of substance use among adolescents. The researchers obtained school records and administered a 400-item personality inventory to 651 children in grades 7 and 8 from a school system in the Boston area. They followed them up four years later when they were in grades 11 and 12. The earlier ratings by peers of individuals' personalities differentiated three groups: marijuana nonusers, those who started using marijuana late, and those who started using marijuana early. Specifically, traits of personal competence and social responsibility – including obedience, diligent work and study habits, determination and persistence, consideration for others, self-control, and orientation toward achievement – were linearly related to stage of initiation.

Low self-control demonstrated in a laboratory setting has also been related to later social competency. Mischel, Shoda, and Rodriguez (1989) showed that preschool children's self-imposed delay of gratification was correlated with their self-regulatory capacities in adolescence as judged by their parents. Ratings on questions such as, "When trying to concentrate, how distractible is your son or daughter?" were predicted by the number of minutes the child elected to wait in an experimental manipulation in which, after being shown rewards, the child was told that he or she could have them only by waiting until the experimenter returned. Children could summon the experimenter back into the room by ringing a bell, but they understood that if they did so before the experimenter came back, they would get a less valuable reward. The number of minutes the child waited predicted a range of social competencies – many known to be related to problem behavior – identified by their parents ten years later.

Impulsiveness and self-control are linked with problem behavior through cognitive processes. Antisocial youths tend to misinterpret social cues. They attribute hostile intentions to peers when none may exist. They have difficulty evaluating the likely consequences of their actions and considering alternatives. They also have trouble regulating behaviors in communication, including using appropriate eye contact and tone of voice. Several studies have linked these cognitive and behavioral deficits with peer rejection (e.g., Dodge, Pettit, McClaskey, and Brown, 1986; McFall, 1982; Perry, Perry, and Rasmussen, 1986; Rubin and Krasnor, 1986), another risk factor to be discussed shortly.

Beliefs and Attitudes Favorable to Delinquency and Drug Use. Belief in the validity of conventional social rules is a central construct in Hirschi's (1969) social control theory of delinquency. According to social control theory, individuals who believe that laws and rules are valid are more constrained by those laws and rules. In Hirschi's (1969) original test of his theory he surveyed a sample of 3,605 high school boys in urban California. Belief was measured by statements such as, "It is alright to get around the law if you can get away with it." Hirschi found that belief in rules and laws was inversely related to both official records and self-reports of delinquent acts, school misconduct, and official records of delinquency. Hirschi's findings were soon replicated in a sample of rural males and females (Hindelang, 1973). Subsequent longitudinal studies (e.g., Elliott, 1994; Thornberry, Lizotte, Krohn, Farnworth, and Jang, 1994) have found that beliefs predict delinquency measured at a later time. Thornberry et al. (1994) found that delinquent beliefs and delinquent behaviors are reciprocally related: delinquent beliefs predict subsequent association with delinquent peers and delinquent behavior. Early delinquency also predicts later expressions of delinquent beliefs.

Numerous studies have linked belief in conventional norms with substance use. Jessor, Chase, and Donovan (1980) reported results from a national sample of adolescents in grades 7 through 12. They observed large concurrent correlations between marijuana use and measures of "intolerance of deviance" (e.g., self-reports of how wrong various generally proscribed behaviors are). Similar correlations were observed with measures of problem drinking. In an earlier longitudinal study, Jessor and Jessor (1977) studied a representative sample of high school youths, first assessed when they were in grades 7 through 9, and then annually for three more years. The study found that intolerance of deviance measured in junior high school predicted the timing of the onset of drinking, marijuana use, and sexual behavior over the next four years. Gottfredson and Gottfredson (1992) studied a large sample of boys and girls, including both black and white adolescents. A seventeen-item scale measuring beliefs in rules was negatively associated with three different measures of substance use. Correlations were similar for males and females.

Beliefs are also often measured as attitudes for and against specific proscribed behaviors. Several longitudinal studies have documented a correlation between attitudes favorable to drug use and later use. Smith and Fogg (1978), in the study described earlier, showed large associations between attitudes toward cigarette smoking and later drug use. Kandel, Kessler, and Marguiles (1978) surveyed high school students in New York State in the fall and spring of the same school year. Fall measures of the students' attitudes toward drugs were correlated with use of hard liquor, marijuana, and other illicit drugs in the following spring.

Testing the generalizability of this association to different race and gender groups, Gottfredson and Koper (1996) showed that both general beliefs about the validity of rules and norms and specific attitudes favoring drug use predict the number of different substances used a year later, and produced correlations that were similar for males, females, blacks, and whites. The correlations were not as consistent across groups when *frequency* of use was the criterion.

Attitudes and Behaviors Related to School

Attachment and Commitment to School. Attachment and commitment to school are also central to Hirschi's (1969) social control theory of delinquency. According to social control theory, individuals with strong bonds to conventional institutions are less likely to engage in delinquent activities than those with weak bonds. Attachment to school refers to emotional attachment and is usually measured with items tapping the extent to which an individual likes school or finds work satisfying. Commitment refers to psychological investment in the pursuit of an educational or occupational goal. A person with high educational aspirations is more committed to school than one who has no such aspiration. He or she has more to lose by violating social norms or participating in delinquent behaviors than the person who lacks such an investment in the future.

Attachment and commitment to school have been shown consistently to be moderately related to delinquency. In Hirschi's original (1969) study (described earlier), attachment to school was measured by questions such as, "Do you like school?" and "Do you care what teachers think of you?" Hirschi found that attachment to school was inversely related to self-reports of delinquent acts, school misconduct, and official records of delinquency. In the same study, commitment was measured by asking respondents questions like "How much education would you like to get?" Hirschi found that commitment to school was inversely related to delinquency. The higher a student's educational aspirations, the less likely he was to have committed delinquent acts according to both self-report and official measures. This was true for both black and white students.

Subsequent longitudinal studies have mostly supported Hirschi's observations. Smith and Fogg (1978) found that liking school and working hard in school predicted later substance use. Jessor and Jessor (1977) found expectations for academic achievement in junior high school predicted the timing of onset of marijuana use and drinking in high school. But Kandel et al. (1978) found no significant correlation between educational expectations and subsequent initiation of drug use. Correlations between attachment or commitment and delinquent behavior (some longitudinal and some cross-sectional) have been replicated in a variety of populations, including Canadian boys (LeBlanc, 1994), Stockholm girls (Torstensson, 1990), Israeli boys (Shichor, 1975) and Israeli boys and girls (Javetz and Shuval, 1982), and Japanese boys and girls (Tanoika and Glaser, 1991). Two studies (Gottfredson and Gottfredson, 1992; Gottfredson and Koper, 1996) found that attachment to school predicts later variety and frequency of substance use similarly for whites, blacks, males, and females. Commitment to school predicts less subsequent use for all groups, but the associations were stronger for whites than for blacks. Cernkovich and Giordano (1992) showed that both attachment and commitment to school were equally predictive of delinquency for these same four demographic groups.

School Performance. Consistent evidence supports an association between poor school performance and drug use and other adolescent problem behaviors. School grades have been shown to be moderately related to delinquency (Bachman, 1975), having a police record (Hirschi and Hindelang, 1977), having a court record (Farrington, 1991; Polk and Halferty, 1972), and engaging in serious juvenile delinquency (Rhodes and Reiss, 1969) and drug use (Jessor et al, 1980; Kandel et al., 1978; Smith and Fogg, 1978) for youths from middle school to college. This literature is summarized in Gottfredson (1981, 1988) and in Loeber and Dishion (1983). As with attachment and commitment to school, the correlation between academic performance and delinquency has been replicated in studies in different countries (e.g., Farrington, 1991; LeBlanc, 1994; Torstensson, 1990).

Interactions with Peers

Peer Rejection in Elementary Grades. Socially competent individuals successfully control anger, aggression, and hostility and recognize and control their emotions. Youths with these skills are more likely to be accepted by their peers than youths without these skills (Coie, Dodge, and Coppotelli, 1982; Coie, Dodge, and Kupersmidt, 1990). Rejection by peers is related to subsequent association with deviant peers (Synder, Dishion, and Patterson, 1986) and problem behavior (Coie, Lochman, Terry, and Hyman, 1992; Kupersmidt, Coie, and Dodge, 1990; Parker and Asher, 1987; Tremblay, LeBlanc, and Schwartzman, 1988). Peer judgments of social competency appear especially predictive of later problem behavior. In a study of more than seventeen hundred boys from Minneapolis, Roff and Sells (1968) found that being actively disliked by peers in grades 5 and 6 predicted having a police record three years later. Ollendick, Oswald, and Francis (1989) studied students in grade 4 who had been rated by their peers. Students who had been rejected by their peers then reported five years later significantly more substance use and conduct problems than average children. Rejected children were also rated as having more behavior problems by their teachers, had significantly higher school dropout rates, and had more court records of offenses than did average students. Dishion (1988) found that 29% of boys rejected at age 10 as compared with 7% of popular boys had records of police contacts by age 11. Dishion (1990) reports that by ages 14 and 15, these percentages have risen to 47% and 11%.

The mechanism through which peer rejection leads to problem behavior is not well understood. Some evidence (Cairns, Cairns, Neckerman, Gest, and Gariépy, 1988; Dishion, 1990) suggests that aggressive youths are often rejected by conventional peers but accepted by other aggressive children. Dishion (1990) shows that at age 10 rejected children are more likely than other children to nominate other rejected children as friends. He concludes on the basis of other evidence that this process of selective association begins as early as age 6. These "coercive cliques" become delinquent peer groups during early adolescence. Parker and Asher (1987) suggest that the peer group is a setting in which socially acceptable behaviors are shaped. Rejected children are actively shunned and so are denied this learning experience over a period of several years. It is also possible that acceptance by prosocial peers buffers the effects of vulnerability to later disorders.

Researchers have debated whether peer rejection has a causal influence on subsequent problem behavior, or whether it is simply a marker for aggressiveness, low self-control, and impulsiveness. Dishion, Patterson, Stoolmiller, and Skinner (1991) tested the causal effect of peer rejection in a longitudinal sample of white boys from Oregon. They related peer rejection to later association with deviant peers, a major risk factor for problem behavior to be discussed next. They noted a high degree of stability of problem behavior from ages 10 through 12, but, even when researchers controlled for prior antisocial behavior, rejected youths were more likely to associate with delinquent peers at age 12.

Exposure to or Association with Delinquent Peers. Exposure to or association with negative peers – usually assessed by examining how many of the respondent's friends use illicit substances or engage in delinquent activities, or the amount of time spent with negative peers – is the largest correlate of adolescent problem behavior. Most research examining negative peer association and involvement in drug use and delinquency has examined high school samples. A few studies show that exposure to negative peers among younger children is also associated with gateway drug use or other problem behaviors.

Jessor and Jessor (1977), in the study described earlier, examined the relation between friends' modeling of problem behavior and the subjects' problem behavior. Friends' modeling of problem behavior showed moderate to high concurrent associations with the number of times adolescents had been drunk in the past year, marijuana involvement, deviant behavior in the past year, and a multiple problem-behavior index. Friends' modeling of problem behavior was a strong predictor for initiation into marijuana use and drinking for both males and females in the longitudinal study. Kandel et al. (1978) also reported that peer drug behaviors were among the strongest correlates of subsequent initiation into drug use behaviors.

Elliott, Huizinga, and Ageton (1985) reported results from the National Youth Survey (NYS) for a sample first assessed in 1977 and followed through 1979, when the youths were ages 13 through 19. A composite index of spare time spent with friends and the proportion of a subject's close friends who engage in ten illegal acts predicted marijuana use, illicit drug use, and several delinquency scales for both boys and girls.

Gottfredson and Gottfredson (1992) assessed the relationship between negative peer associations and alcohol, tobacco, and other drug use among elementary, middle, and high school students. Results showed that peer drug models were correlated with the variety of drugs used in the past year and the frequency of drug use in the past month. For youths in grades 6 through 12, peer drug models were strongly correlated with the last-month frequency of drug use and the variety of drugs ever used.

Association with delinquent peers predicts subsequent problem behavior for males and females and persons of different race and ethnic backgrounds (see, e.g., Tanioka and Glaser, 1991, for evidence that negative peer influence is the largest correlate of delinquency among Japanese adolescents). Gottfredson and Koper (1996), however, found evidence that the association is stronger for whites than for blacks, and is particularly weak for black females.

In sum, association with negative peers is one of the strongest correlates of adolescent problem behavior. Many longitudinal and cross-sectional studies in addition to those cited here confirm this relation. Studies generally confirm this association in samples of adolescents, but measures of peer rebellious, aggressive, or delinquent behavior have also been shown to be associated with the respondent's problem behavior in younger populations.

Personal Characteristics and Experiences Unrelated to Problem Behavior

Some popular beliefs about correlates of problem behavior are not supported by research. These include involvement in extracurricular activities, self-esteem, and anxiety or alienation.

Anxiety or Alienation. Measures of these "internalizing" problems show inconsistent correlations with problem behaviors. Caspi et al. (1994) examined the relation of personality characteristics and crime in two populations: an entire New Zealand birth cohort at age 18 and Pittsburgh boys at ages 12 and 13. They showed significant correlations between a construct they called "Negative Emotionality" and delinquency. But when the construct was disaggregated into its three subscales, the data showed that the Aggression component rather than the Alienation and Stress Reaction components was primarily responsible for the large correlation with delinquency.

Other longitudinal studies have also found little or inconsistent evidence for a correlation between anxiety or alienation and delinquency. Jessor and Jessor (1977) found a measure of social alienation unrelated to most measures of problem behavior. For females only, a significant correlation was found with marijuana use. Another study involving a large, nationally representative sample showed that a scale measuring Negative Affect (anxiety and tension, irritability, general anxiety, depression, anomie, and resentment) had relatively small correlations with delinquency a year later. The Kellam et al. (1980) Woodlawn study is sometimes cited as evidence that shyness (a characteristic associated with anxiety and alienation) is related to higher levels of substance use. In fact the results show that over all first grade children rated as shy by their teachers used drugs *least often* ten years later. Results for some subgroups in their analysis showed that shyness *in combination with aggression* was associated with somewhat higher rates of use of certain substances (but not other subgroups or other substances). Block et al. (1988) showed that anxiety, worrisomeness, and social isolation in nursery school were not significantly related to substance use at age 14. A later study on the same sample (Shedler and Block, 1990) also reported no significant correlation between anxiety at ages 7 and 11 and drug use at age 18, although some related measures (e.g., "tends to withdraw and disengage when under stress") suggested that childhood anxiety and alienation have a curvilinear association with drug use at age 18: whereas youths who experimented with drugs were less anxious than abstainers, youths who were frequent users of drugs had been far more anxious as children than either abstainers or experimenters. Oetting, Swaim, Edwards, and Beauvais (1989) examined the association between measures of emotional distress – including anger (hotheadedness, quick temper), alienation (feeling blamed and rejected), and anxiety (feeling tense, nervous, and worried) – and alcohol use among white and American Indian students in grades 11 and 12. They found only very small correlations with alcohol use for alienation and anxiety for both white and American Indian youths. Two studies (Gottfredson and Gottfredson, 1992; Gottfredson and Koper, 1996) have demonstrated that the null correlation between social integration and later substance use generalized to males and females of different ethnic groups.

Self-Esteem. Self-esteem measures were not predictive of problem behavior in three national longitudinal studies (Jessor and Jessor, 1977; Kandel et al., 1978; O'Malley, 1975) with large sample sizes and high-quality measures. This null finding was replicated in moderately large samples of Anglo and American Indian youths in a study of emotional distress and alcohol use (Oetting, Beauvais, and Edwards, 1988). Gottfredson and Gottfredson (1992) and Gottfredson and Koper (1996) also demonstrated that the very small correlations between self-esteem and drug use apply across different race and gender groupings. Some popular beliefs notwithstanding, very little evidence suggests that low self-esteem is linked with elevated risk for problem behavior. Thinking highly of oneself does not make one less likely to engage in acts of force or fraud, or to act in other self-indulgent ways.

Involvement in Extracurricular Activities. The belief that involving youths in productive or safe activities will reduce delinquent behavior is widespread. Research has examined the plausibility of the "idle hands are the devil's workshop" rationale for explaining delinquency and found it lacking. Hirschi (1969) found that time spent on activities that reflect an underlying commitment to conventional pursuits (e.g., hours spent on homework) is related to the commission of *fewer* delinquent acts, whereas time spent on activities that reflect a (premature) orientation to adult activities (e.g., time spent riding around in cars) is related to the commission of *more* delinquent acts. But the myriad activities of adolescents that have no apparent connection to these poles (e.g., clubs, volunteer and service activities, youth organizations, sports, hobbies, television) are *unrelated* to the commission of delinquent acts. Simply spending time in these activities is unlikely to reduce delinquency.

A recent study (Polakowski, 1994) found evidence that involvement in extracurricular activities may actually *increase* delinquency. Using data from the Cambridge Study in Delinquent Development, Polakowski found that a measure of time spent in leisure activity between ages 8 and 10 (including time spent at the boys' club) predicted lower levels of self-control between ages 12 and 14 and a greater likelihood of criminal convictions between ages 14 and 16. Diminished self-control continued to influence convictions through age 21. The mechanism through which extracurricular involvement might reduce self-control is not clear, but the substantial negative correlation between involvement and parental supervision suggests that involvement in extracurricular activities may in fact free youths from the relatively more watchful eyes of their parents.

Summary

The literature on risk factors firmly establishes that early aggression and conduct problems, early initiation of delinquency and drug use, impulsiveness and low self-control, weak belief in the validity of laws and norms, and, more specifically, attitudes favorable to delinquency and drug use, attachment and commitment to school, school performance, peer rejection in elementary grades, and exposure to or association with delinquent peers predict later problem behavior. It suggests that certain personality characteristics are present in some persons from an early age and that they predict concurrent as well as later problem behavior, and that these characteristics shape important social influences, attitudes, beliefs, and experiences that alter the likelihood of subsequent problem behavior. Because early conduct problems and personality correlates appear so central to the development of problem behavior, I turn next to a review of the structure and stability of personality. This literature helps to organize the research summarized thus far.

Personality Structure and Problem Behavior

Personality Dimensions and Stability

Personality is defined as relatively stable traits or dispositions that differ across individuals. A set of personality dispositions tends to produce consistency in behavior across situations (Epstein and O'Brien, 1985) and to be stable over time (McCrae and Costa, 1990), at least in adulthood.

The scientific literature on personality refers to a very large number of trait terms. This abundance of terms, many of which are near synonyms and others that convey subtle shadings of personality, makes it difficult to summarize or integrate the evidence about links between personality and problem behaviors because often the same or similar trait will be described using different terms. Fortunately, personality researchers have begun to come to a consensus that a small number of robust factors – usually five – are useful in organizing related traits together (Digman, 1990; Goldberg, 1992) so that patterns in the evidence about specific aspects of personality and problem behavior are easier to see. Scientists still disagree over the precise number of useful factors and how some more global factors should be divided (e.g., Halverson, Kohnstamm, and Martin, 1994), but it is clear that three to six factors provide the benefit of usefully organizing the large number of more specific descriptions.

The "Big 5" personality factors, using Goldberg's (1992) and McCrae and Costa's (1990) terms, are:

Conscientiousness (C): Competence, Order, Dutifulness, Achievement Striving, Self-Discipline, Deliberation.
Neuroticism/Emotional Stability (N): Anxiety, Angry Hostility, Depression, Self-Conscientiousness, Impulsiveness, Vulnerability.
Extraversion (E): Warmth, Gregariousness, Assertiveness, Activity, Excitement Seeking, Positive Emotions.

Agreeableness (A): Trust, Straightforwardness, Altruism, Compliance, Modesty, and Tender-Mindedness.
Openness/Intellect (O): Fantasy, Aesthetics, Feelings, Actions, Ideas, Values.

Considerable research (summarized in Costa and McCrae, 1992) shows that these five factors succinctly describe personality from late adolescence through adulthood. The same five factors can be observed in early adolescence (ages 12 and 13; Robins, John, and Caspi, 1994), but it is clear that the personality structure becomes more distinct with age and that personality factors not in the "Big 5" can also be detected at this age. Similar factors can also be detected for younger children, but the studies demonstrating this usually depend on adult ratings of the children's personalities. What is observed may reflect adults' interpretations of childrens' dispositions and behaviors rather than or in addition to patterns in childrens' dispositions and behaviors.

Both cross-sectional comparisons of adolescents and adults and longitudinal studies of individuals as they move into adulthood show the same normative age trends in the development of personality. Young people are higher on Neuroticism, Extraversion, and Openness and lower on Conscientiousness and Agreeableness than are adults. But how stable are individual differences over the life course? Costa and McCrae (1992) show that personality develops throughout childhood, reaches maturity at some point in early adulthood, and remains stable thereafter. Retest stability coefficients for personality dimensions increase from adolescence through early adulthood, but stabilize at about age 30. For example, stability coefficients for personality characteristics over a seven-year period were about .24 for high school students and .35 for college-age students, but for adults they were almost always above .5 and often in the .70s. It appears that individuals continue to change their relative standings on basic personality dimensions through the decade of the twenties. By age 30, maximal stability is achieved. But even then, personality cannot be said to be "fixed." Life events and circumstances continue to accumulate and influence personality. Costa and McCrae estimate that about three-fifths of the variance in individual differences in adult personality is stable. Also, stability coefficients are overestimated to the extent they are correlated with *environmental stability.* Caspi and Bem (1990) summarize research showing that several environmental factors – children's peer networks, parenting practices, teaching and learning experiences – are quite stable over time.

Many theories about how adult personality develops exist. It is not necessary to review this literature in detail here, but only to connect contemporary debates in criminology about the development of personality characteristics (most notably, low self-control) that predict later criminal behavior with the larger literature on personality development. Some personality researchers believe that the early roots of personality can be traced to the interaction of individual differences in temperament during infancy and characteristics of the care-giver: Eder and Mangelsdorf (1997) summarize evidence suggesting that the fit between early child temperamental characteristics (e.g., activity level, emotionality) and parental personality (e.g., sensitivity to the child's needs) predicts the quality of the bond formed between the child and the parent. Secure versus weak attachments to the care-giver predict the child's view of the world (e.g., as safe or unsafe, fun or not fun) and his or her self-concept, which develops during the first three years of life.

Early individual differences are discernible but not highly stable from year to year. Very young children are not yet able to describe themselves in terms of traits. Researchers believe that further development of the self-concept is needed before a stable personality can emerge. According to Eder and Mangelsdorf (1997), full-blown dispositional self-conceptions do not emerge until age 7 or 8. Only then do children begin to recognize dispositions as being consistent across different situations, although they recognize that people have characteristics that endure across time somewhat earlier. Even very young children (e.g., three-year-olds) can choose words that describe themselves, and research shows that these descriptors hang together as identifiable factors. But the factor structures change from ages 3 to 5 to 7.

At approximately age 7 or 8, children do begin to describe themselves in terms of traits and use these self-theories to make decisions. Only at this time does the structure begin to resemble the more complex structure of adult personality. At age 7, an Emotional Stability factor and an Extroversion factor are discernible in childrens' reports of their own dispositions. But the degree of continuity between these early emerging traits and similar adult traits has not been established. All that can be said is that personality development is "at least partially completed" (Eder and Mangelsdorf, 1997) by age 7.

Relation of Personality Factors to Problem Behaviors

Several studies have demonstrated a link between the "Big 5" personality factors and measures of problem behavior. Caspi et al. (1994) examined the relation of personality characteristics and crime in two studies: the New Zealand birth cohort at age 18 and Pittsburgh boys ages 12 and 13. They departed from earlier studies of personality and crime by using personality assessment tools that covered the full range of personality traits identified by personality researchers. Earlier studies tended to use scales that had been developed specifically to differentiate delinquents from nondelinquents.

The New Zealand portion of the study used data from the Dunedin Multidisciplinary Health and Development Study – a longitudinal study of the health, development, and behavior of a cohort of males and females born in 1972 and 1973. Subjects were assessed at age 18 using a modified version of the Multidimensional Personality Questionnaire (MPQ; Tellegen, 1982). This assessment instrument yields ten scales measuring a broad range of personality characteristics that can be combined into three super factors. These three factors map quite closely onto four of the five "Big 5" factors (e.g., see Goldberg and Rosolack, 1994). Table 2.1 shows the concordance between the typologies.

Caspi et al. (1994) correlated the three higher-order and the ten primary factors of personality with official police and court records as well as measures of self-reported and informant-reported delinquency during the twelve-month period preceding the interview, separately for males and females. A consistent pattern emerged. Among both males and females, Constraint predicted lower delinquency and Negative Emotionality predicted higher delinquency in three independent data sources. Positive Emotionality was not related to delinquency. The correlation between Negative Emotionality and delinquency was driven largely by the Aggression subscale (a negative facet of Agreeableness in the "Big 5").

These basic associations between the Conscientiousness and Agreeableness dimensions of personality and problem behaviors have been replicated in samples of different ages, genders, and ethnicities. In the same study, Caspi et al. (1994) reported on data from the Pittsburgh Youth Study, which used a different personality assessment tool that could also be organized according to the three super factors just discussed. Measures of delinquency came from self-reports, teacher reports, and parent reports. This study also found that Constraint predicted lower delinquency and Negative Emotionality predicted higher delinquency across all data sources and for black and white students alike. Robins et al. (1994) used the same data to show that Antisocial Personality, a personality construct known to be highly predictive of criminal behavior, is composed primarily of facets of Conscientiousness and Agreeableness, and that these two personality dimensions predict lower delinquency. They also showed that Conscientiousness is positively related to school performance and IQ. Interestingly, these "Big 5" personality correlates of delinquency are unrelated to socioeconomic status or race.

Studies using different samples and relying on teacher ratings of child personality constructs have also found correlations between these same personality dimensions and measures of social adjustment and problem behavior. Graziano and Ward (1992) studied a mixed-race sample of students ages 11 through 14 from Georgia. Teacher and counselor evaluations of social adjustment were significantly related to teacher ratings of Conscientiousness (.72), Agreeableness (.41), Neuroticism (−.46), and Extraversion (.31). Victor (1994) studied a sample of predominantly African American fifth and sixth graders from rural Virginia and found that

Table 2.1. *Concordance between "Big 5" and MPQ Personality Factors*

"Big 5" Factor	MPQ Scale	Description
Conscientiousness	Constraint	
	Traditionalism	Desires a conservative social environment; endorses high moral standards.
	Harm Avoidance	Avoids excitement and danger; prefers safe activities even if they are tedious.
	Control	Is reflective, cautious, careful, rational, planful.
Neuroticism plus Agreeableness (−)	Negative Emotionality	
	Aggression	Hurts others for own advantage; will frighten and cause discomfort to others.
	Alienation	Feels mistreated, victimized, betrayed, and the target of false rumors.
	Stress Reaction	Is nervous, vulnerable, sensitive, prone to worry.
Extraversion	Positive Emotionality	
	Achievement	Works hard; enjoys demanding projects and working long hours.
	Social Potency	Is forceful and decisive; fond of influencing others; fond of leadership roles.
	Well-Being	Has a happy, cheerful disposition; feels good about self and sees a bright future.
	Social Closeness	Is sociable; likes people and turns to others for comfort.

teacher ratings of Extraversion, Agreeableness, and Conscientiousness all predicted a different teacher's rating of conduct problems. Digman and Inouye (1986) summarized results from three additional studies showing a correlation between Conscientiousness and subsequent measures of achievement.

Personality correlates of problem behavior are clearly evident during childhood and adolescence. Despite the different terminologies and measurement strategies used across studies, the evidence suggests that the Conscientiousness factor (emphasizing self-discipline, self-control) and the Agreeableness factor (emphasizing trustworthiness, compliance, closeness to people) are central to problem behavior across the age span. Openness is not related to problem behavior. The other two personality dimensions in the "Big 5" – Neuroticism and Extraversion – have all been shown to be related to problem behavior, but the strength of the relation depends on the items used to make up the factor in any particular study. Neurotic persons are emotionally unstable. When this instability involves aggression and hostility, problem behavior is more likely. When it involves more internalized forms of emotional instability (e.g., depression, alienation, and stress), it is not as likely to be linked with problem behavior. Extraverts are forceful and decisive but also sociable. Many studies have suggested that these dimensions of personality are closely linked. The sociable aspects of this dimension (liking and caring about people) seems to restrain problem behavior, whereas the "social potency" aspects do not.

Developmental changes in these personality characteristics correspond to developmental changes in delinquent involvement. As noted earlier, Conscientiousness and Agreeableness increase from childhood to adulthood. During childhood, children who are low on these characteristics engage in more antisocial behavior than do their counterparts who rate higher on these characteristics. They are also shunned by other students and are disliked by teachers. As children move into adolescence, delinquent peer groups form and opportunities for delinquent involvements increase. Again, those individuals who measure the lowest on the important personality dimensions succumb most readily to these temptations and join delinquent peer groups. But even during adolescence young people are in the process of developing into more competent individuals. As they become more conscientious and congenial, some undoubtedly attract conventional friends and other sources of social control, and their problem behavior desists. These natural developmental changes in personality, combined with changes in opportunities to commit crimes, may explain the general desistence from crime observed during the twenties.

Relation of Risk Factors to Personality Dimensions

The "Big 5" personality dimensions are useful for organizing and simplifying the risk factors for problem behavior identified earlier. Certain risk factors – early and persistent antisocial behavior (e.g., lying, cheating, stealing, destroying property) and early initiation of delinquency and drug use – are simply early forms of delinquency. Adolescents highly disposed to problem behavior will not only engage in greater quantities and more serious forms of these behaviors during adolescence, but they will also have initiated these behaviors at an earlier age than their peers. Because problem behavior is more likely to be noticed in children if it is extreme, those whose problem behavior is noticed earliest more often display more problem behavior later on. This accounts for the frequent observation that early onset of drug use or other problem behaviors predicts continued problem behavior (Robins, 1978; Robins and Pryzbeck, 1985). These behavioral "risk factors" are therefore simply early signs of the outcomes of interest in this book.

Facets of Conscientiousness. Many of the risk factors identified earlier are facets of Conscientiousness. These include impulsiveness or low self-control, belief in conventional rules, and attitudes unfavorable to drug use and delinquency. Self-control and low levels of impulsiveness are at the heart of the Conscientiousness factor. Persons high on this factor are self-disciplined, dependable, purposeful, persistent, mannerly, cautious, consistent, and conventional. They are not negligent, erratic, foolhardy, rash, reckless, or aimless.

Beliefs in conventional rules and attitudes unfavorable to drug use and delinquency are also facets of Conscientiousness. Persons high on belief in conventional rules endorse or internalize widely shared social rules, norms, proscriptions, prescriptions, or laws. Persons who display high levels of belief are conscientious, conforming, and respectful of authority; they are concerned about meeting their obligations to others; and they follow rules. Attitudes about drug use and delinquency are *specific* beliefs or proclivities that dispose individuals to respond to opportunities to engage in these behaviors in certain ways.

Facets of Agreeableness. Persons high in this personality dimension are adaptable, accommodating, considerate, polite, amiable, pleasant, modest, easygoing, truthful, ethical, honest, warm, and compassionate. They are not belligerent, volatile, dishonest, inconsiderate, impersonal, bossy, rude, cruel, or irritable. These are clearly the kind of people who form attachments with others and with whom others find it easy to form attachments. This dimension encompasses the risk factors that emphasize bonding to others. It also shares aspects of belief in rules (e.g., honesty, truthfulness, and ethical beliefs) with the Conscientiousness dimension.

Social closeness provides an important source of social control. Persons who care about what others think about them are constrained by these attachments to behave in ways that will not risk losing the love, esteem, and respect of significant others. Agreeable people are more likeable. Teachers and other adults care about them, are accepting of them, and are willing to help them. Conversely, teachers often regard students who are low on this dimension as troublemakers and are less willing to nurture them.

The individual-level risk factors for problem behavior, then, are facets of the well-established personality dimensions – Aggression (a facet of Emotional Stability), Conscientiousness, and Agreeableness. These aspects of personality begin to form very early in life, in interaction with parenting styles. They are identifiable but not highly stable at the point of school entry and continue to develop throughout childhood and adolescence. While school and family influence the development of these personality factors, these personality characteristics also shape the environment by influencing reactions of parents, teachers, and peers.

Aside from these personality and attitudinal risk factors, the research establishes associations of problem behaviors with academic performance, commitment and attachment to school, peer rejection, and association with delinquent peers for children in elementary school through high school. These risk factors are also at least in part a function of the personality dimensions discussed earlier. Conscientious people, by definition, are more likely to apply themselves in academic tasks. They are industrious, ambitious, organized, careful, persistent, purposeful, and prompt – all characteristics that are likely to be rewarded in school. They are more likely to invest time and energy in even the most mundane academic tasks. Gottfredson and Hirschi (1990, p. 106) noted that homework completion has always been a correlate of later crime. "Those who do it are by definition thinking about tomorrow. Those who do not do it have a shorter time frame. One mark of socialization is considering the consequences of today's activities for tomorrow. Homework thus indexes and perhaps contributes to socialization." Considerable research (summarized in Patterson, DeBaryshe, and Ramsey, 1989) shows that antisocial and rejected students lack the academic survival skills necessary to perform well in school.

Students high on the Agreeableness dimension are more likely to form attachments to school. Graziano (1994) reports that teacher and counselor evaluations of school adjustment are highly correlated with ratings of Conscientiousness, Agreeableness, and Neuroticism. Hence, attachment to school is at least in part a reflection of the enduring personal qualities students bring to school. Likewise, research summarized earlier shows that early peer rejection and subsequent peer influences are determined by early tendencies toward aggressive, rebellious, and impulsive acts.

Summary

Research on the structure and stability of personality provides an organizing framework for the more diverse research on risk factors for problem behavior. This literature identifies common elements of personality, detectable from early childhood, that continue to develop over the life course. These characteristics shape general demeanor, life views, and problem-solving approaches. Early individual differences on these characteristics influence how peers react to the individual as well as academic success and acceptance by teachers. These early experiences in turn influence the formation of adolescent peer groups, the development of beliefs and attitudes about the acceptability of deviant behaviors, and commitment to more conventional pursuits such as schooling. When self-control is lacking, and social controls fail to fall into place, nothing stands in the way between a youth's impulse to engage in self-indulgent behavior and the behavior.

Relatively stable personality differences alter behavior in combination with environmental conditions that are also relatively stable over time. Caspi and Bem (1990) suggest that the effect of early personality characteristics on later life outcomes is in part mediated by schooling experiences. Although enduring personality differences clearly influence behavior, so do experiences in the family, school, and peer group. Sufficient research has not yet been conducted to draw firm conclusions about the relative strength of individual propensity variables and social control variables as causes of delinquency or to construct precise models of how the two influences interact in the production of criminal behavior. These questions are, however, at the heart of debate in contemporary criminological theory. Literature pertaining to this debate attempts to sort out questions about the nature of the antisocial tendency, its malleability, and whether the conditions that arise from the early tendency (e.g., antisocial peers and weakened school bonds) have independent effects on subsequent crime. I turn now to a summary of this debate.

Theories of Crime Causation

Theories Emphasizing Stable Characteristics of Individuals

Most contemporary theories of crime causation recognize that the absence of self-control (often measured as impulsiveness, short time horizons, antisocial personality, etc.) is an important cause of delinquency, present in some persons from an early age, and relatively stable through the life course. Theories differ, however, in the centrality of this characteristic to the causal process, the extent to which self-control is malleable versus trait-like, and the extent to which other factors play important causal roles. Gottfredson and Hirschi's *General Theory of Crime* (1990) best articulates the view that low self-control is the central cause of delinquency, is more or less fixed at an early age, and that other social factors play minor causal roles at best.

Central to Gottfredson and Hirschi's 1990 theory is the assertion that people vary in their propensity to use force and fraud as a means of obtaining resources. Those on the high end of the propensity scale – those lacking self-control – tend to be impulsive, insensitive, risk takers, thrill seekers, highly physical, shortsighted, and relatively nonverbal. Persons with these qualities do not carefully weigh the pros and cons of delinquent acts before they are undertaken, and are not particularly constrained by the fear of losing the respect or positive regard of loved ones. They have low levels of internal control and manage to erode their sources of informal social control as they develop, if these sources exist at all. People lacking self-control probably never develop the requisite trust and emotional attachments to others necessary for social controls to be effective. These individuals are at increased risk not only for engaging in criminal activity but also for school failure, rejection by prosocial peers, dropout, poor performance on the job, failed marriages, and poor parenting.

This constellation of traits, formed during childhood socialization and persisting throughout the lifetime, arises from ineffective or incomplete socialization. When parents (and other socializing agents) do not watch children, recognize when deviant behavior has occurred, and punish deviant behavior consistently, children do not develop self-control.

Gottfredson and Hirschi's causal process is simple. As children enter adolescence, opportunities to engage in delinquency increase. Youths having reasonable levels of self-control manage to avoid the temptations associated with these opportunities. Those with low self-control do not. For youths with low self-control, nothing stands in the way between the youth and the benefits he will obtain through criminal activity. For other youths, self-control intervenes. The relative rankings of persons on the self-control dimension remain stable even as the desistance process begins. As people mature, changes in activity patterns cause them to be less exposed to criminal opportunities. But even during this process, the rank ordering on self-control is maintained. Self-control continues to explain variation on deviant acts throughout the life cycle.

According to this theory, no other sociological factors (e.g, association with delinquent peers; attachment or commitment to school, work, or a spouse; strain related to school failure) are necessary to explain crime. These other factors, which are primary causal elements of other theories, have only spurious relationships with crime because they also depend on self-control. Persons with low self-control are by nature not interested in schoolwork, which often tends to be boring. They are not likely to work hard at school or perform well. From a very early age, these students are likely to have a difficult time adjusting to their teachers' expectations that they be punctual, quiet, obedient, attentive, and physically inactive for long periods of time. Such students are more likely to be expelled or eventually to drop out of school. They are not likely to have strong attachments to school. But these facts do not increase youths' likelihood for engaging in crime. Rather, low self-control is responsible for all of these negative outcomes.

Students with low self-control are also less likely to form lasting relationships with others. They are liars, cheaters, and bullies, and most people do not care to have them as friends. They are too irresponsible, undependable, and selfish. These students are therefore often rejected by their more conventional peers and tend to gravitate toward one another for companionship. Gottfredson and Hirschi believe that this "birds of a feather flock together" hypothesis explains why delinquents overwhelmingly report that they associate with delinquent peers. Delinquent peer groups do not increase the likelihood that individuals will engage in criminal activity. They simply mark the youths who, by virtue of their low self-control, have a greater propensity for crime.

Similarly, holding down a job and marrying or becoming involved in a love relationship are not likely to reduce crime, according to Gottfredson and Hirschi. The observed correlations are spurious: crime is related to unemployment because those most likely to engage in crime are also the persons least likely to be able to find and keep jobs. And married persons are less likely to be engaged in crime because persons with a high propensity for crime tend to avoid the responsibilities of a long-term relationship. They may also have a difficult time finding a mate willing to marry them. In short, as Gottfredson and Hirschi explain, "people with low self-control sort themselves or are sorted into circumstances that are *as a result* correlated with crime" (1990, p. 119).

This General Theory is sometimes considered a "static" theory because it emphasizes the stability of self-control throughout the life-span. Because low self-control is a product of socialization, interventions aimed at altering early childhood socialization experiences are likely to be far more effective than interventions occurring later in life, including most rehabilitation efforts and efforts of criminal justice agencies. Secondary accounts of the theory (e.g., Cohen and Vila, 1996) have highlighted this feature of the theory, stating that self-control (according to Gottfredson and Hirschi) is more or less "set" at or around age 8 (e.g., around grade 3) and that if families and schools, the primary socializing institutions, have failed to teach self-control by that time, it is unlikely they will in the future. Likewise, a good job of socialization up to this point is unlikely to be undone in the future. But the original statement of the theory seems less deterministic than secondary accounts have suggested. Although Gottfredson and Hirschi clearly viewed parents as the primary socializing agents, they stated that socialization continues throughout childhood and even (to a lesser extent) into adulthood. They stated that policies directed toward enhancing "familial institutions" (1990, p. 273) to socialize children are the only realistic long-term policies with potential to reduce crime, but they did not restrict the meaning of "familial institution" to the traditional family. This term was extended to include "responsible adults committed to the training and welfare of the child."

As for the role of the school in teaching self-control, Gottfredson and Hirschi expected it has one, but that its ability to carry out this role is often crippled by uncooperative families. Schools can effectively monitor behavior, recognize deviant and disruptive behavior, and control it through systems of rewards and punishments. Gottfredson and Hirschi (1990, p. 105) state that "the school could be an effective socializing agency. The evidence suggests, however, that in contemporary American society the school has a difficult time teaching self-control. A major reason . . . appears to stem from the lack of cooperation and support it receives from families that have already failed in the socialization task." Poor parents, they said, cannot even be counted on to get their children to school. But, even without parental support, the net effect of schools is seen as positive. Schools do teach self-discipline. They impose restrictions on students and do not allow the "unfettered pursuit of self-interest." Schools also activate external controls, both in the form of school staff and commitments to future educational and occupational goals. Schools have the potential to teach self-control and to engage informal social controls to hold youthful behavior in check. But they will not always succeed because some schools are less capable than others of performing these socializing functions, and because some children and their families resist or at least fail to take advantage of what is offered.

Because the General Theory was created to explain the large and consistent correlations observed between the indicators of low self-control and criminal activity, it is highly consistent with this evidence. Recent tests of the theory have verified that low self-control (operationalized as suggested by Gottfredson and Hirschi) increases the likelihood that crime will occur in the face of opportunity to commit crime in a predominantly white general adult population (Grasmick, Tittle, Bursik, and Arneklev, 1993), and that low self-control predicts a variety of imprudent behaviors, including drinking and gambling (Arneklev, Grasmick, Tittle, and Bursick, 1993), although it does not affect smoking. The latter study also suggested that the risk taking and impulsivity components of the self-control measures carried most of the weight for the composite measure. Burton, Cullen, Evans, and Dunaway (1994) also studied the effects of self-control in an adult sample of white Americans. In models that included measures of key theoretical constructs from Strain, Social Control, and Differential Association theories as well as controls for age, gender, and income, self-control emerged as the most robust predictor of crime.

The most interesting tests of the theory have focused not on the extent to which low self-control predicts criminal activity (as this was already known) but on the structure and stability of self-control. Polakowski (1994) tested these aspects of the theory using data from the Cambridge Study in Delinquent Development collected in Great Britain between 1961 and 1981. This study provided evidence that, first, self-control, as suggested by Gottfredson and Hirschi, is measured better for boys ages 8 to 10 as a single factor that combines measures of behavioral conduct disorders, hyperactivity, impulsivity, and attention deficits than as multiple separate factors; and, second, this self-control trait is "moderately stable" over time, as evidenced by a correlation of .6 between a factor of low self-control measured at ages 8 to 10 and a similar factor measured at ages 12 to 14. Self-control at the earlier age explained 36% of the variance in self-control four years later. Polakowski noted that this level of correlation provides evidence of consistency in personality over the four-year period but, at the same time, admits to variability over time. The study also found that the lack of self-control is inversely related to elements of the social bond to conventional society, and that even with controls for several predetermined variables and earlier self-control, increases in parental supervision predicted higher self-control between ages 12 and 14 (implying that self-control is not "fixed" at age 8). Interestingly, a measure of involvement (e.g., greater amounts of time spent in leisure activities and involvement in the boys club) between ages 8 and 10 predicted *lower* self-control at ages 12 to 14. Finally, as Gottfredson and Hirschi predicted, self-control predicted future criminal convictions as well as self-reports of serious crime. But contrary to theoretical prediction, self-control did not predict self-reported minor crimes.

Research has also focused on the General Theory proposition that the effects of low self-control on criminal involvement (and related behaviors) remain stable over the life course and that other social conditions have minimal effect on offending. The General Theory notion of invariance in these associations over the life course is easily contrasted with developmental theories of crime causation, suggesting that different causal factors come into play at different points in the life cycle. Perhaps the most extreme developmental view is that of Moffitt (1993), who contends that there are two types of offenders. The "life-course-persistent" offenders resemble Gottfredson and Hirschi's offenders: their high propensity toward antisocial behavior develops early and persists through the life course. "Adolescent-limited" offenders, on the other hand, have no elevated propensity to engage in delinquent activity, but between ages 12 and 15 these youths mimic the delinquent behavior of their deviant peer models in an effort to appear less childlike. These youths desist from delinquent activity as they move into adulthood, while the life-course-persistent offenders continue their antisocial behavior into adulthood. This theory states, in a nutshell, that the causes of delinquency are different for these two groups of offenders and implies that the correlates of crime for very young offenders (who would be primarily life-course-persistent offenders) will be different from the correlates of crime for teens between ages 12 and 15.

Farrington (1986b) provided data pertinent to this theoretical debate in work that predated the debate. This report from the Cambridge Study of Delinquent Development examined which variables were associated with convictions during different age spans. Farrington found that some correlates of offending were the same regardless of the timing of the convictions, but some were different. For example, with minor exception, economic deprivation predicted problem behavior beginning at ages 8 through 10 and continuing through age 24. Family criminality predicted problem behavior beginning at ages 8 through 10 and continuing through age 20. Certain factors (e.g., parental mishandling) predicted early problems (through age 14) but did not continue to predict convictions from young adulthood through adulthood. Certain factors also seemed to come into play only at later times: truancy (at ages 12 through 14) and delinquent friends (at age 14), for example, predicted convictions in the early adult years but not earlier.

More recent tests have been attempted to provide more specific tests of the competing theories. Nagin and Farrington (1992a) also used the Cambridge Study in Delinquent Development data to test whether age of onset of criminal behavior had a causal impact on subsequent behavior, whether the determinants of onset vary with age, and whether the determinants of onset differ from the determinants of continuation of offending. The General Theory predicts that age of onset has no causal impact on subsequent offending net of individual propensity to offend and that the determinants of onset are invariant across age and with the determinants of continued offending. This study examined convictions between ages 10 and 31 and found (consistent with the General Theory) that the inverse association between age of onset (e.g., prior conviction) and continuation of offending is entirely attributable to time-stable individual differences. Results related to the second and third hypotheses were mixed: the effects of personal characteristics (IQ and "daring disposition") on participation in crime did not depend on age of onset. The magnitude of the covariation was also similar for explaining onset and continuation of offending. But the covariation of parental behaviors (separation and the interaction of separation and criminal status) did vary with age of onset, and these parental behaviors predicted onset but not continued offending. Also, poor parental child-rearing behavior was associated with early onset but not late onset. The results imply that whereas the effects of personal characteristics on delinquent behavior are stable over the life course, the influence of parental variables becomes less potent over time. The authors argue that this finding is not necessarily inconsistent with the General Theory. Instead, the declining influence of the parenting variables may be an artifact of the study design: effects of parent and dispositional variables measured at age 8 were related to criminal behavior through age 31. The diminishing effect of the parent variables may reflect the separation of the child from the parent as he aged. Postonset offenders were more likely to occur after the child no longer lived with the parents. Unfortunately, this study did not examine school-related social controls or peer-influence variables.

Bartusch, Lynam, Moffitt, and Silva (1997) also tested competing hypotheses about the extent to which different factors give rise to antisocial behavior at different ages. Using longitudinal data on New Zealand males between ages 5 and 18, they found that a two-factor model of antisocial behavior in which antisocial behavior at ages 13 and 15 loaded on a different underlying factor than antisocial behavior at ages 5, 7, 9, and 11 fit the data better than a single-factor model, although the factors in the two-factor model were highly correlated. They also showed that the correlates of adolescent antisocial behavior were somewhat different from the correlates of childhood antisocial behavior: childhood but not adolescent antisocial behavior was significantly related to low verbal ability, hyperactivity, and negative or impulsive personality, whereas adolescent but not childhood antisocial behavior was significantly related to peer delinquency. The differences in magnitude of the coefficients, although in the direction predicted by Moffitt's developmental theory, did not reach conventional statistical significance levels. The results were therefore more consistent with the General Theory of Crime than with Moffitt's developmental theory.

Paternoster and Brame (1997) also contrasted developmental with general theories of crime in a longitudinal study of predominantly white Americans boys and girls, age 11 or 12 at the time of first measurement. They tested to see if "dynamic" variables (e.g., participation in a serious delinquent act in the prior survey wave and delinquent peers) predicted subsequent delinquency net of demographics and a measure of "criminal propensity," which consisted of other, somewhat less serious problem behaviors (e.g., running away from home, lying, hitting, cheating, drinking alcohol, skipping school) and a composite of negative attitudes (including attitudes toward deviance, commitment and attachment to family, peers, and school), all measured at age 11 or 12. If self-control is the primary cause of later delinquent behavior and it is more-or-less fixed by age 10, Paternoster and Brame argued, subsequent offending and association with delinquent peers should not provide additional explanatory power once early forms of problem behavior and its likely consequences are controlled. The study showed that exposure to delinquent peers and prior offending[1] both predict subsequent delinquency, net of individual

---

[1] This finding replicated an earlier finding by Nagin and Paternoster (1991) using a longitudinal study of South Carolina students in grade 10 and contradicted Nagin and Farrington's (1992b) findings in a sample of younger British boys (ages 8 to 10) that association between prior and future participation in crime is largely attributable to time-stable individual differences.

propensity at age 11 or 12. They also found that the effects of prior delinquency and exposure to delinquent peers does not differ for low-propensity and high-propensity individuals, as anticipated by Moffitt.

Paternoster and his colleagues (Paternoster, Dean, Piquero, Mazerolle, and Brame, 1997) reported similar findings from a sample of North Carolina training school releasees ages 16 to 18. Using logic and methods similar to that reported in Paternoster and Brame (1997), they showed that (a) the magnitude of the effects of prior offending on subsequent offending decreased substantially once measures of stable individual differences were included in the model (supporting Gottfredson and Hirschi's notion of the importance of stable individual propensity to offend); but (b) the effect of prior arrest on future arrest was significant and "substantively important" even after controlling for persistent individual differences (supporting the predictions of "dynamic" theorists who emphasize the importance of transitions and change in criminal careers); and (c) these effects were for the most part similar for high- and low-propensity groups (failing to support the prediction that different processes apply to life-course-persistent and adolescent-limited offenders). On the bases of these two studies, Paternoster and his colleagues concluded that neither extreme theory (Moffitt's developmental nor Gottfredson and Hirschi's General Theory) is consistent with the data. Rather, the data accord more with a middle-ground explanation such as Sampson and Laub's (1993) theory of social control through the life course. Both continuity and change appear important in predicting future crime.

Theories Emphasizing the Influence of Individual and Social Factors

Sampson and Laub's (1993) theory grants the impressive stability in offending behavior over the life course but holds that fluctuations in informal social controls over the life course continue to explain offending behavior throughout adolescence and into adulthood. Social processes throughout the life course, including family discipline and monitoring, attachment to parents, school adjustment, and peer influences and important life events such as the acquisition of spousal and occupational attachments, predict changes in offending behavior, over and above the prediction offered by individual propensities that are stable through the lifetime. Their reanalysis of the Gluecks' data (Glueck and Glueck, 1950) provided evidence that family, school, and peer variables affect delinquent involvements. Attachment to school was a moderately large predictor of lower delinquency for the boys in the Gluecks' sample. This effect persisted when controls for demographics and family background were applied. Academic performance, on the other hand, showed inconsistent and small associations with delinquency. Sampson and Laub also found that early childhood disruptive and antisocial behavior predicted lower attachment to school and academic performance. But even when these strong predictors of delinquency were controlled, attachment to school (but not academic performance) continued to predict delinquency.

Academic Performance and School-Related Attitudes. Sampson and Laub's findings mesh well with findings of other investigations into the causal status of the school-related risk factors. Studies have long also attempted to disentangle the causal process related to academic performance and attitudes toward school. Early studies of the determinants of academic attainment (Bowles and Gintis, 1976; Porter, 1974) demonstrated that grades in school are influenced by students' social competencies as well as their academic performance. Longitudinal studies have likewise demonstrated that teacher and peer ratings of early problem behavior predict later academic performance (Feldhusen et al. 1973; Spivack and Cianci, 1987; Ullmann, 1957) and that drug use in high school leads to dropout, even when academic achievement is controlled (Garnier et al., 1997). Some studies have shown that school failure does not predict delinquent behavior once the behavioral antecedents of both are controlled. In a sample of African American middle school students, for example, Gottfredson, Fink, and Graham (1994) showed that being "held back" has no effect on later rebellious behavior when earlier characteristics that predispose individuals to both delinquency and school failure were controlled. These studies suggest that the association between early academic performance and delinquency is at least not unidirectional, as implied in several popular theories of delinquency causation (e.g., Cohen, 1955; Hirschi, 1969).

This line of inquiry had been most thoroughly examined by a team of Canadian researchers. Tremblay, Mâsse, et al. (1992) review several longitudinal and experimental studies that raise questions as to the causal status of academic success in the development of delinquent behavior. They then directly test competing models in a sample of French Canadian school children, first assessed in grade 1 and followed up at age 14. Academic achievement was measured in grades 1 and 4. The study showed that the link between disruptive behavior in grade 1 and delinquent behavior at age 14 was not mediated by academic achievement in grade 4. Academic performance in grades 1 and 4 was not related to delinquent behavior at age 14 once disruptive behavior in grade 1 was included in the model. For girls only, the model suggested that early disruptive behavior decreases school achievement. The study found a significant causal path between academic performance at age 10 and a constellation of personality characteristics (measured at age 14) thought to be related to delinquent behavior. These included measures of manifest aggression, antisocial values, and negative affect.

A similar study (Tremblay and Mâsse, 1993) compared competing causal models in a different sample of French-speaking Caucasian boys first assessed at age 6 and followed up at ages 10, 13, and 14. This study showed that the main causal path to delinquency in early adolescence was from preschool "externalizing personality problems" (e.g., oppositional behavior, hyperactivity, and fighting) through the same behavior problems measured at age 10. Poor academic performance was associated with these problem behaviors at each time point, but did not independently predict later delinquency when the prior and concurrent behavior problems were included in the model. LeBlanc et al. (1993), on the other hand, studied older French-speaking Canadian boys. They found that academic performance at ages 12 and 14 was the "best and most stable" predictor of criminal offending during early adulthood (between ages 18 and 30). The effect of academic performance on later offending persisted even with controls for early school misbehavior and adolescent delinquency.

Loeber and Maguin (1993) also found evidence that the association between educational performance and later delinquency is spurious. Using data from the Pittsburgh Youth Study, they showed that the association between poor reading performance and the seriousness of delinquency was reduced to nonsignificance when a measure of teacher- and care-giver-rated attention problems (whose items overlap considerably with the low self-control construct discussed earlier) was introduced. The likelihood of delinquency among children with attention problems was about twice that for those without, controlling on several demographic and family background measures.

Using slightly older students, Olweus (1983) found no support for a causal effect of poor grades on subsequent aggressive behavior. Olweus's sample consisted of 444 male Swedish students between ages 13 and 16. Within each time point, grades and aggressive behavior were inversely related, as expected. The cross-lagged correlations revealed that the correlation between early aggressive behavior and later school grades was somewhat higher (p < .1) than the correlation between earlier grades and later aggressive behavior. But the main finding of the study was that all of these cross-lagged correlations disappeared once measures of demographic and family factors were introduced. Olweus concluded that family variables influence both academic achievement and aggressive behavior. The oft-observed association was found to be spurious.

Finally, studies from the Oregon Youth Study have both questioned and supported the role of academic performance in the generation of delinquent behavior. Both studies relied on (different) samples of Caucasian boys from Oregon. Snyder et al. (1986) found that concurrent correlations of academic skills with association with deviant peers (a major risk factor for delinquent behavior) were statistically significant (and negative) in grade 7 but not grade 4 or 10. Measures of social skills and antisocial attitudes were related to negative peer associates at all three age levels. In multivariate equations, academic skills failed to predict association with deviant peers once social skill deficits were controlled. Dishion et al. (1991) examined longitudinal models of involvement with antisocial peers. Academic skills at age 10 were significantly (and inversely) related to peer antisocial behavior at age 12, and this effect persisted after controlling for the previous antisocial behavior of both the respondent and his peers. The investigators speculated that this negative effect might arise as a result of schools grouping academically deficient youths together for instruction.

Taken together, these studies suggest that *during elementary school* academic performance is best predicted by cognitive ability and antisocial behavior is best predicted by early problem behavior. Delinquent behavior in early adolescence (e.g., at age 14) is a function of persistent antisocial tendencies more than poor academic performance. But some studies do find that poor academic performance is one of the factors that predict association with negative peers.

Some studies examining *attitudes* about school measured during high school and delinquency suggest that academic failure *in high school* may indirectly heighten delinquent behavior by reducing prosocial attitudes and beliefs. Liska and Reed (1985) reanalyzed the Youth in Transition data and found that the effects of school attachment on delinquency (both of which were measured in grades 10 and 11) were reciprocal, although somewhat stronger in the delinquency-to-attachment direction than in the attachment-to-delinquency direction. Ward and Tittle (1994) also used the Youth in Transition data to show that the effects of IQ on delinquency are mediated primarily through school attachment. This study found that school performance in grade 10 had no direct effect on delinquency in grade 12, but that its effects were indirect through attachment to school. Thornberry, Lizotte, Krohn, Farnworth, and Jang (1991) confirmed a bidirectional relationship between commitment to school and delinquent behavior for younger youths who participated in the Rochester Youth Development Study. This study reported on data from three different data collection points over a one-year period, beginning when youths were in grade 7 or 8. The study found consistent evidence for a "mutually reinforcing causal relationship over time." Low commitment increases delinquency, and delinquency reduces commitment to school.

The Rochester data were reanalyzed (with two additional data points) and similar data from the Denver Youth Study (which involved annual interviews with youths ages 7 through 15 at the time of the first interview) were examined in a summary report on the Program of Research on the Causes and Correlates of Delinquency. Thornberry, Esbensen, and Van Kammen (1993) confirmed the bidirectional relationship between commitment to school and measures of street crime and drug use in the Rochester sample, but found no evidence that low commitment to school increases delinquency in the Denver sample, perhaps because younger students were included in the study. Only an effect of street crime on commitment was found in that sample. The report concluded that, overall, the results supported a bidirectional causal process and that prevention efforts aimed at improving commitment to school were wellfounded.

The evidence to date suggests that receiving poor grades in school and being held back do not necessarily increase the likelihood of delinquency, especially in childhood and early adolescence. But low attachment and low commitment to school in adolescence do increase the likelihood of later delinquency.[2] The most likely causal mechanism is that early and persistent conduct problems lead to early involvement in delinquent activities, which, along with the persistent personality traits of the individual, reduce subsequent academic performance and attachments and commitments to school.

Association with Delinquent Peers. Sampson and Laub's reanalysis of the Gluecks' data is also pertinent to a long debate in criminology about the relative utility of socialization and selection explanations of the observed correlation between delinquency and association with delinquent peers. The large concurrent correlation has often been interpreted to mean that association with negative peers increases delinquent behavior. One leading theory of delinquency causation states that delinquent behavior is learned through differential association with others who control powerful reinforcements, provide normative definitions, and expose one to behavioral models (Burgess and Akers, 1966). Control theories, on the other hand (e.g., Gottfredson and Hirschi, 1990; Hirschi, 1969), have countered that the association is entirely explained by delinquent youths seeking out or being sorted into delinquent peer groups – the "birds of a feather flock together" argument. Sampson and Laub (1993) showed that delinquent peer attachments in adolescence predicted later delinquency net of early childhood antisocial tendencies, family management practices, parental rejection, and structural factors. These findings accord with research summarized in Akers (1996), with recent research (Paternoster and Brame, 1997) that suggests a causal effect of peers on delinquency, and with the results of an experimental study that manipulated negative peer associations (Feldman, Caplinger, and Wodarski, 1983).[3] Sampson and Laub stop short of fully endorsing Differential Association Theory, however. They

[2] Note, however, that Olweus's (1983) study of Swedish males found no effect of academic performance on school attitudes or of school attitudes on aggressive behavior. All associations were spurious.
[3] This study, although difficult to summarize in detail, randomly assigned boys referred because of their antisocial behavior to receive project services either as part of a mixed group in which most of the participants had not been referred or as part of a homogeneous group of referred youths. Although the number of cases in the relevant groups was small (twenty-five or twenty-six referred boys in each type of group) and the differences often do not reach conventional levels of statistical significance, the results clearly show more positive outcomes for the boys who received services as part of the mixed groups.

point out that the largest predictor of delinquency is early antisocial behavior, which could not have been learned through differential association with peers. Also, sibling delinquency had little effect on delinquent behavior in the Glueck data, a finding that seems inconsistent with a strict version of Differential Association Theory. The scant research that has examined reciprocal effects of peer associations and delinquent behavior finds support for both explanations: delinquent peer associations increase the likelihood of delinquency, and delinquency further isolates the person within delinquent peer networks (see, e.g., Krohn, Huizinga, and Van Kammen, 1993; Thornberry et al., 1994).

Developmental Progressions. In addition to demonstrating that social experiences affect delinquency above and beyond the effects due to enduring individual differences, Sampson and Laub (1993) provided evidence that the effects of social bonds are cumulative over the life course: attachments to school, for example, explain additional variation in delinquency over and above that explained by family variables. Later changes in the nature and strength of social bonds (through, e.g., marriage, military service, and steady employment) continue to explain fluctuations in criminal activity into adulthood. Sampson and Laub's theory is essentially a developmental theory of crime causation that assumes both time-stable and developmental influences on crime. This theory suggests that some causal variables can be expected to predict crime regardless of when they are measured, whereas other causal variables reflect changes in social control over the life course and would not necessarily be persistent causes of crime across the life course.

A recent meta-analysis of predictors of violent and serious delinquency (Lipsey and Derzon, 1997) provides more support for such a developmental perspective. This study summarized evidence from thirty-four independent longitudinal studies (like those described earlier) that measured delinquency in late adolescence and early adulthood. It examined the extent to which predictors of violent and serious crime between ages 15 and 25 differ for youths at different stages of development. Lipsey and Derzon examined some 793 effect sizes from sixty-six reports from these studies. Twenty different predictor variables were identified in these studies. They were grouped into the following categories:

Antisocial behavior: physical violence, aggression, person crimes, general offenses, problem behavior, and substance use.

Personal characteristics: gender, ethnicity, IQ, psychological conditions, school attitude or performance.

Family characteristics: antisocial parents, abusive parents, broken home, parent-child relations, family socioeconomic status, other family characteristics.

Social factors: social ties, antisocial peers.

Correlations of each predictor variable and the criterion were calculated. Correlations derived from early measurements of risk factors (when subjects were between ages 6 and 11, roughly corresponding to the elementary school years) were compared with the correlations derived from later measurements of the risk factors (when subjects were between ages 12 and 14, roughly corresponding to the junior high school years).

The study found that the mean effect size for each of the twenty predictors was significantly different from zero for both age groups, indicating that the predictor variables most frequently studied in prospective longitudinal studies are statistically related to subsequent violent or serious delinquency. Furthermore, the effect sizes for several of the factors were large enough to be of practical importance in prevention work and were variables that are potentially malleable. The study also found evidence that the effect sizes differed for different predictor variables and their rank orders were different for the different age groups.

After controlling for characteristics of the study methodologies, the largest correlates of later violent and serious delinquency for younger subjects were earlier general delinquency and substance use. Correlations of demographic characteristics, having antisocial parents, and aggression with later violent and serious crime were also moderately high. Other risk factors identified here – social ties, problem behavior, school attitude or performance, and antisocial peers – had relatively low predictive power when these variables were measured between ages 6 and 11.

The results were almost reversed when the factors were measured when the subjects were older. In these analyses, social ties and antisocial peers were the largest predictors of subsequent violent and serious crime, followed by involvement in general delinquency. Substance use and demographics (except for gender) barely predicted later violent and serious crime. Aggression was about as predictive as it was for the younger age group, and school attitudes or performance was somewhat more predictive.

What these results do *not* tell us is the extent to which early risk factors have an immediate effect on problem behavior. Peer rejection during the early grades, for example, may in fact reduce problem behavior during these school years even if it does not predict serious and violent delinquency at age 15. Problem behavior across the life-span was not the criterion examined in the Lipsey and Derzon meta-analysis. But the results do suggest that the youths most likely to engage in later serious and violent crime can be identified at an early age, mostly by their early antisocial behavior and aggressive tendencies. Family conditions are also predictive. Early school failure, poor attitudes about school, weak social ties, and association with antisocial peers are not among the strongest correlates of later serious and violent behavior. But during the period just prior to adolescence, general delinquency and substance abuse become more prevalent in the population and less predictive of subsequent violent and serious behavior. By this developmental stage, the most chronic segment of the population has severed ties with conventional others, shed their commitment to school, and formed delinquent peer groups. These variables, along with aggression (whose effect appears stable throughout the lifetime), differentiate serious future offenders from nonoffenders.

Conclusions

This chapter started with a summary of literature on "risk factors" for problem behavior. It called upon research in the personality field to organize this diverse literature with reference to a small number of personality factors that can be identified from childhood onward into adulthood and are fairly stable. Next, it reviewed the terms of and evidence pertaining to a contemporary debate among criminological theorists regarding the static versus dynamic nature of crime causation. In this context, it examined the evidence regarding risk factors related to social controls and experiences – attachment and commitment to school, academic performance, and association with delinquent peers – and found evidence supporting a causal association between delinquent behavior and association with delinquent peers and attachment and commitment to school. The evidence suggested that the correlation between academic performance, at least prior to high school, and delinquency was due mostly to their common reliance on early behavior problems.

Taken together, the evidence from various sources suggests that traits associated with antisocial behavior are evident in some individuals from very early in life. The personality literature shows that early temperamental differences among infants interact with environmental conditions (caregiver behaviors and characteristics) to create early personality dispositions. Although not very stable, these early differences resemble major personality dimensions known to be related to crime later in life. Ineffective parenting[4] (including failure to monitor and supervise the child, harsh and inconsistent discipline practices, and little positive involvement with the child) during the preschool years further interacts with early temperament to produce childhood conduct disorders. These disorders are not transient. Rather, the behavior patterns tend to stick with a child and generalize to the school setting (Ramsey, Patterson, and Walker, 1990).

At about age 6, the school begins to share with the family the responsibility for shaping the child's disposition and behavior. The school's func-

[4] The literature on developmental progressions for antisocial behavior within the family was not reviewed in this chapter. Readers are referred to the work of Gerald Patterson and his colleagues (e.g., Patterson, DeBaryshe, and Ramsey, 1989; Patterson, Reid, and Dishion, 1992).

tion is similar to that of the family. School officials watch for and punish instances of misbehavior. They demand and reinforce conscientiousness and agreeableness. They teach rules and expect them to be followed. Just as families can be effective or ineffective in this function, so can schools. As we will see, all schools and teachers are not equally effective socializing agents, and all students within a given school do not experience equal mixes of effective and ineffective teachers. Some schools, by failing in their socialization function, become training grounds for antisocial behavior. They allow antisocial behavior to escalate through reinforcement. When this happens, antisocial children are more conspicuous and tend to be rejected by prosocial peers who might otherwise provide the necessary training in how to get along with others. Teachers also begin to dislike these youngsters, regard them as troublemakers, and may take steps to isolate them from the rest of the class. These interactions continue throughout the elementary school years, often in conjunction with academic difficulties caused by persistent failure of the child to concentrate and apply himself or herself to the academic task. The most extremely antisocial youth extend their antisocial behaviors to include forms of delinquency even in elementary school.

As youths move into early adolescence, the same predispositions that caused them to be troublesome in their early years continue to cause them to be troublesome, unless the school or the family has successfully intervened to teach the child to control himself or herself. The school continues to shape this behavior, but the task becomes more difficult because of the decreasing assistance from parents and the increasing influence of peers. Evidence suggests that social controls in the form of attachment and commitment to school (and perhaps belief in the validity of social rules and norms) and peers exert causal influence at this developmental stage – in addition, of course, to the persistent effects of personality. Although personality in part shapes the peer group experiences and the levels of social bonding to which one will be exposed, these experiences have predictive power for explaining subsequent delinquency above and beyond that due to the personality characteristics.

Does the school have a role in shaping delinquent behavior? Evidence summarized in this chapter suggests that schools might reduce subsequent delinquency by helping children to develop and maintain self-control and teaching them how to get along with others. These lessons should begin in the early elementary grades and continue through high school. As youths move into adolescence, schools should attend to a broader array of student outcomes, including their academic performance, attitudes about school, and association with peers.

The next chapter reviews literature on school-to-school variation in problem behavior outcomes and in the important individual precursors of delinquency summarized in this chapter. It shows that schools do affect these outcomes and suggests some of the dimensions along which the more and less effective schools differ. Subsequent chapters examine the success of efforts to intervene in school settings to manipulate these factors.

School Effects

KOZOL'S (1992) stark account of the extremes of wealth and poverty in America's school system exposed major inequalities in public schooling. He contrasted schools serving inner city children with those serving more affluent populations in selected cities. Of one school in Chicago, he wrote:

> Teachers use materials in class long since thrown out in most suburban schools. Slow readers in an eighth grade history class are taught from 15-year-old textbooks in which Richard Nixon is still president. There are no science labs, no art or music teachers. Soap, paper towels and toilet paper are in short supply. There are two working bathrooms for some 700 children. (1992, p. 63)

He quoted a "permanent sub" (i.e., a long-term substitute teacher used to keep personnel costs down) who teaches in this school: "It was my turn. I have a room of 39 overage, unmotivated sixth and seventh graders. . . . I am not prepared for this. I have absolutely no idea what to do" (1992, p. 64). Kozol offered an account of a different teacher in the same school:

> Three years ago this teacher received "official warning" at another elementary school. Transferred here, but finding herself unable to control the class, she was removed in March. Instead of firing her, however, the principal returned her to the children for their morning reading class. It is a class of "academically deficient children." But the teacher does not know how to teach reading. (p. 64)

Kozol's work is filled with many such descriptions of schools serving the nation's poor, usually minority, students. He described blatant deficiencies in the physical school buildings, the material resources, and the personnel – teachers and administrators – in these schools, and contrasted them with nearby suburban schools, which enjoy attractive campuses, modern buildings, superior labs, up-to-date technology, small class sizes, and top-notch faculty and administrators.

In this chapter I explore the extent to which exposure to such different schools influences students' educational and social outcomes. I set the stage by exploring the larger community contexts of which schools are a part. Because deteriorated schools often serve economically disadvantaged students, I also discuss technical problems of disentangling school contextual effects from the effects of aggregated individual characteristics and from community contextual effects. I describe a research strategy suited to analyzing the type of nonexperimental survey research data commonly used to study school contributions to student outcomes. Then I summarize evidence from school-level and multilevel studies about characteristics of schools related to problem behavior and its individual-level causes. Finally, I place school effects research within the routine-activities framework presented in Chapter 1.

Schools Embedded in Communities

It is not informative to study between-school variation in crime without also considering community-level contributions to crime. Schools are embedded within communities and, in many ways, reflect larger community-level processes. By far the largest correlates of school disorder are characteristics of the schools' population and community context (Gottfredson and Gottfredson, 1985). Schools in urban, poor, disorganized communities experience much more violence and other forms of disorder than do schools in rural or suburban, affluent, organized communities. The percentage of teachers in a 1990–1991 national survey indicating that discipline problems in their school are serious or moderate is substantially higher for every problem except substance abuse for teachers in city schools than teachers in suburban and rural schools (National Center for Education Statistics, 1991): 37% of city teachers compared with 27%, 25%, and 18% of urban fringe, town, and rural teachers reported that physical conflicts among students are a serious or moderate problem. According to NCVS surveys on crimes against school teachers aggregated from 1992 through 1996 (Kaufman et al., 1998), teachers in urban schools (39 out of every 1,000) were more likely to be victims of violent crime than were teachers in suburban and rural schools (20 out of every 1,000 teachers in suburban schools and 22 for every 1,000 teachers in rural schools). Students in urban areas have also reported more disorder. A 1993 national study of students in grades 3 through 12 showed that 24% of students in urban schools compared with 16% of students in suburban or rural schools thought that the use of knives or guns was a major problem in their school (Louis Harris and Associates, 1993).

The 1996 NCVS also showed that students ages 12 through 18 living in urban areas were more vulnerable to serious violent crime than were students in suburban and rural areas both at and away from school (Kaufman et al., 1998). The rates per 1,000 students were approximately twice as high in urban than in rural schools for out-of-school victimization, and four times as high for in-school victimization.

Studies focusing solely on inner-city areas find exceptionally high rates of disorder. Callahan and Rivara (1992) found that in one urban area 34% of students in grade 11 reported easy access to guns, and 6% reported owning a handgun. In a survey of students in selected inner-city high schools, Sheley, McGee, and Wright (1995) found approximately 20% of students had been assaulted with a weapon, and 66% knew somebody who had been shot at, stabbed, or otherwise assaulted at school; 80% reported that other students carried weapons at school.

Other educational problems are distributed in a similar way: high school dropout rates, school completion rates, and academic performance indicators all imply vastly greater problems for schools in urban areas (Kantor and Brenzel, 1992). In 1980, for example, the dropout rate in urban communities was 19% compared with 12% in the suburbs and 13% in rural areas.

These uneven distributions of school disorder and educational outcomes surely reflect in part the uneven social distribution of problems in general. One of the best-known facts in criminology is that social area characteristics are related to the level of crime. In 1990, the violent crime rate from the FBI's Uniform Crime Report (UCR) ranged from 359 per 100,000 residents for cities with less than 10,000 population to 2,243 for cities with a million or more residents (Reiss and Roth, 1993). Victimization and self-report surveys show the same pattern.

Crime rates vary across locations *within* cities as much or more than they vary by urbanicity. Reiss and Roth (1993) showed that violent crime rates for census tracts within one metropolitan area differ so much that one area's rate was three hundred times that of another. This variation in crime rates across areas is substantially correlated with other social and economic characteristics of the areas. Poverty and income inequality, educational attainment, mobility of the population, ethnic composition, population density, and high proportions of female-headed households are correlated with area crime rates (Block, 1979; Sampson, 1995). These are the same community characteristics shown to predict the level of disorder experienced in schools (Gottfredson and Gottfredson, 1985).

The relative contributions of school and community factors in the generation of crime has received scant attention in the research literature. Some authors (e.g., McDermott, 1983) have argued that the level of crime committed in schools simply reflects the level of crime in the surrounding community. Variation in school crime rates are due to community-level rather than school-level characteristics or processes. He argues that focusing attention on school characteristics and designing school-related interventions to reduce crime will be futile in the long run if the true source of variation in school crime rates lies in the larger community. Others (Gottfredson and Gottfredson, 1985) have argued that what schools do also influences levels of school disorder. According to this perspective, manipulating school environments should reduce crime.

Theoretical support for a school effect is found in the work of Shaw and McKay (1969) and elaborations of their social disorganization theory (Bursick and Grasmick, 1993). Disorganized communities experience higher levels of crime, according to this perspective, because their mechanisms of social control are less effective. Intimate ties among residents are said to be less common, limiting the informal control made possible by threats to withdraw sentiment, support, or esteem of loved ones. Supervision of residents by neighbors is also weakened by population instability and heterogeneity. The key socializing institutions, such as families, schools, and churches, are less effective in disorganized areas.

Shaw and McKay's work and more recent scholarly works (e.g., Kantor and Brenzel, 1992) suggest that schools in high-crime areas are less able to socialize youths effectively because (a) community norms for behavior are ambiguous, inconsistent, or unconventional and educators can neither agree on appropriate standards for behavior nor depend on the community to support their socializing actions; (b) fewer human and other resources can be garnered from the community to work with the school; (c) the social and emotional needs of the students are greater, requiring a higher level of effort for effective socialization; and (d) schools in disorganized areas are less effective at attracting and holding the most talented educators. These social facts contribute to poor educational practices – including the use of irrelevant, fragmented curriculum, rigid retention policies and disciplinary practices, and low teacher expectations for student success – that adversely affect student performance in schools and increase the likelihood of delinquency and dropout. Research summarized later in this chapter shows that these and other features of schools contribute to the explanation of youthful delinquent and other problem behaviors. As one element of community social disorganization, schools play a causal role in the production of crime and can potentially reduce it.

Studying Contextual Effects

The central question for research on the uneven distribution of social problems was raised more than twenty years ago by Kornhauser (1978, p. 104), who asked: "How do we know that differences in delinquency rates result from the aggregate characteristics of communities rather than the characteristics of individuals selectively aggregated into communities? How do we even know that there are differences at all once their differing composition is taken into account?" As Sampson (1987) pointed out, observed correlations between area characteristics and rates of crime cannot necessarily be interpreted as ecological effects. Such large correlations might easily arise simply as a result of the grouping of individuals with similar characteristics in geographical proximity to one another. For example, single mothers with children may be drawn to certain areas because of the availability of low-cost housing. Schools serving these areas are likely to experience higher levels of delinquency than schools serving areas in which a higher proportion of two-parent families reside. In this example, the apparent school-level variation in crime rates may be due entirely to characteristics of the individuals (or their families) who happen to be grouped together in school catchment areas rather than to any contextual effect of the schools or the communities in which they are located. Perhaps attending a school in an inner-city area does not produce school failure, dropout, and delinquency. Rather, students destined for more favorable life outcomes may attend other schools. Before attributing to school- or community-level processes observed variability in aggregate student outcomes, it is important to consider whether meaningful individual-level processes explain the observed correlations.

Several studies have demonstrated that characteristics of the community influence the behavior of individual residents, net of the individuals' own characteristics. Early studies (Gottfredson, McNeil, and Gottfredson, 1991; Simcha-Fagan and Schwartz, 1986) showed that indicators of community social disorganization were related to higher self-reported and official delinquency. More recent studies have extended these findings to show that the level of community affluence predicts IQ at age 3, as well as teenage births and school dropout (Brooks-Gunn, Duncan, Klebanov, and Sealand, 1993); and that residence in an "underclass" neighborhood increases individual-level delinquency (Peeples amd Loeber, 1994). Both of these studies also found that race differences in individual outcomes are accounted for in large part by characteristics of the communities in which individuals live. Elliott et al. (1996) examined the importance of organizational features of neighborhood (low social integration, weak informal networks, and weak informal controls) in mediating the effects of neighborhood disadvantage (poverty, mobility, single-parent families, and ethnic diversity). The study found that organizational features of the community predict adolescent problem behavior outcomes, net of individual and family characteristics. Informal control was most consistently found to mediate the effects of neighborhood disadvantage.

Finally, Sampson, Raudenbush, and Earls (1997) report on the most elaborate community effects study to date. They identified 343 "neighborhood clusters" (NCs) in the city of Chicago. These NCs were formed by combining census tracts in an ecologically meaningful way so that they were internally homogeneous and consistent with geographical boundaries. Residents living in representative households within each neighborhood were interviewed. Measures were taken from the census (concentrated disadvantage, immigrant concentration, and residential stability) as well as from the resident interviews. The investigators hypothesized that the "collective efficacy" of the neighborhood (social cohesion among neighbors combined with their willingness to intervene on behalf of the common good) would mediate the effects of neighborhood socioeconomic disadvantage on violence. Controlling for individual background characteristics associated with higher reports of collective efficacy, they found that concentrated disadvantage and immigrant concentration decreases and residential stability increases collective efficacy. These same neighborhood socioeconomic characteristics were related to community rates of violence and victimization (again, net of personal characteristics). The effects of neighborhood socioeconomic disadvantage, immigrant concentration, and residential instability were substantially mediated by collective efficacy.

Taken together, these studies of community effects on individual problem behavior consistently show that residence in a disadvantaged or disorganized community increases problem behavior, above and beyond what would be expected on the basis of the characteristics of the individuals and families living in those communities, although the percentage of variance in individual problem behavior accounted for by community characteristics is often small, ranging from less that 1% (Gottfredson et al., 1991) to 5% (Elliott et al., 1996). The most recent studies suggest that one important mechanism through which community socioeconomic disadvantage operates to increase crime is informal social control. Neighborhoods differentially activate informal social control. In neighborhoods with high rates of residential mobility and low levels of financial investment, residents do not form social ties and do not have a vested interest in supporting the commonwealth of the community. Trust and solidarity among residents are not built, and residents are not willing to intervene or invest time and effort in solving community problems. Because schools are community institutions, the collective efficacy of the community is likely to influence school social organization as well, causing schools in disadvantaged communities to manage themselves ineffectively.

A second technical problem in studying *school* effects is to separate the contextual effects of the larger community from those of the school. It may be possible to demonstrate that school-level variation in delinquent behavior is not completely accounted for by the aggregated characteristics of the students attending the school – that is, that some between-school variance remains after the predicted delinquency based on an individual-level model has been removed. But some or all of this school-level variation may be due to contextual processes that require no special reference to the school. A student from a middle-class family whose personal and family characteristics do not place him or her at particularly high risk for delinquent behavior may live in a high-crime area of the city. Residence in this area of the city may increase proximity to gangs and reduce adult supervision in general. The school serving this high-crime community might have no impact on this boy's involvement in crime beyond these community-level contributions. Alternatively, the school might have its own contextual effect, and this effect might counteract or exacerbate the effect of the community. Studies that fail to measure and separate *school* from *community* contextual effects provide only a combined estimate of the two effects. This imprecision applies to most studies of community and school contextual effects.

Short of a social experiment in which individuals are randomly assigned to live in different communities and attend different schools, the ideal study of school effects would employ individual-, school-, and community-level data for a large number of social areas. Further, it would measure the specific characteristics of community and school context as well as the specific individual-level factors thought to contribute to the behavior of interest. No study has yet accomplished this combination of measurements and sample size.

School Effects Research

Like the early community contextual effects research, early research on school contextual effects suggested that little variance in individual outcomes was attributable to between-school differences. A pioneering study conducted in the 1960s by Coleman and his colleagues (Coleman et al., 1966) involving 645,000 students in four thousand elementary and secondary schools showed that achievement test scores were hardly related to a number of measured school characteristics such as per-pupil expenditure, class size, and teacher qualifications. Instead, these outcomes were explained primarily by student background characteristics. Jencks et al. (1972) came to similar conclusions after reanalyzing data from a number of different studies, which showed that characteristics of the schools students attend account for less than 1% of the variance in cognitive test scores. Summarizing this early research, Hauser, Sewell, and Alwin (1976, p. 310) declared that "it is abundantly clear that the observed differentiation of educational outcomes among American students has not been traced directly or in large measure to systematic variations in the social environment from school to school." Large differences in educational outcomes by ethnicity and social class were accounted for much more by family factors than by school factors, leading many scholars to conclude that manipulating school organizational or process variables would be fruitless.

This dismaying conclusion spurred researchers to conduct more careful and increasingly sophisticated research on school effects. This research has broadened the set of student outcomes examined, employed more sensitive outcome measures, specified and measured the school factors thought to influence school outcomes, used longitudinal research designs to assess how schools change students over time, and employed multilevel modeling techniques to obtain more refined estimates of school effects. The following pages summarize this research.

School-Level Studies

Early research on school effects compared school means on student outcomes with no or only crude controls for the differing populations served by the school. These studies (Cannan, 1970; Power, Benn, and Morris, 1972; Reynolds, Jones, and St. Leger, 1976), although largely inadequate for assessing the unique contribution of schools beyond those of the families and communities from which students are drawn, were useful for demonstrating the existence of a wide range of variation in school-level outcomes that could not be entirely accounted for by the characteristics of the communities in which the schools were located.

School effects research in the 1980s began to employ more sophisticated measures of school intake characteristics. School-level studies used school averages or rates as dependent variables in equations that explicitly controlled for school-level measures of social background and demographics. A few longitudinal studies also included controls for school averages on relevant outcome variables taken at the time of entry to the school. Many of these studies simply looked for residual variance in the school-level outcome of interest after the effects of school intake had been accounted for. Gray, McPherson, and Raffe (1983), for example, conclude that the variation in school outcomes (achievement test scores, truancy, satisfaction with school, and having been "belted") reflects more than differences in the compositional characteristics of the students served and that the amount of between-school variance differs by outcome. This study was among the first to demonstrate that employing more sensitive measures of the outcomes of schooling might result in larger estimates of school effects than had been observed in the works of Coleman and Jencks, both of which studied only a narrow range of cognitive outcomes measured by tests designed to be most sensitive to individual differences. Such tests discount sources of variation that might arise from school-to-school differences.

Subsequent school-level studies examined a number of different outcomes of schooling, explicitly measured characteristics of the community and the school thought to influence these school aggregate outcomes, and controlled for school-level measures of student input. Two of these (Galloway, Martin, and Wilcox, 1985; Hellman and Beaton, 1986) found no evidence for school effects on student absenteeism or suspension once community characteristics were controlled. In both of these studies, however, the measures of school characteristics were limited to features of the school building (e.g., age of building) and aspects of formal school organization (e.g., school size, use of ability grouping, staff turnover taken from school and school district records) commonly found in archival records. Studies demonstrating more substantial school effects measured aspects of the school social organization as well and included more schools.

The most ambitious study of school effects published in the 1980s examined school factors related to rates of victimization in schools. Gottfredson and Gottfredson (1985) analyzed the Safe School Study data on a 1976 national sample of more than six hundred U.S. secondary schools. Census characteristics of the areas in which each school was located were combined with data from students, teachers, and principals on the level of disorder experienced in the school. This study measured characteristics of the community in which the school is located (community poverty and disorganization, socioeconomic status, and residential mobility from census data; and community crime, population of the area, and distance from the central city from principal reports), as well as sociodemographic characteristics of the students in the school and characteristics of the school environment from student, teacher, and principal surveys. The measures of community context and student input characteristics were highly correlated and in most analyses had to be combined because it was not possible to estimate their effects separately. Interestingly, the correlations between student demographic characteristics and the community characteristics were much higher at the junior high school level than at the senior high school level, probably because senior high schools draw students from a wider geographical area and are therefore more likely to contain a heterogeneous mix of students.[1] The study showed that these externally determined factors explained 54% and 43% of the variance in teacher victimization rates for junior and senior high schools, respectively. But controlling for these externally determined characteristics, characteristics of schools accounted for an additional 12% and 18% of variance in teacher victimization rates in junior and senior high schools.

Statistical models were developed to identify those features of the school environment that directly contributed to the explanation of teacher victimization rates after controlling for exogenous community characteristics and student input characteristics. For junior and senior high schools, the following characteristics met this rigorous test:

[1] This finding was replicated in a 1986 study of school suspension rates in the Boston public schools (Hellman and Beaton, 1986), in which community crime rates were essentially redundant with measures of aggregated student input characteristics and school organization in the explanation of school suspension rates for middle school students, but added substantially to the explanation of suspension rates for senior high schools.

Staffing, size, and resources
Fewer teaching resources.
Larger total enrollment (junior high schools) and larger number of different students taught by the average teacher (senior high schools).

Governance and educational climate
Greater use of ambiguous sanctions (e.g., ignoring misconduct, lowering grades as a disciplinary practice).
More democratic attitudes of teachers (e.g., belief that students and parents should have a say in how the school is run) – junior high schools only.
More punitive teacher attitudes.
Less teacher-administration cooperation – senior high schools only.

Social climate and student socialization
Lower perceptions among students that rule enforcement is firm and clear (junior high schools) and lower student beliefs in the conventional social rules (senior high schools).

In contrast to these findings for teacher victimization rates are the results of similar analyses of student victimization rates. In these analyses, externally determined factors explained only 5% and 21% of the variance in student victimization rates for junior and senior high schools, respectively. In the junior high schools, student characteristics did not significantly predict victimization rates once community characteristics were controlled. But in the senior high schools, the student characteristics were far more predictive of victimization rates than were community characteristics. Controlling for externally determined characteristics, school factors again significantly predicted student victimization rates, explaining an additional 19% and 6% of the variance in student victimization rates in junior and senior high schools, respectively. In both junior and senior high schools, higher student victimization rates were associated with lower student perceptions of fairness and clarity of school rules. As with teacher victimization rates, student victimization rates in junior high schools were also associated with more democratic orientation among teachers.

These results suggest that estimates of school effects relative to community and compositional effects on measures of school disorder may depend on the level of the school (junior vs. senior high) and the source of the data on disorder (student vs. teacher reports). They show that the community context in which the school operates and the average demographic characteristics of the students enrolled in the school are the best predictors of the school's level of disorder, but that characteristics of the way the school is organized also contribute to the level of disorder. The study also demonstrated that characteristics of school organization are highly correlated with characteristics of the community. The schools with the least effective policies and practices tend to be located in the most disorganized communities. The implications of this finding for interpreting school effects research and for practice will be discussed later in this chapter.

Two studies published in the 1990s (Ostroff, 1992; Witte and Walsh, 1990) have verified that carefully measured relevant characteristics of the way schools are organized and managed are related to the problem behavior displayed by the schools' students, controlling on intake characteristics of the students and their communities. Witte and Walsh (1990) showed that "effective school characteristics" (characteristics found in previous research to be statistically related to more positive schooling outcomes) explain variance in achievement outcomes but not dropout, and Ostroff (1992) showed that teacher satisfaction and commitment predict student dropout, attendance, and disciplinary problems. Interestingly, both studies found evidence that measures of school characteristics are themselves highly dependent on the location of the school and the student population of the school. Ostroff reported, for example, that in schools with higher percentages of students receiving free lunch, teachers are less satisfied with and committed to their jobs and the student-teacher ratio is lower.

Multilevel Studies

In the studies just described, data were aggregated to the school level and within-school variance was ignored. Student input characteristics, measured by school averages for certain demographic or prior educational experience variables, and (sometimes) community characteristics were controlled to try to isolate the effects of school from effects of the types of students the school receives. These studies share five weaknesses. First, by removing variance in the outcome variables shared with average student input characteristics and community characteristics, they underestimate the effects of schools to the extent that these compositional characteristics are correlated with important features of the school environment.

Second, by relying only on school-level data, they fail to separate the effects of the compositional context of the school from the effects of purely individual-level processes. Characteristics of the composition of schools (e.g., the balance of academically weak and strong students, racial heterogeneity) are potentially manipulable and may contribute to variance explained in student outcomes above and beyond that due to individual students' backgrounds. In other words, attending a school in which the majority of students come from educationally disadvantaged families almost certainly reduces the likelihood of school success for a child, regardless of his or her own individual level of disadvantage. School-level studies are not able to estimate these two different kinds of effects of background characteristics.

Third, school-level studies assume a constant effect of student input characteristics across all schools. And fourth, they do not allow for the examination of how variables relate to one another within schools. Schools may influence student outcomes by increasing the average outcome (a main effect) or by changing the within-school processes that produce those outcomes. School A's educational practices may accentuate and school B's may mitigate the effects of prior educational disadvantage. School-level studies are not capable of detecting such effects on within-school processes.

Finally, school-level studies tell us nothing about the effect of school characteristics on *individuals*. They tell us only what predicts the performance of the average student. Robinson's (1950) account of the "ecological fallacy" warns that an association discovered in aggregated data may be misleading if interpreted as though it applied to individuals. Individual-level correlations can be zero or opposite in sign of the corresponding ecological correlations. A grouping effect occurs when the membership of the ecological unit (e.g., the school) is statistically linked with one or both of the variables involved in the ecological-level correlation. For example, segregation by socioeconomic level among schools produces a larger correlation between socioeconomic status (SES) and achievement test scores at the school level than is observed at the individual student level. Whereas individual-level correlations between SES and achievement test scores are typically around .3, school average achievement test scores and SES correlate .8 or higher (Cooley, Bond, and Mao, 1981). Ostroff (1993) discusses the conditions under which differences between individual-level correlations and correlations based on aggregates are meaningful or simply represent statistical artifacts, and provides guidelines for interpreting such differences.

Multilevel studies address these shortcomings. Most of these studies use students as the unit of analysis, although a few have used a two-stage process to "correct" school-level equations by incorporating information from individual-level equations. The earlier multilevel studies modeled individual-level schooling outcomes from individual-level student input characteristics as well as school membership or direct measures of school characteristics. These strategies produce estimates of school effects on student behavior net of individual input characteristics and are capable of separating effects of the demographic composition of the school from individual demographics. At the same time, they generally assume a constant effect of student input characteristics across schools and do not allow for the possibility that schools may affect their students by altering the association between student inputs and outputs.

The most sophisticated multilevel studies use hierarchical linear modeling (HLM; Raudenbush and Bryk, 1986). This approach estimates two distinct models: one captures relationships among variables at the student level within each school, and another attempts to explain these individual-level relationships in terms of school-level factors. The first equation might express a measure of student delinquent behavior as a function of the student's age, gender, and social class. This equation is estimated separately for students in each school in the study, yielding three regression coefficients (one for each predictor) and an intercept term representing the student-input-adjusted school average for the outcome variable (if one assumes the predictors have been centered around their means) for each school. In the second step, these coefficients become the dependent variables in a school-level equation that attempts to explain variation between schools in the coefficients in terms of school characteristics. The intercept terms from the individual-level models might be expressed as a function of school size, fairness and consistency of the disciplinary practices, and leadership qualities of the principal. Because the intercept terms for each school represent the dependent variable adjusted for the student input characteristics, this model is conceptually similar to a school-level model that controls for student intake characteristics. It is potentially more precise, however, because the model parameters are estimated separately for each school – input characteristics are not assumed to have a constant effect across all schools – and because the HLM procedures provide for more accurate representation of the complex multilevel error structure.

HLM also permits the examination of school effects on the regression coefficients from the within-school models. Using HLM, for example, one can estimate the effects of school size, disciplinary climate, and principal leadership on school-to-school variation in the effect of social class on delinquency. Some schools may amplify and others may attenuate social class differences. If so, the regression coefficient relating delinquency to social class will vary from school to school, and the school-level correlates of this differentiation could be modeled. Only four studies have used HLM, a relatively recent advance in the study of school effects. Summaries of these HLM studies are followed by discussion of other multilevel studies.

HLM Studies. Bryk (Bryk and Driscoll, 1988; see also Bryk, Lee, and Holland, 1993, chap. 11) used a subset of schools from the nationally representative High School and Beyond (HSB) data to study the effects of school organization on student behavior. They hypothesized that schools with a "sense of community" would have positive effects on student learning and behavior. Indicators of school community included shared values among members of the organization (particularly relating to the purposes of the institution), expectations for learning and behavior, and expectations for student achievement; activities designed to foster meaningful social interactions among school members and to link them to the school's traditions; and a distinctive pattern of social relations embodying an "ethos of caring" and involving collegial relations among adults in the institution and an extended teacher role.

Bryk and Driscoll used HLM to estimate the effects of communal school organization on the academic achievement, social misbehavior, and persistence in school (vs. dropout) of students who were high school sophomores in 1980 and seniors in 1982. These students were drawn from the 357 HSB schools in which special administrator and teacher questionnaires had been administered. The percentage of variance explained by all school characteristics examined in the *intake-adjusted* school means (e.g., the school means that have been adjusted for differences between schools in the social class, academic background, and race or ethnicity of the students enrolled) ranged from 17% for interest in academics to 37% for dropout.

The study separated the effects of school composition (e.g., average academic background, school social class, minority concentration, ethnic and social class diversity of the student population) from the effects of aggregated individual input variables. These compositional variables had large independent effects on each of the outcomes. Larger school size significantly increased behavioral problems (absenteeism, class cutting, classroom disorder, and dropping out) but not mathematics achievement or interest in academics. Communal organization significantly reduced all of the problem behaviors and increased the academic achievement variables, even controlling for school composition, size, parental cooperation, and student selectivity. Effects were larger for measures of student social engagement than for measures of academic achievement. Interestingly, the study found that the effects of composition and school size tend to diminish after the communal organization variable entered the equation. The authors concluded that these other features of the school affect student outcomes indirectly by facilitating or impeding the formation and sustenance of a communal organization. In additional analyses, the authors showed that communal organizations also have important consequences for teachers: teachers in communally organized schools are absent less often, have higher morale, are more satisfied with their work, and are seen by their students as enjoying their teaching more than teachers in schools lacking communal organization.

This study demonstrated that important features of the school organization are correlated with school compositional characteristics and makes clear that the school-level studies that examine residual school effects after controlling for average school inputs underestimated the effects of school organization on student outcomes.

Bryk and Thum (1989) also used HLM to study the effects of high school organization on absenteeism at grade 10 and dropout by grade 12. This study used all Catholic and a random sample of public high schools from the HSB data, for a total of 160 schools and 4,450 students followed from their sophomore through their senior year of high school. The within-school model included measures of gender, race or ethnicity, socio-economic status, and (for dropout analyses only) a measure of academic difficulties prior to high school and "at-risk" behaviors in early high school. Five categories of school variables – teacher quality and commitment, academic press (e.g., higher concentration of academic subjects, more time spent on homework) disciplinary climate (e.g., safe environment, school discipline fair and effective), curricular differentiation (e.g., greater differences among students in the courses they take), and social and academic background composition of the school – were examined in the school-level model. These characteristics of the school were expected to mediate the effect of school sector (public vs. Catholic) on attendance and dropping out. The study showed that adjustments for individual-student gender, social class, ethnicity, and academic background accounted for about 20% of the between-school variance in attendance rates. School-level factors accounted for 13% (teacher quality), 22% (composition), 34% (curriculum differentiation), 47% (academic press), and 59% (disciplinary climate) of the student-intake-adjusted absenteeism rates. Adjusted absenteeism rates were lower in schools with faculty interested in and engaged with students, an emphasis on academic pursuits, and an orderly social environment. Absenteeism was also lower in schools with less internal differentiation of students according to their background characteristics. The final model explained 68% of the variance in the adjusted school absenteeism rate.

School dropout rates proved somewhat less predictable with the final model explaining only 24% of the variance in adjusted dropout rates, but four of the five categories of school characteristics significantly predicted dropout rates. One anomalous finding was that adjusted dropout rates were higher in schools in which students rated the fairness and effectiveness of discipline to be high. The study also found evidence of "differentiating" school effects. That is, certain characteristics of schools were associated with reducing the likelihood of dropout for youths at higher risk of dropping out. For example, lower-class students enrolled in big schools and in schools with many discipline problems were more likely to drop out.

Lee and Croninger (1996) reported on a multilevel study of perceptions of safety among high school students using data from 5,486 students in 377 schools that participated in the 1988 National Educational Longitudinal Survey. The researchers predicted individual student perceptions of safety in school from individual demographic variables (social class, minority status, and gender), school compositional and community characteristics (average school SES, high minority enrollment, and urbanicity), school size, sector (public, Catholic, or elite private school), and a measure of positive social relations in the school. They found that 17% of the variability in individual perceptions of safety lies between schools, and about 29%

of this between-school variance is accounted for by student-level input demographics. Adding the school-level variables to the model explains an additional 42% of the between-school variance. The compositional characteristics of the school (percentage minority and average school SES) explained the most variance in student-intake-adjusted school average perceptions of safety, followed by positive student-teacher relations. School size and urban location did not predict perceptions of safety, and school sector effects were mediated by composition and student-teacher relations.

Only one study of delinquent behavior used hierarchical modeling techniques (Baerveldt, 1992). This study included students ages 15 to 17 in the "low stream" (equivalent to the bottom track on U.S. schools) from fourteen similar Dutch schools. The study used a hierarchical linear modeling approach to separate the effects of individual-, class-, and school-level effects on self-reports of petty crime and on a measure of student integration into school (positive school attitudes, low truancy, and little punishment in school). Less than 1% of the variance in petty theft and only 7% of the variation in integration were between schools. Features of the school organization, teacher attitudes, and lessons did not predict delinquency, but schools paying more attention to students and stressing the improvement of the quality of education had higher integration of students into the school. Larger amounts of variance were explained by classroom-level effects (6% and 9% for crime and integration, respectively). Interestingly, this study found that 5% of the variance in crime was accounted for by differences between schools in the association between integration and crime. Although this association was negative in all schools, its magnitude varied considerably from school to school, with correlations ranging from −.2 in one school to −.8 in another. In other words, bonding to the school was far more protective in some schools than in others. This finding suggests that some schools may be better able to capitalize on individual bonds.

Other Multilevel Studies. The simplest multilevel studies of school effects have generally examined effects on individual-level outcomes, controlling for individual demographic variables expected to predict the outcome (e.g., gender, age, social class) and occasionally more precise indicators of delinquency potential (e.g., degree of involvement in unsupervised leisure activities) or academic performance potential (e.g., test scores at intake to secondary school). These studies have demonstrated that *something* about where one goes to school matters for a wide range of student outcomes, including delinquent behavior or drug use (Caspi, Lynam, Moffitt, and Silva, 1993; Felson, Liska, South, and McNulty, 1994; Gottfredson, 1988; Heal, 1978; Rutter, Maughan, Mortimore, Ouston, and Smith, 1979; Skager and Fisher, 1989), scholastic achievement (Cuttance, 1992; Fitz-Gibbon, 1992; Mortimore, Sammons, Stoll, Lewis, and Ecob, 1988; Nutall, Goldstein,

Prosser, and Rasbach, 1989; Rutter et al., 1979; Smith and Tomlinson, 1989), school misbehavior (Mortimore et al., 1988; Rutter et al., 1979), school attendance (Mortimore et al., 1988; Rutter et al., 1979), and attitudes toward school (Mortimore et al., 1988; Fitz-Gibbon, 1992). These studies demonstrated significant school effects on each of the outcomes listed for both elementary and secondary schools and for students in several different countries, including the Unites States, New Zealand, England, and Scotland.

Only three multilevel studies failed to demonstrate school effects on the individual behavioral outcomes examined. West and Farrington (1973) found that attendance at different secondary schools made no substantial difference to boys' preexisting delinquency potential. Baerveldt (1992), in a study already described, found minimal variance explained by school membership in a relatively homogeneous sample of fourteen Dutch schools. And school-to-school differences were found not to add significantly to the explanation of effort in school (Fitz-Gibbon, 1992) in a sample of ten schools in northern England, although the same study demonstrated school effects on other student outcomes.

The percentage of variance explained in individual student outcomes by school membership differed across studies and outcomes. Estimates of the percentage of variance in delinquency explained by school membership after controlling for individual propensity correlates ranged from less than 1% (Baerveldt, 1992) to 11% (Felson et al., 1994). For measures of scholastic achievement, the estimates ranged from 1% (Fitz-Gibbon, 1992) to 27% (Mortimore et al., 1988); for attitudes toward school, from 8% (Mortimore et al., 1988) to 16% (Fitz-Gibbon, 1992); and for school attendance and school misbehavior, from 6% to 10% (Mortimore et al., 1988). For perceptions of school safety, Lee and Croninger (1996) estimated that 17% of the variance in individual perceptions was between schools. Summarizing the school effects literature in general, Reynolds and Cuttance (1992) estimated between 8% and 15% of the variance in pupil outcomes is due to between-school differences.

Although these estimates of the magnitude of school effects have generally been described as "small," they translate into effect sizes ranging from .59 to .84, indicating that membership in a more effective school is associated with an increase of roughly six- to eight-tenths of one standard deviation unit in a student's outcome. If effect sizes of this magnitude were generated from an experimental or quasi-experimental study, the results might, for example, imply an increase in a binary outcome such as recidivism due to membership in the more effective school of anywhere from 23 to 33 percentage points. These effect sizes are somewhat larger than average effect size (.50, SD = .29) reported by Lipsey and Wilson (1993) in their meta-analysis of 302 reviews of more than 16,000 intervention studies in the social and behavioral sciences and education for many different types of programs and many different outcomes. Although results from nonexperimental studies can be compared only with extreme caution with results from experimental studies, it appears that relative to the effects of other behavioral and social interventions, school effects are at least moderate in size.

A few multilevel studies attempted to measure characteristics of school to learn *what* about schools mattered. A landmark study of London schools was conducted by Michael Rutter and colleagues (Rutter et al., 1979). The study found that, when one controls for individual intake variables,[2] school membership explained variance in academic achievement, attendance, delinquency (having been cautioned or found guilty of an offense in the juvenile court as of the eighteenth year of life),[3] and a scale measuring student self-reports of behaviors such as truanting, arriving late for lessons, disruptive behavior in class, adherence to school rules regarding uniforms, and being on task in lessons.

The study measured a wide range of school characteristics, including physical and administrative features, school processes, and "ecological influences." Measures of physical factors (e.g., size of the school, age of the building, and space available) and broad administrative arrangements (e.g., tracking, house-based vs. year-based organization) were not related to schooling outcomes. But several school process variables as well as student composition did predict success on the four outcomes, net of individual intake variables. The main school features found to be related to positive school outcomes included:

A balance of intellectually able and less able children in the school, since, when a preponderance of pupils in a school was academically unsuccessful, peer group cultures and an antiacademic or anti-authority emphasis may have formed.

The system of rewards *and* punishments – ample use of rewards, praise, and appreciation.

A positive school environment – good working conditions, responsiveness to pupil needs, and good care and decoration of buildings.

Ample opportunities for children to take responsibility and to participate in the running of their school lives.

Good use of homework, clear academic goals, and an atmosphere of confidence in their pupils' capacities.

Teachers who provided good models of behavior by means of good time-keeping and willingness to deal with pupil problems.

Good group management in the classroom – preparing lessons in

---

[2] Analyses of the student behavior outcome were conducted at the school level only. No controls for individual propensity were included.

[3] A school effect was found for boys only.

advance, keeping the attention of the whole class, unobtrusive discipline, and a focus on rewarding good behavior and of swift action to deal with disruption.

Firm leadership and a decision-making process in which all teachers felt that their views were represented.

In general, these school features were related to each of the four outcomes examined, although the strength and consistency of the effects was lower for delinquency than for the other outcomes.

During the late 1980s several large school effects studies were conducted in England to verify and extend the findings from the Rutter et al. study. Mortimore et al. (1988) followed two thousand students from fifty randomly selected primary schools through four years of schooling and found twelve different school process variables were related to the school outcomes, controlling for student input characteristics. Effects were also found for average student composition, such that schools with higher percentages of "advantaged intakes" had more positive outcomes, net of individual intake measures. A study of twenty urban comprehensive secondary schools in England (Smith and Tomlinson, 1989) followed approximately 3,100 students from the beginning to the end of their secondary school careers (from ages 11 to 15) and found substantial differences between schools in examination scores at the end of secondary school, controlling for academic performance at intake. Caspi et al. (1993) showed that school context even mediates biological processes. In a longitudinal study of girls in New Zealand, they found that the impact of menarcheal timing on delinquency was moderated by the sex composition of the school: early-maturing girls in mixed-sex settings were at greatest risk for delinquency.

Two American studies also documented the effects of specific school characteristics on measures of delinquency. Gottfredson (1988) found that, controlling for individual propensity to use substances, the proportion of students reporting that it is easy to buy drugs in the school significantly predicted individual drug involvement in three of four equations examined. Felson et al. (1994) examined the effects of normative school values supporting interpersonal violence on individual interpersonal violence, theft, and vandalism and school delinquency. They found that school norms regarding violence significantly predicted individual involvement in all three forms of delinquent behavior. The percentage of black students in the school was also related to individual interpersonal violence, when individual demographics were controlled. The authors concluded that normative values, in addition to individually held values, provide an additional source of social control.

Kasen, Johnson, and Cohen (1990) studied the effects of school climate on the development of student psychopathology. This study regressed mother reports of child emotional and behavioral problems on student reports of four dimensions of school climate: conflict, academic focus, student autonomy (e.g., choice over academic program), and social facilitation (as indicated, e.g., by teachers leading discussions of emotional or family problems), controlling for earlier mother reports of psychopathology, age, sex, and socioeconomic status. School conflict increased and academic focus decreased the problem behaviors of interest. The percentage variance in the problem behavior outcomes explained uniquely by the school climate variables ranged from 5% to 6%.

Summary

Does school matter? Yes. School-level studies document school effects on school rates of victimization, delinquent involvement, suspension, truancy, dropout, "belting," satisfaction with school, and cognitive skills. Multilevel studies demonstrate effects for delinquent involvement, scholastic achievement, school attendance and truancy, dropout, attitudes toward school, drug and alcohol use, school misbehavior, psychopathology, and student perceptions of safety. School effects have been demonstrated for students at the elementary and secondary levels of education, and for students in different countries. These effects cannot be attributed solely to the grouping of individuals with different propensities and prognoses in schools. School effects persist after outcomes are adjusted for the effects of individual-level demographic and other predictors.

The magnitude of school effects is moderate. In multilevel studies, the percentage of variance in student outcomes attributable to schools usually ranges between 8% and 15%, which translates into effect sizes ranging from .58 to .85. These results from correlational studies suggest that membership in an effective school might increase student success rates anywhere from 29 to 42 percentage points above those of similar students enrolled in less effective schools. School effects are somewhat larger than the average effect sizes observed in interventions in the social and behavioral sciences and education, suggesting that improving the way schools are organized and managed may be more effective than providing special prevention and intervention services for youths.

Just as the magnitude of community context effects are underestimated in studies that do not specify variables at lower levels of aggregation (such as the school catchment area), so school effect sizes are underestimated to the extent that meaningful variation exists within schools. Schools contain important microenvironments, the most important of which is probably the classroom. If classroom effects offset one another, estimates of school effects will be relatively meaningless averages of these more potent effects (Bidwell and Kasarda, 1980). The only study reviewed here that specified classroom level effects found considerably larger effects for classrooms than for schools on individual involvement in delinquency and integration into the school (Baerveldt, 1992).

Does the location of the school matter? Yes, in two ways. Where the school is located determines who goes to the school. The demographic composition and the balance of academically weak to academically strong students, and the diversity of student backgrounds represented in the school all influence student outcomes, even controlling on the students' own demographic and educational background. These "compositional" effects appear to matter more than other school characteristics and more for noncognitive outcomes such as attendance, dropout, and school misbehavior than for academic achievement, which is determined primarily by students' own ability levels. The higher the concentration of educationally and socially disadvantaged students in the school, the poorer the outcomes for individual students in the school, regardless of their own level of disadvantage. The composition of the school determines the normative culture in the school. The demographic composition of the school is primarily determined by characteristics of the community, including urban location, population density, community crime, disorganization, unemployment and socioeconomic status of the population. These two sets of indicators are essentially redundant in terms of their explanation of student outcomes.

A second way that the location of the school affects student outcomes is by influencing school characteristics and processes, which themselves influence students. Evidence for this comes from a handful of studies already summarized. Gottfredson and Gottfredson (1985) reported considerable difficulty in trying to separate empirically the effects of school processes from those of the composition of the school and the characteristics of the community. Exploratory factor analyses were conducted to identify clusters of variables that could be treated as multiple indicators of underlying school and community variables. These factor analyses suggested that characteristics of the composition of the school and community factors loaded on the same factor with characteristics of the way the school is staffed and managed and the social climate of the school. For example, urban location, community crime, unemployment, and poverty loaded with the total enrollment of the school and peer and nonacademic orientation (students reporting that what other students think is important, and much involvement in nonacademic activities). A census measure of community affluence and education level loaded highly with teacher educational level, firm and clear disciplinary climate, delinquent youth culture (students saying that drugs are easily available in the school and that they would cheat or "play hookey" if given the opportunity), and college-prep orientation of the school.

Bryk and Driscoll (1988) showed that greater concentrations of socially and educationally disadvantaged students in the school operated both directly and indirectly to lower student outcomes. In schools with higher proportions of disadvantaged students, schools were less likely to include a system of shared values, a clear mission, high expectations, meaningful social interactions, collegial relations among adults, and extended teacher roles.

Witte and Walsh (1990) also noted that school effectiveness measures are highly dependent on the location of the school and the student population of the school. Their measure of effective school practices correlated −.41 (elementary), −.66 (middle), and −.67 (high) with a measure of city versus suburban school location. Correlations with teacher control over school decision making were even larger.

These results, combined with the results of recent community contextual effects studies (Elliott et al., 1996; Sampson et al., 1997) showing that the level of "collective efficacy" (e.g., cohesion among residents, willingness of residents to intervene on behalf of the common good) not only explains neighborhood crime rates but also substantially mediates the effects of neighborhood disadvantage, point to a "Matthew effect" (Matthew 13:12) in education. To those schools that have [advantaged populations], more will be given. To those that have not, even what they have will be taken away. The schools serving the most disadvantaged populations lack the resources that make other schools effective. These are mostly human resources capable of managing schools in such a way as to create cohesive social organizations. A model in which characteristics of schools are treated as additional indicators of latent community poverty and disorganization rather than the model (used in all school effects research) in which community characteristics are treated as exogenous variables seems appropriate. Schools are community institutions. Disorganized communities have difficulty recruiting high quality teachers and administrators for their schools and garnering community support and other resources. School ineffectiveness can not be easily separated from community ineffectiveness.

School effects research forces such a separation when it statistically controls for community characteristics and student input characteristics, attributing to schools only that portion of variance in outcomes that cannot be explained by these externally determined characteristics, or when it holds community characteristics constant by examining schools in homogeneous communities. These studies use the most conservative model in order to demonstrate that schools matter. Now that school effects have been demonstrated, attention should be redirected to the potentially more important fact that schools are inextricably linked to and influenced by their communities. This theme will be revisited in Chapter 6, which examines factors affecting school capacity to innovate and maintain change.

What about schools matters? School effects research has, for the most part, been conducted without benefit of guiding theory. Results are usually presented in the form of a list of eight to twelve correlates of school effectiveness. These lists vary somewhat depending on which schooling outcomes are examined, how characteristics are measured, where the study schools are located, and what levels (elementary, middle, or high) of schooling are included. But more commonality than divergence is observed.

Figure 3.1 is an attempt to integrate the findings from the school effects research summarized here and an excellent review of school organization factors related to achievement and engagement in the learning process (Lee, Bryk, and Smith, 1993).[4] The individual-level factors directly influencing involvement in problem behaviors have been summarized in Chapter 2. They are a subset of personality, attitude, and experience factors leading to problem behavior most likely to be influenced by schools: academic success, commitment to education, attachment to school, belief in conventional rules, self-control, and exposure to negative peers and criminogenic substances and commodities (e.g., weapons). Problem behavior is influenced directly by these personal characteristics as well as by features of the school administration, specifically discipline management. Schools whose rules for behavior are clear and firmly enforced; whose adults watch for misbehavior, recognize it when it occurs, and immediately punish it; and whose adults model desired behaviors and reward them when they occur experience less problem behavior. Students living in high-crime areas are expected to be involved in more problem behavior through mechanisms not included in this model.

The other school factors in the model are hypothesized to influence problem behavior indirectly by increasing or decreasing the individual-level causes. Peer culture is an important feature of the social organization. When the balance of peer norms supports behaviors such as drug use, violence, and other problem behaviors more than learning and other forms of prosocial behavior, students in the school will be more likely to be exposed to negative influences, their attachments to the prosocial elements in the school will be lessened, their beliefs in the validity of conventional rules will erode, and they will be less likely to exhibit self-control in the face of opportunity or pressure to misbehave. Their commitment to education will decline relative to other activities, and their academic performance will suffer. Delinquent youth cultures flourish in schools that do not or cannot establish and maintain a "communal" social organization. Communal schools are characterized by a system of shared values among members of the organization, particularly relating to the purposes of the institution, expectations for learning and behavior, and expectations for student achievement; meaningful social interactions among school members; and a distinctive pattern of social relations embodying an "ethos

---

[4] Lee et al. (1993) review an extensive array of analytic essays, ethnographic investigations, quantitative research studies, and research syntheses on the organization of secondary schools.

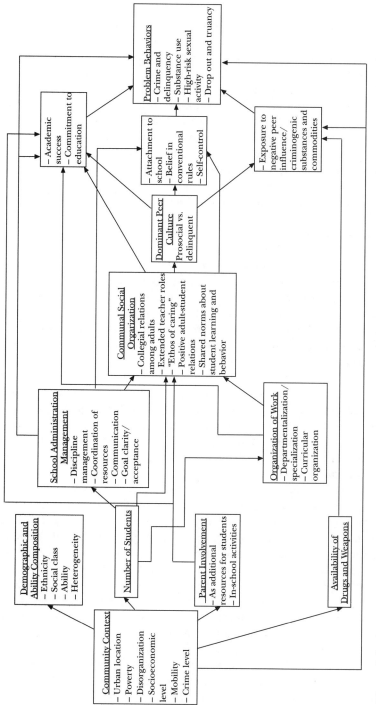

Figure 3.1. Community and School Factors Influencing Student Problem Behavior

of caring" and involving collegial relations among adults in the institution. They also include expanded roles for teachers so that they are responsible for fostering positive social as well as cognitive outcomes for students. Communal schools create a strong normative climate inconsistent with delinquent norms. A delinquent peer culture could not dominate in such a school. Such communal social organizations not only weaken delinquent peer norms, but they also build social bonds (beliefs in conventional rules, attachment to school, and commitment to education) and learning. Although not yet examined, it is likely that increased interaction with adults in a caring role also teaches youths self-control.

Two additional features of the way schools are organized directly influence the development of a communal social organization, according to the model in Figure 3.1: administration and management practices, and the organization of work. Important features of the administration and management of the school include discipline management, coordination and resource allocation, communication, and goal setting and maintenance. Well-managed schools have clear, fair, and consistently enforced rules for behavior. Staff in effective schools use the enforcement of rules as an opportunity to teach students about fairness, justice, and personal responsibility, thereby increasing self-control, beliefs in the validity of conventional rules, and perceptions of procedural justice in addition to enhancing the communal social organization.

Principals in effective schools coordinate the flow of resources and information to teachers as they are needed for school operations, increasing teacher satisfaction and effectiveness and student learning. They maintain relations between the school and external constituencies, garnering needed resources and generating community support; buffer the school from the effects of harmful outside influences; and facilitate informal social interactions within the school. These communication functions increase teacher satisfaction and effectiveness and facilitate the maintenance of the school community. Finally, effective schools have strong instructional leaders. These leaders formulate clear educational goals for the school and foster acceptance of the goals by members of the school community. They articulate and represent the school's mission. This goal setting directly affects student learning and fosters school community.

Work organization includes the extent to which the school is divided into departments or otherwise characterized by specialization of role, and the way the school and classrooms are organized for curricular delivery. The first of these features applies more to secondary than to elementary schools. Schools differ on the extent to which they are departmentalized. In highly departmentalized schools, teachers are more likely to see themselves as subject matter specialists and less likely to feel responsible for non-subject-related aspects of their students' schooling experience. Such departmentalization therefore decreases sense of community by narrowing the role of the teacher and reducing opportunities for meaningful interaction between teacher and students. It further erodes the school community because department loyalties detract from teachers' allegiance to the school and their ability to maintain shared norms and collegiality across departments.

A related feature of school organization is specialization of the teacher role, with or without departments. Lee et al. (1993) describe this specialization function. An early form of specialization involved organization of instruction by grade level. Increasing pressure to accommodate to students' special needs results in increased specialization (e.g., compensatory education, bilingual education, special education), special programming areas (e.g., drug and alcohol abuse education, dropout prevention), and specialized functions (e.g., college counseling, job placement). The addition of special courses tailored to students' abilities and interests increases specialization of the curriculum. Such tailoring, of course, is expected to increase learning by targeting instruction more appropriately. But Lee et al. (1993) reported that such benefits have not yet been empirically demonstrated. Some evidence suggests that specialization fragments students' school experiences and reduces teacher involvement in the personal and social development of the child. It increases the number of different teachers with which the student has superficial contact while decreasing the number of teachers with which the student maintains meaningful and sustained contact. These features of specialization can be expected to reduce the sense of community in the school.

Student learning is most directly influenced by instructional processes and the school structures, policies, and routines that influence instruction, or what Lee, Bryk, and Smith call the "technical core." Schools in which teachers use more effective methods promote more learning among students and also increase attachment to school and commitment to education. The literature on effective instructional strategies is too extensive to review here, but several key elements of effective instruction (Brophy, 1986) can be summarized:

Opportunity to learn and content covered
More curriculum covered

Role definition, expectations, and time allocation
Teachers see instruction as basic to their role; expect students to master the curriculum; and allocate most of the available time to academic activities

Classroom management and student-engaged time
Successful classroom management: activities run smoothly, transitions

are brief and orderly, little time is spent getting organized and dealing
with misconduct

Good preparation of the physical environment

Teaching the rules and procedures in the beginning of the school year

Continuous monitoring of the entire classroom

Smoothness and continued momentum in lesson pacing

Variety and appropriate level of challenge in assignments

Clear accountability procedures and consistent follow-up concerning
work quality and completion

Clarity about how students can get help when they need it and about
what options are available when they finish their work

Consistent success and academic learning time

Organizing instruction so as to maximize the amount of time students
spend engaged in academic tasks that they can perform with a high
success rate

Active teaching

Maximize time students are actively taught or supervised by the teacher
as opposed to working alone or not working

Teacher carries the content to the students personally rather than
depending on the curriculum materials alone

Quality of teaching

Clear, enthusiastic, well structured, sufficiently redundant, and well-
sequenced presentations

More frequent, clear questions, most of which can be answered correctly
by the students.

An additional characteristic of the way schools are organized for
instruction is the process used to allocate students to different courses of
study, including tracking and other course placement decisions. These
decisions, which affect opportunities for learning for entire groups of
students, often result in uneven distributions of such opportunities across
social class and racial or ethnic groups. Research (summarized in Lee
et al., 1993) demonstrates that schools that place a larger proportion of
their students in the "academic track" or in higher level courses have better
learning outcomes. The superior outcomes achieved in Catholic schools
may arise from the fact that almost all students are placed in the same
(largely academic) course of study. Public schools are more likely to use
tracking in order to deal effectively with the greater heterogeneity of
students they receive. Tracking has a differentiating effect on student
outcomes, such that the input characteristics of students are magnified.
One study summarized already (Bryk and Thum, 1989) demonstrated that

nonattendance and dropout are higher in schools with greater curriculum differentiation, and that lower-class students in particular were more likely to drop out of school if they attended schools with more tracking. Becker (1987) observed a similar effect in Pennsylvania schools: attending a school that uses homogeneous tracking to assign students to math classes substantially increases the math test scores of students from more privileged backgrounds. For students from lower socioeconomic backgrounds, test scores were the same whether students were in schools that formed heterogeneous math classes or used homogeneous between-class tracking.

Only a few studies have investigated tracking effects on delinquent behavior. The earliest studies (e.g., Schafer and Polk, 1972) established that youths placed in nonacademic tracks were more likely to engage in delinquent activities. Several different studies (summarized in Kelly, 1978) replicated this association, showing that it was not explained completely by socioeconomic status or prior achievement levels, and exploring some possible mechanisms through which tracking might increase delinquency. Kelly (1978) concluded that the main mechanism was via increased exposure to delinquent peers rather than through decreased academic performance or commitment to education. In a more recent cross-sectional study of substance use among Ontario high school students, Allison (1992) reported that students in the "lower stream" (e.g., preparing for the work force rather than community college or the university) reported higher substance use, and the association maintained even with controls for gender, grade average, drug education lessons, and pressure to use substances. In a more rigorous, longitudinal study of a national sample (of boys), Wiatrowski, Hansell, Massey, and Wilson (1982) contradicted the earlier findings. They showed that the correlation between track placement (in grade 11) and delinquency (in grade 12 and one year past high school), small to begin with, was completely explained by prior delinquency level. Once delinquency (reported in grade 10) was controlled, track placement explained no further variation in later delinquency.

Taken together, the results suggest that any negative effects of tracking probably occur prior to grade 10 (Wiatrowski's base-line year). This is plausible because the practice of tracking begins much earlier than grade 10. A survey of schools in Pennsylvania (McPartland, Coldiron, and Braddock, 1987) showed, for example, that more than 50% of elementary and 90% of schools serving grades 7, 8, and 9 use this practice. Tracking increases exposure to nondelinquent peers for those placed in the academic track. This serves to protect youths so placed – who tend to be the more academically and socioeconomically advantaged students in the first place. Tracking increases attendance and decreases dropout for the most advantaged students in the school. It has little or no effect on the most disadvantaged segment of the population.

A Note on Externally Determined Factors

The foregoing discussion focuses primarily on characteristics that are determined by or under the control of school staff. Yet many important features of schools are externally determined. Some of these external factors – the type of students in the school, the level of parent involvement in the school, and the availability of drugs and weapons in the school – are determined by the community in which the school is located. Others – school district boundaries, school size, grade structures, attendance laws, use of time (e.g., summer school, year-round school, number of days of schooling required), standards for graduation and promotion, testing practices, course requirements, and expulsion policies – are determined by educators at the school district or state levels. School governance structure or "sector" – for example, whether the school is public, private, or religious – is also an important externally determined feature of the school.

These school characteristics are likely to constrain in major ways the effectiveness of schools as socializing agents and are at the heart of much public policy debate about school effectiveness. Probable mechanisms through which they might operate are shown on Figure 3.1. Sorrowfully, space limitations prevent a thorough discussion of research related to them.

Implications for Practice

Much of the literature reviewed in this chapter has implications for the design of interventions to improve the capability of school managers to regulate schools. The research implies that principals and faculty control behavior by setting rules, communicating clear expectations for behavior, consistently enforcing rules, and providing rewards for rule compliance and punishments for rule infractions. Effective school managers also perform general management functions (such as coordination and resource allocation and communication) well, and they establish and maintain clear goals for the organization. Principals and teachers further manage the behavior of students by organizing the delivery of instruction in ways that promote maximal learning and that encourage a sense of community. Effective managers organize the school so that informal social control is maximized through an extended network of caring adults who interact regularly with the students and who share norms and expectations about their students. When managers succeed at creating such "communal social organizations" they increase the number of and effectiveness of "intimate handlers" who can informally control potential offenders.

All of these school management functions are aimed directly at enhancing the enduring disposition or capability of *the school* to function effectively. But most are ultimately aimed at reducing potential offenders' dispositions to engage in problem behavior by (eventually) increasing their self control and their social bonds. By maximizing student learning and engagement, schools increase commitment to education and attachment to school. By modeling appropriate behavior and establishing a fair and just discipline system, school staff enhances student beliefs in the validity of rules and laws. By maintaining a social climate that prevents the emergence of a negative peer group culture, managers effectively separate potential offenders from peer facilitators. Most of these management functions belong to the principal, but a collegial faculty and willing community volunteers also assist. Also, managers are constrained by externally imposed conditions and decisions.

Translating the research reviewed in this chapter into recommendations for policy and practice requires a leap of faith. The nonexperimental research examined here can only provide broad guidelines for policy and practice. It has not demonstrated causality with any degree of confidence, and it can only suggest strategies that might influence the school compositional and organizational variables thought to influence problem behaviors. Recommendations from this nonexperimental research must be tested for efficacy in more rigorous experimental or quasi-experimental studies. The next chapter examines evidence from such experimental and quasi-experimental studies that have attempted to manipulate some of the school characteristics identified in this chapter.

Field Studies of School-Based Prevention: An Overview

THIS BRIEF CHAPTER describes the methodology used to locate and summarize studies of the effectiveness of attempts to prevent or reduce problem behavior. It provides an overview of the studies included in the next two chapters. The chapter begins with a discussion of the importance of experimental and quasi-experimental studies both for refining theories about the causes of problem behavior and for learning how to prevent it.

Correlation versus Causality

Although the risk factors summarized in earlier chapters are *correlated with* current and future problem behavior, most have not been demonstrated to *cause* problem behavior. Even longitudinal studies fall short of the standards necessary to establish causal relations: covariation, temporal priority, and nonspuriousness. Studies summarized in the two preceding chapters always satisfy the first, often the second, but almost never the third requirement.

Correlation does not imply causation. A correlation between an individual risk factor (e.g., academic performance, beliefs in the validity of rules) or a characteristic of the school environment (e.g., collegial relations, fairness, and clarity of rules) and problem behavior cannot be interpreted causally because the problem behavior may have preceded the risk factor in time or because the correlation may arise simply because both the risk factor and the problem behavior are caused by a third factor. Even if the correlation arises from a causal association, the direction of the causation may not be as expected. The direction of associations established in correlational research is often ambiguous. For example, academic failure may increase drug use, but so may drug use increase academic failure. Most studies overestimate the correlation between the risk factor and the outcome by failing to take bidirectionality into account.

Longitudinal studies are sometimes (but not always) helpful for ruling out these alternative explanations. By separating the measurement of the presumed cause from the presumed effect, longitudinal studies can potentially rule out spuriousness and clarify the causal direction of the association. But to do so, the longitudinal study must measure the variables likely to produce spurious correlation and test for bidirectionality. For example, if attachment to school measured in grade 7 predicts delinquency in grade 12, one possible explanation is that delinquency in grade 6 leads both to lower attachment to school and to continued delinquency. Another possibility is that a third variable such as low self-control explains both low attachment to school and later delinquency. And a third possibility is that causal effects are present in both directions. Very few longitudinal studies measure the hypothesized risk factors and variables associated with likely alternative causes early enough in the life course to be able to rule out the possibility that some (earlier) correlated factor (rather than the factor of interest) caused the subsequent outcome. Even fewer test for bidirectionality.

Experimentation increases confidence in causal interpretations. Active manipulation of the hypothesized causal variable and random assignment of subjects to treatment and control groups represent the "gold standard" in experimental research. When these conditions are met, threats to internal validity are minimized because randomization equalizes the treatment and control group on potential "third variables" that might introduce spurious correlation, and because active manipulation creates a definitive sequencing of the potential cause and presumed effect. Random assignment of subjects to treatment and control conditions is not always possible, but several quasi-experimental designs afford reasonable levels of confidence in causal interpretations (Cook and Campbell, 1979). These designs always involve some degree of control over the timing of the presumed cause and provide means of ruling out alternative causal hypotheses.

A potential drawback of experimental and quasi-experimental designs for testing theories about causation is that it is difficult if not impossible to manipulate some variables of interest directly. A scientist can usually not directly manipulate another individual's level of self-control, for example. Instead, he or she must manipulate the environment in ways expected to effect self-control. The subject may be exposed to a behavior modification program or an instructional program that teaches self-control skills. By measuring the variable of theoretical interest (e.g., self control), the researcher can check to ensure that the manipulation was successful.

Aside from their theory-testing uses, experimental methods are of course necessary to test the effectiveness of a proposed intervention. The correlational studies reviewed in previous chapters are helpful for guiding the design of interventions to reduce problem behavior. But the bottom line in prevention must always be the demonstrated effectiveness of a particular strategy for reducing problem behavior. Effectiveness can be demonstrated only through experimental and quasi-experimental methods.

Chapters 5 and 6 summarize what has been learned from quasi-experimental and experimental studies of interventions to reduce problem behavior. The remainder of this chapter provides an overview of all of the studies and explains how they were located and coded.

Methods

Search Methods

A library search was conducted to locate all published studies of school-based prevention programs. Online data bases such as Psychlit, Sociofile, and ERIC (Educational Resources Information Center) were used to gather initial studies. Keywords used in the searches were "delinquency," "prevention," "intervention," "school-based prevention," "drugs," "drug-education," "youth," and "juvenile." The list of studies obtained through the library search was augmented with additional studies cited in recent reviews or identified by reviewers of earlier versions of this summary. The studies obtained through this process were scanned to eliminate studies that did not fit the definition of school-based prevention programs used here. A "school-based prevention program" was defined to include any intervention to prevent or reduce problem behavior that was either located in a school building (even if outside of school hours) or implemented by school staff or under school or school system auspices. Programs for students at the kindergarten, elementary, and secondary school levels were included. Programs for pre-school-aged children were excluded unless they extended into the regular school years. Only studies reporting on active interventions (rather than natural variation in the independent variable) were retained. Finally, studies were limited to those that contained some measure of problem behavior, as broadly defined here, and that compared the preventive intervention group with a comparison group.[1] In all, 174 studies of school-based prevention were identified.

---

[1] The comparison group requirement tended to exclude studies of attempts to alter the behavior of emotionally and behaviorally disordered students, many of which use single-subject designs.

Classifying Programs

Prevention programs can be classified in different ways. They might be sorted according to the specific behaviors targeted (e.g., drug prevention, gang prevention, etc.), by the prevention theory underlying the program (e.g., programs to increase social bonding or self-control or to decrease the stigmatizing labeling of delinquents), or by the strategies employed or activities undertaken (e.g., tutoring, counseling, clarifying school rules). Each of these categorization schemes might prove useful for one purpose or another.

In this work, the basic unit of categorization is the program activity. Classifying programs according to *what is done* to students or school enviroments is useful because it enables testing of presumed links between program activities and program outcomes. Does a program that delivers lessons on self-control actually increase self-control? Does a tutoring program increase commitment to education? Do changes in the targeted intermediate outcomes reduce problem behavior? Answering these questions requires a measure of the actual activities undertaken in each program.

A classification of program content containing seventeen major activities was developed for this purpose. It is based on a similar classification used in the National Study of Delinquency Prevention in Schools (Gottfredson and Gottfredson, 1996). The classification scheme was developed using an iterative process in which coders read program descriptions and attempted to classify each distinct activity mentioned in the project description. Coding discrepancies and activities that could not be coded were discussed, and the classification was adjusted. This process was repeated until the classification captured all activities for each new program. A coding sheet was developed to correspond to the final classification. Four graduate students coded the 174 studies using the classification scheme. Every study was coded by two students, and discrepancies were resolved. After coding all activities, the coders indicated up to three major activity categories that best described the content of the program.

These finer distinctions are sometimes collapsed into two major program types that differentiate programs whose primary goal is to promote individual adaptation or resistance to negative influences from programs aimed at eliminating or attenuating environmental influences that contribute to problem behaviors. A social skills training course aimed at increasing resistance skills is an example of an individually targeted program, whereas increasing the sanctions a school imposes for certain violations is an example of an environmental approach to prevention. We consider first those programs which alter the school or classroom environments and next those which focus primarily on changing the behaviors, knowledge, skills, attitudes, or beliefs of individual students.

Environmental Change Strategies

Managing Classes. Instructional methods are designed to increase student engagement in the learning process and hence to increase their academic performance and bonding to the school (e.g., cooperative learning techniques and "experiential learning" strategies). In addition, classroom organization and management strategies include activities to establish and enforce classroom rules, uses of rewards and punishments, management of time to reduce "down-time," strategies for grouping students within the class, and the use of external resources such as parent volunteers, police officers, or professional consultants as instructors or aides.

Setting or Changing School Norms for Behavior. Schoolwide efforts to redefine norms for behavior and signal appropriate behavior include activities such as newsletters, posters, ceremonies during which students declare their intention to remain drug-free, and displaying symbols of appropriate behavior. Some well-known interventions in this category are "red ribbon week" sponsored through the Department of Education's Safe and Drug-Free Schools and Communities program and schoolwide campaigns against bullying.

Building a Supportive, Caring Community. Interventions to create a more cohesive community within the school and to create a broader base of community support often involve schoolwide campaigns, activities to promote mutual caring, or activities to increase appreciation for the perspectives or traditions of different cultural groups.

Setting Rules and Discipline Policies. Schoolwide efforts to establish or clarify school rules or discipline codes and mechanisms for the enforcement of school rules include efforts to formalize youth roles in the regulation and response to student conduct through peer mediation or student court interventions, for example.

Building School Capacity. Interventions to change the decision-making processes or authority structures to enhance the general capacity of the school often involve teams of staff and (sometimes) parents, students, and community members engaged in planning and carrying out activities to improve the school. These teams often use information to identify problems, develop strategies to address them, and evaluate their efforts. Activities aimed at enhancing the administrative capability of the school by increasing communication and cooperation among members of the school community are also included.

Regrouping Students. Reorganizing classes or grades – to create smaller units, continuing interaction, or different mixes of students, or to provide greater flexibility in instruction – can include changes to school schedule (e.g., block scheduling, scheduling more periods in the day, changes in the lengths of instructional periods); adoption of schools-within-schools or similar arrangements; tracking into classes by ability, achievement, effort, or conduct; formation of grade level "houses" or "teams;" and decreasing class size.

Excluding Intruders. Interventions to prevent intruders from entering the school include the use of identification badges, visitor's passes, security personnel posted at school entrances, locks, cameras, and other surveillance methods.

Excluding Weapons and Contraband. Interventions to prevent weapons and contraband from entering the school include the use of metal detectors, locker searches, and the like.

Individual-Change Strategies

Instructing Students. This is the most common strategy used in schools. These interventions provide instruction to students to teach them factual information, increase their awareness of social influences to engage in misbehavior, expand their repertoires for recognizing and appropriately responding to risky or potentially harmful situations, increase their appreciation for diversity in society, and improve their moral character. Well-known examples include Drug Abuse Resistance Education (DARE), Law-Related Education (LRE), and Gang Resistance Education and Training (GREAT).

Use of Cognitive/Behavioral or Behavioral Modeling Methods. Interventions using these methods rely on modeling, providing rehearsal, and coaching in the display of new skills. A program might use repeated exposure to a modeled behavior with rehearsal and feedback or extended use of cues to elicit the behavior over long periods of time and in varied settings. These methods, which always involve feedback on performance and reinforcement, are most often used in conjunction with a cognitive-behavioral or behavioral intervention but are also sometimes used in instructional programs.

Behavior Modification and Cognitive/Behavioral Strategies. Behavior modification strategies focus directly on changing behaviors and involve timely tracking of specific behaviors over time, behavioral goals, and feedback or positive or negative reinforcement to change behavior.

These strategies rely on reinforcers external to the student to shape student behavior. Larger or more robust effects on behavior might be obtained by teaching students to modify their own behavior using a range of cognitive strategies research has found lacking in delinquent youth. Efforts to teach students cognitive-behavioral strategies involve modeling or demonstrating behaviors and providing rehearsal and coaching in the display of new skills. Students are taught, for example, to recognize the physiological cues experienced in risky situations. They rehearse this skill and practice stopping rather than acting impulsively in such situations. Students are taught and rehearsed in such skills as suggesting alternative activities when friends propose engaging in a risky activity. And they are taught to use prompts or cues to remember to engage in behavior.

Other Counseling, Social Work, Psychological, or Therapeutic Strategies. Individual counseling, case management, and similar group-based interventions are included in this strategy.

Tutoring, Mentoring, and Other Individual-Attention Strategies. Mentoring is distinguished from counseling because mentoring is generally provided by a lay person rather than a trained counselor and is not necessarily guided by a structured approach. Tutoring includes individualized assistance with academic tasks.

Providing Recreational, Enrichment, and Leisure Activities. These activities are intended to provide constructive and fun alternatives to delinquent behavior. Drop-in recreation centers, after-school and weekend programs, dances, community service activities, and other events are offered in these programs as alternatives to the more dangerous activities. The popular "Midnight Basketball" is included here.

Methodological Rigor

The studies used a variety of methods, some more scientifically defensible than others. In an effort to describe the range of scientific rigor and to give more weight to the conclusion of the most rigorous studies, scientific rigor was quantified. The method for scoring methodological rigor was adapted from that used in the National Structured Evaluation (Center for Substance Abuse Prevention, 1995), a meta-analysis of 309 substance use prevention programs conducted between 1986 and 1991.

Seven aspects of the methods used in each study were rated to arrive at an overall rating of methodological rigor. The elements that weighed most heavily in the determination of the overall rigor score were control of extraneous variables (e.g., the extent to which influences of independent variables extraneous to the purpose of the study had been minimized – usually through random assignment to conditions, matching treatment and comparison groups carefully, or statistically controlling for extraneous variables); and minimization of error variance (e.g., the extent to which key variables are measured reliably). Sufficiency of statistical power to detect meaningful differences is another important element of the methodology, which is not explicitly considered in the methodological rigor score. Because so many studies are based on fewer cases than are needed to reject successfully a false null hypothesis in favor of a true alternative hypothesis, insufficient power is an alternative explanation for many of the null findings in the literature. The issue of statistical power will be addressed separately from overall methodological rigor.

Other aspects of the methodology (such as attrition) were considered, and the rigor score was lowered if problems were observed. Rigor scores ranged from "1" to "5." Typical characteristics of studies scoring at each level are described in Table 4.1. Each study was coded by two trained graduate students. All discrepancies were discussed and resolved.

The rigor code applies only to the scientific rigor of study and emphasizes primarily internal validity. Among the other important dimensions of rigor are the programmatic rigor of the prevention program studied (an element of what Cook and Campbell call "statistical conclusion validity"), and the extent to which the findings of the particular study can be generalized to other persons, settings, or times (external validity). Programs and policies are implemented differently across occasions, settings, and implementors. This variation can be thought of as error in the measurement of the independent variable of interest when we assume that a standard program has been applied. For example, when one study finds that a program (such as DARE) is effective for reducing substance use, and another finds that it is not, the discrepancy may be because in one instance the program was implemented in a less rigorous fashion than in the other. Studies very rarely actually measure the independent variable. This type of invalidity affects the study's conclusion but is not taken into account in the methods rating scale.

Likewise, external validity, an issue discussed at length in Chapter 7, is not explicitly considered in the methods rating. Carefully controlled laboratory-like studies are often high in internal validity and, hence, earn high ratings on our scale but have low levels of generalizeability to more natural settings. Preventive strategies implemented in natural school settings over longer periods of time, using staff readily available to the schools, and employing methods that have been embraced by regular school staff are more likely to generalize to new settings. A conundrum for school-based prevention research is that programs with a higher degree of external validity are the most difficult to study using rigorous methods. Long-term interventions are more likely to suffer from attrition problems.

Table 4.1. *Typical Methods Used at Each Level*

Methods Rating	Number of Studies	Typical Method(s)
1	0	No comparison group No systematic reproducible approach to the measurement of key outcome variables
2	17	Nonequivalent comparison group design – no control or limited controls for preexisting differences No indication of how outcome measures were constructed or obtained
3	27	Nonequivalent comparison group design – statistical controls used, but some important differences not ruled out Attention to constructing or obtaining high-quality measures of outcome variables
4	54	Nonequivalent comparison group design with no important preexisting differences left uncontrolled Reliability of outcome measures reported, most are reliable
5	12	Random assignment to treatment and control conditions Reliable and valid measurement of outcome variables

Note. Because studies lacking a comparison group were excluded at the outset, no level 1 studies are included among the studies summarized.

In natural settings it is not always possible to assign subjects randomly to treatment and control conditions, thus lowering confidence in the interpretation of any differences observed as due to the effects of the intervention. The programs with the greatest likelihood of actually being used by educators therefore are usually not studied with the highest level of scientific rigor.

Among the studies summarized in the next two chapters, those reviewed in Chapter 5 (the environmental change strategies) are more often implemented in natural settings using regular school staff because changes to the school or classroom environment require more collaboration with school staff than do efforts to provide services to individuals. Only nine independent studies reviewed in Chapters 5 and 6 were rated as level 5 on the methods rating scale. Of these, only one was an attempt to alter the school or classroom environment. Most of the level 5 studies involved outsiders in the application of behavioral techniques or cognitive-behavioral training to relatively small groups of students. Most did not involve school staff at all. These studies are extremely important for testing causal hypotheses, but they tell us little or nothing about the programs' likely effect in more realistic settings. Once programs have passed the internal validity test, they should be tested in more natural settings.

Study Effects

Measures of Effectiveness. School-based prevention programs include interventions to prevent a variety of forms of problem behavior, ranging from illegal acts of aggression to truancy. The problem behavior was coded and can be divided into six dimensions.

Delinquent or criminal behavior is any behavior that is against the law. Delinquency is criminal behavior committed by a young person. Laws, and therefore the precise definition of behaviors in violation of the law, vary across countries and states. Crime and delinquency include the full range of acts for which individuals could be arrested. They include crimes against persons ranging in seriousness from murder to robbery to minor assault and an array of crimes against property ranging from arson to felony theft to joyriding. Crime and delinquency also include possession, use, and selling of drugs. For juveniles, they include status offenses such as running away. Dimensions of crime that are often measured distinctly in evaluations include age of first involvement, status as a delinquent ever in one's life, current criminal activity, and frequency of delinquent involvement. Delinquency is more often measured using youth self-reports than official records of arrest or conviction in evaluations of school-based prevention programs.

Ingestion of alcoholic beverages and any illicit drug are considered *substance abuse*, at least for juveniles. Dimensions of use that are often measured distinctly in evaluations of prevention programs include age of first use (age at onset); status as having used alcohol or another drug at least once; and current use, including frequency of use and amount typically used. Substance use is most often measured using youth self-reports in evaluations of school-based prevention programs.

Risky sexual behaviors include multiple sexual partners; sex with persons not well known to the individual, known to inject drugs, or known to be sexually engaged with others; unprotected sex; and anal sex. Having had sexual intercourse at all is also correlated with other problem behaviors for adolescents.

Dropping out – leaving school prior to graduation (from grade 12 in the United States) – is used as a measure of success in some prevention programs. The precise definition of truancy differs according to location. For practical purposes it is often measured as the number of days absent from school.

Studies of school-based prevention often measure *conduct problems, rebellious or antisocial behavior, defiance, disrespect, and aggression* in addition to or in lieu of actual delinquent behavior because (1) the subjects are too young to have initiated delinquent behavior, (2) the questions are less controversial because they are not self-incriminating, or (3) teachers and parents are more able to rate youth on these characteristics than on actual delinquent behavior, which is often covert. Suspension from school is categorized here unless the suspension is for a specific behavior included in one of the preceding categories.

Truancy is usually measured as days absent from school without a valid excuse. Excessive truancy is a less serious form of school withdrawal.

As noted in earlier chapters, these different forms of delinquent behavior are highly correlated and share common causes. Many of the programs considered in this chapter were not specifically designed to prevent the problem behaviors but instead to affect presumed causal factors such as academic performance, attachment to school, or other correlates that are expected to increase protection against or decrease risk toward engaging in problem behaviors at some later date.

As with the dimensions of problem behavior, intermediate outcomes measured in each study were coded. The intermediate outcomes included are listed in Table 4.2 along with the measures of problem behaviors.

Effect Sizes and Significance Tests. The effectiveness of a program or practice is usually assessed using statistical significance tests. If subjects receiving the program or service of interest are "significantly different" from subjects not receiving the program or service on an outcome measure, and if the direction of the difference favors the program participants, the program is usually said to be "effective." But critics (Cohen, 1994; Schmidt, 1996) have demonstrated that overreliance on statistical testing can produce misleading if not erroneous results. Significance levels are influenced by the size of the sample used in the study, and studies often lack the power necessary to detect meaningful differences when they exist. The tendency among social scientists to apply traditional statistical tests (i.e., controlling type I errors while allowing type II errors to be determined by the number of cases included in the analysis and using the arbitrary – and, some argue, too strict – alpha levels of .05 or .01) often results in the erroneous conclusion that no difference exists when in fact a meaningful difference exists. Meta-analytic techniques, which rely on effect size estimates rather than nominal significance levels, are preferred.

Program effects on measures of problem behavior are sometimes expressed in the next two chapters in terms of "effect sizes" (ESs) as well as levels of statistical significance. The ES is a measure of change due to the treatment as a proportion of the standard deviation for each measure

Table 4.2. *Outcome Measures Used in Studies of School-Based Prevention*

Outcome Measure	Number of Studies
Problem behaviors	
Delinquent and criminal behavior	35 (32%)
Alcohol, tobacco, and other drug use	26 (24%)
High-risk sexual behavior	2 (2%)
Withdrawal from school/school dropout	11 (10%)
Conduct problems, rebellious or antisocial behavior, defiance, disrespect, and aggression	87 (79%)
Truancy and school tardiness	35 (32%)
Individual characteristics, attitudes, beliefs, and experiences	
Association with delinquent, drug-using peers	10 (9%)
Academic performance	60 (54%)
Educational attainment (except dropout by persons required by law to attend school)	9 (8%)
Employment	3 (3%)
Knowledge (e.g., about laws, harmful effects of drugs)	9 (8%)
Social competencies or skills	33 (30%)
Cognitive ability or aptitude	0 (0%)
Personality disposition, attitude, belief, or intention	
Emotional stability, psychological health or adjustment	50 (46%)
Extroversion	7 (6%)
Openness	6 (5%)
Agreeableness or likability	27 (24%)
Conscientiousness, self-control, or impulsiveness	44 (40%)
School and classroom characteristics	
Rules, norms, expectations for behavior	13 (12%)
Responsiveness to behavior	14 (13%)
Opportunity to engage in problem behavior in and around school	4 (4%)
Organizational capacity for self-management not included in preceding outcomes	5 (4%)
Family characteristics	
Parental supervision	5 (4%)
Family or parental behavior management practices	7 (6%)

Note: Based on 110 studies.

employed. ESs usually range from −1 (indicating that the treatment group performed one standard deviation lower than the comparison group) to +1 (indicating that the treatment group performed one standard deviation higher than the comparison group). Rosenthal and Rubin (1982) show that ESs can be translated for ease of interpretation into success rate differentials between the program and comparison groups. For example, an ES of .5 translates into a success rate of 62 percent for the program group and 38 percent for the comparison group, a success rate differential of 24 percent. Lipsey and Wilson (1993), summarizing effect sizes from 302 reviews of psychological, behavioral, and educational interventions, reported an average effect size across these reviews of .50 (SD = .29) for many different types of programs and many different outcomes. By comparison, Lipsey (1992) showed the average effect size in 397 studies of delinquency treatment and prevention was .17 (SD = .44). Delinquent behavior appears more difficult to change than more conventional behaviors. The practical significance of an effect size depends largely on the seriousness of the outcome for the population. Lipsey argues that even small ESs (e.g., .10) for serious criminal behavior have practical significance.

The Studies

This section describes the studies to be reviewed in the next two chapters. Two types of prevention studies – studies of prevention of cardiovascular risk and studies of drug prevention curricula – were omitted from all summary tables. Studies of prevention of cardiovascular risk often focus on changing diet, exercise patterns, and smoking behavior. Although overeating may be considered an indicator of low self-control, and cigarette smoking a deviant behavior or a measure of low self-control, the line had to be drawn somewhere if this book was ever to be completed. Instructional drug prevention curricula are clearly within the scope of this book. Because several meta-analyses and reviews of the effectiveness of school-based drug prevention instruction have been conducted recently (Botvin, 1990; Botvin, Baker, Dusenbury, Botvin, and Diaz, 1995; Dryfoos, 1990; Durlak, 1995; Hansen, 1992; Hansen and O'Malley, 1996; Hawkins et al., 1995; Institute of Medicine, 1994; Tobler, 1986, 1992; Tobler and Stratton, 1997), I decided to rely primarily upon those reviews rather than summarizing each of these studies. Chapter 6 draws heavily upon earlier reviews of this type of program, updating as necessary with recent studies not included in the earlier reviews, and highlighting certain studies covered in the reviews as necessary. Forty-one studies that reported on interventions that were primarily drug prevention curricula or programs to reduce cardiovascular risk (and measured no problem behavior other than substance abuse) were excluded from the pool of 174 studies.

Also, several of the studies were reports of the same prevention activity. Although each study is considered separately in subsequent chapters, the following section summarizes only the eighty-six "unduplicated" studies.

Level and Domains Targeted

The eighty-six unduplicated studies of school-based prevention programs are fairly evenly distributed across the middle and elementary[2] levels, but studies of high-school-age populations are relatively rare.

The most common types of intervention studied are those targeting only individual student attitudes, beliefs, or behaviors by providing direct service to students through instruction, cognitive-behavioral or behavioral modeling training, behavior modification, counseling, tutoring, mentoring, and recreational services. This is true despite the exclusion of drug prevention curricular interventions, which constitute a high percentage of studies of instructional programs. No major effort to alter features of the environment (other than by providing these direct services)[3] is included in this group of studies, which comprises 63% of the studies. Only two programs included interventions aimed at changing family practices (not surprising given the focus on school-based prevention), and these studies included younger populations.

Twenty-two (26%) of the studies were of prevention programs that contained a major focus on changing features of the classroom or school environment. These programs did not directly target students, but instead attempted to alter classroom management or instructional methods, school norms, intergroup communication or interactions, school rules, rule enforcement strategies, school management, grade or class organization, access to the school by intruders, availability of drugs or weapons in the school, or the actual student composition of the school. An additional eight studies (10%) combined one or more of these environmental interventions with direct services to students.

No clear patterns emerge in terms of the cross-classification of major domain by level. Each type of program has been studied at each educational level, except that family interventions are found only among studies of elementary school children. Also, studies of high-school-age students are less likely to involve changes to the classroom environment – probably

---

[2] Studies limited to preschool populations were not considered. Only studies of preschool interventions that extended into the elementary school years were included.

[3] This classification by major activity is problematic because some purely instructional programs are designed to alter schoolwide normative beliefs. These programs are often distinguished from other instructional programs by their target population (i.e., they are generally delivered to the entire school population or to an entire grade-level cohort), their content (i.e., they contain lessons aimed at altering normative beliefs about acceptable behavior), and level of assignment to experimental conditions (i.e., entire schools rather than individuals are assigned). The instructional category includes these "universal" programs as well as programs that are more like traditional instruction (e.g., relying largely upon conveying information). These special instructional programs are highlighted in Chapter 6.

because students travel from class to class in high school rather than staying in one classroom for an extended period.

Outcomes Measured

Table 4.2 shows the number and percentage of studies measuring each of the problem behaviors and intermediate outcomes discussed earlier. This table includes multiple studies of the same program when they exist because often different published accounts report on different outcomes. The most frequently used category of outcome measure is the large category including conduct problems, rebellious or antisocial behavior, defiance, disrespect, and aggression. Of all the studies, 79% use this type of outcome measure. Other types of measures frequently used include measures of academic performance (54%), emotional health (e.g., self-esteem, anxiety; 46%), and conscientiousness, self-control, or impulsiveness (40%). Delinquent behavior is used as an outcome measure in 32% of the studies, and among these delinquency measures, measures of what most would call "serious" delinquency are rare. Approximately 10% of studies measured serious violent crimes such as murder, rape, robbery or aggravated assault, or serious property crimes such as burglary, larceny-theft, and motor vehicle theft. Most of the delinquency measures used in studies of school-based prevention are of less serious or unspecified criminal behavior. Note that measures of school or classroom environment are seldom used to measure success in school-based prevention programs.

Different outcomes are studied at different grade levels. As expected, delinquency, truancy, and school dropout are less likely to be used in studies of elementary school children. Conduct problems are less often used as outcome measures in studies of high school populations. Among the intermediate outcomes measured in these studies, a few (association with delinquent peers; educational attainment; and conscientiousness, self-control, or impulsiveness) are found more often in studies of older youths. Measures of social competency skills and agreeableness or likability are found more often in studies of younger students. These differences across school-level in the types of outcomes measured most likely correspond to implicit hypotheses about developmental differences in the importance of certain risk factors found in the studies.

The following chapters summarize these studies of school-based prevention. The studies are divided by major domain so that the thirty-nine studies whose interventions attempted to alter characteristics of the class or school environment are discussed in Chapter 5, and the seventy-one studies focusing on individual and family interventions only are summarized in Chapter 6 along with studies of drug prevention curricula. Within each chapter, studies are organized by developmental level.

Changing School and Classroom Environments: The Field Studies

CHAPTER 3 identified a number of features of school and classroom environments related to problem behavior. Many are characteristics of the way the school is organized and managed. The research implies that principals and faculty can control behavior by setting rules, communicating clear expectations for behavior, consistently enforcing rules, and providing rewards for rule compliance and punishments for rule infractions. They can also perform general management functions (such as coordination and resource allocation and communication) well, establish and maintain clear goals for the organization, deliver instruction in ways that promote maximal learning, and encourage a sense of community. They can create an extended network of caring adults who interact regularly with the students and who share norms and expectations about their students. The research implied that when educators succeed at creating such "communal social organizations," they increase social control and therefore reduce the likelihood that youths will engage in problem behavior.

Can these findings from nonexperimental research be translated into specific policies and practices that can be implemented in schools? Are such programs effective for reducing problem behavior? This chapter examines evidence from experimental and quasi-experimental studies of attempts to implement changes to the way schools and classrooms are organized and managed.

Overview of Studies

Although the intent in this chapter is to focus on school- or classroom-level interventions, the multicomponent nature of school-based prevention makes it impossible to isolate these types of programs or practices. Classifying these activities by content is difficult because most school-based prevention programs contain a mix of different types of activities. A large percentage (29%) of the studies containing major efforts to change school and classroom environments also contain major components of direct service to individuals.

Comprehensiveness in prevention programs, although a thorny issue for researchers trying to isolate effective strategies, is perfectly reasonable given the nested nature of the schooling experience and the multiple routes to problem behavior. Student behavior is most directly influenced by the attitudes, beliefs, and characteristics of the student and his or her peers. Individually targeted interventions such as instructional or behavior modification techniques that teach students new ways of thinking and acting may be effective in changing these individual factors. But students interact in the context of classrooms, each of which has its own normative climate encouraging or discouraging certain behaviors. And classrooms exist in school environments that establish larger contexts for all activities in the school. An instructional program teaching students to resolve conflicts nonviolently is not likely to be as effective for reducing violence in a school setting in which fights are regularly ignored as in one that immediately responds to such incidents. Prevention strategies designed to take these interconnections into consideration are *likely* to be more effective than programs targeting single domains (Elias et al., 1994), although we have little hard evidence to support this hypothesis.

Most programs reviewed in this chapter are multicomponent in nature. The research designs utilized in most studies do not permit examination of *which* of the several major components included in these comprehensive programs is responsible for any observed change. Programs are necessarily viewed as "packages," whose contents cannot be analyzed separately.

Among the programs selected for their emphasis on changing school or classroom environments, the most common type of intervention strategy involves changes to the instructional or classroom management methods in the classroom. Sixty-one percent of the programs include this activity, and the studies that use these strategies tend to be conducted at the lower educational levels. This uneven distribution probably comes about because students in elementary grades (and sometimes in the middle grades) tend to stay in the same classroom for their entire school day. Therefore, changes to the classroom rather than the school environment would be expected to affect students most directly.

The next most common activities included in these studies are instruction, changing rules and policies regarding student behavior, and changing school management practices, which constitute nearly 20% of the programs. Changes to school management and administration practices are the next most commonly studied strategy.

Several environmental change strategies are not represented among the strategies that have been studied. The effects on problem behavior of preventing intruders from entering the school, excluding weapons[1] or contraband, and altering school composition (e.g., by using selective admissions) are not known.

Studies of Programs in Elementary Schools

Table 5.1 shows the content of twelve different programs conducted at the elementary school level whose evaluations have appeared in the literature. These twelve programs, or minor variants of them, have been the subject of the twenty-five studies listed in Table 5.2.

All but two of the programs (Comer's School Development Process and Olweus's Bullying Prevention Project) included a major emphasis on altering instructional or classroom management methods or practices with the intention of increasing student interest, attention, and learning and decreasing off-task, disruptive behavior. These changes often involved instructional strategies such as cooperative or mastery learning, or the application of specific behavioral principles to classroom discipline management. They were augmented in some studies with specific curricular changes (e.g., the addition of a social skills component or a new reading curriculum). One program extended beyond the classroom by employing cross-grade grouping of students for instruction, and two used a team of school faculty and other professionals to develop schoolwide programs and practices to reduce problem behavior. The Comer Process was unique in its intense focus on the school and its organization and management. The following sections describe each elementary program and the related studies.

Classroom Interventions

ClassWide Peer Tutoring. Greenwood, Terry, Utley, Montagna, and Walker (1993; methods rating = 4) studied the effects of a four-year program that taught teachers in grades 1 through 4 to use a structured peer-tutoring method. Consultants trained teachers to use the method and monitored the implementation of the method to assure quality implementation. Teachers were not considered "trained" until they produced a classroom implementation score of at least 85% on a procedural checklist used by the consultants. ClassWide Peer Tutoring (CWPT) was introduced incrementally in reading, math, and spelling instruction. Teachers randomly

[1] One study of metal detectors in the New York City public schools (Centers for Disease Control, 1993) found that students who attend schools with metal detector programs report carrying weapons less often in school. No differences were found for weapon carrying in general or threats and physical fights at any location. The study was not included in this chapter summary because it used survey research methodology.

Table 5.1. *Elementary School Programs with Environmental Change Focus*

Program (Study)	Grades Targeted	Program Content[a]																Duration of Program
		1	2	3	4	5	6	7	8	9	10	11	12	13	14	15	16	
"ClassWide Peer Tutoring" (Greenwood et al., 1993)	1–4							X										4 school years
"Effective Classroom Management" (Schaps et al., 1984; Moskowitz et al., 1984a)	4–6	✓						X										1 school year
"Magic Circle" (Moskowitz et al., 1982)	3							X										1 school year
"Cooperative Learning – Jigsaw" (Moskowitz et al., 1983)	5–6							X										1 school year
"Good Behavior Game and Mastery Learning" (Dolan et al. 1993; Kellam et al., 1994)	1–2			X				X										2 school years
"Success for All" (Madden et al., 1993)	K–3					✓		X	✓			✓	✓					3–4 school years
"Seattle Social Development Project" (Hawkins et al., 1991; Hawkins et al., 1992; O'Donnell et al., 1995; Hawkins et al., 1998)	1–6	X	✓					X	✓								X	6 years

Program	Grades	1	2	3	4	5	6	7	8	9	10	11	12	13	14	15	16	Duration
"Child Development Project" (Battistich et al., 1996)	K–6	✔							X	✔								3 school years
"Child Development Project" (Solomon et al., 1988; Battistich et al., 1989)	K–4	✔	✔					✔	X	✔	✔							5 school years
"Behavioral Consultation to Reduce Violence/Vandalism" (Mayer and Butterworth, 1979; Mayer et al., 1983)	4–8	✔	✔						X	X								7 months
"Bullying Prevention" (Olweus, 1991, 1992; Olweus and Alsaker, 1991; Smith and Sharp, 1994)	4–7				✔	X			✔	✔								2 years
"School Development Program (Comer Process)" (Comer, 1985; Haynes, 1994; Comer et al., 1989; Cook et al., 1998)	K–5	X				✔			✔	X								Up to 5 school years

[a] Program content key: 1. Instructing students. 2. Cognitive-behavioral change/behavior modeling. 3. Behavioral or behavior modification. 4. Counseling, social work, other psychological or therapeutic interventions. 5. Tutoring, mentoring, or other individual attention. 6. Recreational, enrichment, and leisure. 7. Changing instructional or classroom management methods or practices management. 8. Changing norms or expectations for behavior. 9. Building a sense of community, morale, caring, support, or pride. 10. Changing rules, policies, regulations, or laws about behavior or discipline. 11. Changing school management structure or process. 12. Reorganizing grades or classes. 13. Preventing intruders from entering the school. 14. Excluding weapons or contraband. 15. Altering school composition. 16. Changing family supervision or family behavior. ✔ = contains some of this content; X = major focus of program.

Table 5.2. *Evaluations of Elementary School Programs with Environmental Change Focus*

Program (Study)	Subjects	Method Rating/ Follow-up (mos.)	Correlates of Problem Behavior	Outcomes[a] Problem Behavior
"ClassWide Peer Tutoring" (Greenwood et al., 1993)	303 low SES, at-risk boys and girls in 9 schools	4/24	Standardized academic skills test scores (+) Grade retention (0)	Special education placement (+)
"Effective Classroom Management" (Schaps et al., 1984)	997 boys and girls in 39 classes in 8 largely white, suburban schools	4/0	Standardized reading and math achievement test scores (0) Perceived alcohol costs (individual level: 0) (class level: + boys; 0 girls) Perceived pot costs (individual level: 0 boys; + girls) (class level: 0) Attitudes to school (individual level: 0) (class level: + boys; 0 girls) Peer attitudes to school (individual level: 0) (class level: + boys; 0 girls)	Absences (0) Minor and major discipline problems (individual level: N/A) (class level: 0) *Alcohol involvement (individual level: 0) (class level: + boys; 0 girls)* *Pot involvement (0 boys; + girls)*
"Effective Classroom Management" (Moskowitz et al., 1984a)	441 boys and girls in 22 classes in 13 schools	4/0	Standardized reading achievement test scores (+ boys; 0 girls) Standardized math achievement test scores (0) Alcohol and pot costs (+ boys; 0 girls) Attitudes to school (0) Peer attitudes to school (0)	Absences (0) Minor discipline problems (0) *Alcohol and pot involvement (0)*

Program (reference)	Sample	Duration/follow-up (months)	Outcome measures	Results
"Magic Circle" (Moskowitz et al., 1982)	467 boys and girls in 28 classes in 13 largely white, suburban schools	4/0	Standardized reading and math achievement test scores (0) Attitudes to school (0) Peer attitudes to school (0)	Absences (0) Minor discipline problems (– boys; 0 girls) Major discipline problems (0)
"Cooperative Learning-Jigsaw" (Moskowitz et al., 1983)	261 boys and girls in 13 classes in 8 schools	4/0	Standardized reading and math achievement test scores (0) Attitudes to school (0) Attitudes to peers (0)	Absences (0)
"Good Behavior Game and Mastery Learning" (Dolan et al., 1993)	864 boys and girls in 42 classes in 19 schools (follow-up at end of grade 1)	4/0	ML vs. control: standardized reading achievement test scores (+) GBG vs. control: standardized reading achievement test scores (0)	ML vs. control: Teacher-rated aggressive behavior (0) Peer-rated aggressive behavior (0) GBG vs. control: teacher-rated aggressive behavior (vs. external control: + boys; 0 girls) (vs. internal control: 0 boys; + girls) Peer-rated aggressive behavior (vs. external control: 0 boys; 0 girls) (vs. internal control: + boys; 0 girls)
"Good Behavior Game" (Kellam et al., 1994)	590 boys and girls in 41 classes in 19 schools (follow-up at end of grade 6)	4/48		GBG vs. ML and controls: teacher-rated aggression (0) (but + for boys most aggressive at base line)

Table 5.2. (*cont.*)

Program (Study)	Subjects	Method Rating/ Follow-up (mos.)	Outcomes[a]	
			Correlates of Problem Behavior	Problem Behavior
"Success for All" (Madden et al., 1993)	342 boys and girls in 10 disadvantaged, Chapter I schools	3/0	Reading proficiency (+) Retention (+ nr)	Attendance (+ nr)
"Success for All" (Jones et al., 1997)	167 boys and girls in 2 schools	3/0	School affect (0) Normal grade progression (mixed) Achievement test scores (kindergarten: +) (other grades: mixed)	Behavior rating (0)
"Seattle Social Development Project" (Hawkins et al., 1991)	458 boys and girls in 21 classrooms in 8 schools	3/0	Teacher-rated popularity (0)	Teacher-rated, aggressive behavior (+ boys; 0 girls) Teacher-rated externalizing antisocial behavior (+ boys; 0 girls)
"Seattle Social Development Project" (Hawkins, Catalano, Morrison, et al., 1992)	853 boys and girls in 18 schools	2/3	Achievement test scores (−) School attachment and commitment (+) Belief in moral order and attitudes about substance use (0) Family management (+) Family discipline (0) Attachment to family (+)	School misbehavior (0) *Alcohol initiation (0)* **Delinquency initiation (0)**

Study	Sample		Mediators	Outcomes
"Seattle Social Development Project" (O'Donnell et al., 1995)	106 high-risk, low-income boys and girls in 18 schools	2/0	Antisocial peers (student reports: 0) (teacher reports: + boys; 0 girls) Grades and standardized achievement test scores (+ boys; 0 girls) Substance abuse refusal skills (0) Social and study skills (+ boys; 0 girls) Belief in moral order and substance use norms (0) Attachment to friends (0) Bonding to parents (0) Attachment to school (0 boys; + girls) Commitment to school (+)	*Alcohol and marijuana use (0)* **Delinquency initiation (0)**
"Seattle Social Development Project" (Hawkins et al., 1998)	643 boys and girls in 18 schools	2/76	Bonding to school (+ full; 0 late) School achievement (+ full; 0 late) GPA (0) Repeated a grade (0) Standardized test score (0) Opportunities to get marijuana (0 boys; + girls) Family management (0)	Dropped out (0) Past year school misbehavior (+) Official disciplinary action report (0) Suspended or expelled (0) **Violence (+ full; 0 late)** **Nonviolent crime (0)** **Arrested (0)** **Court charges (0)** *Substance use (0)* Sexually active (+ full; 0 late) Multiple sex partners (+ full; 0 late) Been/gotten a woman pregnant (0) Had/fathered a baby (0)
"Child Development Project" (Battistich et al., 1996)[b]	1,400–1,800 per year – boys and girls in 24 schools	3/0		Skipping school (0) *Marijuana use (0)* *Alcohol use (+)* **Prevalence of delinquent behaviors (0)**

Table 5.2. (cont.)

Program (Study)	Subjects	Method Rating/ Follow-up (mos.)	Correlates of Problem Behavior	Outcomes[a] Problem Behavior
"Child Development Project" (Solomon et al., 1988; Battistich et al., 1989)	133 to 191 middle- to upper-middle-class boys and girls in 67 classes in 6 schools	3/0	Standardized achievement test scores (0) Conflict resolution skills: prosocial skills (+), antisocial strategies (0) Object acquisition and peer group entry skills (2 measures: +) (7 measures: 0)	Observer tallies of negative classroom behavior (0) Observer tallies of positive classroom behavior (+)
"Behavioral Consultation to Reduce Violence/ Vandalism" (Mayer and Butterworth, 1979)	228 boys and girls taught by 38 teachers in 19 schools	4/0		Money spent on vandalism (+) Observations of attending behavior (+ nr) Observations of nontask behavior (0) Observations of disruptive behavior (+ nr)
"Behavioral Consultation to Reduce Violence/ Vandalism" (Mayer et al., 1983)	216 at-risk boys and girls taught by 36 teachers in 18 schools	4/0		Money spent on vandalism (+) Observations of off-task behavior (+)

"Bullying Prevention" (Olweus, 1991, 1992; Olweus and Alsaker, 1991)	2,500 boys and girls in 112 classes in 42 schools (4 cohorts)	3/0	Self-reports of being exposed to bullying (+ nr) Self-reports of bullying others (+ nr) **Self-reports of antisocial behavior (+ nr)**
"Bullying Prevention" (Smith and Sharp, 1994)[b]	8,309 boys and girls in 27 schools	2/0	Being bullied: percentage not bullied (primary school: + nr) (secondary school: − nr); frequency of being bullied (+ nr); number of students bullied (primary school: + nr) (secondary school: − nr) Bullying others: percentage not bullying others (primary school: + nr) (secondary school: − nr); frequency of bullying others (primary school: + nr) (secondary school: − nr); number of students bullying others (+ nr)
"School Development Program (Comer Process)" (Comer, 1985)	48 low-income boys and girls in 2 schools	3/36	Standardized achievement test scores (+) GPA (+) Self-perceptions of school competence (+)

Table 5.2. (cont.)

Program (Study)	Subjects	Method Rating/ Follow-up (mos.)	Correlates of Problem Behavior	Problem Behavior
			Outcomes[a]	
"School Development Program (Comer Process)" (Haynes, 1994)	315 boys and girls in 14 schools	1.5/0	Reading and math grades (mixed, mostly 0) Standardized reading and math test scores (mixed) Teacher-rated attitude to authority (mixed) Parent-rated social competence (0) Cognitive ability (0)	Teacher-rated classroom behavior (mixed) Parent-rated behavior problems (0) Self-reported behavior (0)
"School Development Program (Comer Process)" (Comer et al., 1989)	306 low-income, minority boys and girls in 14 schools	3/0	Grades: reading (+), math (0) Classroom order and organization (children's report: +) School climate: (teacher assessment: 0) (parent assessment: +)	Percentage of days absent (+)
"School Development Program (Comer Process)" (Cook et al., 1998)	1,685 boys and girls in 19 schools (longitudinal sample)	4/0	Standardized math and reading test scores (+) Disapproval of misbehavior (+)	Acting out (+) *Substance use (0 school level; + individual level)*

Notes. Follow-up period begins at end of intervention. The number of subjects is the maximum number present for any of the analyses reported in the table. [a] 0 = no significant effect (p < .05); + = significant positive effect (p < .05); – = significant negative effect (p < .05); nr = two-tailed significance level not reported. Outcomes for substance use and for crime and delinquency measures appear in italics and in bold, respectively.
[b] Results vary for subsets of schools or classrooms that differed on level of program implementation.

assigned students to partners for peer tutoring. The partners changed each week. Partners worked together using teacher-prepared exercises to test and correct each other on academic material. Tutees earned points for each correct answer. At the end of each session, students reported their scores to the teacher, who summed the partners' scores to create a team score. The winning teams were recognized, and the losing teams encouraged to do better next time. CWPT was used for a four-year period.

CWPT had immediate positive effects on engagement in the classroom and achievement test scores. Greenwood et al. (1993) reported long-term effects two years after the end of the program, at the end of grade 6. In the original study, nine schools were randomly assigned to receive the program or not. Analyses were conducted at the individual level, comparing students from Chapter I schools (e.g., low-SES, high-risk students) assigned to the experimental group with students from the Chapter I schools assigned to the comparison group as well as with students from non–Chapter I schools assigned to a second comparison group. Of the 416 students in grade 1 included in the original study, 303 (73%) were located for the follow-up study six years later. The follow-up study found that achievement test score gains continued to favor the CWPT group over the comparison high-risk group (with ESs ranging from .39 to .57), and that the CWPT group had significantly fewer members (69% vs. 96%, ES = .58) placed into special-education programs between grades 1 and 6. A disaggregation of the special-education categories resulting in placement showed that the CWPT group was placed less often into the social maladjustment, learning disabled, and educable mentally retarded categories, the first two of which are highly related to subsequent delinquent behavior. No significant group differences in grade retention rates were found.

Several classroom management strategies were tested in a series of studies conducted in Napa, California, in the late 1970s and early 1980s. Because the strategies, study designs, and outcomes are similar, they are considered as a group.

Effective Classroom Management (ECM), Magic Circle, and Cooperative Learning. Schaps, Moskowitz, Condon, and Malvin (1984; methods rating = 4) and Moskowitz, Malvin, Schaeffer, and Schaps (1984a; methods rating = 4) reported on two different tests of an in-service course in which fourth through sixth grade teachers were taught communication skills (e.g., tailored feedback, "I-Messages," clarifying responses, reflecting feelings, and reflecting content), problem-solving (e.g., creating problem statements, brainstorming, evaluating alternative solutions, force field analysis, and developing an action plan), and self-esteem enhancement techniques (e.g., techniques that create opportunities to describe and receive recognition for a positive trait, skill, or experience) for use in their classrooms.

In another in-service training workshop (Moskowitz, Schaps, and Malvin, 1982; methods rating = 4) , third grade teachers were trained to lead structured small-group discussions ("Magic Circle" classroom meetings) about a variety of interpersonal and intrapersonal topics. Another in-service workshop (Moskowitz, Malvin, Schaeffer, and Schaps, 1983; methods rating = 4) taught fifth and sixth grade teachers to use one of several cooperative learning strategies (Jigsaw) – a technique whereby students work in small "expert groups" to learn academic material, and then each member is responsible for teaching this same material to a different small group of peers. The technique is intended to increase engagement in the learning task, attachment to school, social competencies, and constructive peer relationships. Each of these teacher training activities was intended to make the classroom environment more responsive to students' affective and cognitive needs in order to eventually reduce students' acceptance and use of drugs. The programs were expected to operate indirectly by changing students' attitudes, behaviors, and perceptions of norms.

In each study, schools were randomly assigned to treatment and control conditions. Teachers in the experimental schools were invited to participate in the training sessions, but not all teachers agreed. Analyses were generally conducted at the classroom and the individual levels, comparing immediate outcomes for all students in the classrooms of all treatment and control teachers, controlling for any preexisting differences between the groups. When high percentages of teachers failed to participate, additional analyses compared only the participating teachers with the control teachers. To check on selection effects, in the study of Cooperative Learning, a backup "randomized invitation" design was used. In this design, only teachers in the experimental and control schools who initially expressed an interest in attending the in-service workshop (seven in the treatment and six in the control schools) were included in the final evaluation. This strategy helped to remove some of the self-selection effects of voluntary participation.

Table 5.2 shows the detailed results from the studies. The preponderance of evidence suggests that the training activities had no effect on measures of problem behavior. The only significant differences between the groups on teacher ratings of misbehavior favored the Magic Circle control group. Measures of involvement with substances showed some positive effects: for ECM boys, classroom-level analyses showed a significant ($p <$ .01) positive effect for alcohol involvement, but the individual-level analyses did not confirm this effect. No effect was observed for male marijuana involvement. For ECM girls, individual-level analyses revealed a significant positive effect on marijuana (but not alcohol) involvement ($p < .01$), and these results were confirmed in the classroom-level analyses ($p < .05$). Note, however, that the involvement scales contained perceptions of peer attitudes and peer use as well as own attitudes and use. Occasional significant effects were found on measures of correlates of problem behavior, but they were generally not replicated across studies or even across genders within studies.

Mastery Learning and the Good Behavior Game. Dolan et al. (1993; methods rating = 4) and Kellam, Rebok, Ialongo, and Mayer (1994; methods rating = 4) reported on trials of two different elementary school classroom interventions. The first intervention – Mastery Learning (ML) – consisted of a strengthened reading curriculum for the entire class and a group-paced instructional approach whereby the class was tested after each unit and was retaught the material until 80% of the class achieved mastery. A flexible corrective process was used to help individual learners achieve mastery. The second intervention – the Good Behavior Game (GBG) – was a group-based behavior management program based on sound behavioral principles. Small student teams are formed within each classroom, and the teams are rewarded for achieving behavioral standards. Because the team reward depends on the behavior of each member of the team, peer pressure is used constructively in this program to achieve positive behavior.

These strategies were tested in separate trials in which nineteen schools were randomly assigned to receive ML, GBG, or no program. Within each treatment school, first grade classrooms were randomly assigned to receive or not receive the program. Also, the incoming first graders were randomly assigned to these conditions. Hence, two comparison groups – one internal and one external – were available. This design feature allowed a control against the possibility of spillover effects to control classrooms in the same schools. The program lasted for two years. Only students who stayed in their schools for an entire year (n = 864) were included in the analysis of first-year outcomes, which measured academic achievement and aggressive behavior, rated by both teachers and peers.

At the end of the first year of the program, students in the ML condition scored significantly higher on reading achievement tests than did comparison group children, but no differences were observed on measures of aggressive behavior. The results for the GBG were somewhat inconsistent both across genders and depending on which measure of aggressiveness and control group was used. Compared with control students from other classrooms in the same school, GBG males were rated by their peers but not by their teachers as less aggressive at the end of grade 1. The opposite pattern was found for females: teacher ratings but not peer ratings of aggression were significantly lower for GBG students. Compared with control students from classrooms in different schools, GBG males were rated by their teachers but not by their peers as less aggressive at the end of grade 1, and none of the comparisons of GBG females with the external controls showed significant differences. Kellam and Rebok (1992) recommended caution in interpreting the teacher ratings, as the teachers were responsible for delivering the intervention. The study also showed some evidence that the GBG was most effective for reducing aggressive behavior among the most aggressive children, but the internal validity of these results based on supplementary analyses is not as strong as the results based on the original design.

Kellam et al. (1994) reported the results of a follow-up at grade 6. Only students who had experienced two full years of the intervention (in grades 1 and 2) and took part in the six-year follow-up assessment (n = 590) were retained in the analysis. As anticipated, no effects on aggressive behavior due to participation in ML were detected. The early positive effects of GBG on aggression were no longer evident for the total population of females or males. When subgroups of subjects who differed on their levels of teacher-observed aggression in grade 1 were examined, a significant reduction in teacher-rated aggression at grade 6 was observed, but only for males, and only for males at or above the median on aggressive behavior in grade 1. But, as in the analysis of grade 1 outcomes, these post hoc subgroup findings are based on a weaker design than the findings for the total population.

Class and School Interventions

The following programs are broader in scope than those described so far, which include only one or two different types of strategies (e.g., using a different instructional or classroom management method). The studies that follow tend to combine these strategies with changes to school schedules, school management processes, special instruction, or attempts to enhance intergroup relations; not surprisingly, the methodological rigor of these studies is somewhat lower. When interventions involve changes to school-level processes, the scientist generally has less control over the details of the evaluation than when only classroom-level processes are involved. More compromise in the scientific methods is generally required for studies of more complex interventions.

Success for All (SFA). SFA reorganizes instruction in the early elementary grades in order to teach *all* students to read at or near grade level by grade 3. It involves reading instruction, periodic assessments and regrouping for instruction, reading tutors, and family support. The components of the program are:

"Story Telling and Retelling" reading curriculum ("STaR"): Teachers read stories to children and have them retell or act out the stories to increase involvement and comprehension. The program includes Peabody Language Development Kits in kindergarten and the first half of first grade, and beginning reading instruction in the second half of kindergarten.

Cooperative Integrated Reading and Composition (CIRC): This is a form of cooperative learning in which students work in teams, receive recognition for their teams' progress, and use specially developed materials designed to maximize comprehension of the stories (grades 1 through 3).

Regrouping for reading instruction: Initial reading group placement is determined by a reading assessment. Students are assessed in reading every eight weeks. These tests are used to shift students into a higher or a lower reading group to tailor the reading instruction to the child's current reading level. Because reading groups are composed according to reading level rather than grade level, cross-grade grouping is used.

Reading tutors: The reading assessments are used to identify which students need additional tutoring, in which area. One-on-one tutoring is provided to students who are not performing well.

Family support: This component often involves a social worker who provides specific services to families on an as-needed basis.

SFA has undergone several evaluations, most recently summarized in Jones, Gottfredson, and Gottfredson (1997). Evaluations conducted by the program developers have found generally positive results of the program on language development and reading. For example, Madden, Slavin, Karweit, Dolan, and Wasik (1993; methods rating = 3) report effects of SFA after three years (four schools) and four years (one school) of implementation in five Baltimore city schools. Students in the SFA schools were matched (using standardized achievement test scores) with students in comparison schools selected for their similarity to the SFA schools. Only students who had been enrolled in their schools since first grade were included in the analysis. Reading scores, attendance, and grade retentions were gathered for the SFA students, but only reading test scores were available for the control school students as well. The comparisons favored SFA students on most of the reading measures. Over-time comparisons of retentions and attendance rates in the SFA schools showed drastic reductions in retention rates (but reducing retentions is a feature of the program implementation rather than an outcome) and reductions in attendance rates. In the absence of a comparison point, these attendance data are ambiguous.

Other evaluations (by researchers other than the program developers) have also usually found positive results on reading, but the results have not been as consistent. Evaluations have suggested that the positive results may be limited to kindergarten or the first grade (in which the STaR component is delivered), and that they depend largely on the level of implementation of the program, which varies considerably across schools. Jones et al. (1997; methods rating = 3) report on an independent evaluation of SFA conducted in two elementary schools (one treatment and one control). The program was implemented under difficult conditions (e.g., in a school district that was hit by a major hurricane during the implementation), and it departed from the SFA standard practice of selecting only schools in which 80% or more of the faculty vote in favor of bringing the program into the school. Two cohorts of students were studied for three years and a third cohort for two years as they progressed through early elementary school. As in earlier evaluations, students who were only partially exposed to the program were omitted from the analyses.

This evaluation found large positive effects of the kindergarten program on first grade reading achievement, but the results on reading achievement in the later grades were inconsistent. Effects on math achievement were as often negative as positive. No effects were observed on teacher ratings of student behavior or a measure of student school adjustment. Teacher ratings of student achievement were positive in grade 1 but negative in grades 2 and 3.

Seattle Social Development Project. Another longitudinal field study of the effect of upgrading classroom instructional and management methods on subsequent substance use and delinquent behavior is the Seattle Social Development Project (Hawkins et al., 1992; Hawkins, Von Cleve, and Catalano, 1991; O'Donnell, Hawkins, Catalano, Abbott, and Day, 1995; Hawkins et al., 1999). The intervention involved cooperative learning strategies, proactive classroom management, and interactive teaching. Proactive classroom management consisted of establishing expectations for classroom behavior, using methods of maintaining classroom order that minimize interruptions to instruction, and giving frequent specific contingent praise and encouragement for student progress and effort. Interactive teaching involved several instructional practices generally accepted as effective (e.g., frequent assessment, clear objectives, checking for understanding, and remedial work). Cooperative learning used small heterogeneous learning groups to reinforce and practice what the teacher taught. Recognition and team rewards were provided to the teams, contingent on demonstrated improvement. In addition, first grade teachers provided cognitive problem-solving instruction, and parent training in family management practices was also provided in grades 1 through 3. This program was implemented continually from grade 1 through 6 in several elementary schools beginning in 1981.

The study began as a quasi experiment in which eight Seattle elementary schools were selected to participate. Of these, one was assigned to be treatment only, one control only, and entering students in grade 1 in the remaining six schools were randomly assigned to intervention and control conditions. During grades 1 through 4, newly entering students were randomly assigned in these schools to treatment and control conditions. In 1984, when the initial subjects entered grade 5, the design changed: the study expanded to include all fifth grade students in eighteen elementary schools. The groups were reformulated at this point. The "full intervention" group (n = 199) consisted of students exposed to at least one semester of the program in grades 1 through 4, and the control group included the original control group plus unexposed students added to the panel in 1984 (n = 709). Students exposed to the program for less than one semester were excluded from the study. All studies report analyses conducted at the individual level.

Several different reports have been issued on this project. Hawkins et al. (1991; methods rating = 3) report results for second graders after two years of the program, before the new panel was added. Teacher reports of aggressive behavior and externalizing problem behaviors favored the treatment group, but only for males. Results in grade 5 (Hawkins, Catalano, Morrison et al., 1992; methods rating = 2) showed consistent significant positive effects on attachment and commitment to school, the absence of such effects on belief in moral order and attitudes about substance use, and a significant effect on achievement test scores favoring the control students. Measures of alcohol use favored the treatment group in grade 5 (marginally significant at p < .10), but measures of school misbehavior and minor delinquency initiation showed no significant effects.

O'Donnell et al. (1995; methods rating = 2) reported results for sixth graders after six years of the program, but only for a subsample of 177 low-SES students. This study reported significant effects favoring treatment students on attachment to school (girls only), commitment to school, grades (boys only), and achievement test scores (boys only), and no significant effects on belief and attitudes favoring substance use. Some measures of problem behavior tended toward a positive effect for the program for certain groups: measures of alcohol and marijuana use favored the treatment girls (marginally significant at p < .10), but were not significant for boys. A lower delinquency initiation was observed for the treatment group (p < .10), but only for males.

The most recent report from the study (Hawkins et al., 1998; methods rating = 2) compares participants who received the program in grades 1 through 6 and those who received it later (in grades 5 and 6) with students who did not receive it at all. The report found that students who received the full intervention (e.g., beginning in grade 1) reported significantly less school misbehavior, lower prevalence of violent delinquent behavior, and less frequent alcohol consumption than students not receiving the intervention. Students receiving the intervention in grades 5 and 6 were no different from the control group. In summary, the SSDP produced positive effects on antisocial behavior. It also registered effects on crime, substance use, and school dropout, but these results are more tenuous than the results from the more conclusive early comparison of randomly assigned treatment and control students. At any rate, positive effects are observed only for the full intervention condition delivered beginning in grade 1 and continuing through the elementary school years.

Child Development Project. The Child Development Project (CDP) was conducted with several cohorts of elementary school students in twelve elementary schools for three consecutive years beginning in 1992 (Battistich, Schaps, Watson, and Solomon, 1996; methods rating = 3). It included the following components:

"Cooperative learning" activities: intended to encourage student discussion, comparison of ideas, and mutual challenging of ideas on academic and social topics.

"Values-rich" literature-based reading and language arts program: intended to foster understanding of diversity.

"Developmental discipline": a positive approach to classroom management that stresses teaching appropriate behavior rather than punishment, involving students in classroom management, and helping them to learn behavior management and conflict resolution skills.

"Community-building" activities: aimed at increasing appreciation for diversity or students' sense of communal involvement and responsibility.

"Home-school" activities: intended to foster parents' involvement in their children's education.

A similar program was conducted in three elementary schools for five consecutive years beginning in 1982 (Battistich, Solomon, Watson, Solomon, and Schaps, 1989; Solomon, Watson, Delucchi, Schaps, and Battistich, 1988; both with methods rating = 3). Students in grades K through 4 participated. The earlier demonstration lacked the values-rich curriculum and the home-school activities, and instead included efforts to draw attention to, model, and explain prosocial behavior through the use of literature, films, and television; and "helping activities," in which students were given the opportunity to help others in a variety of ways (e.g., tutoring, chores, school improvement, and community service activities).

In the Battistich et al. (1996) study, twenty-four elementary schools from six districts were assigned (nonrandomly) to treatment and control conditions. Those students in the three upper grades in these twenty-four participating schools for whom parental consent was obtained participated in the research each year. The number of cases ranged from 5,331 to 5,502 (between 77% and 82% of the upper-grade students), but the number of cases available for specific analyses varied by measure. Measures of drug use and delinquency, for example, were obtained only for students in grades 5 and 6 (numbers ranged from 1,400 to 1,800, depending on the year). Students were measured at base line and once per year for two additional years. Analyses were conducted at the individual level.

Year-by-year comparisons of prevalence rates for measures of delinquency and drug use showed that the program had no effect on skipping school, delinquency, or marijuana use, but alcohol use among the treatment youths in grades 5 and 6 was significantly lower than among the control students. In this study, supplementary analyses that take into account varying levels of implementation across schools showed that marijuana use and two of the ten delinquency items were significantly lower among treatment youths in the schools with the highest level of implementation, but these results are ambiguous because the high implementation schools also have strikingly higher levels of marijuana use and delinquency at all time points. Regression to the mean is not ruled out as an alternative explanation for the observed pattern of results.

In the earlier study, six schools were randomly assigned to treatment and control conditions. Individual-level analyses (Battistich et al., 1989) of program effects on conflict resolution and problem-solving skills showed that the program increased prosocial conflict resolution skills but did not decrease negative conflict resolution skills among students in grades K through 4. Significant positive effects were also observed for certain cognitive problem-solving skills (e.g., interpersonal sensitivity and means-ends thinking). Consistent with these findings were the classroom-level (n = 67) analyses of behavioral observations reported by Solomon et al. (1988). Participating students displayed significantly more positive behavior (e.g., supportive, friendly, and helpful behaviors) but no significant differences were observed on measures of negative behavior (including aggression, anger, and noncompliance).

Behavioral Consultation to Reduce Violence and Vandalism. Mayer and Butterworth (1979; methods rating = 4 for the classroom-level analyses) studied a program that trained teams of school personnel to use behavioral strategies for reducing student vandalism and disruption. Two teachers of grade 4, 5, or 6 from each of nineteen elementary schools were selected by their school principal to participate as team members in a schoolwide effort to reduce violence and vandalism. These teachers participated on a school team with the school psychologist, counselor, and principal to plan and implement programs that would teach students alternative behavior to vandalism and disruption. The team members attended twenty hours of training workshops to learn about applied behavioral analysis techniques. They developed management programs for the lunchroom, playground, and classroom that stressed the use of specific positive reinforcement. Strategies involving aversive control were not used in the project. Graduate student consultants worked with each teacher a half day per week and conducted about two team meetings per month during the school year.

Schools were randomly assigned to treatment and control conditions. Most analyses were based on observations of a random sample of students from the two participating teachers' classes. These analyses were conducted at the classroom level (n = 38). School vandalism costs were also compared for the treatment and control schools. The study showed that changes in rates of student disruptive behavior decreased over the school year and attending behavior increased significantly (only one-tailed tests were reported) in the treatment as compared with the control schools. Changes in rates of nontask behaviors were not significantly different. Vandalism costs plummeted in the project schools as they increased dramatically in the control schools. Although the vandalism analysis suggests a schoolwide effect of the program, the reliance on student data only from the target teachers' classrooms does not permit conclusions about effects of the program on nontarget teacher students.

In a replication of this study, Mayer, Butterworth, Nafpaktitus, and Sulzer-Azaroff (1983; methods rating methods rating = 4) randomly assigned eighteen schools (ten elementary and eight junior high) to treatment and control conditions. As in the earlier study, teams of school personnel were trained to use behavioral strategies in planning and implementing programs for reducing student vandalism and disruption. Graduate student consultants worked with each teacher about twice per week and conducted about two team meetings per month during the school year.

Behavioral observations by graduate students were compared for two different treatment and comparison groups. One consisted of randomly selected students from classrooms of the teachers who participated directly in the project as a team member. The second consisted of randomly selected students from classrooms of randomly selected teachers in the same grades as the team members. All participating students were selected randomly from a larger group of students identified as low-achieving and disruptive students. The study showed that rates of student disruptive behavior from the beginning until the end of the school year declined significantly more for students in treatment schools than for students in the control schools. This was true both for the students of team members and the students in randomly selected classrooms. Also, vandalism costs declined in the second half of the school year in significantly more treatment than control schools.

Bullying Prevention Program. Olweus (Olweus, 1991, 1992; Olweus and Alsaker, 1991; methods rating = 3) developed and implemented an intervention to limit conflict in schools. Olweus noted that certain adolescents

– "bullies" – repeatedly victimized other adolescents. This harassment was usually ignored by adults who failed to intervene actively and thus provided tacit acceptance of the bullying. A program was devised to alter environmental norms regarding bullying and redefine the behavior as wrong: a booklet defining and listing ways to counteract bullying was directed to school personnel; parents were sent a booklet of advice; and a video illustrating the problem was made available. Surveys to collect information and register the level of the problem were fielded. Information was fed back to personnel in forty-two schools in Bergen, Norway. Among the recommended strategies to reduce bullying were establishing clear class rules against bullying, contingent responses (praise and sanctions), regular class meetings to clarify norms against bullying, improved supervision of the playground, and teacher involvement in the development of a positive school climate.

The program was evaluated using data from approximately 2,500 students (ages 11 to 14) belonging to 112 classes in 42 primary and secondary schools in Bergen. Data were collected in the spring of three successive years. The first data collection occurred prior to the beginning of the intervention. The design involved time-lagged contrasts between successive cohorts of students at the same grade level. For example, the grade 5 cohort at time 1 was compared with the time 2 data for the grade 4 cohort. All comparisons were for same-age youths who had experienced different dosages of the program (none, one year, or two years). Possible confounding differences on time-related unmeasured variables remain unexamined. The results indicated that bullying decreased by 50 percent. Program effects were also observed on self-reports of delinquent behavior, including truancy, vandalism, and theft. These effects on delinquency were smaller in magnitude.

The antibullying program was replicated in a study of seventeen primary and ten secondary schools in Sheffield, England (Smith and Sharp, 1994; methods rating = 2). Pre- to postintervention measures of being bullied and bullying others showed positive change for the primary schools, but many of the measures changed in the undesired direction for the secondary schools. Comparisons with nontreatment schools were not very helpful in this study, because there were too few such schools and some had been exposed to elements of the antibullying program through other sources.

School Development Process. The School Development Program (SDP; Comer, 1985; Comer, Haynes, and Hamilton-Lee, 1989; Haynes, 1994; Cook, Hunt, and Murphy, 1998) stands alone among evaluated elementary school programs as a comprehensive school organization development intervention seeking to broaden the involvement in school management of stakeholders in the school. The program creates a representative governance and management team composed of school administrators, teachers, support staff, and parents that assesses school problems and opportunities, identifies social and academic goals for the school, plans activities to address the goals, monitors activities, and takes corrective action to keep the activities on track. This team oversees other program components, which include: (1) a social calendar that integrates arts and athletic programs into school activities, (2) a parent program in support of academic activities and extracurricular activities that fosters interaction among parents, teachers, and school staff by paying parents to work in classrooms, encouraging them to volunteer in the school, and having them serve on the School Advisory Council; and (3) a multidisciplinary health team that works on global school climate issues, provides direct services to students, and provides consultation to individual teachers in managing student behavior problems. The program, designed to enhance urban elementary schools, had been implemented in more than 550 schools and 80 school districts as of 1995.

Preliminary evaluations of this program were not rigorous. Haynes, Emmons, Gebreyesus, and Ben-Avie (1996) summarize results of early evaluation activities on academic achievement. Aggregate achievement test score data from three different districts show that schools participating in the SDP have higher achievement gains than their district averages. One study (Comer, 1985; methods rating = 3) compared twenty-four seventh graders who had attended SDP elementary schools with twenty-four demographically matched seventh graders who had not attended an SDP elementary school. Significantly higher grade-point averages and achievement test scores were observed for the students from the SDP schools.

Another study (Comer et al., 1989; methods rating = 3) compared 176 elementary students who attended SDP schools with 130 who did not on measures of perceptions of the classroom and school climate, attendance, and classroom grades. Measures taken at the beginning of the school year were compared with the same measures taken at the end of the school year, separately for each group. Generally, children in the SDP schools showed larger changes in the positive direction than students in the control schools. These differences were observed for reading (but not math) grades and attendance. SDP students' perceptions of the classroom climate (e.g., perceptions of affiliation, involvement, teacher support, order, and organization) improved, whereas those of the comparison students did not. Other less rigorous studies have also been reported (see Table 5.2). Taken together, these studies are not of sufficient rigor to justify conclusions about the effectiveness of the model.

A more rigorous study was recently conducted by researchers at the Institute for Policy Research at Northwestern University. Cook, Hunt, and Murphy (1998, methods rating = 4) evaluated SDP in ten inner city Chicago schools over a four-year period. These schools were compared with nine randomly selected no-treatment comparison schools. Student ratings (but not teacher ratings) of the school's social climate improved significantly. Both teachers' and students' perceptions of the academic climate improved significantly. SDP school children gained about three percentile points on math and reading tests. Most importantly for the purpose of this book, students' rate of increase in reports of acting out (measured by an eleven-item scale of mischievous and delinquent behaviors) and substance use were significantly lower in the SDP than in the comparison schools.

Summary

These twelve elementary programs differ on several dimensions, including the age level of the students targeted, comprehensiveness, structure, reliance on social science theory and research, and intensity. The evaluation methods used run the gamut from school-level to individual-level comparisons, and the rigor of these methods varies considerably from study to study. These differences make comparisons across studies difficult. Studies of elementary school programs generally do not assess the "harder" problem behavior outcomes of crime or substance use. Those few that included these measures most often find no significant (p < .05) effect, or inconsistent effects across measures or subgroups. It stands to reason that these measures would not show program effects because these behaviors are quite rare among such young populations. Measures of conduct disorder show more variance and can be expected to be more sensitive to intervention for this age group. Using these measures, some programs appear effective for reducing problem behavior and some do not. Ineffective programs tend to be narrow in scope, diffuse, and lacking in a specific focus on reducing problem behavior. Classroom discussions, mastery learning, cooperative learning (by itself), and relatively diffuse in-service training for teachers on classroom process appear to have no effect on students' problem behavior. But even relatively narrow classroom management strategies that incorporate behavioral principles (specifically, monitoring or specific behaviors, reward and recognition of desired performance) appear effective for reducing special-education placements that often reflect behavior problems (e.g., the classwide peer tutoring program) and aggressive behavior (e.g., the Good Behavior Game). The Behavioral Consultation Project (aimed at reducing violence and vandalism using behavioral strategies) involved schoolwide strategies as well as classroom management strategies and was successful for reducing disruptive behavior.

Studies of broader classroom programs that combine instructional and classroom management strategies show mixed results, in part because the rigor with which they have been studied is relatively low. Both the CDP and

Seattle projects found evidence of positive effects on substance use initiation, but the effects were usually only marginally significant and were inconsistent across different substance use measures and gender groups. Also, although these strategies appear effective for increasing some social behaviors and skills and a number of protective factors, the preponderance of evidence weighs against these programs producing a reduction in general delinquent behavior. On the other hand, early evidence from the Seattle Social Development Program showed significant reductions in aggression (for males only) directly after the first two years of the program, during which a cognitive social problem-solving curriculum was taught as part of the program.

The SFA program, with its strong emphases on increasing reading achievement, shows a positive effect on attendance but not on behavioral ratings. But the evaluations to date have not measured problem behavior with much precision. More rigorous studies of these broader instructional and classroom management processes must be conducted to produce more definitive evidence of their effectiveness.

Programs that alter school management practices at the elementary level are rare. Only the SDP involves major alterations in the way the school is managed, and aims to create the type of "communal" social environment recommended in the nonexperimental studies summarized in Chapter 3. The only evaluation of its effect on problem behavior suggests that it is effective. The successful Behavioral Consultation project also contains elements of organizational change (e.g., the team approach to local program development). This program was successful, but it is not clear to what extent the team approach as opposed to the behavioral strategies employed accounted for its success.

The antibullying programs have broad scope compared with most other elementary-level programs. They include individual-level interventions, changes to classroom management practices, changes to schoolwide norms for behavior, and changes to school rules. Although the Olweus evaluation does not differentiate effects for elementary versus secondary schools, the Smith and Sharp replication indicated that effects were stronger at the elementary than at the secondary level. Except at the secondary level in the replication study, the results suggest the program can work to reduce problem behavior. But more rigorous evaluations employing comparable control groups are required.

Studies of Programs in Middle and Junior High Schools

Studies of two of the programs discussed so far – the Bullying Prevention and Behavioral Consultation to Reduce Violence and Vandalism programs – include students at the middle or junior high school level. Table 5.3 shows the content of eight additional programs conducted at the middle or junior

Table 5.3. *Middle and Junior High School Programs with Environmental Change Focus*

Program (Study)	Grades Targeted	Program Content[a]																Duration of Program
		1	2	3	4	5	6	7	8	9	10	11	12	13	14	15	16	
"Seattle Social Development Program" (Hawkins and Lam, 1983; Hawkins et al., 1988)	7	X						X										1 school year
"Effective Classroom Management" (Malvin et al., 1984)	7–9	✔						X										3 school years
"Behavioral Consultation" (Fuchs and Fuchs, 1989)	5–6			X				X				✔						8 weeks
"BASIS" (Gottfredson et al., 1993)	6–8	✔		✔				✔			X	✔						2 school years
"PATHE" (Gottfredson, 1986)	6–12	✔			✔		✔	✔	✔	✔	✔	X						2 school years
"Effective Schools Project" (D. Gottfredson, 1987)	7–9	✔		✔			✔	X	✔	✔	X	X						2 school years
"Law Related Education" (Johnson and Hunter, 1985)	1–12	X						X										1 semester
STATUS (Gottfredson, 1990)	7, 9	X	✔				✔	X		✔			X					1 school year

[a]Program content key: 1. Instructing students. 2. Cognitive-behavioral change/behavior modeling. 3. Behavioral or behavior modification. 4. Counseling, social work, other psychological or therapeutic interventions. 5. Tutoring, mentoring, or other individual attention. 6. Recreational, enrichment, and leisure. 7. Changing instructional or classroom management methods or practices management. 8. Changing norms or expectations for behavior. 9. Building a sense of community, morale, caring, support, or pride. 10. Changing rules, policies, regulations, or laws about behavior or discipline. 11. Changing school management structure or process. 12. Reorganizing grades or classes. 13. Preventing intruders from entering the school. 14. Excluding weapons or contraband. 15. Altering school composition. 16. Changing family supervision or family behavior. ✔ = contains some of this content; X = major focus of program.

high school levels whose evaluations have appeared in the literature. These eight programs, or minor variants of them, have been the subject of the nine studies listed in Table 5.4. Two of the eight programs (the Seattle Social Development Program, and Effective Classroom Management) discussed earlier were tested separately in middle school populations in the studies listed in Table 5.4. Results for these additional tests are summarized here, but the reader is referred back to the previous descriptions of the program strategies.

Programs

Seattle Social Development Project (SSDP). Hawkins and Lam (1983) and Hawkins, Doueck, and Lishner (1988) report on additional tests of the classroom management elements of the SSDP (proactive classroom management, cooperative learning, and interactive teaching, described earlier) implemented without the parent training element that was present in the elementary version of the program. Hawkins and Lam (1983; methods rating = 3) reported results for thirty-three teachers who had been assigned to receive or not receive training in the classroom management strategies. These teachers taught seventh graders in five different schools. All teachers in one school received training, all teachers in a second school did not, and all teachers in the other three were assigned for the most part randomly to experimental or control conditions. These teachers taught a total of 113 classes. Seventh grade students in the three schools containing both conditions were assigned more or less randomly to treatment and control teachers.

Hawkins and Lam (1983) reported primarily correlations between measures of program implementation and measures of outcomes taken at the end of one year of the program. Comparisons of teacher observations showed significant differences between treatment and comparison teachers' use of the experimental methods, but these differences were not evident in students' reports of perceptions of opportunities and rewards in the classroom. Also, no significant differences were observed between experimental and control subjects on attachment to school. Results for all other outcomes are reported in the form of correlations, which are not helpful for establishing program effects because comparison group teachers also used the experimental practices, although to a lesser extent than the treatment group teachers.

Hawkins et al. (1988; methods rating = 3) did report treatment–control group differences, but only for the 160 low math achievers in the seventh grade. No significant effects were observed on measures of academic achievement, delinquency, or drug use. But the treatment group had significantly higher liking for school (two of six indicators significantly favored the treatment group), commitment to education (one of two measures

Table 5.4. *Evaluations of Middle and Junior High School Programs with Environmental Change Focus*

Program (Study)	Subjects	Method Rating/ Follow-up (mos.)	Outcomes[a] Correlates of Problem Behavior	Problem Behavior
"Seattle Social Development Program" (Hawkins and Lam, 1983)	1,012 boys and girls in 113 classes in 5 schools	3/0	From regression analysis: Grades and standardized test scores (mostly 0) From T/C student comparison: Attachment to school (0) Like classes (mixed) Educational aspirations (+)	From regression analysis: School misbehavior (+) Truancy (0) *Self-reported drug use at school (−nr)* **Theft from lockers or desks (0)**
"Seattle Social Development Program" (Hawkins et al., 1988)	158 low-achieving boys and girls in 113 classes in 5 schools	3/0	Grades (0) Standardized test of academic skills (0) Bonding to school (+) Expectations for education (+) Aspirations for education (0)	Times suspended/expelled for school misbehavior (+) *Self-reported drug use (0)* **Self-reported serious crime (0)**
"Effective Classroom Management" (Malvin et al., 1984)	273 boys and girls in 2 schools	4/0	Grade-point average (0) *Drug attitudes (− boys; 0 girls)* School attitudes (− boys; 0 girls) Peer drug attitudes (− boys; 0 girls)	Unexcused absences (+ boys; 0 girls) *Alcohol involvement (− boys; 0 girls)* *Marijuana involvement (0)*
"Behavioral Consultation" (Fuchs and Fuchs, 1989)	48 difficult to teach students (mostly boys) in 9 schools	4/0		Teacher ratings of problem behavior (+ for higher dosage levels) Observations of problem behavior (0)

Table 5.4. (*cont.*)

Program (Study)	Subjects	Method Rating/ Follow-up (mos.)	Outcomes[a]	
			Correlates of Problem Behavior	Problem Behavior
"BASIS" (Gottfredson et al., 1993)[b]	5,281 boys and girls in 288 classes in 8 schools	4/0	Student attention to academic work (0) Classroom rule clarity (+) Rewards for behavior (+) Clarity/fairness of school rules (0) Teacher support (0)	Rebellious behavior (−) Disruptive classroom behavior (0) Avoidance of punishment (+) Classroom order (student reports: +) (teacher reports: 0)
"PATHE" (Gottfredson, 1986)	2,602 boys and girls in 9 schools	4/0	Self-reported grades (middle school: −) (high school: 0) Attachment to school (middle school: +) (high school: 0) Educational expectations (0) Student alienation (+) School climate (nr): clarity of rules (+); fairness of rules (middle school: +) (high school: −); safety (+); morale (+); smooth administration (+)	Suspensions (+) School punishments (middle school: 0) (high school: +) School nonattendance (middle school: 0) (high school: +) *Self-reported drug involvement (middle school:0) (high school: +)* **Serious delinquency (middle school: 0) (high school: +)**

136

"Effective Schools Project" (D. Gottfredson, 1987)	1,975 boys and girls in 122 classes in 2 schools	3.5/0	Positive peer associations (0) Attachment to school (0) Educational expectations (−) Academic rewards (+) Teacher morale (+) Planning and action (+) Smooth administration (+)	Rebellious behavior (0) Classroom orderliness (+) Suspensions (between school: + nr) (within school: +) **Delinquent behavior (between school: +) (within school: 0)**
"Law Related Education" (Johnson and Hunter, 1985)[b]	857 boys and girls in 35 classes in 8 schools	3.5/0	Delinquent peer influence (19 classes: 0) (2 classes: − nr) Exposure to delinquent peers (21 classes: 0) Completion of assignments/class preparation (9 classes: + nr) (8 classes: 0) (4 classes: N/A) Time spent on homework (5 classes: + nr) (12 classes: 0) (4 classes: N/A) Support offered by teachers (5 classes: + nr) (16 classes: 0) Attitudes toward personal violence (9 classes: + nr) (8 classes: 0) (4 classes: − nr)	School rule infractions (9 classes: + nr) (11 classes: 0) (1 class: − nr) *Drinking alcohol (9 classes: + nr) (12 classes: 0)* *Smoking marijuana (21 classes: 0)* *Hard drug use (17 classes: 0) (4 classes: N/A)* **Index offenses (2 classes: + nr) (18 classes: 0) (1 class: − nr)** **Violence with a weapon (21 classes: 0)** **Minor theft (1 class: + nr) (19 classes: 0) (1 class: − nr)**

Table 5.4. (*cont.*)

Program (Study)	Subjects	Method Rating/ Follow-up (mos.)	Outcomes[a]		
			Correlates of Problem Behavior	Problem Behavior	
			Attitudes toward the police (5 classes: + nr) (15 classes: 0) (1 class: − nr) Equity in the application of rules and grades (11 classes: + nr) (10 classes: 0)	Percent withdrew from school (0) Number of months enrolled (junior high: 0) (high school: +) Percent suspended or expelled (0) School punishments (+) Nonattendance (0) *Self-reported drug involvement* (+) **Self-reported serious delinquency (junior high: 0) (high school: +)** **Number of court contacts (0)**	
"STATUS" (Gottfredson, 1990)	247 high-risk boys and girls in 4 classes in 2 schools	4/0	Negative peer influence (+) Grades (+) Attachment to school (+) Educational expectations (0) Belief in rules (0)		

Notes: Follow-up period begins at end of intervention. The number of subjects is the maximum number present for any of the analyses reported in the table.

[a] 0 = no significant effect (p < .05); + = significant positive effect (p < .05); − = significant negative effect (p < .05); nr = two-tailed significance level not reported; N/A = not analyzed. Outcomes for substance use and for crime and delinquency measures appear in italics and in bold, respectively.

[b] Results vary for subsets of schools or classrooms that differed on level of program implementation.

significantly favored the treatment group), and fewer suspensions from school.

Effective Classroom Management. Malvin, Moskowitz, Schaeffer, and Schaps (1984; methods rating = 4) report on the ECM teacher training intervention described earlier but implemented with junior high school teachers. All teachers in one treatment school were offered ECM training in three consecutive school years. About half of the teachers in the school completed an ECM course over the three-year period. Only a small percentage of the teachers (13%) completed all three courses. Students (n = 273) in both schools who were present both for the seventh grade pretest and the ninth grade post-test and who were not participants in another evaluation were included in the analysis. When pretreatment differences were statistically controlled, males in the treatment school reported significantly *more* drug and alcohol involvement, attitudes more favorable to substance use, and more negative attitudes toward school. These boys also had significantly fewer unexcused absences from school. No effects were found for girls. The authors attributed the negative effects of the program to differential attrition and concluded the program had no effect on any of the targeted outcomes.

Behavioral Consultation. Fuchs and Fuchs (1989; methods rating = 4) reported on an effort to use behavioral consultation to help middle school teachers teach "difficult-to-teach" students. In this study, ten school-based consultants were assigned to work with four schools. These consultants were special-education resource room teachers, school psychologists, and pupil personnel specialists. Two graduate students also worked as part of the consultation team. The team members worked with individual teachers and their most difficult student to help them identify the problem, analyze the problem, develop and implement a plan to reduce the problem, and monitor the effectiveness of the plan. The consultation relied heavily on behavioral principles to identify antecedent conditions and consequences of the problem behavior, and to manipulate these conditions in order to reduce the intensity, duration, or frequency of the behavior.

Four schools were selected to participate in the program. Five control schools were matched on the basis of demographics, achievement, and referrals to school psychologists. Within each treatment school, eight fifth and sixth grade teachers were selected to participate (nonrandomly) and they were asked to identify their "most difficult-to-teach" nonhandicapped student – one who was at risk for special-education referral or grade retention. Within each control school, an equal number of teachers and students were recruited using a similar selection process. Teachers in the participating schools were randomly assigned to receive one of three different intensity levels of behavioral consultation. No significant differences were found across conditions on measures of demographics, behavior, or achievement prior to the beginning of the consultation period.

Both teacher ratings and observations of the problem behaviors (mostly off-task behavior) were collected. Teacher ratings of student behaviors improved significantly more from pre- to post-intervention for the teachers in the two most intensive levels of behavioral consultation (compared with the control teachers). However, observation data did not corroborate this finding.

BASIS. Gottfredson, Gottfredson, and Hybl (1993; methods rating = 4) tested a discipline management intervention in six urban middle schools. The BASIS program included the following components:

Increasing clarity of school rules and consistency of rule enforcement through revisions to the school rules and a computerized behavior tracking system.

Improving classroom organization and management through teacher training.

Increasing the frequency of communication with the home regarding student behavior through systems to identify good student behavior and a computerized system to generate letters to the home regarding both positive and negative behavior.

Replacing punitive disciplinary strategies with positive reinforcement of appropriate behavior through a variety of school- and classroom-level positive reinforcement strategies.

School teams of administrators, teachers, and other school personnel were responsible for implementing the program. The researchers provided quarterly feedback to the teams on the quality of program implementation and on changes in the behaviors targeted by the program.

Six schools were selected by the school district to participate. The researchers selected two additional middle schools for comparison. No training was provided for the comparison schools, but feedback was provided to their administrators on the targeted outcomes at the same time the treatment schools received feedback, and the administrators of the two comparison schools attended quarterly feedback and planning sessions with the treatment schools. Each quarter (beginning with the year prior to the beginning of the program), teachers and students in all eight schools completed a brief survey measuring the outcomes most directly targeted: classroom orderliness, classroom organization, classroom rule clarity, and teacher supportiveness. These data were aggregated to the classroom level for analysis (n = 288). In addition, all teachers rated the behavior of each student quarterly, and records of all disciplinary referrals were maintained.

Finally, students completed an annual assessment to provide additional measures of outcomes targeted by the program, including rebellious behavior, school rewards and punishments, school rule clarity and fairness, and respectful treatment of students. Different levels of analysis (students and classrooms) were used for different measures. For all measures, changes in school means were examined from baseline until the end of the second year of program implementation.

When the combined school mean change for all six treatment schools was compared with the school mean change for the two comparison schools, significant changes in the expected direction were observed from the beginning to the end of the program on the measures most directly targeted: classroom orderliness, classroom organization, classroom rule clarity, and student reports of rewards and (fewer) punishments. However, student reports of rebellious behavior, a scale measuring minor delinquent acts, *increased* significantly over the three-year time frame for students in both treatment and comparison schools, and slightly more so in treatment schools than in the comparison schools. This increase was probably due to the countywide aging of the middle school student population which resulted when the implementation of higher grade-to-grade promotion standards resulted in a huge increase in grade retentions. No overall effects were observed on teacher ratings of attention to academic work and disruptive behavior.

Data show that the components of the program were implemented with high fidelity to the original design in only three of the six program schools. In these three schools, the positive changes reported were more marked. Also, teacher support increased, student perceptions of the fairness of school rules increased, teacher reports of student attention to academic work increased significantly, and their ratings of student classroom disruption decreased significantly. The increase in rebellious behavior was smallest in these three schools.

Positive Action through Holistic Education (PATHE). Project PATHE was one of eighteen school-based prevention program models tested as part of the Alternative Education Initiative of the Office of Juvenile Justice and Delinquency Prevention (OJJDP) in the early 1980s. It was implemented in the context of an organizational development method called Program Development Evaluation (PDE; Gottfredson, 1984; Gottfredson, Rickert, Gottfredson, and Advani, 1984) that had been developed for use with schools participating in the OJJDP alternative education initiative. This method was developed to help organizations plan, initiate, and sustain needed changes. Researchers and practitioners collaborate, using specific steps spelled out in the program materials, to develop and implement programs. Researchers continuously provide data feedback during the implementation phase to the practitioners.

PDE was used to develop and implement project PATHE, a comprehensive school improvement intervention that altered the organization
and management structures in seven secondary schools between 1981 and
1983 (Gottfredson, 1986, methods rating = 4). District-level administrators
used PDE to develop a general plan for all seven schools and then to structure specific school-level planning interventions. These efforts increased
staff and student participation in planning for and implementing school
improvement efforts. Changes resulting from the planning activity
included efforts to increase clarity of rules and consistency of rule enforcement and activities to increase students' success experiences and feelings
of belonging. These activities targeted the entire population in each
school. An individually targeted intervention for high-risk youths was also
developed and implemented as part of the project. This portion of the
intervention is discussed in the next chapter.

The evaluation of the project focused on change for an array of measures, comparing data from the year prior to the treatment into those one
year (for four high schools)[2] and two years (for five middle schools)
into the intervention. One school at each level was a comparison school
selected from among the nonparticipating schools to match the treatment
schools as closely as possible. The students in the participating high
schools reported significantly less delinquent behavior and drug use, had
fewer suspensions, and had fewer school punishments after the first year
of the program. Students in the comparison high school did not change
significantly on these outcomes. A similar pattern was observed for the
middle schools after two years. As serious delinquency increased significantly in the comparison school, it decreased (nonsignificantly) in the
program middle schools. Suspensions also declined significantly in the
program middle schools, but a similar decline was observed in the comparison school. Several indicators of the school climate directly targeted
by the program (e.g., safety, staff morale, clarity of school rules, and
effectiveness of the school administration) also increased in the program
schools.

Effective Schools Project. D. Gottfredson (1987; methods rating = 3.5)
reported the results of a similar effort – the Effective Schools Project – in
a difficult Baltimore City junior high school. PDE was used with a team of
school- and district-level educators to plan and implement changes to
instructional and discipline practices. Schoolwide and classroom-level
changes were made to the disciplinary procedures to increase the clarity
and consistency of rule enforcement, and to substitute positive reinforcement strategies for strategies that relied solely on punishment. Instruc-

---

[2] A district consolidation of high schools prevented continued evaluation at the high school
level.

tional innovations including cooperative learning and frequent monitoring of classwork and homework were put in place, an expanded extracurricular activities program was added, and a career exploration program that exposed youth to positive role models in the community, took them on career-related field trips, and provided instruction on career-related topics was undertaken.

The evaluation of the project involved a comparison of pretreatment measures to post-treatment measures taken two years later for the one treatment school and a second school that was intended to receive the program but instead chose to develop a school improvement plan with minimal assistance from the researchers. Also, because many of the program interventions were targeted at one grade level at the school, the researchers were able to compare this "experimental" cohort with a cohort of same-aged students from the year before. This comparison cohort had not been targeted for the program. Indicators of organizational health (e.g., staff morale, cooperation and collaboration between faculty and administration, and staff involvement in planning and action for school improvement) improved dramatically in the treatment school. Only the Planning and Action scale improved in the comparison school. Significant reductions from pre- to post-treatment on delinquency and increases in classroom orderliness were observed for the treatment school. A reduction in student reports of rebellious behavior in the treatment school was observed (not significant), whereas a significant increase was observed in the comparison school. The reductions in delinquency and rebellious behavior were not corroborated in within-school comparisons, however. Although students in the experimental unit reported significantly more social integration, more academic rewards, and fewer school suspensions, their self-reports of delinquency and rebellious behavior were not significantly different than students in the nonexperimental units.

Law-Related Education (LRE). Law-related education curricula are designed to familiarize youths with the country's laws, develop appreciation of the legal process, encourage responsible political participation, develop moral and ethical values, and develop analytical skills. Lack of knowledge about the law, citizenship skills, and positive attitudes about the law and the role of the government are cited in LRE materials as causes of juvenile crime.

In 1979, the justice department's National Institute for Juvenile Justice and Delinquency Prevention (NIJJDP, the OJJDP's research arm) funded five organizations to develop and demonstrate LRE methods. An evaluation of these efforts, also funded by NIJJDP, examined the effects of the program on delinquency and factors related to delinquency. Most of the results of this evaluation are summarized in Johnson and Hunter (1985; overall methods rating = 3.5). The evaluation included sixty-one LRE elementary, junior, and senior high classrooms and forty-four comparison classrooms in thirty-two schools in six states. The rigor of the methodology varied from year to year and across location. Results for 1981, the first year of the evaluation, were regarded as formative. It compared ten LRE classrooms with eight comparison classrooms and showed that LRE did not always produce positive effects, and that the quality of implementation was correlated with the amount of positive change from pre- to post-test on many measures. The second-year evaluation (for 1982) compared thirty LRE classrooms with twenty-two comparison classrooms. Results were more positive, but the effects were, according to the authors, "severely diminished" except in one site in Colorado in which generally positive outcomes were observed. The strongest program implementation occurred in 1983. Johnson and Hunter (1985) summarize the results comparing outcomes, separately by teacher, for students in twenty-one LRE classes and fourteen comparison classes (most of which were nonrandomly assigned). Out of 132 effects reported for the eleven delinquency items, 15 showed a significant effect (13 would have been expected by chance using the one-tailed test of significance reported); 9 of these differences favored the LRE students, and 6 favored the comparison students. Significant program effects on attitudes toward deviance and violence favored the comparison students. Positive effects were found for school rule infractions, knowledge about the law and legal practices, and other outcomes that might be expected from improved classroom management techniques (e.g., completion of assignments, reduced "clock watching," and consistency of classroom rule enforcement).

Johnson (1984; method rating = 4) focused on the nine LRE classes in the site for which randomization to treatment and control conditions was obtained. He showed that the nine LRE classes fared significantly better than the two control classes on more than half of the forty-one possible measures. Three of the eleven items measuring delinquency were reported as significantly favoring the LRE group. The effect sizes for all eleven items ranged from 0 (for violence against other students) to .66 (for school rule infractions, such as cheating on tests and skipping school). The average effects size for the eleven delinquency items was .22.

In summary, these evaluations on LRE showed positive program effects on school rule infractions, law-related factual knowledge, and classroom behaviors. Effects on other outcomes were minimal. In one particularly strong site, consistent positive effects were observed on certain risk factors for delinquency (e.g., attachment to school and attitudes toward violence and deviance) but not others (e.g., association with delinquent peers), and small positive effects were found on certain measures of delinquency but not others.

The part of the evaluation focusing on the entire national sample was the weakest methodologically (methods rating = 3) and showed no reason for optimism about LRE's effect on delinquency. The "substudy" of Colorado sites was stronger methodologically, and more positive outcomes were observed; however, the extent to which results for these "well-implemented" schools can be generalized to other schools implementing LRE programs is unclear. Because the LRE intervention at this site included a large dose of general instructional and classroom management training for teachers in addition to law-related activities it is not possible to rule out the possibility that any positive effects of the program are due to these general techniques rather than to the law-related content of the curriculum. Because LRE programs are not necessarily augmented with these additional strategies, the positive evaluations may not be relevant to understanding the effects of typical LRE programs.

Student Training through Urban Strategies (STATUS). D. Gottfredson (1990; methods rating = 4) studied another program, STATUS, which was included in OJJDP's alternative education initiative. This program combined several different strategies. High-risk youths in grades 7 and 9 (in two different schools) were grouped together to receive an integrated social studies and English program that involved a law-related education curriculum and used instructional methods emphasizing active student participation. Students stayed together for two hours each day for one school year. The curriculum included five units covering the functions of different institutions in American society: the school (the function of rules, decision-making processes, student rights and responsibilities), human nature and interpersonal relations (informal codes of conduct and formal rules of behavior), family (personal, social, and legal perspectives), social contracts and their basis in the need for order in society, and the criminal justice system (how informal contracts are expressed as laws in our society). The high school curriculum substituted units on job markets and life planning for the human nature and family units. The classroom methods were intended to encourage active student participation. Field trips, guest speakers, and student role playing and simulations were used frequently. Cooperative learning strategies (including rewards for individual and group progress) and cooperative research projects were used.

Random assignment of approximately 120 students in each of the two participating schools who had self-referred or been referred by school staff was attempted, but scheduling difficulties required some shifting of students after randomization. Nonequivalent groups resulted. Analyses statistically controlled for the known differences. Results implied that STATUS reduced delinquency and drug use (ESs range from −.07 to −.42) and changed in the desired direction several factors related to delinquency, including attachment to school, academic achievement, and negative peer influence. Treatment students in the high school also persisted in school longer than the control students.

Summary

Several studies of students in the middle grades show evidence of positive effects on problem behaviors, but the conclusions most often must be tempered because the results are not consistent across all measures, or because positive results are obtained only for a subset of settings in which the program was best implemented.

The most consistently positive results are for the STATUS program, which grouped high-risk youths together for two periods per day and interwove a law-related education curriculum with activities intended to keep students interested and actively engaged. The positive results for this program are corroborated to a certain degree by results from a national evaluation of LRE that showed some reduction in delinquency but only when the LRE curriculum was combined with innovative classroom management and instructional strategies. It would appear that neither improvements to classroom management and instructional technologies nor curriculum content targeting problem behavior work *by themselves* to reduce delinquency or substance use. Both are needed.

Another consistent trend emerges: programs that focus on clarifying expectations for behavior, monitoring and providing consequences for behavior, and especially providing positive reinforcement for desired behavior appear moderately effective. Behavioral Consultation for teachers in the use of these techniques in their classrooms work to reduce problem behavior for difficult-to-teach children and for children in general (Fuchs and Fuchs, 1989). Studies of the effects of training for school staff in behavioral principles and techniques, and the establishment of schoolwide systems to clarify expectations, monitor behavior, and reward compliance (Gottfredson et al., 1993; D. Gottfredson, 1986, 1987) all showed some evidence of effectiveness for reducing problem behavior, although the evidence was not as consistent across different education levels and different subgroup comparisons as would be desired. But these secondary school interventions rely on many of the same strategies as the bullying prevention, behavioral consultation, and Good Behavior Game studies reviewed in the elementary section that provided evidence of effectiveness. Additional research using stronger designs is needed to further develop and test this type of intervention and to compare its effectiveness in multiple contexts and for different age groups.

The focus on schoolwide discipline policies and practices is often confounded with other innovations, most notably the use of school teams and a structured organization development method to focus the school's attention on identifying its problems, developing strategies to overcome these problems, and using data feedback to guide the implementation of these plans over a multiyear period. These enhancements improve the school's general management functions as well as indicators of organizational health, such as teacher morale and teacher involvement in planning and action to improve the school. Studies of attempts to use structured organization development models to build the infrastructure necessary for schools to initiate and maintain innovations have proved moderately successful at reducing problem behavior (D. Gottfredson, 1986, 1987). These indicators of organizational health overlap considerably with the indicators of "communal social organization."

Studies of Programs in Senior High Schools

The studies of PATHE, LRE, bullying prevention, and STATUS were all tested in high schools as well as in the junior high or middle schools in the studies summarized in the preceding section. Table 5.5 shows the content of five additional programs conducted at the senior high school levels whose evaluations have appeared in the literature. These five programs have been the subject of the six studies listed in Table 5.6.

Programs

School Transitional Environment Project (STEP). Felner, Ginter, and Primavera (1982) and Felner and Adan (1988; both methods rating = 4) studied the School Transitional Environment Project, a one-year program for students making the transition to a large high school. Incoming students were assigned to small "schools within the school" consisting of 65 to 100 students. Students remained in intact small groups for their homeroom and academic subject periods. These classrooms were physically close. The role of the homeroom teacher was redefined so as to include more responsibility for meeting the administrative, counseling, and guidance needs of the students.

Sixty students were randomly selected for participation from a pool of approximately 450 entering freshman who were showing satisfactory school adjustment and were not in need of special mental health programming. A comparison group of 120 subjects who met the same eligibility criteria and were matched on demographic variables to those selected for treatment was identified. Midyear and end-of-year assessments measured students' self-concepts, perceptions of the school environment, attendance, and grade point averages.

STEP improved students' perceptions of the school environment. Using many of the same measures of classroom environment as were used in the PATHE and Social Development Program studies discussed earlier, the STEP study showed that participating students perceived their environments as having greater clarity of expectations, more orderliness and organization, and higher levels of teacher support and involvement. Relative to

Table 5.5. *Senior High School Programs with Environmental Change Focus*

Program (Study)	Grades Targeted	Program Content[a]																Duration of Program
		1	2	3	4	5	6	7	8	9	10	11	12	13	14	15	16	
"School Transition Environment Project" (Felner et al., 1982; Felner and Adan, 1988)	9				✔			✔				✔	✕					1 school year
"School Transition Environment Project" (Reyes and Jason, 1991)	9					✔		✔			✔		✕				✔	1 school year
"School Safety Program" (Kenney and Watson, 1996)	11	✕						✔			✕	✕						1 school year
"Peer Mediation Program" (Tolson et al., 1992)	9–12							✔			✕							1 school year
"Dropout Prevention Program" (Trice et al., 1982)	10			✕	✔	✕		✔			✔		✕					1 school year

[a]Program content key: 1. Instructing students. 2. Cognitive-behavioral change/behavior modeling. 3. Behavioral or behavior modification. 4. Counseling, social work, other psychological or therapeutic interventions. 5. Tutoring, mentoring, or other individual attention. 6. Recreational, enrichment, and leisure. 7. Changing instructional or classroom management methods or practices management. 8. Changing norms or expectations for behavior. 9. Building a sense of community, morale, caring, support, or pride. 10. Changing rules, policies, regulations, or laws about behavior or discipline. 11. Changing school management structure or process. 12. Reorganizing grades or classes. 13. Preventing intruders from entering the school. 14. Excluding weapons or contraband. 15. Altering school composition. 16. Changing family supervision or family behavior. ✔ = contains some of this content; ✕ = major focus of program.

control students, the STEP students had higher grades and better attendance records.

Felner and Adan (1988) reported on progress of the subjects through the high school years. The STEP students had higher grades and better attendance than students in the comparison schools through tenth grade, although the gap closed in later grades. However, the dropout rate for the STEP students was only half that of the comparison students (43% vs. 21%). The program's success at keeping students at risk for dropout in school probably explains the closing of the gap in attendance and grades for those who remained in school.

Reyes and Jason (1991; methods rating = 4) reported results for a similar program, which also contained an attendance-monitoring component. The program differed slightly from that reported by Felner: students took only three primary academic classes (rather than four) in their "school-within-a-school" setting, and the classrooms were not located in physical proximity to one another.

Participants (n = 77) were randomly selected from a group of 130 eligible students during the summer prior to the beginning of the program. Comparison subjects were the 53 students left in the pool of eligible subjects, plus 24 eligible additional subjects who did not enroll until just prior to the start of school. The two groups were for the most part equivalent prior to treatment. The one known nonequivalence was statistically controlled. Midyear and end-of-year assessments showed no differences between the groups on grade-point average or classes failed, absence, class cutting, or five of six achievement test scores. One achievement test score favored the treatment subjects. Neither were the groups different in terms of dropout rates or rates of referral to guidance counselors.

School Safety Program. Kenney and Watson (1996; methods rating = 3) report on an intervention to empower students to improve safety in schools. This study involved eleventh grade students (Ns range from 372 to 451) in the application of a problem-solving technique to reduce problems of crime, disorder, and fear on the school campus. As part of their government and history class, students implemented a four-step problem-solving method commonly used in problem-oriented policing interventions to identify problems, analyze possible solutions, formulate and implement a strategy, and evaluate the outcomes of the intervention. The investigators anticipated that empowering students to serve as change agents in the school would produce safer schools. Among the problems selected by the students to work on were streamlining lunchroom procedures and monitoring the restrooms.

Base-line surveys used by the planning groups to identify school problems were used also as base-line measures for the evaluation of the project. Change over two semesters was examined for the treatment school and one

Table 5.6. *Evaluations of Senior High School Programs with Environmental Change Focus*

Program (Study)	Subjects	Method Rating/ Follow-up (mos.)	Outcomes[a]		
			Correlates of Problem Behavior	Problem Behavior	
"School Transition Environment Project" (Felner et al., 1982; Felner and Adan, 1988)	172 primarily low-income, minority boys and girls in 1 school	4/36	Immediate follow-up: GPA (+) Perceptions of school's social climate, including rule clarity (+); orderliness and organization (+); teacher support (+) Three-year follow-up: Grades (0)	Immediate follow-up: Absenteeism (+) Three-year follow-up: Absenteeism (0) Dropout (+)	
"School Transition Environment Project" (Reyes and Jason, 1991)	154 primarily Hispanic, low-income boys and girls in 1 school	4/0	GPA (0) Course failures (0) Class rank (0) Standardized writing and math achievement test scores (0) Standardized reading achievement test scores (+)	Absences (0) Class cuts (0) Dropout (0)	
"School Safety Program" (Kenney and Watson, 1996)	451 boys and girls in 2 schools	3/0	Student fear in school (+) Teacher fear in school (3 measures: +) (3 measures: 0)	**Teacher victimization (student reports: +) (teacher reports: 0)** **Student fighting (+)**	

Program	Subjects	N		Outcomes
"Peer Mediation Program" (Tolson et al., 1992)	52 boys and girls involved in interpersonal conflict in 1 school	3/2.5		Number of referrals for interpersonal problems (+) Number of disciplinary referrals (0)
"Dropout Prevention Program" (Trice et al., 1982)	66 disruptive students (mostly male) in 1 school	3/24	GPA (R > M > S) Achievement test scores (R > S)	Attendance (R > M > S) Suspension (S > M > R) Percent completing the year (0) Percent reenrolling the following year (R > S > M) Percent enrolled 2 years hence (R > S > M)

Notes: Follow-up period begins at end of intervention. The number of subjects is the maximum number present for any of the analyses reported in the table.

R = resource room; S = self-contained; M = mainstreamed.

^{a}0 = no significant effect (p < .05); + = significant positive effect (p < .05); − = significant negative effect (p < .05); nr = two-tailed significance level not reported.

Outcomes for substance use and for crime and delinquency measures appear in italics and in bold, respectively.

comparison school. The study found that students in the treatment school reported significantly less fighting and less teacher victimization and were less fearful about being in certain places in the school at the end of the two-year period compared with their base-line responses. Students in the comparison school did not change on these outcomes. A few of the items measuring teacher fear and victimization experiences were significantly lower at the end of the program, but positive effects were more evident in student than in teacher reports.

Peer Mediation Program. Peer mediation programs rose in popularity in the 1980s. These programs use students to assist in dispute resolution when conflicts arise among students. Trained peer mediators assist in developing alternative solutions to fighting and provide an alternative to traditional interventions by a school administrator (e.g., warnings, suspensions, or demerits). Lam (1989, cited in Brewer, Hawkins, Catalano, and Neckerman, 1995) reviewed fourteen evaluations of peer mediation programs. The methodological rigor of all but three of the programs was too weak to justify any conclusions about the effect of the programs. According to Brewer, none of the three studies in the Lam review employing quasi-experimental designs showed significant effects on observable student behavior (e.g., fighting, disciplinary referrals). One additional study of peer mediation published after Lam's review (Tolson, McDonald, and Moriarty, 1992; methods rating = 3) suggested that students assigned to receive peer mediation had the same number of referrals for disciplinary problems in the 2.5 months following the program as students assigned to receive traditional responses to misbehavior, but the peer mediation group had fewer referrals for interpersonal conflicts during this period.

A recent review of conflict resolution and peer mediation programs (Johnson and Johnson, 1996) thoroughly discusses the conceptual bases for, development of, and studies assessing effects of these programs on a wide array of student and school outcomes. They show that the studies generally are low in internal validity. Many of the studies are short-term case studies with no control conditions and use suspect outcome measures. The review concludes that whether these programs are needed or effective remains unknown.

Dropout Prevention Program. Trice, Parker, and Safer (1982; methods rating = 3) reported on a school reorganization effort in the senior high school that grouped disruptive tenth grade students together into a self-contained classroom to receive special services. The study compared outcomes for three successive cohorts of disruptive tenth grade students attending one school. During one school year, disruptive students were grouped together for their major subject instruction (four periods). Behavior modification techniques were used to reward students for being prepared for class, remaining on task, and completing work. Daily progress reports were sent home to parents, and sometimes these reports were used to support a home-based reinforcement program. Students received vocational training in the afternoons, for which they were paid during the second semester.

Outcomes for students in this self-contained program were contrasted with outcomes for similar students receiving no services (e.g., disruptive students who were mainstreamed with no special services) and for students in a resource program. During the year in which the resource room was used, disruptive students were mainstreamed, but they could be referred by their teachers to a resource room in which they would receive tutoring, counseling, and in-school detention. Much of the time in the resource room was spent on intensive, remedial instruction. Resource teachers also monitored student behavior and academic performance. During the year in which the resource room was in place, disruptive students were also given the opportunity for paid work each afternoon, but this opportunity was contingent upon favorable reports from all four major subject teachers each day.

The study compared identified disruptive students each year (N = 26, 18, and 22 for the three years) on attendance, grade-point-average, persistence in school, suspension rates, and achievement test scores. The groups differed significantly on each measure. The resource room participants outshone the self-contained and control conditions on all measures.

Summary

Prevention studies conducted at the senior high school level are relatively uncommon. Of the few programs summarized in earlier sections – LRE, antibullying campaigns, STATUS, and PATHE – that were also tested at the high school level, STATUS and PATHE showed some evidence of effectiveness for reducing problem behavior when implemented in the high schools. The STEP program, which reorganized students into smaller groups for most of their instruction and enhanced the role of the homeroom teacher, was effective for reducing truancy and dropout in one study, but the effects were not replicated in the Reyes and Jason (1991) study. The earlier intervention reported by Felner seemed to work by altering students' perceptions of their environment. They reported more orderliness, greater clarity of expectations, and a more social support. Unfortunately, we do not know whether the Reyes and Jason intervention succeeded in altering these same perceptions. The physical proximity of classes that was part of the first and not the second trial may have been an essential element. The success of the Felner study is encouraging, especially in light of the success of STATUS, which also created somewhat of a "school-within-a-school" atmosphere for students. Programs that reorganize students into smaller, more communal groups are promising but should be tested in additional studies.

The positive findings for the School Safety Program (Kenney and Watson, 1996) are also encouraging. The reductions in fighting, fear, and victimization experiences found in this study are consistent with the findings from PATHE and the Effective Schools Project, both of which also employed structured school planning interventions. These studies, taken together, suggest that interventions aimed at building school capacity for initiating and sustaining change reduce problem behavior.

Alternative Schools

None of the studies discussed so far test deliberate attempts to alter the composition of the students in a school. Examples of such strategies include the use of selective entry and exit criteria, and the use of alternative schools in separate physical settings. Alternative schools for disruptive youths are often proposed as a solution to the problem of disorder in schools.

Few rigorous studies of the effects of alternative schools have appeared in the literature. Probably the best known is a study by Gold and Mann (1984) of three alternative schools. Gold and Mann hypothesized that to the extent alternative schools could increase students' successful versus unsuccessful experiences and provide for warm, accepting relationships with one or more adults, they would reduce delinquent behavior. They compared approximately eighty-three mostly high-school-age youths attending each of three alternative schools with approximately ninety-seven eligible youths who did not attend. Several subject characteristics were measured at each of three time points: about halfway through the first school year, at the end of the first school year, and six months later. While the alternative students' in-school disruptive behavior declined relative to the controls', no such trend was observed for delinquent behavior in general. Analyses were also conducted comparing subsets of students displaying negative affect (anxiety, depression) at time 1 with students who did not. Of twelve comparisons of delinquent and disruptive behavior for three different schools and two different groups, only one comparison showed a statistically significant difference favoring the alternative schools' students. The small number of cases in these subanalyses resulted in extremely underpowered tests, however.

Subsequent studies of alternative schools have also lacked power and are for other reasons lacking in credibility. Five alternative schools were funded as part of OJJDP's alternative education initiative. All were small schools for students who had not flourished in the regular school setting. After reviewing the content of these programs, G. Gottfredson (1987a) concluded that they are far too variable in nature, student composition, structure, and purpose to warrant any blanket statement about their effectiveness. He reviews two of the five models – one based on a theory that intense personal involvement of the educators with the youths would reduce delinquency through increased bonding, and the other based on the theory that rigorous discipline and behavior modification techniques would result in decreased delinquency. The evaluation of the first program found remarkable improvements in several risk factors for delinquency, including commitment to school, attachment to school, and belief in rules. It also found significantly less self-reported drug use (but not self-reported delinquency or arrest records) among alternative school students than among controls. The evaluation of the second alternative school implied that the program was effective for increasing several measures of academic persistence, but that students liked school less and reported significantly more delinquent behavior than the comparison students. The varied models employed in alternative schools suggest that the question, Are alternative schools effective? is too simplistic. The components of the interventions involved in alternative schools must be disentangled in future evaluations.

Size and Durability of Effects

Because effect sizes were not calculated for all studies, it is not possible to compare the size of the effects across studies. Table 5.7, however, shows a sampling of effect sizes for some of the studies that demonstrated positive effects on measures of problem behavior. The sizes of the effects vary considerably by study and outcome measures. Rarely do they reach the average magnitude for effects of interventions in the social and behavioral sciences and education reported by Lipsey and Wilson (1993; .50), but most of the effects on the table are larger than the average effect for studies of delinquency treatment and prevention reported by Lipsey (1992; .17). The effects reported in this chapter are certainly in the "important" range.

Only six studies summarized in this chapter followed students more than three months beyond the end of the intervention period to assess the duration of effects. Of these, only three (the studies of ClassWide Peer Tutoring, STEP, and the Good Behavior Game) had strong enough initial designs (e.g., methods ratings greater than 3) to support confident conclusions about their effects. Two of these programs involved the application of behavioral principles in classroom management. Two years after the end of a long (four-year) intervention, students who had received peer tutoring were less likely to have been placed in special-education classes. Four years after the end of a two-year intervention, students who had participated in classrooms using the Good Behavior Game were no less aggressive than students who had not received this treatment. Three years after being placed in a smaller, less alienating ninth grade unit, students'

Table 5.7. *Selected Effect Sizes from Environmental Change Studies*

Outcome Measure (Study)	Effect Size
Special-education assignment	−.58
(Greenwood, Terry, Utley, Montagna, and Walker, 1993)	
Teacher-rated aggressive behavior	−.34[a]
Teacher-rated externalizing behavior	−.29[a]
(Hawkins, Von Cleve, and Catalano, 1991)	
Alcohol use	−.15
(Battistich, Schaps, Watson, and Solomon, 1996)	
Suspensions	−.23
(Hawkins, Doueck, and Lishner, 1988)	
Delinquent behavior	−.15, −.31[b]
Drug use	−.15, −.33[b]
School punishments	−.21, −.16[b]
(Gottfredson, 1986)	
Delinquent behavior	−.31
Classroom orderliness (classes)	.57
(Gottfredson, 1987)	
Delinquency (average ES for 11 items)	−.22
(Johnson, 1984)	
Serious delinquency	−.42, −.33[b]
Drug involvement	−.35, −.42[b]
School punishments	−.48, −.82[b]
(Gottfredson, 1990)	
Dropout	−.53
(Felner and Adan, 1988)	

Note: Study citation follows cluster of outcomes for each study.
[a]Males.
[b]High schools and middle schools.

dropout rates were lower than those of students in the regular ninth grade. This is very weak evidence on which to base any conclusions at all about the durability of the effects of environmental interventions. More rigorous longitudinal follow-up studies of initially promising interventions are required.

Conclusions

Program Strategies

The studies discussed here provide evidence that changing the school and classroom environment can work to reduce problem behavior leading up to and during the adolescent years. However, a few quandaries for future research were uncovered. Although the studies are not ideal for examining the mechanisms through which a school-based intervention affects problem behavior, several of the studies summarized in this chapter suggested that the link between certain school-based risk factors and problem behavior is not straightforward. Consistent effects on attachment and commitment to school and on achievement do not often translate into reductions in problem behavior. This is evident in the Mastery Learning evaluation, in which effects on academic achievement do not "cross over" to the social behavior domain, and in the SSDP studies, which show consistent effects on attachment and commitment to school, but only inconsistent effects on problem behavior outcomes. Also, the most intensive instructional program, SFA, shows mixed results. Its effects on behavioral outcomes have not been the focus of much investigation, but the available evidence suggests that achievement score gains do not translate into behavioral improvements. Future research should attempt to further understand these apparent disconnects between cognitive and affective risk factors and problem behavior.

Also, the introduction to this chapter stated that more comprehensive approaches to prevention are more likely to be effective than programs targeting single domains. Although the evidence shows that several of the more comprehensive programs are effective for reducing problem behavior, counterevidence also exists. The evidence suggests that programs with a narrow focus are effective when they use behavioral and cognitive-behavioral approaches, and that broader programs are unsuccessful when they lack this focus. But more research is needed to understand better the relative contributions of scope and content to program effectiveness.

Several generalizations about effective and ineffective programs can be drawn from the studies. These generalizations must remain tentative until more rigorous studies confirm them:

1. Ineffective programs tend to be narrow in scope, diffuse, and lacking in a specific focus on reducing problem behavior.

Classroom discussions, and primarily instructional innovations such as Mastery Learning and Cooperative Learning (by themselves), and relatively diffuse in-service training for teachers on classroom process appear to have no effect on students' problem behaviors. Evidence for this generalization was found in studies targeting both elementary and middle schools.

2. Classroom management strategies that incorporate behavioral principles (specifically, clarifying expectations for behavior, monitoring of specific behaviors, reward and recognition of desired performance) appear effective for reducing problem behavior.

Evidence was found at both the elementary and middle school levels that teaching teachers to use behavioral approaches reduces student problem behavior. These strategies work under different delivery conditions, including behavioral consultation and more general staff development models. Among the relatively narrow-in-scope programs, only those containing this strategy work.

3. Broader, schoolwide approaches appear effective for reducing problem behavior when they contain an emphasis on behavior management, social-cognitive development, or normsetting.

For example, Olweus's antibullying program includes individual-level interventions, changes to classroom management practices, changes to school-wide norms for behavior, and changes to school rules. PATHE and the Effective Schools Project employed many of the same approaches, including schoolwide efforts to train school staff in behavioral principles and techniques, and the establishment of schoolwide systems to clarify expectations, monitor behavior, and reward compliance. STATUS reorganized the classroom environment and changed instructional and classroom management practices as well as the curriculum. The Seattle Social Development model, particularly as it was implemented in the early grades, included social competency skill instruction, family management training, and changes to classroom instruction and management. Evidence suggests these broad approaches work at all school levels.

4. Programs that group students into smaller units for instruction appear to work, especially when they include drastic changes to instructional and classroom management strategies.

Evidence comes from the STEP studies of reorganizations of high school freshman classes (although one replication did not support that efficacy of the program) and the STATUS program in both junior and senior high schools.

5. The use of school teams and a structured organization development method to focus the school's attention on identifying its problems, developing strategies to overcome these problems, and using data feedback to guide the implementation of these plans over a multiyear period reduces delinquency. These enhancements improve the school's general management functions as well as indicators of organizational health such as teacher morale and teacher involvement in planning and action to improve the school.

Evidence comes from studies at the elementary level (SDP), at the middle school level (PATHE, Effective Schools Project), and at the senior high school level (School Safety Program).

Methods

The methodological rigor of the studies summarized in this chapter is variable. Methods ratings range from 1.5 to 4. One study was ranked at the bottom of the scale, and four were assigned a rating of 2. Most (86%) were in a range of 3 to 4. The modal score was 4, and the average about 3.4.

The number of schools involved in the studies ranged from 1 to 42 (mean = 12), and the number of students ranged from 48 to 8,309 (mean = 1,685; median = 330). In most cases, some of the schools received a program and others did not. The schools were randomly assigned to conditions in only three studies. The investigator generally collected relevant data prior to and at the end of the intervention. Only six studies (15%) collected follow-up measures more than three months beyond the end of the program. Usually, analyses compared the subjects in the treatment schools with those in the comparison schools, using individual-level analyses and controlling on whatever pretreatment data were collected.

Most of the studies share a methodological shortcoming: schools are allocated to experimental conditions, but individual students are used as the unit of data analysis. Many school-based prevention programs – especially those summarized in this chapter – are delivered to entire classrooms or schools rather than to the individuals nested within these units. Of the studies summarized in this chapter, 87% used schools or classrooms as the unit of allocation to treatment and control conditions, but only 38% of the studies used these larger units for analysis. Two-thirds of the studies analyzed data at a lower level than was used for allocation.

Boruch and Foley (in press) argue that designs using sites (such as schools, classrooms, or communities) as the unit of allocation and analysis are to be preferred in many evaluations of social interventions. They argue for the superiority of these designs on grounds of precedent, substantive theory, statistical theory, and government policy. But they show that when analyses are conducted at the individual level when allocation to experimental conditions has occurred at a higher level, the assumption of independence of observations is violated. When standard statistical tests are employed in these situations (as they almost always are), the estimate of the variance is lower than it actually is because of the clustering of subjects within units, and the estimated test statistic is higher than it should be. Boruch and Foley estimate that such studies conclude that the treatments are different when they are not (a type I error) more than would be expected given the alpha-level of the statistical test. The chance of error increases as the similarity of the individuals within each group increases. Effect size estimates are also often incorrect when the wrong unit of analysis is used because they, too, rely upon an incorrect estimate of the variance.

Scientists analyze their data using individuals rather than classrooms or schools as the unit of analysis because too few of the larger units are available for study. Boruch and Foley provide estimates of the number of such units likely to be required to detect small differences in outcomes due to the intervention. This number depends upon the size of the difference to be detected, the number of subjects available within each unit, and the degree of clustering among subjects within the unit. In the scenarios provided, the number of units required ranges from 44 to 107 per treatment condition.

None of the studies summarized in this chapter have as many as forty-four schools. Most (85%) involve fewer than twenty schools, and the average number of schools is only twelve. If studies were conducted using the appropriate unit of analysis, they would certainly be underpowered. Investigators trade type II for type I errors when they choose to analyze data at a lower level to increase the sample size.

It is not surprising that only tentative conclusions can be drawn from the studies summarized in this chapter. Environmental change strategies are a promising avenue for delinquency prevention, but far more rigorous studies involving much larger numbers of schools must be conducted to further develop and test the promising approaches identified.

Chapter 6 continues the scrutiny of evidence from experimental and quasi-experimental studies, but focuses on programs and practices intended to alter individual students' behaviors, attitudes, or beliefs through direct services provided to these individuals.

Changing Student Personality, Attitudes, and Beliefs: The Field Studies

NONEXPERIMENTAL RESEARCH reviewed in Chapter 2 suggests that personality characteristics, beliefs, and attitudes held by individuals are robust predictors of delinquency. Two relatively stable personality characteristics – conscientiousness (e.g., competence, order, dutifulness, achievement striving, self-discipline, and deliberation) and agreeableness (e.g., trust, straightforwardness, altruism, compliance, modesty, and tender-mindedness) – predict less problem behavior. Aside from any direct influence these characteristics have on problem behavior, they also indirectly influence it by determining the extent and intensity of social control (e.g., attachments to school and others, commitment to education and work, and beliefs in rules), as well as the kinds of influences (especially peer) to which the individual is exposed. Evidence for a causal link between academic performance and problem behavior is weaker. Chapter 2 suggests that the correlation between academic performance and delinquency, at least prior to high school, is due mostly to their common reliance on early behavior problems. This chapter examines experimental and quasi-experimental studies for evidence that active manipulation of these presumed causal factors through interventions provided directly to students does in fact reduce problem behavior.

Presumably, prevention strategies aimed directly at changing one or more of these presumed causes of delinquency will be more effective and those targeting other factors will be less effective. Direct attempts to teach, model, and reinforce the emotional, cognitive, and behavioral skills necessary for self-regulation should be more effective for reducing problem behavior than attempts aimed at factors such as self-esteem or anxiety. This chapter examines several different individually targeted prevention strategies in order both to confirm results from the nonexperimental studies and to explore which of the causal factors can be manipulated through social interventions.

Overview of Studies

Twice as much research has been published on interventions to change individuals than on interventions to change school and classroom environments. None of the programs reviewed in this chapter includes a major focus on changing the environment. Rather, each seeks to reduce problem behavior by directly changing students' thoughts, beliefs, attitudes, or behaviors. Seventy-one studies of such programs will be reviewed. Fifty-five of these are reports of unique studies; sixteen are additional reports of studies included among the fifty-five. As in Chapter 5, the studies are organized by education level of the students targeted. Within large sections, studies are further organized by type of intervention.

Each of the major types of service to students has been studied, but studies of instructional interventions using cognitive-behavioral change methods are most common among the evaluated programs. Studies of recreational and other alternative activities programs, very popular among practitioners, are the least studied type of program.

Behavior modification and recreational studies are fairly evenly spread across levels, but the other types of programs are not: Studies of programs involving instruction and the use of cognitive behavioral methods are far more likely to involve younger populations, whereas studies of counseling, tutoring, mentoring, and similar programs are more likely to involve older populations. These large differences by education level in the types of programs that have been studied render ambiguous comparisons of general prevention program effectiveness across ages.

Studies of Programs in Elementary Schools

Table 6.1 shows the content of the interventions tested in the ten unique studies[1] of early elementary programs (e.g., those targeting mostly students in grades 3 and below), and Table 6.2 does the same for the thirteen unique studies of upper elementary grades (e.g., those targeting mostly students in grades 4 and 5). Tables 6.3 and 6.4 display information about the thirty-two different studies of these twenty-three programs. These tables are organized more or less by the age of the students targeted. Note that programs targeting only preschool children were beyond the scope of this book, but those few studies that included both preschool and early elementary grades were included. Although several studies of students in preschool have been conducted, only rarely do such studies assess program

---

[1] A unique study is one involving a distinct population. Replication studies are unique studies, but separate reports of the same study are not.

Table 6.1. *Early Elementary School Programs with Individual Change Focus*

Program (Study)	Grades Targeted	Program Content[a]								Duration of Program
		1	2	3	4	5	6	7	16	
"Interpersonal Cognitive Problem Solving" (Shure and Spivack, 1979, 1980, 1982)	Preschool and K	X	X							Up to 6 months
"Montreal Longitudinal Study" (Tremblay et al., 1991; Tremblay, Vitaro, et al., 1992; Tremblay et al., 1994)	2–3	X	X			✔		✔	X	2 school years
"Improving Attendance" (Barber and Kagey, 1977)	1–3			X						6 months
"Playground Aggression Prevention" (Murphy et al., 1983)	K–2			X			✔	✔		13 days
"Second Step Violence Prevention" (Grossman et al., 1997)	2–3	X	X					✔		6 months
"Social Problem Solving Training" (Weissberg, Gesten, Rapkin, et al., 1981)	3	X	X					✔		4 months
"Social Problem Solving Training" (Weissberg, Gesten, Carnrike, et al., 1981)	2–4	X	X					✔		4 months
"Promoting Alternative Thinking Strategies (PATHS)" (Greenberg and Kusché, 1993)	1–6	X	X	✔						1 school years
"Promoting Alternative Thinking Strategies (PATHS)" (Greenberg et al., 1995; Greenberg, 1996)	2–3	X	X	✔		✔	✔	✔		Up to 2 school years
"Families and Schools Together, FAST Track" (Dodge and Conduct Problems, 1993; Conduct Problems Prevention Research Group, 1992, 1997; Coie, 1997)	1–2	X				✔	✔	✔	✔	Spans 7 years[b]

[a]Program content key: 1. Instructing students. 2. Cognitive-behavioral change/behavior modeling. 3. Behavioral or behavior modification. 4. Counseling, social work, other psychological or therapeutic interventions. 5. Tutoring, mentoring, or other individual attention. 6. Recreational, enrichment, and leisure. 7. Changing instructional or classroom management methods or practices. 16. Changing family supervision or family behavior management. ✔ = contains some of this content; X = major focus of program.

[b]Most intense phase lasts 2 years.

163

Table 6.2. *Upper Elementary School Programs with Individual Change Focus*

Program (Study)	Grades Targeted	Program Content[a]								Duration of Program
		1	2	3	4	5	6	7	16	
"Cognitive Behavioral Training" (Forman, 1980)	3–5	X	X	X						6 weeks
"Academic and Social Skills Training" (Coie and Krehbiel, 1984)	4	✓	X			✓		✓		6 months
"Social Relations Training for Aggressive Behavior" (Coie et al., 1991)	4	X	X			✓		✓		7 months
"Social Skills Training" (Rotheram, 1982)	4–6	X	X	✓				✓		3 months
"Assertiveness Training" (Rotheram et al., 1982)	4–5	X	X	✓				✓		3 months
"Anger Coping Plus Goal Setting" (Lochman et al., 1984; Lochman et al., 1985; Lochman, 1985)	4–5	X	X	✓						8–20 weeks[b]
"Anger Coping Intervention and Anger Coping Self-Instruction Training" (Lochman and Curry, 1986)	4–5	X	X	✓						18 weeks
"Cognitive Behavioral Therapy" (Lochman, 1992)	4–6	X	X	✓						12–18 weeks
"Anger Coping and Anger Coping with Teacher Consultation" (Lochman et al., 1989)	4–6	X	X	✓				✓		18 weeks
"Social Problem Solving Project" (Elias et al., 1991)	4–5	X	X	✓						2 school years
"Children of Divorce Intervention Program" (Pedro-Carroll et al., 1986)	4–6	X	X					✓		11 weeks
"Earlscourt Social Skills Group" (Pepler et al., 1991)	2–6	X	X	✓		✓		✓	✓	12–15 weeks
"ADEPT Drug and Alcohol Community Prevention Project (ADACPP)" (Ross et al., 1992)	K–6	X	X				X	✓	✓	7 months

[a] Program content key: 1. Instructing students. 2. Cognitive-behavioral change/behavior modeling. 3. Behavioral or behavior modification. 4. Counseling, social work, other psychological or therapeutic interventions. 5. Tutoring, mentoring, or other individual attention. 6. Recreational, enrichment, and leisure. 7. Changing instructional or classroom management methods or practices. 16. Changing family supervision or family behavior management. ✓ = contains some of this content; X = major focus of program.
[b] Varies by condition.

Table 6.3. *Evaluations of Early Elementary School Programs with Individual Change Focus*

Program (Study)	Subjects	Method Rating/ Follow-up (mos.)	Correlates of Problem Behavior	Outcomes[a] Problem Behavior
"Interpersonal Cognitive Problem Solving" (Shure and Spivack, 1979, 1980, 1982)	219 African American, youths in federally funded day care	4/12	Alternative solution thinking (each follow-up: +) Consequential thinking (each follow-up: +)	Behavioral adjustment from too impulsive or too inhibited (each follow-up: +)
"Montreal Longitudinal Study" (Tremblay, Vitaro, et al., 1991; Tremblay, et al., 1992; Tremblay et al., 1994)	166 disruptive, at-risk, low SES boys	5/72	Class placement (significantly favored treatment in 2 of 4 follow-up assessments) Peer-rated likability (no differences in 3 of 3 follow-up assessments) Parental discipline and monitoring (no differences in 3 of 3 follow-up assessments)	Teacher-rated inattentiveness, hyperactivity, and disruptive behavior (no differences in 3 of 3 follow-up assessments) Mother-rated inattentiveness and disruptive behavior (significantly favored control in 1 of 4 follow-up assessments) Mother-rated hyperactivity (no differences in 3 of 3 follow-up assessments) Peer-rated disruptive behavior (no differences in 3 of 3 follow-up assessments) School adjustment (significantly favored treatment in 1 of 2 follow-up assessments) **Teacher-rated fighting (significantly favored treatment in 1 of 4 follow-up assessments)**

Table 6.3. (cont.)

Program (Study)	Subjects	Method Rating/Follow-up (mos.)	Correlates of Problem Behavior	Outcomes[a] Problem Behavior
				Mother-rated fighting (significantly favored control in 2 of 4 follow-up assessments)
				Self-reported fighting outside the home (significantly favored treatment in 1 of 2 follow-up assessments)
				Self-reported fighting in the home (significantly favored treatment in 1 of 2 follow-up assessments)
				Self-reported theft in the home (significantly favored treatment in 1 of 2 follow-up assessments)
				Juvenile arrest records (0)
"Improving Attendance" (Barber and Kagey, 1977)	212 boys and girls in 10 classes in 1 school (9 schools served as controls)	3/0		Attendance (+)
"Playground Aggression Prevention" (Murphy et al., 1983)	220 boys and girls in 1 school	5/0		Number of aggressive/inappropriate playground incidents (+)
"Second Step Violence Prevention" (Grossman et al., 1997)	649 boys and girls in 49 classes in 12 schools	4/6	Parent- and teacher-rated social competence (0)	Parent- and teacher-rated aggressive behavior (0) Observations of overall negative behavior (0)

Program (Reference)	Sample		Outcome measures	Observations of physical negative behavior (+) **Parent- and teacher-rated delinquent behavior (0)**
"Social Problem Solving Training" (Weissberg, Gesten, Rapkin, et al., 1981)	243 boys and girls in 12 classes in 3 schools	4/1.5	Problem solving skills (9 measures: +) (1 measure: −) (9 measures: 0) Class sociometric (0) Teacher-rated peer sociability (0 suburban schools) (− urban schools)	Teacher-rated acting out (+ suburban schools) (− urban schools) Teacher-rated problem behavior (+ suburban schools) (0 urban schools)
"Social Problem Solving Training" (Weissberg, Gesten, Carnrike, et al., 1981)	563 boys and girls in 24 classes in 8 schools	4/1	Problem solving skills (7 measures: +) (4 measures: 0) Teacher-rated peer sociability (0) Teacher-rated likability and global school adjustment (+) Peer-rated likability (0)	Teacher-rated acting out (0)
"Promoting Alternative Thinking Strategies (PATHS)" (Greenberg and Kusché, 1993)	53 hearing-impaired boys and girls in 11 classes in 6 schools	5/24	Standardized reading achievement test scores (+) Interpersonal cognitive problem solving skills (+) Teacher-rated peer sociability (study group 1: 0) (study group 2: +)	Parent-rated behavior problems (0) Teacher-rated behavior problems (0)
"Promoting Alternative Thinking Strategies (PATHS)" (Greenberg et al., 1995; Greenberg, 1996)	286 regular and special-needs boys and girls in 30 classes	4/24	Interpersonal problem-solving skills (regular: significantly favored treatment in 2 of 3 follow-up assessments; special needs: significantly favored	Self-reported conduct disorder (significantly favored each treatment group in 1 of 3 follow-up assessments) Teacher-rated externalizing problems (regular: significantly favored treatment

Table 6.3. (cont.)

Program (Study)	Subjects	Method Rating/ Follow-up (mos.)	Correlates of Problem Behavior	Outcomes[a] Problem Behavior
			treatment in 1 of 3 follow-up assessments)	in 1 of 3 follow-up assessments; special needs: no differences in 3 of 3 follow-up assessments)
			Standardized math achievement test scores (0)	Parent-rated externalizing problems (0)
"Families and Schools Together, FAST Track" (Dodge and Conduct Problems, 1993; Conduct Problems Prevention Research Group, 1992, 1997; Coie, 1997)	First Cohort (At-Risk Students): 320 high-risk boys and girls	4/15	Social-cognitive skills (+)	Observations of problem behavior (+)
			Peer-rated likability (+)	Rates of observed aggressive behavior (0)
	Three Cohorts (General Population): 385 classes		Social competence (0)	Teacher-rated problem behavior (0)
			Positive classroom atmosphere (+)	Teacher-rated conduct problems (+)
				Peer-rated aggression and hyperactivity (+)
			Teacher-rated peer liking (+)	Observations of aggressive, disruptive, oppositional behavior (grade 1: +)
			Reading comprehension (grades 1 and 2: +)	Teacher- and parent-rated *change* in aggressive, disruptive, and disobedient behavior (grade 1: +)
	Three Cohorts (At-Risk Students): 891 high-risk boys and girls in 385 classes		Problem solving skills and social, cognitive, and emotional coping skills (mostly +)	Teacher- and parent-rated *actual* antisocial behavior (grade 1: 0)
			Parental discipline (mostly +)	Peer-rated aggressive behavior (grade 1: 0)
			Parental warmth and involvement (+)	Teacher- and parent-rated conduct problems (grade 3: +)
			Peer-rated likability (+)	Diagnosed with behavior disorder (grade 4: +)

Notes: Follow-up period begins at end of intervention. The number of subjects is the maximum number present for any of the analyses reported in the table.

[a] Key for study outcomes: 0 = no significant effect (p < .05); + = significant positive effect (p < .05); − = significant negative effect (p < .05); nr = two-tailed significance level not reported. Outcomes for substance use and for crime and delinquency measures appear in italics and in bold, respectively.

Table 6.4. *Evaluations of Upper Elementary School Programs with Individual Change Focus*

Program (Study)	Subjects	Method Rating/Follow-up (mos.)	Outcomes[a] Correlates of Problem Behavior	Problem Behavior
"Cognitive Behavioral Training" (Forman, 1980)	18 aggressive boys and girls in 1 school	4/0		Aggressive behavior: observations, teacher records, and teacher ratings (+)
"Academic and Social Skills Training" (Coie and Krehbiel, 1984)	40 socially rejected, low-achieving, boys and girls	5/12	Academic achievement (2 of 4 comparisons favor academic skills training group – immediate and 12 month follow-up; 1 of 4 comparisons favors social skills training group – immediate only) Peer acceptance: Peer rating of social status (+) Peer nomination of social preference (academic skills training group: +; social skills training group: 0)	Observations of conduct (2 of 5 measures favor academic skills training group; social skills training group: 0)
"Social Relations Training for Aggressive Behavior" (Coie et al., 1991)[b]	49 aggressive, rejected children in 11 schools	3/12	Peer social preference (0) Peer acceptance (0) Peer prosocial ratings (0)	Peer and teacher aggression ratings (0)

169

Table 6.4. (cont.)

Program (Study)	Subjects	Method Rating/ Follow-up (mos.)	Outcomes[a]	
			Correlates of Problem Behavior	Problem Behavior
"Social Skills Training" (Rotheram, 1982)	101 boys and girls in 8 classes in 1 school	4/12	Grade-point average (+) Teacher rating of achievement (+) Assertion quiz (+) Social problem-solving assertive responses (+) Peer popularity (0)	Comportment (+)
"Assertiveness Training" (Rotheram et al., 1982)	343 boys and girls in 10 classes	4/12	Grade-point average (+) Teacher rating of achievement (immediate: 0) (1 year follow-up: +) Social problem-solving assertive responses (+) Popularity (peer-rated: 0) (teacher-rated: +)	Comportment (+)
"Anger Coping Plus Goal Setting" (Lochman et al., 1984; Lochman et al., 1985)	76 aggressive boys in 8 schools	4/1	Social problem-solving number of alternatives (0) Social acceptance (0)	Disruptive and aggressive off-task behavior (+) Aggression (parent and teacher rated: +) Sociometric aggressive nomination (0) Passive off-task behavior (0)

Program	Sample	Ratio	Measures	Outcomes
"Anger Coping Plus Goal Setting" (Lochman, 1985)	98 aggressive boys in 8 schools	4/0		Disruptive aggressive off-task behavior (+); Solitary passive off-task behavior (+)
"Anger Coping Intervention and Anger Coping SelfInstruction Training" (Lochman and Curry, 1986)	20 aggressive boys in 4 schools	4/0	Social competence scale (0); Cognitive competence scale (0)	Disruptive off-task behavior (+ only for Anger Coping Only group); Passive/solitary off-task behavior (0); Classroom on-task behavior (+); Parent report of aggression (+); Teacher report of aggression (0)
"Cognitive Behavioral Therapy" (Lochman, 1992)	145 aggressive boys	4/36	Problem-solving skills (+)	Disruptive off-task behavior (0); Passive off-task behavior (0); *Substance use* (+); **General behavior deviance including crimes against persons and theft (0)**
"Anger Coping and Anger Coping with Teacher Consultation" (Lochman et al., 1989)	32 aggressive boys in 6 schools	3/0		Change in disruptive/aggressive off-task behavior (+); Change in teacher reports of aggression (0)
"Social Problem Solving Project" (Elias et al., 1991)	426 boys and girls	2/60	Comprehensive Test of Basic Skills (+); Social competence (0); Unpopularity (+)	Aggression (0); Absences (3 tests: 0) (1 test: +); *Use of alcoholic beverages* (+); **Vandalism (+)**; **Hitting or threatening (+)**; **Attacking others with intent to injure (+)**; **Delinquency (0)**

Table 6.4. (cont.)

Program (Study)	Subjects	Method Rating/ Follow-up (mos.)	Outcomes[a]	
			Correlates of Problem Behavior	Problem Behavior
"Children of Divorce Intervention Program" (Pedro-Carroll et al., 1986)	132 boys and girls from divorced families in 6 schools	3/.5	Social competence (+) Peer sociability (0) Internal control (0)	Acting out problems (0)
"Earlscourt Social Skills Group" (Pepler et al., 1991)	40 aggressive boys and girls	3/3	Social problem-solving skills (0)	Externalizing behavior problems (teacher rating; +) (parent rating: 0)
"ADEPT Drug and Alcohol Community Prevention Project (ADACPP)" (Ross et al., 1992)	667 latchkey boys and girls in 24 schools	4/1	Standardized achievement test (0) Impulsivity and risk taking (−)	Acting out (0)

Notes: Follow-up period begins at end of intervention. The number of subjects is the maximum number present for any of the analyses reported in the table.

[a] Key for study outcomes: 0 = no significant effect ($p < .05$); + = significant positive effect ($p < .05$); − = significant negative effect ($p < .05$); nr = two-tailed significance level not reported. Outcomes for substance use and for crime and delinquency measures appear in italics and in bold, respectively.

[b] Results vary for subsets of schools or classrooms which differed on level of program implementation.

effects on problem behavior outcomes. The focus is more often limited to cognitive development.[2]

Early Elementary and Preschool Interventions

Spivack and Shure's Interpersonal Cognitive Problem-Solving Skills (ICPS) program was one of the earliest attempts to apply cognitive training to very young children. This program helps the child to learn to generate alternative solutions to problems, become aware of the steps required to achieve a certain goal, consider consequences of actions, understand how events are causally related, and become more sensitive to interpersonal problems. The program is designed for use with children as young as four years old. More sophisticated skills are taught to children in the early elementary school grades. Using the program, teachers work with small groups of children for about twenty minutes per day, using scripts prepared for each lesson. The intervention lasts approximately three months.

Shure and Spivack (1979, 1980, 1982; methods rating = 4) tested the program with 219 inner-city African American nursery school children. One hundred thirteen of these subjects continued with the study through kindergarten. Some children received the training in nursery school only, others in kindergarten only, and others in both years. A fourth group received no training. The investigators measured both the specific interpersonal cognitive problem-solving skills targeted by the program and teachers' ratings of overt behavioral problems. Results showed that (1) students trained in nursery school improved significantly more than controls both on measures of ICPS skills and behavioral adjustment; (2) these improvements were still evident a year following training, even when no additional training was provided; (3) students trained for the first time in kindergarten improved significantly more than controls both on measures of ICPS skills and behavioral adjustment; and (4) students trained for two consecutive years scored higher than any other group on measures of ICPS, but a second year of training made no difference in terms of behavioral ratings (i.e., one year of training was sufficient and equally effective either year).

In the Montreal Longitudinal Experimental Study (Tremblay et al., 1991; Tremblay et al., 1992; Tremblay, Kurtz, Mâsse, Vitaro, and Pihl, 1994; methods rating = 5), disruptive boys identified as having low socioeconomic status were randomly assigned to receive a preventive intervention

---

[2] Yoshikawa (1994) provides an excellent review of preschool programs. He reviews research relating early childhood characteristics to antisocial behavior and shows that "multicontextual" interventions combining comprehensive family support and early education reduce later problem behavior by altering the quality of parenting, early cognitive development, and socioemotional competence. His review suggests that early cognitive and emotional functioning in school as well as parenting have causal influences on later problem behavior.

or to be part of an attention control group or a no-contact control group. Disruptive boys for the pool were identified through kindergarten teacher ratings. The intervention began in grade 2 (when the boys were seven years old) and continued for two years. The program combined a successful model of parent training in family management (developed by the Oregon Social Learning Center; Patterson, 1982) with a social skills training program delivered by professionals in the schools. Approximately seventeen home visits per family were conducted over the two-year period. These sessions focused on teaching parents to monitor their son's behavior, reinforce positive behavior, punish negative behavior without being abusive, and manage family crises. Parents were also given a reading program. The social skills sessions (nineteen over the two-year period) grouped the disruptive boys with prosocial peers for sessions that focused on prosocial skills and self-control. Effective cognitive-behavioral strategies (e.g., coaching, peer modeling, self-instruction, behavioral rehearsal, and reinforcement contingencies) were used during the sessions. The study followed the boys for six years after the end of the treatment.

Teachers rated treatment boys as less likely to fight. The difference was marginally significant (p = .07) immediately following treatment, faded over the next two years, was apparent again at follow-ups between ages 12 and 13, only to disappear at age 14. Mothers of treatment boys perceived their sons as *more* disruptive and inattentive immediately following the treatment. Most of these differences had faded two years later, but the differences in mothers' reports of fighting persisted. Although early self-reports of problem behavior showed no differences among the groups, by the second year after the treatment ended some treatment effects were evident. Out of twenty-seven different delinquent acts, significantly fewer treatment boys reported ever having been involved with four (all relatively minor property crimes) by age 12. Also, scales measuring fighting (both outside the home and inside the home) and theft in the home in the last year favored the treatment group by 1989, when the boys reached age 11. The treated boys reported significantly less delinquent behavior (on a scale including measures of stealing, vandalism, and substance use) than the control group one to six years after treatment. Juvenile court records, however, did not show the same pattern. In summary, the preponderance of results support a positive effect of the two-year early intervention. But they highlight the importance of using multiple data sources. The apparently contradictory mother reports may reflect a positive effect on the mothers' awareness of and sensitivity to the boys' negative behaviors.

Two studies of early elementary school children were primarily behavioral interventions. Barber and Kagey (1977; methods rating = 3) showed that the attendance rate for students in grades 1 through 3 improved dramatically through the use of daily attendance charts posted in each room, with monthly student parties for students whose attendance the prior month exceeded a criterion. Murphy, Hutchison, and Bailey (1983; methods rating = 5) showed that altering antecedent conditions reduces aggressive behavior on the playground for students in kindergarten through grade 2. They found that instances of aggression declined precipitously when organized games were used in place of no structured playground activity. A two-minute time-out procedure was also used for particularly unruly behavior. These studies are important because they suggest that relatively simple behavioral interventions can have immediate effects on precursors of later problem behavior.

School-based violence prevention curricula are becoming increasingly popular. Several have been developed and marketed, but few have been evaluated rigorously. Only one relatively rigorous evaluation of such a program designed for young children has appeared in the literature. Grossman et al. (1997; methods rating = 4) studied the Second Step violence prevention curriculum.[3] The program is available for students in preschool through grade 8, but only the early elementary-level curriculum materials were evaluated in this study. The curriculum consists of thirty lessons covering social skills related to anger management, impulse control, and empathy. It attempts to decrease aggressive behavior by increasing prosocial behaviors, including competence in peer interactions and interpersonal conflict resolution skills. Role playing, modeling of the new skill by the teacher, skill practice, feedback, and reinforcement for appropriate skill use were used. Six schools were randomly assigned to treatment and six to the control condition. Classrooms were then recruited from these schools to participate in the study. Parent and teacher ratings of behavior and direct observations of behavior were collected prior to, directly following, and six months following the course. Analysis of the parent and teacher reports of antisocial, aggressive, and delinquent behaviors revealed no differences between the students who received and did not receive the program. The observation data revealed marginally significant differences[4] between the treatment and comparison groups on rates of physical negative behaviors and neutral or prosocial behaviors but not on verbal negative behaviors or a composite of all negative behaviors. The positive effects were found to be primarily due to improvements in behavior on the playground and in the cafeteria rather than in the

---

[3] The Second Step program was developed and evaluated by the Committee for Children. These early evaluations (Committee for Children, 1988, 1989, 1990, 1992) tested four different age-grade versions of the program with students in preschool through grade 8. The evaluations used nonequivalent comparison group designs with pre- and post-tests. These studies varied in methodological rigor (ranging from 2 to 4 on the methods rating scale), had small numbers of cases (ranging from 35 to 123 per study), and included no measure of actual problem behavior. The results generally supported a positive effect of the program on the social skills targeted, including empathy, interpersonal problem solving, and anger management.

[4] Only one-tailed tests of significance were reported.

classroom, which may explain the absence of effects based on the teacher ratings. Effects diminished somewhat over the six month post-treatment follow-up period.

Weissberg developed and tested a somewhat broader social competency development curricula. This social competence promotion program covers an array of social competency skills without tying them directly to any specific problem behavior, although problem-specific modules aimed at preventing antisocial and aggressive behavior, substance use, and high-risk sexual behavior are available. The program has evolved through a number of tests with students in grades 3 through 8. An early version of the program, tested with students in grade 3, is described here. Weissberg, Gesten, Rapkin et al. (1981; methods rating = 4) implemented a fifty-two-lesson social problem-solving course to third graders in three schools – two in the suburbs and one in an urban neighborhood.

The program was highly structured, and contained multiple lessons on each of the following:

Recognizing feelings in ourselves and others.
Identifying problem situations and associated feelings.
Generating alternative solutions to social problems.
Anticipating the likely consequences of different actions.
Integrating these problem-solving skills to choose the best course of action and successfully enact the solution.

Small-group role playing was extensively used and augmented with videotape modeling exercises, cartoon workbooks, competitive games, and class discussions. All activities focused on teaching students to use a set sequence of steps for resolving interpersonal conflicts. Positive effects of the intervention were evident on several measures of the specific cognitive skills targeted, including problem identification, alternative-solution thinking, and consequential thinking as well as behavioral problem-solving performance (in a contrived situation). Overall, no significant differences were observed on sociometric ratings of student behavioral adjustment or three different teacher ratings of problem behavior. Separate analyses of the urban and suburban samples, however, revealed positive effects for the suburban treatment students on measures of inattentiveness, acting out, and a total problem behavior index. Negative effects were found on the acting out measure for urban school students, but methodological problems resulting in the loss of one of the urban control teachers from the analysis undermine confidence in this counterintuitive result.

The program was modified to reduce the number of lessons to forty-two (taught in fourteen weeks), keeping the same content and methods, and retested in a sample of grades 2 through 4, suburban and urban classrooms (Weissberg, Gesten, Carnike et al., 1981; methods rating = 4). Positive effects on specific cognitive skills targeted in the program (e.g., offering solutions to hypothetical problem situations, attempting to resolve simulated behavioral peer conflicts, and expressing confidence about handling interpersonal difficulties) were again observed. As in the experiment involving children in grade 3, no significant differences were observed on sociometric peer ratings. Teacher ratings showed significant improvements in shy-anxious behavior, likability, and global school adjustment. A total problem scale also showed significant improvement, but this was due to improvements in the shy-anxious subscale. No improvements were observed for the acting-out subscale, which is more predictive of subsequent problem behavior. Importantly, this study found that the program was equally effective in suburban and urban settings.

Greenberg, Kusché, Cook, and Quamma (1995) and Greenberg (1996; methods rating = 4) report on the PATHS (Promoting Alternative Thinking Strategies) curriculum on emotional competence for elementary-school-age children. This project used a sixty-lesson version of the curriculum composed of units on self-control, emotions, and problem solving. Lessons were sequenced according to increasing developmental difficulty and included didactic instruction, role playing, class discussion, modeling by teachers and peers, social and self-reinforcement, and worksheets. Extensive generalization techniques were included to assist teachers in applying skills to other aspects of the school day. The PATHS lessons were taught approximately three times per week, with each lesson lasting twenty to thirty minutes. Specifically, the curriculum included:

A Feelings and Relationships Unit: Thirty-five lessons on emotional and interpersonal understanding cover approximately thirty-five different affective states and were taught in a developmental hierarchy, beginning with basic emotions (e.g., happy, sad, angry) and proceeding to more complex emotional states (e.g., jealous, guilty, proud).

Self-control and initial problem solving: The development of self-control, affective awareness and communication, and beginning problem-solving skills were integrated during the Feelings Unit with the introduction of the Control Signals Poster (CSP), which had a red light to signal "Stop – Calm Down," a yellow light for "Go Slow – Think," a green light to signal "Go – Try My Plan," and at the bottom, the words "Evaluate – How Did My Plan Work?" In a series of lessons, the children were taught skills to use with the different signals of the poster. For purposes of generalization, a copy of the CSP was placed in the classroom and teachers were coached on how to use this model for active problem solving during the classroom day.

Interpersonal cognitive problem solving: Twenty to thirty lessons sequentially covered eleven problem-solving steps, similar to those discussed as part of Weissberg's program.

Generalization procedures: A variety of generalization techniques were included throughout the curriculum to foster transfer of the skills and ideas taught.

The program was initially tested with hearing-impaired children in grades 1 through 6. Greenberg and Kusché (1993; methods rating = 5) found the program led to significant improvements in social-cognitive skills and teacher-reported social competence, but no effects were observed on teacher ratings of problem behavior. The intervention was later field-tested in Washington State using random assignment of schools serving "regular education" students to treatment and control conditions as well as random assignment of classrooms of "special needs" children (in a different school from that of the regular education students) to treatment and control conditions. In all, 426 (286 after attrition) students participated in the study. Students were in grades 1 and 2 at the time of the pretest, and in grades 2 and 3 at the time of the first post-test, which occurred approximately one month after the end of the intervention. Two additional follow-up assessments were conducted to examine maintenance of effects one and two years after the intervention.

Immediate positive effects of the program were observed for both regular and special education students on measures of the specific social competency skills targeted. No differences in externalizing behavior were observed immediately following the intervention for either group. Greenberg (1996) reports on the longer-term effects of the program. At the final follow-up, significant differences favoring the regular-education treatment students (but not the special-education students) emerged on teacher ratings of externalizing behaviors, a measure of serious conduct problems highly related to later delinquent behavior. Intervention students in both groups also self-reported significantly lower rates of conduct problems at the later follow-up points. No differences were observed on parent ratings of externalizing behaviors.

The most ambitious school-based prevention effort aimed at young school children to date is FAST Track (Families and Schools Together; Coie, 1997; Conduct Problems Prevention Research Group, 1992, 1997; Dodge and the Conduct Problems Prevention Research Group, 1993; methods rating = 4). The program was developed by a consortium of social scientists on the basis of developmental theory about the causes of conduct disorder in children and previous evaluations of specific, theory-based program components. It integrates five intervention components designed to promote competence in the family, child, and school and thus prevent conduct problems, poor social relations, and school failure – all precursors of subsequent criminal behavior – during the elementary school years. The program targets children in grade 1 at risk for developing conduct disorder and continues at an intensive level through the end of grade 2. After grade 2, several of the interventions continue but at less intensive levels. The program involves training for parents in family management practices; frequent home visits by program staff to reinforce skills learned in the training, promote parental feelings of efficacy, and enhance family organization; social skills coaching for children delivered by program staff (based on Lochman's anger management program to be described in the next section); academic tutoring for children three times per week; and a classroom instructional program (delivered to all students, including those targeted by the program) focusing on social competency skills (a variant of the PATHS curriculum described earlier) coupled with classroom management strategies for the teacher. The program therefore includes several effective school-based strategies as well as the most effective family-based strategies.

The participating schools and families work closely with the research team to implement the program in a strong fashion and support its evaluation. Several preliminary reports from this ongoing project have been presented at professional conferences. A recent report (Conduct Problems Prevention Research Group, 1997) on outcomes of the first year of intervention for three successive cohorts of children (445 treatment and 446 control students) showed consistent positive effects of the program on cognitive skills as well as several measures of emotional development (e.g., mature coping responses) and problem-solving skills. Importantly, sociometric measures showed that the intervention children were more liked and less disliked by their peers than were the control children. Parents of the target students used more effective discipline strategies, reported less use of physical punishment on hypothetical vignettes (although no difference was observed on other measures of harsh and coercive discipline), and were rated as showing more warmth and involvement with their children. Early effects on antisocial behavior are mixed: As in the Grossman et al. (1997) evaluation of the Second Step violence prevention program, observations by blinded observers during lunch and on the playground revealed positive effects of the intervention for both aggressive-disruptive behavior and prosocial behavior. Both teachers and parents rated the intervention children as having made significantly more positive changes over the year than control students, but their ratings of actual antisocial behavior at the end of the first year were not significantly different. Neither were peer nominations for aggressiveness for treatment and control students any different. Effect sizes for the immediate positive effects ranged from .25 to .35.

Few longer-term effects from FAST Track have been reported, but Coie (1997) reports results through the end of grade 3 on teacher ratings of problem behavior and parent daily reports of conduct problems. Linear

Growth Curve modeling shows that the treatment and control groups, initially equivalent on these measures, gradually diverged over the three-year period following base line. Teacher ratings showed increasing problems for the control but not for the experimental group. Parent ratings showed decreasing problems for both groups but more so for the treatment group. The intervention's significant effects on teacher-rated conduct problems were mediated in part by measures taken at the end of grades 2 and 3 of peer acceptance, nonhostile attributions, and reading comprehension. Peer acceptance and positive changes in parent discipline and support partially mediated the positive effects on parent ratings of conduct problems.

The 1997 report cited earlier also shows significant positive effects of the program on decisions by the school to provide the child with an Individualized Education Plan (IEP). This decision is based primarily on diagnoses of Behavioral Disorder by school psychologists. By grade 4 37% and 48% of the treatment and control students had received IEPs. Further examination showed that most of the results were due to the mediating effects of six individual social and cognitive skill variables: emotional recognition skills, emotional coping skills, social problem-solving skills, reading comprehension, and peer social preference. Measures of the targeted parenting variables were also related to the special-education decision, but these factors did not significantly increment the prediction beyond that afforded by the child factors, suggesting that the parenting component affects child outcomes indirectly by altering the crucial child factors.

The classroom-level effects of the PATHS curriculum are more consistently positive. The same (1997) report compares 201 classrooms receiving a fifty-seven-lesson modified PATHS curriculum (80% of the lessons were drawn from the original curriculum described earlier) in grade 1 with 184 matched comparison classrooms. Intervention teachers rated their classrooms as having fewer conduct problems (but their ratings of cognitive concentration and social competence did not differ). Sociometric measures showed lower ratings for peer aggression and hyperactivity in the intervention classrooms. Finally, classroom observers rated the atmosphere in the intervention classrooms as more positive and conducive to learning. All three data sources therefore converged in suggesting a positive effect of the curriculum on antisocial classroom behavior.

FAST Track appears to reduce problem behavior for both the general population and for youths selected for their high risk for problem behavior. Although effects of the universal curriculum (for the general population) appear immediately, effects on problem behavior for high-risk youths are more gradual and follow changes in social competency skills, reading comprehension, and peer relations.

Upper Elementary Interventions

The most popular school-based prevention program, Drug Abuse Resistance Education, or DARE, targets primarily upper-elementary-age children. This program is discussed along with several other substance abuse curricula in the next section. Non-DARE studies of programs for students in grades 4 and 5 are also abundant. As with the early elementary programs, most involve efforts to improve cognitive skills thought to be necessary for solving problems of an interpersonal nature. Because the studies are similar in terms of strategies studied, research methods utilized, and results obtained, they are not discussed in detail here. Interested readers may find a detailed summary of these studies in a recent report to the U.S. Congress on crime prevention (Gottfredson, 1997). Tables 6.2 and 6.4 show the characteristics and results for all of the studies.

Briefly, three of the strategies targeted high-risk populations. Forman (1980; methods rating = 4) showed that brief cognitive training and behavioral interventions decrease aggressive behavior relative to a brief tutoring condition, although the behavioral intervention decreased disruptive behavior to a somewhat greater extent than the cognitive intervention. Coie and Krehbiel (1984; methods rating = 5), on the other hand, compared much more intensive academic skills and social skills training programs. In their work, academic skills training improved academic achievement and peer acceptance, and improved classroom behavior. The social skills training group improved only on reading achievement, an effect not sustained, and a peer rating of social status. Neither group improved significantly in terms of their disruptive behavior, although the academic skills training group tended in the positive direction.

Lochman's work with highly aggressive boys is reported in a series of research articles beginning in the mid-1980s. The intervention included the following elements:

Establishing group rules and contingent reinforcements.
Using self-statements to inhibit impulsive behavior.
Identifying problems and social perspective taking.
Generating alternative solutions and considering the consequences to social problems.
Modeling videotapes of children becoming aware of physiological arousal when angry, using self-statements, and using a set of problem-solving skills to solve social problems.
Having the boys plan and make their own videotape of inhibitory self-statements and social problem solving.
Dialoging, discussion, and role playing to implement social problem-solving skills with children's current anger arousal problems.

The intervention also applied behavioral techniques to reward compliance with group rules. Several studies found immediate positive effects of the treatment on measures of disruptive, aggressive, off-task behavior in school and aggressive behavior as rated by parents. A three-year follow-up study conducted when the boys were fifteen years old (Lochman, 1992; methods rating = 4) found a significant effect on self-reported alcohol and substance abuse (ES = −.38) but no significant effect on self-reported criminal behavior (ES = −.11). It can be argued that a reduction in delinquency of this magnitude (approximately equivalent to a 5 percentage point difference in the crime rate between the treatment and control group) in a highly delinquent population is practically meaningful even if it is not statistically significant. Also, the treatment group in this follow-up study was significantly younger than the comparison group, which worked against finding program effects as age was inversely associated with rates of delinquency.

Rotheram's work shows that cognitive behavioral approaches to prevention are effective with general populations of upper elementary school students. In her work, cognitive training was provided to all students in classrooms in the context of small-group drama situation "games" involving group problem solving. In one study (Rotheram, 1982; methods rating = 4), high-risk students in the social skills training condition generated significantly more assertive and significantly fewer passive and aggressive problem-solving responses than did the control group directly after treatment, and had larger increases in their grade-point averages over pretreatment one year after the treatment. Teacher ratings of comportment also improved significantly more from pretreatment to immediately following the treatment as well as one year after the treatment. Rotheram, Armstrong, and Booraem (1982; methods rating = 4) showed similar positive effects for all students in the class.

Only one study of an elementary school program lacking an emphasis on cognitive or behavioral skills was located, and it is a study of an after-school care program. The program (Ross, Saavedra, Shur, Winters, and Felner, 1992; methods rating = 4) involved instruction and supervised homework, self-esteem-building exercises, free play, and creative dramatics in a school-based after-school program for children in kindergarten through grade 6. Although the study found no effects on a teacher rating of acting out behavior, it *increased* risk taking and impulsiveness, an important negative side effect most likely due to grouping high-risk youths with lower-risk youths in the absence of a strong intervention.

Summary

Each of the programs targeting children in kindergarten through grade 3 used either purely behavioral or a combination of cognitive and behavioral approaches to reduce problem behavior, and at least one version of each program was found to be effective for reducing some form of problem behavior, although the results were not consistent across all measures and studies. Most of the studies registered immediate effects on problem behavior, but others (e.g., the Montreal program and the FAST Track intervention for high-risk youths) showed that the effects of early intervention may become more evident over time, especially for high-risk populations. Most of the programs studied were "universal," targeting entire student populations. A few (e.g., the Montreal program and most components of FAST Track) targeted students selected for their predisposition to problem behavior. Greenberg's study of the PATHS curriculum compared the effectiveness of the program for regular and special-education students. Each of these studies demonstrated some effectiveness for high-risk students, although the effects were not consistently observed across all time points and across all measures of problem behavior.

Another important finding that emerges from these studies is that the choice of data source is important. Because reliable self-reports of problem behavior are difficult to obtain for young children, evaluations must rely on adult ratings and observations of problem behavior. The few studies reviewed that used both adult behavior ratings and blinded observations of behavior found positive effects based on the observation data but not on the adult ratings. This was also a major finding of a recent meta-analysis (Stage and Quiroz, 1997) of school-based interventions to reduce disruptive classroom behavior. That review of ninety-nine studies (most of which used single-subject or group time series designs) showed that studies relying on teacher rating scales were less likely to evidence reductions in disruptive classroom behavior than were studies rating on behavioral observations. The studies reviewed here also demonstrate that the choice of observation setting is important: problem behavior is relatively uncommon in classroom settings, and the effects of an intervention are not likely to be observed there unless the observers were present in the classroom for an extended period. The choice of adult rater is likewise important: if parents are involved in an intervention designed to heighten their awareness of their children's problem behavior, they observe more problem behavior than comparison group parents not exposed to the training.

The studies of upper elementary school children appearing in the literature are also primarily of programs using a combination of behavioral and cognitive approaches. They, too, generally show positive results. The studies show that teaching cognitive interpersonal problem-solving skills to upper elementary school children is effective for reducing disruptive behavior in school when the intervention is delivered universally (as in the Rotheram studies) as well as when it is delivered to extremely aggressive youngsters (as in the Lochman and Forman studies). The studies also demonstrate that effects are observed both immediately following the treatment and as long as three years later. The Lochman study shows that a cognitive-behavioral intervention with highly aggressive elementary school children reduces harder measures of problem behavior during the adolescent years.

The Coie and Krehbiel study is the only study discussed here whose social skill intervention did not result in decreased disruptive behavior. But in this study, the intervention focused primarily on teaching social skills appropriate during play periods, whereas the outcome measures were observations of classroom periods. It is possible that skills for play were learned, but that they did not generalize to the classroom setting. The Coie and Krehbiel study is particularly important for demonstrating that an intensive tutoring intervention can increase appropriate classroom behavior and improve students' peer acceptance, important protective factors against later delinquency. The study results suggest that an academic intervention may reduce subsequent delinquency by altering peer influence.

Studies of Programs in Middle and Junior High Schools

More varied approaches to delinquency prevention have been tested at the middle and junior high school level. Among the studies are twelve tests of ten behavioral and cognitive-behavioral and instructional programs and twelve tests of programs providing counseling, mentoring, recreation, and other "alternatives" to delinquency. One test of a broad, multicomponent program is also included.

Primarily Behavioral Interventions

Behavior modification interventions focus directly on changing behaviors by rewarding desired behavior, punishing undesired behavior, or altering antecedent conditions to reduce unwanted behavior. Several well-known (non-school-based) programs for delinquent youths (e.g., Achievement Place) rely on these methods, as do many educational programs – especially those serving special-education populations. Meta-analyses (Garrett, 1985; Izzo and Ross, 1990; Lipsey, 1992) have also concluded that the most effective delinquency prevention and treatment programs incorporate behavioral strategies.

Several interventions with a major emphasis on behavior modification have also been tested at the middle and junior high school level. Table 6.5 provides information about the content of these programs, and Table 6.6 describes the studies. Bry's work is the most methodologically sound. She conducted two studies, both involving random assignment of high-risk youths to receive behavioral monitoring and reinforcement or not. A third study reported on the long-term follow-up of the subjects from the earlier

Table 6.5. *Middle and Junior High School Programs with Behavioral, Cognitive-Behavioral, and Instructional Content*

Program (Study)	Grades Targeted	Program Content[a]																Duration of Program
		1	2	3	4	5	6	7	8	9	10	11	12	13	14	15	16	
"The Early (Secondary) Intervention Program" (Bry and George, 1979, 1980; Bry, 1982)	7–8[b]	✓	✓	×	✓			✓			✓						✓	1.5–2 school years[c]
"Preparation through Responsive Educational Programs (PREP)" (Filipczak and Wodarski, 1982; Wodarski and Filipczak, 1982)	7–8	×		×		×											✓	1 school year
"Contingency Management Program for Disruptive Adolescents" (Heaton et al., 1982; Safer et al., 1982)	7–9			×				✓									✓	~1.5 school years[d]
"Behavior Modification and Parent Training" (Patterson, 1974)				×				✓									×	8 weeks
"Anger Control Training" (Feindler et al., 1984)	7–9	×		✓				✓	✓									7 weeks
"Think First" (Larson, 1992)	8 on avg.	×	×	✓														5 weeks
"Positive Youth Development" (Caplan et al., 1992)	6–7	×	×															15 weeks
"Positive Youth Development" (Weissberg and Caplan, 1994)	5–8	×	×					✓										12 weeks
"Moral Reasoning Development and Decision Making Intervention" (Arbuthnot and Gordon, 1986; Arbuthnot, 1992)	7–10	×	×					✓										4–5 months

Table 6.5. (cont.)

Program (Study)	Grades Targeted	Program Content[a]																Duration of Program
		1	2	3	4	5	6	7	8	9	10	11	12	13	14	15	16	
"Gang Resistance Education and Training (GREAT)" (Esbensen and Osgood, 1996)	7	X							✔									9 weeks
"The Youth Development Project" (Reckless and Dinitz, 1972; Dinitz, 1982)	7	X						✔					✔					1 school year

Notes: Substance abuse prevention curricula are excluded from this table.

[a] Program content key: 1. Instructing students. 2. Cognitive-behavioral change/behavior modeling. 3. Behavioral or behavior modification. 4. Counseling, social work, other psychological or therapeutic interventions. 5. Tutoring, mentoring, or other individual attention. 6. Recreational, enrichment, and leisure. 7. Changing instructional or classroom management methods or practices management. 8. Changing norms or expectations for behavior. 9. Building a sense of community, morale, caring, support, or pride. 10. Changing rules, policies, regulations, or laws about behavior or discipline. 11. Changing school management structure or process. 12. Reorganizing grades or classes. 13. Preventing intruders from entering the school. 14. Excluding weapons or contraband. 15. Altering school composition. 16. Changing family supervision or family behavior. ✔ = contains some of this content; X = major focus of program.

[b] With booster in grade 9.

[c] Plus booster sessions.

[d] Plus 2 months transition to the regular population.

Table 6.6. *Evaluations of Middle and Junior High School Programs with Behavioral, Cognitive-Behavioral, and Instructional Content*

Program (Study)	Subjects	Method Rating/ Follow-up (mos.)	Outcomes[a]	
			Correlates of Problem Behavior	Problem Behavior
"The Early (Secondary) Intervention Program" (Bry and George, 1979)	40 high-risk boys and girls in 2 schools	5/0	Grade point total: School A (+); School B (7th grade: −/8th grade: 0)	Attendance: School A (+); School B (7th grade: 0/8th grade: +) Tardiness: School A (0); School B (0) Discipline referrals: School A (+ nr); School B (0)
"The Early (Secondary) Intervention Program" (Bry and George, 1980)	30 high-risk boys and girls in 1 school	4/0	Grade-point total (+)	Attendance (+) Tardiness (0) Discipline referrals (0)
"The Early (Secondary) Intervention Program" (Bry, 1982)[b]	66 high-risk boys and girls	4/60	18-month follow-up: Unemployment (+)	12-month follow-up: School-based problems (+) (includes suspensions, absenteeism, school failure, and tardiness) 18-month follow-up: *Self-reported drug, marijuana, and alcohol abuse (0)* **Self-reported criminal behavior (0)** 60-month follow-up: **Court records (+)** **Drug-related court records (0)**

187

Table 6.6. *(cont.)*

| Program (Study) | Subjects | Method Rating/ Follow-up (mos.) | Outcomes[a] | |
			Correlates of Problem Behavior	Problem Behavior
"Preparation Through Responsive Educational Programs (PREP)" (Filipczak and Wodarski, 1982; Wodarski and Filipczak, 1982)	60 boys and girls with academic and social problems	4/48	Immediate follow-up: Reading comprehension and language skills (+) Vocabulary development (−) Mathematics computation and application (+) Class grades (+) Four-year follow-up: Difference between aspirations and expectations (0)	Immediate follow-up: Number of disciplinary referrals (+) School suspensions (0) School attendance (0) One-year follow-up: School suspensions (+) School attendance (+) Four-year follow-up: **2 of 33 measures of juvenile problem behavior (+)**
"Contingency Management Program for Disruptive Adolescents" (Heaton, Safer, and Allen, 1982; Safer, Heaton, and Parker, 1982)	87 disruptive boys and girls from 2 cohorts	2/48	Immediate follow-up: Percentage receiving passing grades (+) Four-year follow-up: Entry into high school (+) High school grades (0) High school graduates (0)	Immediate follow-up: Absence rates (0) Expulsions (+) Behavioral suspensions (+) Days out of school for discipline reasons (+) Four-year follow-up: Attendance during high school (+) Daily office visits (0) Daily suspension rate (0) High school classroom conduct ratings (+) **Recidivism (0)**

Program (citation)	N	Ratio	Mediating variables	Outcomes
"Behavior Modification and Parent Training" (Patterson, 1974)	28 boys	3/6		Immediate and 6-month follow-ups: Proportion of appropriate classroom behavior (+)
"Anger Control Training" (Feindler, Marriott, and Iwata, 1984)	36 high-risk boys	4/1	Teacher-rated self-control (+) Means-ends problem solving (+)	Mild aggressive behavior (+) Severe aggressive behavior (0)
"Think First" (Larson, 1992)	37 high-risk boys and girls	2/1		Referrals for school misconduct (+) Self-reports of anger, aggression, and antisocial behavior (0) Teacher reports of aggressive classroom behavior (0)
"Positive Youth Development" (Caplan, Weissberg, Grober, Sivo, Grady, and Jacoby, 1992)	282 boys and girls	4/0	Problem-solving ability (+) Stress management (+) Teacher ratings of conflict resolution with peers, impulse control, and popularity (+) Intentions to use drugs (mixed) Attitudes toward substance use (mixed)	Self-reports of behavioral conduct (0) *Substance use frequency (0)* *Excessive alcohol use (+)*
"Positive Youth Development" (Weissberg and Caplan, 1994)	421 boys and girls	4/0	Problem-solving skills and solutions (+) Positive involvement with peers (+) Attachment to prosocial peers (0)	Ratings of behavioral conduct by teachers (+) Ratings of behavioral conduct by peers (0) *Use of gateway substances (0)* **Minor delinquent behavior (+)**

Table 6.6. (*cont.*)

Program (Study)	Subjects	Method Rating/ Follow-up (mos.)	Correlates of Problem Behavior	Problem Behavior
				Outcomes[a]
			Ratings of social acceptance by teachers (primary: 0) (secondary: +)	
			Ratings of social acceptance by peers (0)	
"Moral Reasoning Development and Decision Making Intervention" (Arbuthnot and Gordon, 1986; Arbuthnot, 1992)	48 high-risk boys and girls	4/12	Immediate follow-up: Grade-point average in English, humanities, and social sciences (+)	Immediate follow-up: Behavior referrals to the school office (+)
			Grade-point average in math, physical sciences, and non-academic classes (0)	Teacher evaluations of student behavior (0)
			Sociomoral reasoning (+)	Tardiness (+)
				Absenteeism (0)
				Recorded contact with the police or juvenile courts (+)
			12-month follow-up: Grade-point average in English, humanities, and social sciences (+)	12-month follow-up: Behavior referrals to the school office (+)
			Sociomoral reasoning (+)	Teacher evaluations of student behavior (0)
				Tardiness (+)
				Absenteeism (+)
				Recorded contact with the police or juvenile courts (0)

Study	N			
"Gang Resistance Education and Training (GREAT)" (Esbensen and Osgood, 1996)	5,836 boys and girls in 315 classes in 42 schools	2/12	Commitment to school (+) Peer influence (mostly +) Safe school environment (0) Impulsivity (+) Risk seeking (0) Parental attachment (+) Attitudes favorable to police (+) Attitudes unfavorable to gangs (+) Belief in laws/rules (mixed)	Gang membership (0) *Drug use* (+) **Total self-reported delinquency (+)**
"The Youth Development Project" (Reckless and Dinitz, 1972; Dinitz, 1982)	1,094 high-risk boys	4/36	Grades (0) Attitudes about school variables (0) Attitudes about the law variables (0)	School dropout (0) Attendance (0) **Number of boys experiencing police contact (0)** **Frequency of police contact (0)**

Notes: Follow-up period begins at end of intervention. The number of subjects is the maximum number present for any of the analyses reported in the table.

Substance abuse prevention curricula are excluded from this table.

[a]Key for study outcomes: 0 = no significant effect; + = significant positive effect (p < .05); − = significant negative effect (p < .05); nr = two-tailed significance level not reported. Outcomes for substance use and for crime and delinquency measures appear in italics and in bold, respectively.

[b]Follow-up of both earlier study populations.

studies. In each of the initial studies, students' tardiness, class preparedness, class performance, classroom behavior, school attendance, and disciplinary referrals were monitored weekly for two years. Students met with
program staff weekly and earned points contingent on their behavior that
could be used for a class trip of the students' choosing. Frequent parent
notification was used. In the first study of students in two suburban schools
(Bry and George, 1979; methods rating = 5), experimental students in one
of the two schools had significantly better grades and attendance at the end
of the program than did controls. In the replication study involving an
urban school, experimental students received significantly better grades
and had better attendance, but the positive effects did not appear until
the students had been in the program for two years (Bry and George,
1980; methods rating = 4). Bry (1982; methods rating = 4) reports that in
the year after the intervention ended, experimental students displayed
significantly fewer problem behaviors at school than did controls and
significantly less substance abuse and criminal behavior. These differences
were marginally significant (p < .10) in this underpowered study. Five years
after the program ended, experimental youth were 66% less likely to have
a juvenile record than were controls.

A different behavioral intervention was tested by Filipczak and Wodarski
(1982). The program – Preparation through Responsive Educational
Programs, or PREP – served disruptive and alienated students in grades 7
and 8. The program lasted five years, but each student participated for one
year only (except in one site in which the students participated for two
consecutive years). Between sixteen and twenty-four high-risk students
came to a "skills center" daily during their English and math periods for
academic and social skills training. The academic training mostly relied on
self-instructional materials and was individually paced. The topics covered
in the social skills training included appropriate verbal and nonverbal
behavior, small-group interaction and leadership, personal behavior management, test taking, and instruction following. Family processes, career
preparation, practical skills, and teenagers' rights and responsibilities were
also covered. A family skills training component also provided training to
parents in family management skills and encouraged increased involvement of parents in the school. The content of this component varied year
to year, and it is not clear how many of the students' parents were involved.
Contingency management was used across all program components. Students were rewarded systematically for successful academic work and behavior throughout the day. Activity, food, material, and social reinforcers were
provided. Many students were evaluated daily by their regular teachers.
These daily evaluations formed the basis for routine feedback to parents
and contingent rewards for students.

Wodarski and Filipczak (1982; methods rating = 4) report on the long-
term follow-up results for a group of suburban school children served

during the first year of the program. Students in this trial (n = 60) were randomly assigned to receive one year of the program or to serve as no-treatment controls. Comparisons of the two groups at the end of the treatment year showed a clear benefit on several indicators of academic performance for the treatment group. No differences were observed on school attendance. The treatment group had significantly fewer disciplinary referrals, but the number of suspensions did not differ. A comparison of school records for the two groups one year following the end of the treatment showed that the treatment group had attended school more days and had fewer suspensions and disciplinary referrals than the control group. A four-year follow-up showed that these early gains were not maintained. Of thirty-three self-report delinquent behavior items, only two differentiated the groups. The experimental students reported that they had participated in fewer gang fights and attempted to avoid trouble significantly more than the controls, but several other measures (including police detention, arrests, probation, time served in correctional institutions, and several types of delinquent activities) were similar for the two groups.

These studies of targeted behavior modification for disruptive students demonstrate that these techniques are effective for improving problem behavior in the short run. Effects on problem behavior were maintained on some measures after five years in the Bry study, and after one year in PREP and the Patterson study (see Table 6.6). Effects on delinquency were not observed at the four-year follow-up point for either of two programs that segregated high-risk students for treatment. It is possible that some of the potential benefits of behavioral interventions are lost when they are used in the context of a program that groups high-risk youths together for long periods of time.

Cognitive-Behavioral/Instructional Interventions

Schools are designed to provide instruction, usually in classroom settings. Most school-based prevention programs involve some form of classroom instruction, and this type of program has received the most research attention. During the past two decades we have seen an explosion of classroom-based prevention curricula – first for substance abuse prevention and more recently for violence prevention. Several reviews and meta-analyses of drug prevention curricula have been published recently. This section summarizes these existing reviews of drug prevention curricula, updating as necessary and providing some examples. Fewer studies of violence prevention and other types of delinquency prevention curricula are available. These individual studies are summarized here.

Substance Abuse Prevention Curricula. Several meta-analyses and reviews of the effectiveness of school-based drug prevention instruction have been conducted (Botvin, 1990; Botvin et al., 1995; Center for Substance Abuse Prevention, 1995; Dryfoos, 1990; Durlak, 1995; Hansen, 1992; Hawkins et al., 1995; Institute of Medicine, 1994; Tobler, 1986, 1992; Tobler and Stratton, 1997). Tobler (1986) meta-analyzed 143 drug prevention programs. A subsequent reanalysis included a subset of 91 of these studies, corrected to include only one effect size per study. These meta-analyses found "peer" programs (a broad category of programs aimed at reducing susceptibility to negative peer influence, often involving peer teaching, peer counseling, and other forms of peer participation and including training in refusal, social, and life skills) were by far the most effective for reducing drug use (ES = .40). But the broad "alternatives" category also showed small to moderate effects on reducing drug use (ES = .22).

Botvin (1990) traced the historical development of substance abuse prevention programs. He showed that "information dissemination" approaches that teach primarily about drugs and their effects, "fear arousal" approaches that emphasize the risks associated with tobacco, alcohol, or drug use, "moral appeal" approaches that teach students about the evils of use, and "affective education" programs that focus on building self-esteem, responsible decision making, and interpersonal growth are *largely ineffective* for reducing substance use. On the contrary, approaches that include resistance skills training to teach students about social influences to engage in substance use and specific skills for effectively resisting these pressures alone or in combination with broader-based life skills training do reduce substance use. Components of social resistance skills instruction include:

Increasing student awareness of the social influences promoting substance use.
Teaching skills for resisting social influences from peers and the media.
Correcting normative expectations concerning the use of substances.

Additional skills targeted in life skills instruction include:

Problem solving and decision making.
Self-control or self-esteem.
Adaptive coping strategies for relieving stress or anxiety.
Interpersonal skills.
Assertiveness.

Curricula that focus on general life skills are typically longer than those which focus only on social resistance skills.

Subsequent reviews have not disagreed with Botvin's conclusions. Hansen (1992) meta-analyzed studies of school-based substance abuse prevention curricula published between 1980 and 1990. He categorized program content into more detailed categories than had been used in previous reviews and took account of several methodological variables (e.g., selection bias and statistical power) that varied across studies. The review found that social influence programs (e.g., those focusing on resistance skill training and often including norm-setting activities and pledges to remain drug-free) and comprehensive programs (e.g., those similar to the broadest social influence programs but also targeting other skills, such as more general decision-making skills) were most successful for reducing substance abuse.

More recently, the National Structured Evaluation (NSE; Center for Substance Abuse Prevention, 1995), a major study of the effectiveness of prevention activities, examined hundreds of different alcohol and substance abuse prevention programs in operation during or after 1986. The study examined published and unpublished reports of drug prevention programs including but not limited to school-based programs. Program modules were grouped into seven different prevention approaches representing distinct combinations of activities. The most effective approach for reducing alcohol and other drug use was the psychosocial skills approach, which included personal skill development or task-oriented skill training and *no* emphasis on providing information about drugs. The least effective approaches were counseling (including individual and family counseling and didactic information about drugs) and health and safety education (which often included some personal skills development along with didactic drug information and safety education). The "multidirectional" approach, which often combined personal skills development with didactic and drug-free alternative activities, was among the least effective. Only when drug-free activities or wilderness challenge experience programs appeared as a secondary component in programs primarily aimed at psychosocial skill development were they effective for reducing drug use and related risk and protective factors.

The most recent meta-analysis of school-based drug prevention programs (Tobler and Stratton, 1997) examined 120 published and unpublished studies of school-based drug prevention programs appearing between 1978 and 1990. Only programs available to the entire student body and targeting grades 6 through 12 were included, thereby omitting programs targeting only high-risk youths. More refined meta-analysis strategies were used to control for methodological differences across studies. The main conclusion of the study was that "interactive" programs (e.g., those affording much opportunity for interaction among the adolescents) were more effective than "noninteractive" programs (e.g., didactic presentations). This analysis showed that program content categories (e.g., social influence, information only, affective) are correlated with mode of delivery (interactive vs. noninteractive) and suggested that some of the positive effect previously attributed to program content may in fact be due to the delivery method. Multivariate analyses, however, showed that content focusing on interpersonal competence was a necessary factor in the success of drug prevention curricula. Programs including interactive delivery methods but focusing on such intrapersonal factors as self-esteem or personal values were ineffective.

The results of these reviews and meta-analyses are easily understood in terms of the content categories used in the present review. The literature suggests that effective substance abuse prevention programs contain (a) substantive content related to social competency skills (one category of content contained under the instructional category in our classification), and (b) use cognitive-behavioral or behavioral modeling methods of instruction (e.g., the methods contained in the "cognitive-behavioral" category of our classification). What Tobler names "interactive" programs are programs that make use of methods such as behavioral models (peers or videotapes) to demonstrate new skills, role playing, rehearsal, and practice. Programs using these methods rely less on lecture and individual seat work and appear more interactive. Tobler's terminology, although accurate, neglects to highlight the more important aspect of the approach: its reliance on psychological learning principles. One might imagine an "interactive" teaching method that relies on unstructured brainstorming and group discussion. The research does not suggest that such a method would be effective. Rather, it suggests that modeling behaviors, providing opportunity for practice of behaviors, giving specific and frequent feedback about new behaviors, providing cues to prompt the behavior, and using techniques to generalize the new behavior to different settings, will work. Programs that use these techniques tend also to be interactive.

Using the data base compiled for the present review, one can identify instructional programs that vary on these dimensions. Instructional programs low on social competency content are relatively rare. Almost all programs that use cognitive-behavioral teaching methods also contain social competency content. A few programs, however, are *low on both social competency content and cognitive-behavioral teaching methods*. One example is provided by Stuart (1974; methods rating = 4) who randomly assigned junior high school students to an experimental drug education course or a control group. The experimental group received ten sessions of fact-oriented drug education. The method included lectures by teachers and presentations by students designed to communicate facts about the physiology and pharmacology of drug use and its legal, social, and psychological ramifications. The study showed that the intervention *increased* drug use among the treatment students. Sarvela and McClendon (1987; methods rating = 3) compared an information-only curriculum to an experimental one that included drug information as well as "affective" education. The affective lessons included lectures and discussions about different life-styles, values, alternatives to drug use, and decision making. The main emphasis was on values clarification. The youths exposed to this experimental curriculum (which was delivered primarily lecture-style with discussions) also *used alcohol more* at the end of the program than the control group did. No other significant program effects were observed.

Instructional programs with *social competency content but lacking cognitive-behavioral teaching methods* are common. One example is the popular DARE program (Drug Abuse Resistance Education).[5] Although the program includes several different components, the seventeen-lesson core curriculum delivered to students in grade 5 or 6 has always been the most frequently used form of the program (Ringwalt et al., 1994).

The core DARE program is taught by a uniformed law enforcement officer. The original core curriculum focuses on teaching pupils the skills needed to recognize and resist social pressures to use drugs. It also contains lessons about drugs and their consequences, decision-making skills, self-esteem, and alternatives to drugs. Teaching techniques include lectures, group discussions, question-and-answer sessions, audiovisual materials, workbook exercises, and role playing. The curriculum was revised in 1993 to substitute a lesson on conflict resolution and anger management skills for one on building support systems and to add more interactive teaching methods.

Several evaluations of the original seventeen-lesson core have been conducted. Many of these are summarized in a meta-analysis of DARE's short-term effects (Ringwalt et al., 1994). This study located eighteen evaluations of DARE's core curriculum, of which eight met the methodological criterion standards for inclusion in the study. The study found that the short-term effects on drug use are, except for tobacco use, nonsignificant; the sizes of the effects on drug use are slight (effect sizes average .06 for drug use and never exceed .11 in any study); and certain other programs targeting the same age group as DARE – upper elementary pupils – are more effective than DARE. The report reiterated Tobler's finding that more "interactive" programs than DARE generally achieve larger effects on drug use measures. More recent studies have verified that the program registers no effect on measures of cigarette, alcohol, or marijuana use either during grade 7 or at any later point.

A few instructional programs are on the top of the distribution of both *social competency content* and *cognitive-behavioral teaching methods*. One of these is Life Skills Training (LST; Botvin, Baker, Botvin, Filazzola, and Millman, 1984; Botvin, Baker, Renick, Filazzola, and Botvin, 1984; Botvin, Batson et al., 1989; Botvin and Eng, 1982). LST is a comprehensive program focusing on resistance skills training as well as the general life skills mentioned earlier, and incorporating a significant amount of

---

[5] Interested readers are referred to D. Gottfredson (1997) for a more detailed summary of the DARE program and its research.

cognitive-behavioral teaching methods. This program consists of sixteen sessions delivered to students in grade 7 followed by eight session "boosters" in grades 8 and 9.

LST has also undergone rigorous tests in an ongoing series of studies first published in 1980, conducted by Botvin and his colleagues. The more recent studies examined the effect of the program on alcohol and marijuana use (in addition to cigarette use) and tracked long-term program effects. Botvin, Baker, Renick, et al. (1984; methods rating = 4) examined the effectiveness of a twenty-session course delivered to seventh graders from ten suburban New York junior high schools. The subjects were primarily white, from middle-class families. Schools were randomly assigned to receive the program as implemented by older students, by regular classroom teachers, or to serve as controls. All analyses were reported using individuals as the unit of analysis. Results measured immediately after the program showed that program students compared with control students were significantly less likely to report using marijuana and engage in excessive drinking, but these positive effects were found only for the peer-led condition. Botvin, Baker, Filazzola, and Botvin (1990; methods rating = 4) reported on the one-year follow-up of this study, which contrasted not only the teacher- and peer-led conditions but also the presence or absence of a ten-session booster course delivered during grade 8. The effects of the program diminished without the booster. In the peer-led condition with the booster session, significant effects were maintained at the end of grade 8 on the amount of alcohol and marijuana use. Again, positive effects were found only for the peer-led condition.

In a larger study involving fifty-six public schools, the same twenty-session program in grade 7, ten-session booster session in grade 8, and an additional five-session booster in grade 9 was studied for long-term effects on substance use at grade 12 (Botvin, Baker, Dusenbury, Botvin, and Diaz, 1995; methods rating = 5). In this study, the fifty-six schools (serving mainly white, middle-class populations) were stratified according to base-line levels of cigarette smoking and geographic location and randomly assigned to experimental conditions. All results were reported using individual students as the level of analysis. This study involved only teacher-led classrooms. The grade 12 results for the full sample of 3,597 subjects revealed significant positive effects on the prevalence of drunkenness but not for other measures of alcohol use. Significant effects were not reported for marijuana use, although the effect size for the prevalence of weekly marijuana use is about as large as the effect sizes for the significant effects on excessive drinking. The lower base rate for marijuana use reduces the likelihood of finding statistically significant results for this outcome. When only subjects who received a reasonably complete version of the program were examined, the results were more positive. Additional research (Botvin, Batson et al., 1989; Botvin, Dusenbury, James-Ortiz, and Kerner,

1989) showed that the positive effects generalize to African American and Hispanic American populations.

Another important aspect of instructional drug prevention programs seems to be a focus on *normative change*. We saw in the previous chapter that environmental-change strategies focusing on normative change are generally successful at reducing problem behavior. The research on instructional substance abuse prevention programs provides additional support for the importance of norm-setting activities. Instructional programs can contribute to broader normative change in two ways: they can include specific content aimed at establishing conservative norms regarding use, and they can be delivered to all students in a cohort to increase the likelihood of changing peer norms.

Curricula that promote norms against drug use often portray drug use as socially unacceptable, identify short-term negative consequences of drug use, provide evidence that drug use is less prevalent among peers than children think, encourage children to make public commitments to remain drug-free, and use peer leaders to teach the curriculum (Institute of Medicine, 1994, p. 264). These activities are present in 29% of drug prevention curricula (Hansen, 1992) but always in conjunction with other components such as conveying information about risks related to drug use and resistance skills training. Norm setting and public pledges to remain drug-free are usually elements of the most effective drug education curricula, but meta-analyses have not been able to disentangle the effects of the various components. In a study designed to do just that, Hansen and Graham (1991; methods rating = 4) found that positive effects on marijuana use and alcohol use were attributable more to a normative education than to a resistance skills training component.

Instructional Programs Not Specific to Substance Use. The Law-Related Education program, which attempts to reduce delinquency by teaching students about the law and good citizenship, is discussed in Chapter 5 because it involves changes to the way classrooms are organized and managed.[6] Features of the remaining six[7] instructional programs not

---

[6] To summarize, evaluations of this curriculum showed that as typically implemented, the program does not reduce delinquency. When embedded in a broader program to improve the classroom environment, the program reduces delinquency. It is not possible to determine from the existing studies whether the content of the LRE instruction contributes to the positive findings.

[7] A seventh program, PACT, evaluated by Hammond and Yung (1991) emphasized important interpersonal competency skills, provided incentives for active participation, and was specifically tailored for African American youths. The program appears promising but the weak evaluation design limits confidence in any conclusions that might be drawn about its effectiveness. Also, an evaluation of the Washington (D.C.) Community Violence Prevention Program (Gainer, Webster, and Champion, 1993) has also been published, but effects on problem behavior were not assessed. Effects on social problem-solving skills and attitudes about violence were mixed. This program targeted students in grades 5 and 7.

specific to substance use are shown in Table 6.6. Two are violence prevention programs, one is a gang prevention program, one focuses on moral reasoning, one on self-esteem, and one is a general social competency development program. Each targets on middle or junior high school population, but one is designed for high-school-age students as well. Like the substance abuse prevention curricula, these programs can be ordered along the two potentially important features of social competency skill development content and use of cognitive-behavioral methods. The violence prevention curricula, which we discuss first, are relatively high on both dimensions. Table 6.6 shows the characteristics of the eleven studies of these programs. These instructional programs are designed to improve students' social, problem-solving, and anger management skills; promote beliefs favorable to nonviolence; and increase knowledge about conflict and violence. Only one of these studies is methodologically strong.

Feindler, Marriott, and Iwata (1984; methods rating = 4) studied an anger control training program delivered to junior high school boys who were participating in an existing program for disruptive youths. These students had been suspended for offenses other than smoking or truancy at least twice during the previous year. The thirty-six most disruptive of these youths were selected and randomly assigned to receive anger management training or not. The program consisted of ten fifty-minute sessions delivered by a trained therapist over a fairly brief (seven-week) period. The sessions taught (in small groups of six youths) both behavioral and cognitive controls. The social competency skill content in this program was among the highest of any program reviewed in this book. Students were taught to analyze the components of the provocation cycle – the antecedent anger cues, aggressive responses, and consequent events – using self-monitoring and written logs. They learned to impose their own time-out responses and to relax themselves. They learned to replace aggressive responses (e.g., threatening gestures, harsh tones) with appropriate assertive verbal and nonverbal responses. They learned specific cognitive behaviors, including self-instructions (e.g., thinking, "I'm going to ignore this guy and keep cool"), reinterpretation of potentially aggression-eliciting situations, self-evaluation during conflict situations (e.g., thinking "how did I handle myself?"), and thinking ahead. They also learned a sequence of problem-solving steps to take in difficult situations instead of reacting impulsively. The therapist relied almost entirely on behavioral modeling, role playing, rehearsal, cues, and other cognitive-behavioral strategies to teach the new skills. Participants also received immediate reinforcers (e.g., snacks, activities) for participation.

The experimental students improved more than controls on an interview measure of problem-solving skills and on teacher ratings of self-control. Daily records of "fines" for misbehavior (a measure both of the student behavior and the staff's recording practices) were collected for six weeks prior to, seven weeks during, and five weeks following the intervention. They showed a significant positive treatment effect on the more frequent category of fines for mild verbal and physical misbehaviors such as cursing, arguing, shoving, and throwing small objects. For more serious infractions, the trend favored the treatment subjects but the differences were not statistically significant, perhaps due to the relative infrequency of these behaviors, the short duration of the experiment, and the small number of subjects.

Other prevention curricula focus less on violent behavior per se and are therefore more appropriate for use with general middle and junior high school populations (as opposed to youth at high risk for aggressive behavior). Weissberg's social competence promotion program, for example, covers the entire array of social competency skills without tying them directly to any specific problem behavior. Problem-specific modules aimed at preventing antisocial and aggressive behavior, substance abuse, and high-risk sexual behavior are available. The program ranges in length from sixteen to twenty-nine sessions, depending on the version. This program is an extension upward of the elementary school curricula ranging from forty-two to fifty-two sessions (also developed by Weissberg) discussed earlier, so its content is not described again. Note that the social competency content found in this curriculum is comparable (in terms of the number of different skills covered) with the violence prevention programs just described, and the reliance on cognitive-behavioral teaching methods is considerable, although not quite as high as is possible in small group training interventions.

Caplan et al. (1992; methods rating = 4) studied the effect of a twenty-session version of the "Positive Youth Development" program on 282 sixth and seventh graders in an inner-city and a suburban middle school in Connecticut. Classrooms were randomly assigned to receive the program or not. Results were reported using individuals as the unit of analysis. Students in program classes improved relative to students in the control classrooms on measures of problem-solving ability and stress management. Teacher ratings of the participating students improved relative to the controls on measures of conflict resolution with peers and impulse control, both important protective factors for later delinquency, and popularity. Students' self-reports of their behavioral conduct were not affected by the program, and effects on self-reports of intentions to drink alcohol and use drugs were mixed. No significant difference was found for a self-report measure of frequency of cigarette, alcohol, and marijuana use, but program students reported significantly less excessive drinking than controls. The program was equally effective for students in the inner-city and the suburban schools.

In another study involving 421 students from twenty classes in four urban, multiethnic schools, Weissberg and Caplan (1994; methods rating

= 4) evaluated a similar sixteen-session social competence promotion program for students in grade 5 through 8. This version of the program did not include lessons on substance use. Random assignment to treatment and control conditions was not accomplished in this study. Program students improved more than controls on problem-solving abilities and prosocial attitudes toward conflict resolution. Teacher ratings indicated that the training improved impulse control, problem solving, and academic motivation and decreased teasing of peers, important risk and protective factors for later delinquency. Self-reported delinquency of a relatively minor form (stealing, starting fights, vandalism, skipping school, etc.) also increased less for the program participants (2.8% increase) than for comparison students (36.8% increase) between the beginning and the end of the program. No significant effects were observed for self-reports of substance abuse in this study. Weissberg and Greenberg (1997) summarize another study that shows that the positive effects of the program are maintained in the year after the program only when the training is continued into the second year.

Arbuthnot and Gordon (1986) and Arbuthnot (1992; both methods rating = 4) tested an intervention aimed at accelerating moral reasoning development in boys and girls (mostly in grades 8 and 9) who had been nominated by their teachers as behaviorally disordered. The intervention consisted of small discussion groups (size ranging from five to eight students) held weekly for one class period for sixteen to twenty weeks. Researchers led the groups. Most of the discussions were "guided moral dilemma" discussions. Role playing of moral dilemmas was also used. Moral reasoning and perspective taking were the main foci of the discussions, although a couple of sessions were spent developing specific listening and communication skills deemed necessary for effective discussion. Problem-solving skills (generation of alternatives, consideration of consequences, choice, and action) were practiced throughout the intervention, and consideration of the rights, perspectives, and obligations of the characters involved in the dilemmas was encouraged. The program contained content related to the development of social competency skills and used cognitive-behavioral methods such as behavioral modeling and role playing.

Subjects (n = 48) were randomly assigned to treatment and control groups. Treatment subjects' moral reasoning improved significantly (relative to control subjects) during the intervention. Official measures on misconduct and delinquency (office referrals and police contacts) also improved for the treatment subjects. Teacher evaluations of student misbehavior were not affected by the treatment. Grades in some classes and a measure of tardiness (but not absenteeism) also improved significantly during the period for the treatment subjects relative to those measures for the controls. Twelve months following the end of the treatment, positive effects on moral reasoning, certain grades, tardiness and absenteeism, and disciplinary referrals were still evident, although the police contact data converged for the two groups. The study was weakened, however, by severe attrition. Fewer than half of the subjects were measured at the one-year follow-up, and there was a considerable problem with missing data at both the pretest and the measurement immediately following the treatment.

In contrast to the instructional curricula just described are two programs that incorporate little or no material on social competency development, and which do not make use of the cognitive-behavioral teaching strategies. Gang Resistance Education and Training (GREAT), another popular violence prevention curriculum, falls in this category. A preliminary evaluation of the program (Esbensen and Osgood, 1996; methods rating = 2) found several statistically significant associations between a measure of participation in the program, delinquency, drug use, and several correlates of these problem behaviors. But the effect sizes for the significant delinquency and drug use outcomes were all less than .10 (e.g., the difference between the participants and nonparticipants on outcome measures is less than one-tenth of one standard deviation), suggesting that even if the effects can be safely attributed to the program, they are small. Also, the broad range of outcomes for which significant effects were found seems inconsistent with the relative brevity of the program. More definitive results can be expected from the more rigorous evaluation design currently being implemented. In the meantime, the program is being revised to incorporate content and methods more consistent with what research has demonstrated effective.

Reckless and Dinitz (1972) and Dinitz (1982; both methods rating = 4) reported on a major school-based delinquency prevention intervention implemented in the Columbus, Ohio, schools between 1963 and 1966. This program was based on a self-esteem theory of delinquency prevention – that delinquent behavior is a result of stigmatizing experiences that cause youngsters to think of themselves as "worthless, unproductive, unimportant, nameless and faceless, and without much future" (Dinitz, 1982, p. 280). A year-long self-contained class was developed for delinquency-prone boys to try to reverse this stigmatizing process. For three years, boys rated as vulnerable to delinquency by their sixth grade teachers were randomly assigned to an all-male experimental or to a regular seventh grade class. A total of 1,094 vulnerable boys were randomly assigned during the three-year period. The experimental class was taught by male teachers specially selected to approximate the role of a significant other in the boys' lives. In addition to the regular curriculum, the experimental class received a "role model supplement." In this supplement, the following five topics were covered: The World of Work; The School and You; The House We Live In (a presentation of government services); Getting Along with Others; and The Family. Role models were presented in each segment.

In addition, a nonstigmatizing method of classroom discipline was used. Misbehaving boys were never sent to the office but instead were asked to sit apart from the class until they felt ready to rejoin the class. Remedial reading strategies were also employed in the class. Finally, during the third year of the program, the teachers made home calls to the families of the participating boys.

Volumes of data were collected on the experimental and control boys' delinquent behavior, attitudes toward school, academic performance, educational attainment, interpersonal competence, and self-concepts before the beginning of the class, during the class, and for three years following the class. The results can be summarized succinctly: "On none of the outcome variables were the experimental subjects significantly different from the controls" (Dinitz, 1982, p. 288). This rigorous study supports the definitive conclusion that grouping high-risk boys together for a year in a class in which little emphasis is placed on social competency skill development, and a deliberate attempt is made to make boys feel good about themselves, neither reduces their level of risk for problem behavior nor their actual problem behavior.

Summary of Cognitive-Behavioral Instructional Programs. Certain instructional programs designed to reduce problem behavior have produced consistent evidence of positive effects in rigorous studies, and others have consistently shown no effects. Among programs specifically targeting substance abuse prevention, "information dissemination" instructional programs that teach primarily about drugs and their effects, "fear arousal" approaches that emphasize the risks associated with tobacco, alcohol, or drug use, "moral appeal" approaches that teach students about the evils of use, and "affective education" programs that focus on building self-esteem, responsible decision making, and interpersonal growth are *largely ineffective* for reducing substance use.

Approaches that include resistance skills training to teach students about social influences to engage in substance use and specific skills for effectively resisting these pressures alone or in combination with broader-based life skills training do reduce substance use. But the effects of even these programs are small and short-lived in the absence of continued instruction. Hansen and O'Malley (1996) report average effect sizes for social influence training programs ranging from .14 to .27 (on alcohol, marijuana, and cigarette use), but Gorman (1995) shows these programs have little or no effect on drinking behavior. More comprehensive programs such as LST and Weissberg's Positive Youth Development programs have effect sizes ranging from .08 to .37.

More comprehensive social competency promotion programs work better than programs that do not focus on social competencies or focus more narrowly on resistance skill training. Also, the more extensive the reliance on cognitive-behavioral training methods such as feedback, reinforcement, and behavioral rehearsal rather than traditional lecture and discussion, the more effective the program.

Programs that focus on violence prevention per se have not been rigorously evaluated. Some of these programs have a high level of social competency skill development content. Many also use the same cognitive-behavioral strategies used in the most effective substance abuse programs summarized earlier. These programs seem plausible, and some positive effects have been observed on the social competencies directly targeted (e.g., self-control and problem-solving skills) and on measures of problem behavior. But the results are mixed – probably more because the studies of these programs have not been rigorous and have been based on particularly small numbers of cases. More definitive results should emerge from several ongoing evaluations.

Several instructional programs adopt a more general approach to prevention. They focus not on a specific type of problem behavior but directly on the intermediate factor thought to lead to a variety of problem behaviors. Weissberg's Positive Youth Development, Arbuthnot's moral reasoning, and Dinitz's self-concept programs fall into this category. Evaluations of these programs quite clearly show that the programs do reduce delinquency and substance use *when they incorporate an emphasis on social competency development and use cognitive-behavioral teaching methods.*

Counseling and Mentoring

Tables 6.7 and 6.8 show the characteristics and evaluation results from twelve studies of counseling, mentoring, recreation, and other "alternatives" to delinquency. These tables also include an example of a broad, multicomponent program. The studies of individual and peer group counseling and the provision of other individualized attention to individuals are summarized next. In this discussion, counseling is distinguished from mentoring, because mentoring is generally provided by a lay person rather than a trained counselor and is not necessarily guided by a structured approach.

Many studies have examined the effect of counseling interventions on delinquency. Lipsey's (1992) meta-analysis of juvenile delinquency treatment effects shows that, for juvenile justice and nonjuvenile justice interventions alike, counseling interventions are among the least effective for reducing delinquency. Twenty-four studies of individual counseling in nonjuvenile justice settings yielded an effect size of −.01 on measures of recidivism.

Four studies of school-based counseling were located. The most rigorous of these (Gottfredson, 1986; methods rating = 5) examined effects on delinquent behavior of a program of services provided to high-risk students in middle and high school. Students' behavioral and academic problems

Table 6.7. *Middle and Junior High School Programs with Counseling, Mentoring, Recreation, and Other Alternatives Content*

Program (Study)	Grades Targeted	Program Content[a]																Duration of Program
		1	2	3	4	5	6	7	8	9	10	11	12	13	14	15	16	
"Social Workers in Schools" (Rose and Marshall, 1974)	Secondary school				X			✓										Up to 3 school years
"Positive Action Through Holistic Education (PATHE)" (Gottfredson, 1986)	6–12			✓	X	X												2 school years
"Peer Culture Development" (G. Gottfredson, 1987b)	6–12				X													15 weeks
"Rational Behavior Therapy" (Zelie et al., 1980)	7–9		X		X			✓			✓							One session
"Across Ages Mentoring" (LoSciuto et al., 1996)	6	X	✓				✓										✓	1 school year
"RAISE" (McPartland and Nettles, 1991)	6–8	✓				X	✓											Up to 6 years
"Kansas City Work/Study Experiment" (Ahlstrom and Havighurst, 1971, 1982)	8–12	✓				X		✓					✓					Up to 5 years
"Cross Age Tutoring/School Store" (Malvin et al., 1985)	8–9	✓					X											1–2 semesters

Program	Grades		Duration
"Teen Outreach" (Allen et al., 1990)	7–12	X ✔	1 school year
"Magic Me" (Cronin, 1996)	6–8	X X ✔	1 school year
"Gang Prevention" (Thompson and Jason, 1988)	8	X X ✔ ✔ ✔	3 months
"Multimodel School Based Prevention Demonstration" (Gottfredson et al., 1996)	6–8	X ✔ ✔ ✔ ✔	3 school years

[a] Program content key: 1. Instructing students . 2. Cognitive-behavioral change/behavior modeling. 3. Behavioral or behavior modification. 4. Counseling, social work, other psychological or therapeutic interventions. 5. Tutoring, mentoring, or other individual attention. 6. Recreational, enrichment, and leisure. 7. Changing instructional or classroom management methods or practices management. 8. Changing norms or expectations for behavior. 9. Building a sense of community, morale, caring, support, or pride. 10. Changing rules, policies, regulations, or laws about behavior or discipline. 11. Changing school management structure or process. 12. Reorganizing grades or classes. 13. Preventing intruders from entering the school. 14. Excluding weapons or contraband. 15. Altering school composition. 16. Changing family supervision or family behavior. ✔ = contains some of this content; X = major focus of program.

Table 6.8. *Evaluations of Middle and Junior High School Programs with Counseling, Mentoring, Recreation, and Other Alternatives Content*

Program (Study)	Subjects	Method Rating/ Follow-up (mos.)	Outcomes[a]	
			Correlates of Problem Behavior	Problem Behavior
"Social Workers in Schools" (Rose and Marshall, 1974)	1,644 at-risk boys and girls in 4 schools	2/0		Attendance (– nr) **Persisting delinquency (– nr)** **Initiating delinquency (– nr)**
"Positive Action Through Holistic Education (PATHE)" (Gottfredson, 1986)	869 high-risk boys and girls in 6 schools	5/0	Self-reported grades (+) Grade-point average (0) Standardized achievement test scores (+) Grade promotion (1981–1982: +) (1982–1983: 0) Percent seniors graduated (+) Attachment to school (0) Educational expectations (0)	Percent withdrew from school (0) Suspensions (0) Expulsions (0) Nonattendance (0) *Self-reported drug involvement* (–) **Serious delinquency (0)** **Number of court contacts (0)**
"Peer Culture Development" (G. Gottfredson, 1987b)	360 boys and girls	3/0	Negative peer influence (0) Grade-point average (0) Interpersonal competency (0) Work index (0)	School problems (0) Waywardness (elementary school: 0) (high school: –) Fall tardies (0)

Program	Sample	Ratio			
"Rational Behavior Therapy" (Zelie et al., 1980)	60 boys and girls in 1 school	4/1	Attention to class and homework (+)		Disciplinary referrals (+) Assessment of problem behavior for which the child was referred (+) General classroom behavior (0)
"Across Ages Mentoring" (LoSciuto et al., 1996)	562 boys and girls in 9 classes in 3 schools	3/0	Reactions to situations involving drug use (+) Problem-solving efficacy (0) Reactions to stress (0) Attitudes toward school future and elders (+)	School rewards (0) Attachment to parents (elementary school: 0) (high school: −)	Spring tardies (elementary school: 0) (high school: −) Nonattendance (0) *Delinquent behavior/drug subscale (elementary school: 0) (high school: −)* **Delinquent behavior/serious subscale (0)** **Police contacts (0)** Absences from school (+) *Frequency of substance use (0)*
"RAISE" (McPartland and Nettles, 1991)	7,606 at-risk boys and girls	3/0	Grade-point average (0) Reading/math standardized test (0) Grade retention (0)		Absence rate (+)
"Kansas City Work/Study Experiment" (Ahlstrom and Havighurst, 1971, 1982)	167 socially maladjusted boys	3/0	Adaptive school behavior (cohort 1: − nr) (cohort 2: 0) Adaptive work behavior (+ nr)		Maladaptive school or work behavior (0) **Arrest (0)**

Table 6.8. (*cont.*)

Program (Study)	Subjects	Method Rating/ Follow-up (mos.)	Outcomes[a] Correlates of Problem Behavior	Problem Behavior
"Cross Age Tutoring/ School Store" (Malvin et al., 1985)	88 boys and girls in 1 school	4/12	Grade-point average (mostly 0) Attitudes toward school (0) Drug attitudes (0) Peer drug use (0)	Unexcused absences (0) Nondrug problems (0) *Alcohol and marijuana use (0)*
"Teen Outreach" (Allen et al., 1990)	1,430 boys and girls in 30 schools	3/0	School failure (0)	Pregnancy (+) School dropout (+) Suspension (+)
"Magic Me" (Cronin, 1996)	297 at-risk boys and girls	4/0	Grades (0) Attachment to school (0) Commitment to education (0) Belief in prosocial behavior (0) Attitudes concerning alcohol, tobacco, and other drug use (0) Responsibility (0) Attachment to prosocial adults (0)	Rebellious behavior (0) Truancy (0) *Last-year drug use (−)*

"Gang Prevention" (Thompson and Jason, 1988)	117 youths at-risk for gang membership in 3 schools	2/0	Gang membership (0)	
"Multimodel School Based Prevention Demonstration" (Gottfredson et al., 1996)[b]	1,282 boys and girls in 2 schools	4/0	Association with delinquent peers (0) Grade-point average (+) Commitment to school (0) Attachment to school (0) Belief in rules (0) Alcohol, tobacco, and other drug attitudes (−) Parental supervision (−)	Rebellious behavior (0) In-school suspensions (0) Out-of-school suspensions (0) Conduct disorder (0) *Drug use frequency (0)*

Notes: Follow-up period begins at end of intervention. The number of subjects is the maximum number present for any of the analyses reported in the table.

[a] Key for study outcomes: 0 = no significant effect ($p < .05$); + = significant positive effect ($p < .05$); − = significant negative effect ($p < .05$); nr = two-tailed significance level not reported. Outcomes for substance use and for crime and delinquency measures appear in italics and in bold, respectively.

[b] Results are given for 1994.

were diagnosed, and individual plans were developed by school specialists (either teachers or counselors assigned to work individually with the high-risk students for this project). Counseling and tutoring services were provided consistent with the individual plans, and the specialists also acted as advocates for the students, worked with the students' parents, and tried to involve the students in extracurricular activities to increase bonding to the school. On average, school specialists met twice per month directly with the target students and the students also participated in peer counseling and "rap" sessions with other students. Random assignment of 869 eligible high-risk youths to treatment and control conditions yielded equivalent groups.

After two years of treatment, the targeted youths were significantly better off than the control students on several measures of academic achievement and educational persistence. Treatment students reported receiving higher grades (although this was not born out in the official grade records), they were promoted to the next grade at a higher rate after the first year in the program (ES = .15), graduation rates were higher (ES = .68), and the percentage of students scoring in the bottom quartile of a standardized achievement tests scores was lower (ES = −.19). However, the services did not result in a reduction in delinquency. Gottfredson (1986) examined six indicators of delinquent behavior, including self-reports, school records, and police records. For only one of the measures were significant differences observed. Treatment students reported significantly *more* drug use (ES = −.23). In all, two measures showed no difference, two favored the treatment group (ESs = −.08 and −.14), and two favored the control students (ESs = .02 and .23). The study suggests that even relatively small doses of tutoring led to improvements in academic outcomes. It is probable that the poor showing on the delinquency measures was due to the counseling intervention, which brought high-risk youths together to discuss (and therefore make more salient to others) their poor behavior.

Peer group counseling is popular in schools and is often used in prevention programs for at-risk youths and adjudicated delinquents. This type of counseling usually involves an adult leader guiding group discussions in which participants are encouraged to recognize problems with their own behavior, attitudes, and values. Peer pressure to adopt prosocial attitudes is expected to occur. In an evaluation of the Peer Culture Development (PCD) program implemented in the several Chicago elementary and secondary schools, G. Gottfredson (1987b; methods rating = 3) found no reason for optimism. First Gottfredson reviewed a series of published and unpublished prior evaluations of the PCD program implemented in residential homes and public school settings. Then he reported a new evaluation of the program. His study, which involved random assignment of subjects to experimental conditions, "lends no support to any claim of benefit of treatment, with the possible exception that the treatment may enhance internal control for elementary school students. For the high school students, the effects appear preponderantly harmful" (G. Gottfredson, 1987b, p. 708). Specifically, high school treatment youths reported significantly *more* delinquent behavior, more tardiness to school, less attachment to their parents, and more "waywardness," a scale measuring a constellation of antisocial attitudes, beliefs, and behaviors including rebelliousness, lack of attachment to school, low beliefs in rules, delinquency, and association with delinquent peers. Presumably, these interventions backfire when students are brought into closer association with negative peers during the peer counseling sessions. Gottfredson also notes that frequent discussions of parent-home issues in the groups may have led to a weakening of parental bonding and a subsequent increase in delinquency.

One final study of a counseling intervention (Zelie, Stone, and Lehr, 1980; methods rating = 4) tested a counseling model with cognitive-behavioral content. Sixty students in a junior high school who were referred to the assistant principal's office for behavior problems either received the regular disciplinary treatment (e.g., seeing the assistant principal) or saw a counselor who administered rational behavior therapy to the student prior to his or her visit to the assistant principal. The counseling consisted of an interview with the student emphasizing the following: (1) students have behavioral alternatives at all times; (2) some of these alternatives are in their best interest; and (3) students have the power to choose alternatives and are responsible to do so in their best interest. Short-term effects of this brief intervention were assessed with teacher ratings made two days following the treatment and with subsequent referrals to the office for behavior problems. Teacher assessments of current behavior problems were lower, teacher ratings of attention to school work and home work were higher, and subsequent office referrals were lower for treatment than for control students. Treatment students were referred to the office at about one-third the rate of the control students during the follow-up period. This study shows that even a brief intervention with cognitive-behavioral content can be effective.

The evidence suggests that counseling programs in general are ineffective for reducing problem behavior. Peer counseling interventions for high-risk youths appear harmful. One ray of hope for counseling is found in the Zelie et al. (1980) study, but extended follow-up data collection is needed to see how long the positive effect lasts, and replication is required.

A handful of studies involved individual attention other than counseling. One type of individual attention is mentoring – one-on-one interaction with an older, more experienced person to provide advice or assistance. This type of program has become increasingly popular as a delinquency prevention strategy due to a rigorous study (Tierney,

Grossman, and Resch, 1995) of a highly structured, non-school-based mentoring model. This randomized experiment showed positive effects of the program on initiation of substance use and selected self-reported delinquent behaviors. The U.S. Office of Juvenile Justice and Delinquency Prevention recently invested $19 million in juvenile mentoring programs, as mandated by the U.S. Congress.

Only two studies of school-based mentoring programs targeting junior high school students are available (see Table 6.7). Neither is rigorous, but both (Across Ages: LoScuito, Rajala, Townsend, and Taylor, 1996, methods rating = 3; RAISE: McPartland and Nettles, 1991, methods rating = 3) suggested a positive effect of mentoring on school attendance.

In summary, school-based mentoring programs for middle school students reduce nonattendance, but have not been studied with sufficient rigor to justify confident conclusions about its effectiveness for reducing delinquency or substance use. Work-study programs involving a high level of individualized attention from work supervisors and employment counselors (Kansas City: Ahlstrom and Havighurst, 1971, 1982; methods rating = 3; see Table 6.7) also do not reduce delinquency.

Recreation and Community Service Activities

Providing adolescents with "positive alternatives" has been a popular prevention strategy. This strategy includes a wide variety of activities that exclude alcohol, drug use, and other delinquent behavior: Drug-free activities such as dances, sports, and recreational activities, creative arts and cultural enrichment activities, field trips, wilderness challenge experiences, community drop-in centers, and community service activities. The underlying rationale linking these activities to lower problem behavior is that involvement in constructive, healthy activities reduces the likelihood of delinquent involvement. Different mechanisms have been suggested, including keeping the youth busy (the "idle hands" theory), providing rewards and recognition to substitute for the rewards and pleasure experienced with drugs or other criminal activity, raising self-esteem by reinforcing competencies of a nonacademic nature, and providing constructive group activities to replace unstructured, negative group activities. These strategies – especially the use of recreation centers and community service activities – have been used in attempts to prevent a wide range of problem behaviors, including substance use, delinquency, dropout, and pregnancy.

Alternative activities programs have been examined in several reviews of the effectiveness of drug prevention strategies. Tobler's (1986) meta-analysis provided early (guarded) support for these programs. This study used a broad classification for alternative programs, including drug-free activities as well as programs aimed at increasing competency skill deficits for high-risk populations. The former consisted of community service, youth centers, volunteerism, jobs, entertainment with opportunities for recognition and reward, and nondrug leisure activities such as sports and recreation. The latter included activities aimed at increasing a wide array of competency skills through activities such as tutoring, job skills training, one-on-one relationships, and physical adventure programs such as Outward Bound.

Tobler reported a small to moderate positive effect on reducing substance use for the broad "alternatives" category (ES = .22). She noted that the positive effects for the alternatives programs may be due to the reliance on acquisition of skills (an element common to the "peer" and "alternatives" categories), or to the targeting of high-risk populations with uncommonly intensive programs (85% of the programs in this category targeted high-risk populations, with very high intensities). Other reviews of the effectiveness of alternative programs concluded that when these programs are defined more narrowly to exclude a focus on social skills training, they do not prevent or reduce drug use (Botvin, 1990; Schaps, Bartolo, Moskowitz, Palley, and Churgin, 1981; Schinke, Botvin, and Orlandi, 1991). A recent meta-analysis (NSE; Center for Substance Abuse Prevention, 1995, described earlier) also found that alternative activities *alone* do not reduce drug use, drug-related knowledge and attitudes, or other risk and protective factors related to drug use. When these drug-free activities or wilderness challenge experience programs appeared as a secondary component in programs primarily aimed at psychosocial skill development, however, they were effective for reducing drug use and related risk and protective factors.

Several alternative activities programs for junior high school students have been evaluated. They are summarized in Tables 6.7 and 6.9. As suggested in the preceding summary of meta-analytical findings, alternatives programs have been fairly well studied as drug prevention strategies. The Malvin, Moskowitz, Schaps, and Schaeffer (1985; methods rating = 4) study of the effects of participation in community service courses on substance use is not discussed here because its null results are included in the meta-analyses already described. Only three studies have examined effects of alternative activities programs on outcomes other than substance use, and only one of these measures actual delinquent behavior and had suitable methodological rigor.

Cronin (1996; methods rating = 4) reported on Magic Me, a community service model involving reflection and discussion sessions for "processing" the service experience. This study involved intact classrooms of sixth grade students in orientations to prepare the students for their community service, visits to nursing homes (at least twelve per school year), and reflection and discussion periods (at least nine per year). Cronin found no program effects on self-report measures taken at the end of the school year on rebellious behavior, drug use in the last month, grade-point average, attachment to school, commitment to school, belief, attitudes favoring drug use, or nonattendance. Participating students reported significantly more drug use in the past year, however. Cronin also reported that the program was not particularly well implemented.

The evaluations of the other two community service programs are somewhat more positive, providing some evidence that such programs may improve grades and reduce dropout, but these results are not consistent across studies. Taken together, the results suggest that community service programs are unlikely to reduce delinquency or drug use. No rigorous study has examined the effects of purely recreational school-based alternative activities on problem behavior. This is unfortunate because of the popularity of programs such as "midnight basketball."

A Word about Comprehensive, Multicomponent Approaches

Recently, evaluations of comprehensive program "packages" have appeared in the literature. These multicomponent programs are based on the theory that problem behavior has many causes, and that programs targeting a wider range of these factors will be more effective. A disappointing test of such a multifaceted school-based prevention program implemented in a troubled urban middle school over a four-year period was reported in Skroban, Gottfredson, and Gottfredson (1999; methods rating = 4). The program included several components aimed at increasing social competency skills as well as components aimed at increasing social bonding and school success. Most pieces had been demonstrated in prior research to reduce problem behavior or factors leading to it, and are included among the program strategies that "work," summarized earlier. It included three different curricula (implemented at different grade levels), each focusing on developing self-control skills and problem-solving skills. It included school-based mentoring and tutoring programs, a career education and decision skills program, and a segment to teach students cognitive self-instruction skills related to academic work (such as self-monitoring and evaluation). The five-year study tested the transportability of these plausible intervention strategies into a more comprehensive program that could be implemented in a natural school setting as part of a multiyear school-based prevention demonstration. The evaluation of the five-year effort showed that the program never reached its expected level of implementation and no reliable effects on youth behaviors were observed. Scattered effects on student attitudes, both positive and negative, found in certain years were not replicated in other years. Reasons for this failure are discussed in Chapter 7.

Summary

Several strategies to alter the behaviors, thoughts, attitudes, or skills of youths of middle school or junior high school age have been shown to reduce problem behavior. Behavior modification for disruptive students is effective for improving behavior in the short run, and some but not all of the studies suggest these improvements last for years beyond the period of intervention. Evaluations of instructional programs for this age group are abundant. They consistently show more positive effects for programs with more social competency promotion content and for those that use cognitive-behavioral training methods such as feedback, reinforcement, and behavioral rehearsal rather than traditional lecture and discussion. This is true for drug prevention curricula as well as for programs that do not target a specific problem behavior. Curricula focusing specifically on violence prevention are newer and have not yet been as extensively studied. The jury is still out on the effects of these programs. Instructional programs lacking social competency content and cognitive-behavioral methods generally fail.

Counseling programs in general are ineffective for reducing problem behavior, peer counseling interventions for high-risk youths appear harmful, and school-based mentoring programs for middle school students have not been studied with sufficient rigor to justify confident conclusions about their effectiveness for reducing delinquency or substance use, although they appear to improve school attendance. Work-study programs involving a high level of individualized attention from work supervisors and employment counselors do not reduce delinquency. Finally, community service programs are unlikely to reduce delinquency or drug use.

Studies of Programs in Senior High Schools

Fewer prevention programs have been tested with high school populations, and several that target both middle or junior high school students and high school students have already been discussed. These include Ahlstrom and Havighurst's work-study program; Allen, Philliber, and Hoggson's Teen Outreach program; G. Gottfredson's peer counseling; and Arbuthnot and Gordon's moral reasoning program. The content of the remaining nine programs is shown in Table 6.9, and information about the nine studies of these programs is shown in Table 6.10.

Behavioral and Instructional Programs

One of the high school programs (Brooks, 1975; methods rating = 5) studied a contingency management approach to reducing truancy among high school students. Students carried daily attendance cards, had all of

Table 6.9. *High School Programs with Individual Change Focus*

Program (Study)	Grades Targeted	Program Content[a]								Duration of Program
		1	2	3	4	5	6	7	16	
"Contingency Management for Truancy" (Brooks, 1975)[b]	9–12	✓		X						8 weeks
"Dealing with Conflict" (Bretherton et al., 1993)	9–10	X								2.5 months
"Personal Growth Class – Drug Prevention" (Eggert et al., 1994)	9–12	X	✓							5 months
"Personal Growth Class – Suicide Prevention" (Eggert et al., 1995)	9–12	X	X		X					5 or 10 months
"Cognitive/Social Skills Training" (Sarason and Sarason, 1981)	9	X	X							1 school semester
"Minnesota Youth Advocate Program" (Higgins, 1978)	10 on avg.				X	✓		✓		Up to 15 months
"Mentoring" (Slicker and Palmer, 1993)	10					X		✓		6 months
"Dropout Prevention Program" (Longstreth et al., 1964)	10–12	✓			✓	X		✓		Up to 3 years
"Quantum Opportunities Program" (Hahn et al., 1994)	9–12	✓			X	X	X	✓		~41 months

[a]Program content key: 1. Instructing students. 2. Cognitive-behavioral change/behavior modeling. 3. Behavioral or behavior modification. 4. Counseling, social work, other psychological or therapeutic interventions. 5. Tutoring, mentoring, or other individual attention. 6. Recreational, enrichment, and leisure. 7. Changing instructional or classroom management methods or practices. 8. Changing norms or expectations for behavior. 9. Building a sense of community, morale, caring, support, or pride. 16. Changing family supervision or family behavior management. ✓ = contains some of this content; X = major focus of program.

[b]Program content also includes changing rules, policies, regulations, or laws about behavior, or discipline.

Table 6.10. *Evaluations of High School Programs with Individual Change Focus*

Program (Study)	Subjects	Method Rating/ Follow-up (mos.)	Outcomes[a]	
			Correlates of Problem Behavior	Problem Behavior
"Contingency Management for Truancy" (Brooks, 1975)	40 boys and girls at-risk for truancy in 1 school	5/0		Days absent (+)
"Dealing with Conflict" (Bretherton et al., 1993)	89 boys and girls in 5 classes in 3 schools	3/0	Social problem-solving skills (mostly 0) Beliefs supporting aggression (0)	Use of violence to resolve conflict (0)
"Personal Growth Class – Drug Prevention" (Eggert et al., 1994)	198 high-risk boys and girls in 4 schools	3/5–7	Grade-point average (+) Deviant peer bonding (0 boys; + girls) School bonding (+)	Absences (0) Drug use (0) Drug control problems and consequences (+)
"Personal Growth Class – Suicide Prevention" (Eggert et al., 1995)	105 boys and girls at-risk of suicide in 5 schools	4/5	Self-reported anger (in program 5 mos.: +) (in program 10 mos.: 0)	
"Cognitive/Social Skills Training" (Sarason and Sarason, 1981)	108 boys and girls in 6 classes in 1 school	3/12	Immediate follow-up: Means-end problem-solving skills (+) Ability to generate alternatives (+)	One-year follow-up: Absences (mixed) Tardiness (+) Number of behavior referrals (+)

Table 6.10. (cont.)

Program (Study)	Subjects	Method Rating/ Follow-up (mos.)	Outcomes[a]		
			Correlates of Problem Behavior	Problem Behavior	
"Minnesota Youth Advocate Program" (Higgins, 1978)	74 boys and girls released from state or county correctional institutions	3/0	Grade-point average (+ nr boys; 0 girls)	Attendance (0) School enrollment (+ nr) **Number and seriousness of offenses committed (0)** **Percentage of days in a correctional institution (0)**	
"Mentoring" (Slicker and Palmer, 1993)	58 boys and girls at-risk for dropout in 2 schools	2/0	Grade-point average (0)	Dropout (0)	
"Dropout Prevention Program" (Longstreth et al., 1964)	136 boys and girls at-risk for dropout in 2 schools	4/0	Attitudes about school (+)	Dropout (0) **Police contact (0)**	
"Quantum Opportunities Program" (Hahn et al., 1994)	158 boys and girls from families receiving public assistance	4/3	Enrolled in postsecondary school (+) Received honors or awards in past 12 months (+)	Graduated from high school (+) Dropout (+) Had a child (0) **Self-reported trouble with police in past 12 months (0)**	

Notes: Follow-up period begins at end of intervention. The number of subjects is the maximum number present for any of the analyses reported in the table.

[a] Key for study outcomes: 0 = no significant effect (p < .05); + = significant positive effect (p < .05); − = significant negative effect (p < .05); nr = two-tailed significance level not reported. Outcomes for substance use and for crime and delinquency measures appear in italics and in bold, respectively.

their teachers sign them, and were rewarded with tickets at the end of each day according to the number of teacher signatures and positive comments they received. Tickets were periodically exchanged for chances to win prizes. The intervention period lasted eight weeks. Truancy dropped dramatically for the treatment students and increased for a randomly assigned control group.

Studies of three high school instructional programs are available for summary. Recall that the Law-Related Education Curriculum and a similar program (STATUS) were summarized in the previous chapter. Both of these programs were evaluated for effects on high school students. The overall study showed that the LRE curriculum was successful for reducing delinquency when it was well implemented and coupled with changes to the instructional methods used in the classroom. Effects for high schools were similar to effects for the typical junior high and elementary schools: positive effects were found on a number of outcomes not necessarily related to problem behavior, such as factual knowledge about law and the legal process. Three out of thirty-three possible significant effects on the items measuring actual delinquency were found, two favoring the treatment and one the comparison group. These significant differences may have arisen by chance, given the one-tailed tests used.

The STATUS curriculum, implemented in the context of a fairly major reorganization of the school schedule to facilitate the team teaching and other changes in instructional techniques that accompanied the curriculum, was successful for reducing delinquency, drug use, and a number of factors related to these behaviors for junior and senior high school students. Arbuthnot's moral reasoning program also showed positive results on measures of problem behavior for ninth grade students.

Among the studies not previously reviewed, Eggert's work stands out as most rigorous. Eggert and colleagues (Eggert, Thompson, Herting, and Nicholas, 1995; Eggert, Thompson, Herting, Nicholas, and Dicker, 1994; methods ratings = 3 and 4) reported on different versions of a "Personal Growth Class" offered to high school students. In the first study, students at risk for school dropout (as identified through school records and referrals from school staff) were targeted for a one-semester course focusing on group support and life skills training. The teacher-student ratio was 1:12. Students met daily for ninety school days. The curriculum consisted of four units: self-esteem enhancement, decision making, personal control, and interpersonal communication. The curriculum was structured by a manual but was less standardized than many that have been summarized: the skills training sessions were expected to emerge in response to the specific real-life problems raised by the youths. Support behaviors (e.g., acceptance, respect, encouragement, and praise for contributions, willingness to help others, and active participation) were an important component of the class and were modeled daily by the teacher. Teachers were expected to establish and maintain "therapeutic" relationships with the students.

Subjects were randomly assigned to treatment and control conditions, but many of the treatment subjects opted to take a two-semester course and were excluded from the analysis. The remaining subjects were tested prior to and immediately following the course and again five to seven months later. The treatment subjects improved relative to controls on measures of grade-point average (but not attendance), deviant peer bonding (females only), self-esteem, drug control problems and consequences, and school bonding. Differences on self-reports of drug use were in the desired direction and marginally significant (p < .10).

A similar program was tested for its effects on risk factors related to suicide in Eggert et al. (1995). A second-semester follow-up course was also offered. It had the same goals and structure but extended the lessons from the first semester. For example, while the first-semester course emphasized bonding to others in the class, the second-semester course emphasized school bonding by encouraging joining and participating in school clubs and activities. The second course also moved to practicing skills in more difficult real-life situations and fostered involvement in a variety of social and recreational activities to counter suicidal thoughts.

Three groups were compared: one group received an in-depth suicide risk assessment only; another received the assessment and only the first-semester course; a third received the assessment and both semester courses. Students self-selected into these categories. Several outcomes related to suicide were measured, including anger, which reflected irritability, a loss of control when angry, and striking out physically. Reductions in anger from base line to the end of the first semester were evident for all three groups. A significant difference across groups in the trend from base line until the end of the school year was observed: Those completing two semesters showed the least decline, those completing the first semester only showed the greatest decline, and those receiving the assessment only were in between. The expected dosage response was not observed.

Counseling, Mentoring, and Other Individual Attention Interventions

Several studies of high school populations have examined variations of counseling, mentoring, or other individual attention interventions. One well-known study (Meyer, Borgatta, and Jones, 1965) of an unsuccessful social casework intervention for high-risk adolescent girls is not reviewed in detail here because the casework services were provided outside of the school by a community-based social work agency. Three other studies shown on Table 6.10 reported on programs involving counseling, mentoring, or other individualized attention. The rigor of these studies is too weak to justify strong conclusions, but the results generally suggest no effect on measures of problem behavior.

In contrast to these unsuccessful attempts to provide special attention in the form of counseling, mentoring, or job experience is the successful Quantum Opportunities Program (Hahn, Leavitt, and Aaron, 1994; methods rating = 4). This program provides both in- and out-of-school services to disadvantaged high school students. This program stands out from all others of its type (that have been evaluated) by providing intensive, long-term services as well as cash and scholarship incentives for participants. The program spans the four high school years (including summers) and includes 250 hours *each year* of each of the following services: academic assistance (e.g., computer-assisted instruction, peer tutoring, homework assistance), service activities (e.g., community service activities, jobs), and a curriculum focusing on life or family skills and planning for college and jobs. Services are provided in the community during the after-school hours and in some sites the school provided space for the program. Participating students receive hourly stipends and bonuses for their participation.

A randomized experiment was used to evaluate the program. After one year of services, no differences were observed between the treatment and control students. After two years, differences favoring the treatment subjects appeared on measures of academic and functional skills as well as on educational expectations. A survey conducted in the fall following scheduled high school graduation showed that experimental students graduated at higher rates, dropped out of school at lower rates, and continued on to postsecondary education at higher rates than did control students. Experimental subjects were more likely to report that their lives had been a success and that they were hopeful about the future. Marginal positive effects ($p < .10$) on self-reports of "trouble with the police" and having children were also observed. A separate report (Taggart, 1995; cited in Greenwood, Model, Rydell, and Chiesa, 1996) reports a 70% reduction in arrests for the treatment subjects relative to the control subjects by the time of expected high school graduation.

Summary

Fewer tests of individually targeted school-based prevention models have been tested with high school populations than with populations of elementary and middle or junior high school age, and the models that have been tested are more likely to target high-risk than general populations. As with other age groups, behavioral interventions are effective for altering the targeted behavior (as in the Brooks truancy prevention model), and counseling interventions are generally ineffective (recall Gottfredson's evaluation of Peer Culture Development, summarized in the previous section, which *increased* delinquency for high school students, and the Higgins study summarized earlier showing no effect on problem behavior for an "advocacy" program for youths returning to school from a correctional setting). Similarly, no evidence is found in these high school studies to support school-based mentoring programs or work-study programs for at-risk populations. In these respects, results from the high school studies mirror results for younger populations.

Also consistent with results for other age groups is the superior performance of classroom-based programs focusing on developing social competency skills and employing cognitive-behavioral teaching methods. The Sarason and Sarason study showed that a program that relied on modeling and role playing to teach cognitive and social skills to the general population of high school students reduced behavior problems. The Eggert model showed that a curriculum focusing on social competency promotion but relying less on behavioral modeling and rehearsal than Sarason and Sarason's model had some positive effects on problem behavior in a high-risk population, but they were marginally significant or inconsistent.

The Quantum Opportunities Program stands out as a particularly promising approach for disadvantaged populations, although it is not fair to compare it with programs delivered in or by schools. I include it primarily to provide a standard against which services provided in school-based programs can be compared. This program achieved better outcomes than the typical school-based program but only by providing quantum services.

Size and Durability of Effects

As was true in Chapter 5, effect sizes were not calculated for all studies, so only a sampling of effect sizes is available. Table 6.11 shows effect sizes for several studies that demonstrated significant positive or negative effects on measures of problem behavior. As was true of the studies of environmental change strategies, the magnitude of the effects for individually focused interventions varies considerably from study to study. Effects for programs involving social competency promotion and the use of cognitive or behavioral strategies are often in the range found by Lipsey and Wilson (1993) to be typical for general social, behavioral, and educational intervention (e.g., around .50). Effects for substance abuse prevention curricula are generally smaller, with DARE studies yielding the smallest effects. Effects for the exceptionally intensive FAST Track program (delivered to high-risk youths in the early elementary grades) are moderate in size, and effects for counseling programs and the one community service program for which an effect size for problem behavior is available range from close to zero to moderate in the wrong direction. Effects of behavioral and cognitive-behavioral interventions are certainly large enough to warrant attention.

Table 6.11. *Selected Effect Sizes from Individual Change Studies*

Outcome Measure (Study)	Effect Size
Observations of problem behavior (Conduct Problems Prevention Research Group, 1997)	−.25
Drug use (Ringwalt et al., 1994)[a]	−.06 (average ES)
Marijuana use	−.27 to −.58
Alcohol use (Botvin, Baker, Renick, et al., 1984)[b]	−.07 to .03
Marijuana use	−.05 to −.21
Alcohol use (Botvin et al., 1995)	−.19 to .03
Excessive drinking (Caplan et al., 1992)	−.27 to −.51
Substance abuse for social influence programs	−.14 to −.27
Substance abuse for comprehensive programs (Hanson and O'Malley, 1996)[c]	−.08 to −.37
Self-reported delinquency	−.07
Self-reported drug use (Esbensen and Osgood, 1996)	−.04
Teacher ratings of comportment	−.42 (immediate)
	−.40 (1-year follow-up)
(Rotheram, 1982)	
Disruptive off-task behavior	−.55
Aggressive behavior	−.61
Self-reported alcohol and substance use (Lochman et al., 1984; Lochman et al., 1985; Lochman 1992)	−.38
Juvenile records (Bry, 1982)	−.76
Self-reported drug use (Cronin, 1996)	.13 to .19 (a negative effect)
Recidivism for counseling programs (Lipsey, 1992)[d]	−.01
Drug involvement (Gottfredson, 1986)	.23 (a negative effect)

Note: Study citation follows cluster of outcomes for each study.
[a]Meta-analysis of eight DARE studies.
[b]Peer-led condition with booster.
[c]Review of substance abuse prevention programs for alcohol, marijuana, and cigarette use.
[d]Meta-analysis.

Several of the studies summarized in this chapter reported on the durability of program effects six months or longer after the end of the program. Among early elementary school programs, positive effects persisted one year (ICPS) and up to fifteen months (FAST Track) after the program. In other studies, long-term effects were mixed (e.g., the Montreal Longitudinal study and the Second Step violence prevention program). Positive effects were observed for cognitive self-management programs delivered to upper elementary school children for up to one year (the Rotheram studies) and three years (Lochman's anger management intervention). More rigorous longitudinal follow-up studies of initially promising interventions are required.

Studies of middle school populations show that behavioral intervention can have lasting effects for up to five years (Bry, 1982). But when behavioral programs are delivered in schools to segregated groups of high-risk youths, long-term as well as short-term effects are mixed at best. Studies involving cognitive-behavioral training or instruction at the middle school level have typically shown that effects diminish over time without a booster in later grades, but that with boosters effects maintain. Only one middle school study of an individual-attention intervention followed youths for more than six months. This study showed no enduring effects of mentoring on problem behavior.

Studies of prevention efforts for high school students are rare, and long-term follow-ups are more so. But the studies that followed youths for more than six months found that the positive program effects persisted for up to one year. Both of these studies were aimed at developing social competency skills.

The evidence from all education levels supports the conclusion that effects of prevention endure beyond the program when the program is strong to begin with. But effects become less consistent over time and diminish in strength. This suggests that continued services are necessary to maintain larger effects.

Conclusions

Program Strategies

Experimental and quasi-experimental studies of school-based programs providing direct services to individual students suggest the following:

1. School-based programs aimed at altering individual behaviors, skills, attitudes, or beliefs have been shown to reduce problem behavior for all age groups and for both general populations and high-risk populations within each age group.

2. The content of the program matters, and the most effective program content is the same across all age groups. Behavioral programs (e.g., those

which identify and track specific behaviors over time, and use positive or negative reinforcement to change behavior systematically) work to change the behaviors, at least in the short run. Programs that focus on teaching students self-control and social competency skills are most effective. Self-control instruction includes self-management and emotional control instruction. Social competency instruction includes instruction on recognizing and resisting social influences, social problem-solving skills, communication, and emotional perspective taking.

3. The delivery methods used in instructional programs matter, and the most effective methods are the same across all age groups. Instructional programs that incorporate behavioral modeling, role playing, rehearsal and practice of new skills, and use of cues are more effective than programs relying on didactic presentation, seat work, and other non-cognitive-behavioral methods.

4. Counseling programs, school-based mentoring programs, community service, and work-study programs are generally ineffective for reducing problem behavior, although some have improved school attendance.

5. Studies of programs targeting elementary school students more often report positive results. This may be because (a) they more often include the more effective prevention strategies, including an emphasis on social competency skill development and the use of effective behavioral or cognitive-behavioral strategies; (b) early forms of problem behavior are more malleable than later (more serious) forms; or (c) the measures of problem behavior employed in these studies (e.g., teacher ratings, observations) are more reliable than the measures used in studies of older populations (e.g., police contacts).

6. Program effects are usually not long-lasting. Roughly half of the studies included in this chapter examined whether program effects persisted after the end of the intervention period. The follow-up period ranged from one week to six years (average, 1.5 years). Generally, program effects became less consistently observed over time. Those programs with the most durable outcomes were generally of social competency development programs that had used cognitive-behavioral delivery strategies.

Methods

Not surprisingly, the studies summarized in this chapter are more rigorous than those summarized in Chapter 5. Ten (14%) were ranked as level 5 studies, and 69% were in the top two categories. The average rigor rating was 3.7, compared with 3.4 for the environmental studies. These studies used more equivalent comparison groups and better statistical controls to increase the comparability of the groups. The quality of the measurement of variables was equivalent in both types of studies, but control for attrition was better in the individual-level studies. Also, these studies employed long-term follow-up more often. About half of the individual-level but only 6 (15%) of the studies of environmental change employed follow-up data collection. This fact, that methodological rigor is easier to accomplish in less complex interventions, was discussed in Chapter 4. Many of the studies summarized in this chapter involved single interventions (e.g., tracking and reinforcing behavior or mentoring) or a class of some sort. Many were implemented in the school setting by personnel who did not work for the school. It is in many respects easier to conduct research under these conditions than when the researchers collaborate with educators who agree to implement a preventive intervention while maintaining control over their school. Studies involving such researcher-practitioner collaboration, although generally less rigorous, are useful for probing the generalizability of program effects under more natural conditions.

The number of students in the studies reviewed in this chapter ranged from 14 to 7,606 (mean = 473; median = 113). Sixty-five percent of the studies used fewer than 200 subjects. In approximately three-fourths of the studies, individuals were assigned to receive the intervention or not. The remaining studies used schools or classrooms as the unit of assignment to experimental conditions. Random assignment was used in approximately one-third of the studies. The investigator generally collected relevant data prior to and at the end of the intervention. In all but four studies, individual-level analyses were used to compare treatment and comparison subjects.

Three methodological shortcomings were common in these studies: small numbers of cases, assignment to conditions at the school or classroom level rather than at the individual level, and (especially for studies involving younger students) insensitive measures. As noted already, the majority of studies used fewer than two hundred cases. Without estimating the power of each study to detect the desired differences, it is not possible to judge the adequacy of each. But one hundred cases per group generally do not provide sufficient power to detect even large differences in outcomes. For example, to have an 80% chance of detecting a 50% drop in a form of minor delinquency – the percentage of students reporting that they had stolen something worth under $50 – from 30% to 15% would require 134 cases *per group* (with an alpha level of .05). Most of the studies reviewed in this chapter had insufficient power to detect such a change. The situation is more serious when the outcome of interest is a more serious and less prevalent behavior. For example, the same 80% chance of detecting a 50% drop in the percentage of students who had gotten into a serious fight (from, say 20% to 10%), would require 219 cases *per group*. The results of such underpowered studies can be misleading – generally in the direction of underestimating the effectiveness of the intervention. The GREAT study, for example, involving nearly six thousand students found statistically significant beneficial effects on drug use and delinquency for effect sizes of $-.07$ and $-.04$. Yet in the Bry study of a behavioral intervention involving sixty-six subjects, effect sizes as large as $-.89$ on substance use among high-risk youths did not reach conventional levels of statistical significance.

It is fairly common in school-based studies for classes or schools to be selected into treatment and control conditions, but individual subject data analyzed. This problem was much more prevalent among environmental change studies but was also found in fourteen of the studies summarized in this chapter. Of some concern is the fact that in several of the more effective programs summarized in this chapter, data were analyzed at the individual level after having been assigned at the school (e.g., the analyses of high-risk students in the FAST Track program, early studies of the PATHS curriculum, and some of the Lochman studies) or at the classroom (e.g., Weissberg's Positive Youth Development program, and Sarason and Sarason's cognitive-social skills training) level. The arguments for analyzing data at the level of assignment or for using more sophisticated multi-level modeling techniques discussed in Chapter 5 also apply to the studies reviewed in this chapter.

Finally, study results seem to vary depending upon the type of outcome measures used. Studies of young children often rely on adult ratings and observations of problem behavior. Studies that used both adult behavior ratings and blinded observations of behavior found positive effects based on the observation data but not on the adult ratings. Ratings may also be biased by the raters' involvement in the study or by their knowledge of the subject's involvement. One study found that the problem behavior ratings of children by parents who had been involved in family management training actually increased after the training, presumably because the intervention heightened their awareness of their children's problem behavior. Also, studies that collected observations in a variety of settings were more likely to observe effects on problem behavior in unstructured settings (such as the lunchroom or playground) than in the classroom. Studies relying only on one of these biased data sources might therefore produce misleading results.

Correspondence with Studies from Other Fields

The results of experimental and quasi-experimental studies reviewed in this chapter accord with findings from studies of interventions to reduce problem behavior among behaviorally and emotionally disturbed children. Studies of interventions for behaviorally and emotionally disordered children, underrepresented in this chapter because of their frequent use of single-subject designs, also find that behavioral and cognitive-behavioral programs work reasonably well to control classroom behavior. Stage and

Quiroz (1997), in a meta-analysis of interventions to reduce disruptive classroom behavior, reported an average effect size of −.78 on a variety of measures of disruptive behavior from ninety-nine mostly elementary programs relying on behavioral and cognitive-behavioral interventions. Walker et al. (1996) summarize the usual approaches – counseling and disciplinary removal – taken by school psychologists and other school personnel to deal with antisocial behavior and suggest a new conceptual model for school-based prevention in which universal interventions (e.g., schoolwide discipline plans, instruction in anger management and social competency development using programs such as Second Step, summarized earlier) are provided to all students, and more intensive interventions (e.g., instruction in moral reasoning, anger management, and self-control using programs such as FAST Track and variants of home-based reinforcement, a behavioral method) are provided to selected at-risk children. These services are coordinated using a schoolwide behavioral consultation model similar to Mayer's effective model (employed in that case to reduce vandalism) described in Chapter 5. Obviously, this proposed model for preventing antisocial behavior developed partly on the basis of the literature on emotional and behavioral disorders and their treatments is consistent with, indeed nearly identical to, the model that emerges from the literature summarized in this chapter (and to a certain extent the previous chapter on environmental interventions).

Finally, woven through the summaries of studies in this and the previous chapter is evidence of extreme variability in the quality of implementation of school-based programs. Some programs are implemented with so little integrity that a reasonable reader would conclude that no positive effects could be expected. Other programs – for example, the Quantum Opportunities and FAST Track – are meticulously delivered with a high degree of strength and fidelity to the plan. As the next chapter shows, understanding the nature and causes of this variation is key to building prevention programs that can be implemented outside the boundaries of the laboratory-like settings created by researchers to test their interventions.

CHAPTER SEVEN

Lost in Translation: Why Doesn't School-Based Prevention Work as Well as It Should?

SCHOOLS ARE particularly well situated to provide prevention services: they provide regular access to students during the developmental years and may represent the *only* reliable access to large numbers of crime-prone youths. Children spend approximately 18% of their waking hours in school. Schools are staffed with individuals trained to help youths develop into healthy, happy, productive citizens and the community is generally supportive of schools' efforts to socialize youths. On these grounds alone, schools have crime prevention potential.

The preceding chapters paint a fairly optimistic view of the ability to realize this potential through school-based prevention. The nonexperimental studies summarized in Chapters 2 and 3 show that several of the likely causes of problem behavior are school-related, and that features of schools are related to the level of disorderly behavior they experience. The experimental studies summarized in Chapters 5 and 6 show that many of these factors can be manipulated, and that when they are manipulated, a reduction in problem behavior often results. These studies generally accord with the research on the causes of problem behavior by showing that attempts to alter the most likely causal factors (according to nonexperimental research) are more successful than attempts to alter other factors.

This chapter examines the generalizability of the research findings summarized in previous chapters. It describes the conditions under which the research supporting the efficacy of school-based prevention has been conducted, summarizes the scant evidence about variability of implementation quality and how this variability affects study outcomes, and reviews what is known about the correlates of implementation strength. It applies this knowledge to urban school settings, places problems of urban education in historical context, and reflects upon the generalizability of the research for these more challenging settings. Finally, the chapter recommends preliminary steps that can be taken to overcome these problems and discusses ways to improve the state of knowledge about creating conditions more conducive to change.

Generalizability of Research Findings

Programs operated as part of research endeavors are generally implemented under unusual conditions. Many schools are not amenable to rigorous research studies, and no researcher would choose to attempt to conduct research in them. Only the rare principal and faculty are willing to relinquish control to researchers and undergo the scrutiny required in research studies.

In many studies, external consultants or other professionals are used to deliver services in lieu of regular school staff. This occurs much more frequently with programs designed to provide direct services to individual students (like those summarized in Chapter 6) than with those designed to change the school or classroom environment (like those summarized in Chapter 5). Many of the most effective programs summarized in Chapter 6 were programs delivered by researchers, graduate students, or mental health professionals employed outside the school. Coie and Krehbiel's (1984) academic and social skills training, Rotheram et al.'s (1982) assertiveness training, Feindler et al.'s (1984) anger-control training, Arbuthnot and Gordon's (1986) moral reasoning programs, Sarason and Sarason's (1981) cognitive-social skills training, and Hahn et al.'s (1994) Quantum Opportunities Program – all shown to reduce problem behavior – were delivered by external staff. Other effective programs, including the in-school component of Patterson's (1974) behavior modification intervention, Caplan et al.'s (1992) Positive Youth Development intervention, and Lochman, Burch, Curry, and Lampron's (1984) anger coping intervention were delivered by outside professional staff working with school staff. When school staff members do implement programs in research studies, they are typically provided with extensive training and technical assistance that far exceeds the level of assistance typical in school settings. For example, Weissberg and Caplan (1994) reported that classroom teachers implemented their social competency development program with assistance from undergraduate aides. Ten ninety-minute workshops were provided by the program developers, and on-site consultation and coaching were routinely provided by the research staff. This level of training and technical assistance is typical in research studies but rare in school-based staff development interventions.

These findings are not unusual. Tobler's (1992) meta-analysis of substance abuse prevention programs showed that among the ten most effective programs identified in the literature, only one was implemented by regular classroom teachers, and that program was unusual because extraordinary amounts of training and consultation were provided for the teachers.

The conditions under which research studies are operated should be of no concern if the intent of the research is to demonstrate that a particular strategy can work to reduce problem behavior. Even if we were concerned with programs' generalizability beyond the particular demonstration, the conditions need only concern us if we have reason to believe that the quality of programs delivered under "research" conditions was unlike the quality of programs implemented under more usual conditions. Unfortunately, the quality of programs conducted as part of research studies does differ from the quality of programs implemented under more usual circumstances, and study outcomes seem to vary with the quality of implementation. Lipsey's (1992) meta-analysis of juvenile delinquency prevention and treatment programs found that the strength or implementation (or "dosage") of the treatment programs was associated with the size of their effects, and programs delivered by researchers were more effective than those delivered by practitioners. Researchers presumably attend more to issues of strength and integrity of the programs they are testing.

Little is known about the distribution of strength and quality of implementation of school-based prevention programs. Usually, project reports describe the program in narrative form only. Actual program implementation is almost never quantified and reported along with the outcomes of the program. This practice is unfortunate because data on implementation quality are essential for interpreting null results (null results might mean that an effective program was poorly implemented or that the program was ineffective) and for understanding the extent to which the results of the study are generalizable to "real-world" conditions.

A few of the studies summarized in the previous chapters provided details about level of program implementation. The studies were all of large-scale efforts to change the school or classroom environment (or, in the Botvin study, the curriculum), using existing school personnel. They therefore have a higher level of ecological validity than many of the studies summarized in the previous chapters. These studies (Allen, Philliber, and Hoggson, 1990; Battistich et al., 1996; Botvin, Baker, Dusenbury, et al., 1990; Gottfredson, Gottfredson, and Skroban, 1998; Johnson and Hunter, 1985; Smith and Sharp, 1994) all produced evidence that the level of implementation varies considerably across settings, and that the quality of implementation is related to the program's eventual effectiveness.

Perhaps the most informative of these studies is Botvin, Baker, Dusenbury, et al. (1990). In this study, nearly 4,500 students from fifty-six schools were involved in a three-year study to test the effectiveness of the Life Skills Training (LST) program. Trained observers collected information on the amount of curriculum material actually covered in randomly selected classrooms, and a summary implementation score was calculated for each class. An implementation score was computed for each student based on classes attended over the three-year period. Two different LST conditions were compared in this study – one involving formal training and implementation feedback, and the other involving videotaped training and no feedback. The average percentage of material covered was 67% and 68% for the respective conditions, ranging from 27% to 97%. Only 75% of the students in the experimental conditions were exposed to 60% or more of the material, the cutoff used by the investigators to determine who had actually received a sufficient dosage of the program to warrant testing the program effectiveness. After controlling on pretest substance use measures, implementation scores were found to be significantly (and negatively) related to outcomes for cigarette smoking, drinking frequency, frequency of getting drunk, and marijuana use.

Smith, Ross, and Nunnery (1997) showed even more compelling evidence for the importance of implementation quality in a Success for All (SFA) program implementation. This study was not included in the Chapter 5 discussion of Success for All because it did not include a measure of problem behavior. It involved twelve schools participating in a school restructuring effort in a metropolitan school district. Eight of the schools implemented the Success for All model described in Chapter 5 – a school-wide program designed to overhaul reading instruction. Four schools implemented a different restructuring model. Raters rated the quality of implementation of the first-grade reading curriculum, and the use of tutoring, cross-grade regrouping, and overall teacher effectiveness. The ratings were summed, and the eight SFA schools were divided into two groups according to these rating scores.

The results were strikingly different depending on the level of implementation. Schools that implemented the program poorly actually showed significant *negative* effects on three of the four outcome measures, whereas those that implemented the program well had significant positive effects on one outcome measure.

Each of these studies shows that implementation quality varies from setting to setting and that this variation is related to program outcomes. Of course, the associations are based merely on correlations. Although the level of implementation is correlated with positive change in these studies, the studies do not rule out the possibility that these correlations are spurious. Characteristics of the organization such as leadership, morale, or general school climate may lead both to strong implementation and the positive changes in problem behavior. In other words, these studies do not provide strong evidence for a dosage effect because schools are not randomly assigned to different dosage levels. Only one of the studies reviewed in Chapters 5 and 6 (Fuchs and Fuchs, 1989) conducted an experiment in which the dosage of the intervention was randomly assigned. This study showed that as the dosage increased, so did the improvements from pre- to postintervention in teacher ratings of student behavior. The level of implementation is key to understanding variability in program effectiveness.

No data source yet exists to inform us about the full variation in quality and quantity of program implementation across schools and across different implementers within schools. The studies summarized here provide just a glimpse of what might be, but it is probably an optimistic glimpse because each of the studies was part of a research undertaking. Although the programs were implemented primarily by school staff, these school staff were likely to have had more support and resources than would a typical school staff person implementing a prevention program.

Research Triangle Institute (Silvia and Thorne, 1997) reported on prevention programs implemented as part of the U.S. Department of Education's Safe and Drug-Free Schools and Communities Program. These programs are most likely closer to what is typically implemented in the name of school-based prevention because they are funded through federal block grants for which evaluation is not required. The study found that not only did schools rarely implement the types of programs that have been identified as most effective in research, but their level of implementation was remarkably variable. The amount and content of program delivery varies among classrooms within schools and among schools – even in districts trying to deliver consistent programs. Teachers reported that they had received insufficient training, were not comfortable with the material or teaching methods recommended, and that prevention-related material was of low priority. If this report provides any indication of the quality and quantity of prevention practices typically implemented in schools, we can be fairly certain that these programs usually do *not* work.

This is a sobering fact. Very few of the programs tested as part of research endeavors are retested under more usual circumstances before they are widely disseminated to schools for use in programs such as the Safe and Drug-Free Schools and Communities Program. Jones, Gottfredson, and Gottfredson's (1997) study of Success for All implemented as part of a district's own improvement plan (summarized in Chapter 5), Smith et al.'s (1997) study of Success for All implemented as part of the school district's "New American Schools" restructuring initiative (discussed earlier), and Gottfredson et al.'s (1998) study of a Center for Substance Abuse Prevention (CSAP) demonstration project (summarized in Chapter 6) involving one troubled middle school attempting to implement a set of programs shown in previous research to reduce problem behavior are all examples of what often happens in the translation of research into practice: it fails.

The best estimates of the level of implementation of prevention programs in research studies range from about 42% (Smith and Sharp, 1994) to 68% (Botvin, Baker, Dusenbury, et al., 1990) intensity. Intensity levels in efforts not part of research studies are most likely below 60%. If the level of program implementation determines program effectiveness, an obvious way to improve program effectiveness is to strengthen program implementation. Improving the quality of implementation may prove more fruitful for improving outcomes than altering the type of prevention program schools use. Understanding what kinds of programs are more easily implemented and what kinds of schools more effectively implement programs is a first step in learning how to improve the quality of implementation.

Correlates of Quality of Program Implementation

Aside from the Research Triangle Institute study just summarized, there has been no systematic investigation into the quality of implementation of delinquency prevention programs as they are typically implemented in schools.[1] Fortunately, some research has been conducted on implementation of educational innovations in general. This research occurred in a flurry of evaluative activity in the late 1970s and early 1980s culminating in an influential report (National Commission on Excellence in Education, 1983). Probably the best-known study of this period was the Rand Change Agent Study (Berman and McLaughlin, 1978), which involved a nationwide survey in eighteen states of nearly three hundred federally funded "change agent" projects. Interviews were conducted with numerous people at different levels (from superintendent to classroom teacher) in districts operating these programs to learn about the factors influencing the outcomes of the projects. These interviews were augmented with site visits and interviews with federal and state officials working with the programs.

Staff development studies are another source of information about correlates of successful implementation and maintenance of new practices. Little's (1981) research in six schools focuses on school norms and work conditions conducive to staff development and improvement. Another influential body of research examined the role of principals in the change process. Hall and his colleagues conducted a series of such investigations (summarized in Hall, Hord, Huling, Rutherford, and Stiegelbauer, 1983) to identify principal leadership styles as they relate to the change process. Several case studies of schools or school districts implementing a major change have also contributed to this knowledge base. For example, Huberman (reported in Huberman and Miles, 1984) conducted a case study of one school district's use of a structured reading instruction

---

[1] This section is based on an earlier version, which appeared in Gottfredson, Fink, Skroban, and Gottfredson (1997).

program available through the National Diffusion Network. Taken together, these studies indicate that implementation varies across the country and between individual schools (Berman and McLaughlin, 1978; Liberman and Miller, 1984; McLaughlin, 1990) and that this variance affects outcomes (Stallings, 1985).

Information regarding features of programs and schools that influence the level of implementation and hence program outcomes can be gleaned from quantitative evaluations of school improvement efforts as well as qualitative research involving interviews and case studies. Several reviews – Clark, Lotto, and McCarthy, 1980; Fullan, Miles, and Taylor, 1980; Fullan and Pomfret, 1977; Fullan and Steigelbauer, 1991; Purkey and Smith, 1983 – have related characteristics of the innovation and of the organization to the strength and integrity of program implementation.

Characteristics of Innovations

Need. School staffs must perceive the need for the innovation before they will implement it. Often, innovations are undertaken without a careful examination of the needs of the school or the school district (Fullan and Stiegelbauer, 1991). If teachers do not believe the innovation will solve a problem they are experiencing, they will have little motivation for changing existing practices. This is particularly true when the innovation is complex and time-consuming.

Complexity. In their review of implementation of curriculum innovations, Fullan and Pomfret (1977) found that successfully implemented curricula were explicit and not confusing to teachers (see also Kennedy, 1978). In addition, Fullan et al. (1980) found greater implementation of changes regarded as "practical" to teachers than of changes that affected the classroom only indirectly.

Implementation seems to vary with program complexity. In an analysis of twelve case studies, Huberman and Miles (1984) found that schools often attempt to implement innovations that are beyond their ability to carry out, and massive failure ensues. Projects in the twelve schools tended to be downsized and adapted, resulting in greater alteration of projects that began more broadly based. On the other hand, research has found that the more attempted, the more accomplished. Complex programs with many components are likely to be down-sized and modified, but they still often result in more change than do simpler programs. Multicomponent programs seem to be high-risk, high-gain ventures for schools. The risk is inversely related to the initial capacity of the school.

Clarity and Staff Training. Many innovations are not made clear to teachers or other school staff at the outset and, hence, fail (Fullan and

Stiegelbauer, 1991). Diffuse program goals and unspecified means of implementation are huge problems in school innovation and happen more frequently when a particular innovation is adopted suddenly in response to a perceived crisis.

Clarity can be improved with high-quality materials, simpler programs (but see earlier discussion), and staff training. One study (Wyant, 1974) quantified the length of effective training as measured by communication variables on teacher questionnaires. The study found that training had consistent positive effects on communication, but only after twenty-two hours of staff involvement. Small amounts of training served to open up communication, but did not allow enough time to progress toward dealing with problems. One of the clearest findings in organizational psychology is that high-ability workers require less training time than less able workers – and they perform better on complex jobs. It comes as no surprise, therefore, that research on effective program implementation in education has found that higher-ability teachers learn to implement programs according to plan better than do lower-ability teachers (Good and Brophy, 1987).

A large-scale evaluation of school health education programs (Connell, Turner, and Mason, 1985) also found evidence that the quality of implementation increased with the amount of staff training. Teachers who received no in-service training were compared with teachers who received full and partial in-service training on measures of the percentage of the program taught and program fidelity. On the average, fully trained teachers delivered a larger percentage of the program with greater fidelity than teachers with partial training, who in turn implemented the programs more fully than teachers with no training. But because the amount of training received was not a manipulated variable, its effects on the level of program implementation may be confounded with the effects of other teacher qualities related to the amount of training received. Also, the study found that even with no training, 70% of the lessons were delivered with 60% fidelity to the program.

Teacher Involvement. Teacher participation in the process of change, training, and planning appears to affect implementation (Berman and McLaughlin, 1978; Liberman and Miller, 1981, 1984; Loucks, 1983; Social Action Research Center, 1979). Berman and McLaughlin (1978) identified teachers as key to the "mutual adaptation" that occurs with successful implementation of innovations in their four-year, two-phase study of 293 federally funded programs in eighteen states. Teachers played an important role in "local input" into planning and acted as "internal change agents" necessary for implementation (Fullan et al., 1980).

At the same time, *mere* participation is unlikely to be useful or necessary. Research by industrial organizational psychologists (Jackson, 1983) implies that providing opportunities for worker participation can increase workers' sense of involvement but produce little else. Teacher participation will be useful when teachers can provide needed information about practical obstacles or potential opportunities for improvement, or when their consent or commitment is needed for a project that they could otherwise sabotage (see Vroom and Yetton, 1975).

Characteristics of Organizations

Staff. Berman and McLaughlin (1978) found that several teacher characteristics affected implementation of innovations. A questionnaire given to superintendents, program managers and directors, principals, and teachers – supplemented by follow-up site visits – showed that teachers' sense of their own efficacy affected how they carry out changes in their classrooms. Several other studies imply that teacher morale is related to teacher support of innovative projects (Fullan and Pomfret, 1977; Social Action Research Center, 1979). Runkel and Bell (1976) found that teachers' skill at communicating during emotional periods predicted their readiness for collaborative action. Miles (1986) found teachers' skill deficits to be a barrier to change in five extensive case studies of urban high schools. Huberman and Miles (1984) surveyed students and teachers and found that mastery of innovation that occurred over time reinforced implementation of change in program. Even difficult changes could be mastered with sufficient administrative assistance, which in turn would lead to teacher commitment to the process.

Leadership. One of the most consistent findings points to leadership as crucial to implementation of educational change. Fullan et al. (1980) found leadership by school principals a factor in all three phases of implementation: entry, start-up, and maintenance. Berman and McLaughlin (1978) found that principals gave the innovations local legitimacy and acted as gatekeepers. Hall and colleagues (Hall, 1987; Hall, Hord, Huling, Rutherford, and Stiegelbauer, 1983; Hall, Rutherford, Hord, and Huling, 1984) identified three styles of principals and correlated them with degree of implementation. Principals high in initiating style, those who accommodate and become involved in the change process, achieved higher levels of implementation than did the "responders," principals who stay behind the scene and show interest in change only for the short term, or the "managers," principals who carry out change when dictated but do not initiate or add local input.

Leadership is not limited to the principal. Several studies found central office support crucial to implementation (Fullan et al., 1980; Fullan and Pomfret, 1977; Huberman, 1983). Others found teams of central support necessary for change (Louis, 1986; Purkey and Smith, 1983). One study of teams of innovators found that teams accomplished more effective implementation of programs when administrators or principals were members of the planning team.

Resources. Another type of support identified with innovation can be generally termed "resources." Concentrating on urban high schools, Louis (1986) surveyed 248 principals in schools involved in successful effective school programs for at least one year and found that lack of resources, time, and money were often listed as barriers to implementation. Reviews of research also identified resources, physical and monetary, as limiting to implementation (Fullan et al., 1980; Fullan and Pomfret, 1977). Other evidence implies that resources do not play an important role in the variation of implementation (Berman and McLaughlin, 1978; Clark et al., 1980; McLaughlin, 1990), or that resource affects implementation indirectly through financial support for training (Fullan and Pomfret, 1977; Miles, 1986). Whether resources are externally or locally provided may also affect the implementation and probably has more effect on how innovation is maintained (Holmes, Gottfredson, and Miller, 1992).

School Climate or Culture. Each school's culture is shaped by its community, its central office, its staff and students, and its physical structure. A cultural perspective on schoolwide change (Rossman, Corbett, and Firestone, 1988) views the nature of change at the school level in terms of "sacred" and "profane" norms. Change aimed at changing "sacred" norms will encounter resistance from the forces that make up the school. Behavior may change, but the norms may remain.

Organizational capacity and school climate also affect *how* implementation occurs. Problem-solving focus, staff morale, perceptions of support, and readiness for change are related to level of implementation (Derr, 1976; Fullan, Miles, and Taylor, 1980; Purkey and Smith, 1983). Stability of staff, especially principals, is another element of school climate cited by teachers (Huberman, 1983), in case studies (Mann, 1978), and by studies compiled for review (Purkey and Smith, 1983). Overall, school environments that do not feel "turbulent" or overwhelmed with basic problems have a better chance of implementing "extra" programs. Clinical experience implies that schools with low morale or an impaired infrastructure are difficult places to put innovation in place (Gottfredson, 1984; Gottfredson and Gottfredson, 1987).

One author (Miles, 1986) noted in his case studies of urban high schools that "Improvement happens to those who seek it" (p. 8). Fullan et al. (1980) noted that schools had lower levels of implementation when they had a record of previous failures in innovation. Runkel and Bell (1976) surveyed twelve elementary school staffs about the innovations recently attempted and categorized them into five types varying in difficulty of implementing from innovations that barely affect teachers to basic structural changes. The research indicated that teachers perceived their schools attempting flurries of innovation in descending order of difficulty. Schools failing at one innovation may not try a more difficult change but may attempt a simpler one.

Local adaptation may be crucial to implementation (Berman and McLaughlin, 1978; Huberman and Miles, 1983; McLaughlin, 1990). Schools with the necessary readiness for innovation seem to be able to adapt an innovation to the local culture, thereby increasing the level of program implementation. Adaptation is a double-edged sword, however. If local adaptation omits key features of an innovation (as often happens), a limited or ineffective adaptation may be all that is put in place. In fact, one study (Rosenblum and Louis, 1979) showed that high levels of classroom autonomy in a school district work against implementation of districtwide programs.

To summarize, a greater degree of implementation integrity can be expected with explicit, user-friendly innovations for which a great deal of training is offered and when teachers perceive that the innovation meets a need and have participated in the planning for the innovation. If the program is complex, more effort must be expended to increase clarity and perceived need. Greater integrity can be expected in schools that have highly skilled teachers who communicate well and have high senses of self-efficacy, cultural norms that do not reject the innovation, strong district- and school-level leadership, staff stability, central office support, and a climate supporting change (e.g., problem-solving focus, high staff morale and commitment to change, no history of failed implementation, and a relatively low level of turbulence). Finally, local adaptation is likely to occur, especially with more complex programs. This adaptation process, although necessary, has the potential to alter the program drastically.

External Factors

Schools do not operate in vacuums. They operate in the contexts of local school districts, state education agencies, and federal government policies, practices, and funding streams, and are influenced by local politics and community pressures. Because these external agents have traditionally had little access to information about or control over the day-to-day operations in a school building, they have had minimal direct effect on the quality of implementation. They have instead affected implementation indirectly by choosing or making funds available only for high-quality programs, clarifying the need for the program, establishing conditions that provide for sufficient staff development and technical assistance time, and so on. But the schools' level of use of these resources ultimately depends on the local culture. A recent trend in the U.S. federal government[2] toward requiring implementation monitoring of prevention programs that are funded as part of the Safe and Drug-Free Schools and Communities Act may introduce more pressure toward high-quality implementation but only if local schools feel the pressure and accept the challenge.

External factors are more influential at the initiation stage. Fullan and Stiegelbauer (1991) cite advocacy from the central administration, availability of funds, and community pressure as three important influences on a school's decision to initiate an innovation. Although most communities do not actively participate in change decisions about educational programs, the community generally prevails when it is involved. Highly educated communities pressure their schools to adopt high-quality academic-oriented changes, and they oppose changes they do not like. Less educated communities are less likely to initiate change or pressure educators to initiate change, and therefore change is less likely.

These external factors determine to some extent the local school climate with respect to change. When district resources are lacking, central administration is weak, and community pressure is absent, schools are less likely to adapt innovations. The next section examines how these factors influence the implementation of prevention programs in those geographic locations most in need of prevention services – inner cities.

Change in Urban Schools: A Special Case

Rates of problem behavior are higher in urban than in suburban and rural areas. Research summarized in Chapter 3 suggests that schools may contribute to the relative high levels of delinquency and other problems faced in these communities – that weak schools are one component in the overall social disorganization experienced in urban areas. Several mechanisms through which community social disorganization contributes to poor educational practices and fails to control problem behavior were discussed. Parents in disorganized areas are less active in the school and less likely to exert external pressure to improve schools. Cultural differences among administrators, teachers, parents, and students make it more difficult to develop shared norms about behavior. Delinquent peer cultures are more likely to flourish in the absence of shared norms for behavior. Principal leadership functions are likely to be more difficult in urban schools simply

---

[2] The 1986 Drug-Free Schools and Communities Act provided substantial funds to states to develop and operate drug prevention programs. In 1994, the legislation was expanded to authorize expenditures on school-based violence prevention as well. After several critical reports suggested that the funds were not being utilized effectively at the local level, the U.S. Department of Education (Federal Regulations, July 16, 1997) began to require that schools expend the funds only on "proven" strategies, and that they monitor the quality of implementation.

because there are more crisis situations with which to deal. Teachers respond to student heterogeneity by lowering expectations for some students, grouping students within classrooms by ability level, and altering the pace of instruction. Schools respond by allocating different students to different tracks or courses. These grouping functions serve to fragment the school experience and reduce the likelihood that higher-risk youths will be exposed to more prosocial peer models. Schools serving lower-class students focus on basic skills to a greater extent than schools serving more advantaged populations.

Evidence from the school-change literature suggests that schools in urban areas also suffer because they have less capacity to implement innovations effectively. If this is true, urban schools not only suffer because they are at the bottom of the distribution of the characteristics linked to student success but also because attempts by staff in urban schools to change these conditions will more often fail. If true, the likelihood of finding successful school-based prevention programs is lowest in the communities most in need of such programs.

The distribution of implementation quality across different areas and types of school is not well understood. What little evidence exists points to unequal distribution, with schools in the most troubled, urban areas having the least capacity for innovation. The following paragraphs summarize the scant evidence showing that organizational capacity to implement new programs and policies effectively is not equally distributed across locations.

Capacity to Innovate in Urban Schools

Only one national survey sheds light on differences across schools in implementation capacity. The National Center for Education Statistics (1991) asked teachers to report not only about the level of problems related to drugs, violence, and other forms of disorder, but also about certain resources available to them for dealing with these problems. Table 7.1 shows responses, by location, of questions related to school capacity. It shows that teachers in urban schools report receiving roughly the same amount of in-service training as teachers in other areas, but that they perceive a lack of adequate training. More striking are the differences in perceptions that lack of administrative support and fear of student reprisal (an indicator of poor school climate) interfere with teachers' work.

Corcoran, Walker, and White (1988) interviewed more than four hundred teachers, school administrators, central office personnel, district officials, board members, and union officials from thirty-one schools in five urban areas in order to understand the working conditions in these schools. The report is rich in quotations about and observations of conditions in the schools. Among the findings of the study were that the physi-

Table 7.1. *Indicators of School Capacity, by Location*

Item	Location of School			
	City	Urban Fringe	Town	Rural
Percentage of teachers ever receiving training regarding school's general discipline programs and policies	60 (3.0)	63 (2.9)	58 (2.8)	58 (3.4)
Average number of in-service hours (in 1990– 1991) for teachers receiving training	5.0 (.46)	4.5 (.41)	5.3 (1.02)	3.7 (.42)
Percentage of teachers indicating that certain factors limit to a great or moderate extent their ability to maintain order and discipline in their school				
Lack of or inadequate teacher training in discipline procedures and school law	22 (2.2)	18 (2.1)	16 (2.1)	17 (1.8)
Lack of support from administration	33 (2.2)	26 (2.8)	26 (2.3)	24 (2.1)
Fear of student reprisal	11 (1.2)	6 (1.5)	6 (1.3)	8 (1.4)

Note: Standard errors appear in parentheses.

cal conditions in urban schools are substandard. In only three of the thirty-one schools (10%) in Corcoran et al.'s study were the physical conditions rated as "good." Maintenance issues (e.g., neglect of needed repairs, lengthy repair processes, general uncleanliness) were cited as problems in most schools.

Resources for implementing changes are generally lacking in urban settings. The overall adequacy of resources was rated as "inadequate" in nineteen of the thirty-one schools. One teacher commented that "Part of every paycheck goes toward buying supplies." Many teachers said they had to sneak to use the copier machine, and that they had to purchase ditto masters and paper from their own pockets. These conditions erode morale.

Urban schools also face personnel resource problems because they are less able to attract qualified teachers than surrounding suburban schools. Their ratio of teaching vacancies was three times as high as other districts in 1983. Among the reasons why urban districts find it difficult to recruit good teachers are (a) greater bureaucratic control over the content and timing of teaching, (b) more student discipline problems, (c) a greater share of students with whom it is difficult to achieve results, and (d) poor physical working conditions.

Corcoran also asked school staff about the extent of teacher participation in school decision making, an important factor in determining the level of implementation of innovations. Teachers in a third of the schools said their influence over school decisions was low. No teacher reported a high degree of influence, and only three (10%) said their influence level was moderate to high. More than half of the schools were rated low in collegiality, and Corcoran observed a correlation between the ratings of collegiality and the level of participation in decision making reported by teachers. Teachers in noncollegial schools reported major factions in the school, poor communication between the faculty and administrators, and autocratic school leaders. By contrast, teachers in schools rated higher on collegiality reported the existence of strong committees, team planning with time allocated for teams to meet, and good faculty-administrative relations.

On the topic of administrative support, teachers agreed that principal leadership was critical. But only 29% of the schools had effective school leaders, according to the teacher interviews. Perceptions of the quality of principal leadership declined as the size of the school increased. Urban teachers also had little confidence in the supervision, staff development, or central office leadership. These teachers generally felt that district-level improvement efforts had not been well communicated to teachers.

Corcoran's description of working conditions in urban settings suggests that these conditions are not conducive to strong implementation of new programs and practices. The schools included in the study certainly appear deficient on a number of indicators of school capacity. Yet, without comparisons with suburban and rural schools, we cannot be certain that all schools are not as deficient. A handful of studies in the school change literature have compared schools in different locations on indicators of school capacity.

Principal Leadership. We have seen that principal leadership and support is one of the most important determinants of high-quality implementation. Gottfredson and Hybl (1989) asked principals in schools in suburban, rural, and urban areas to describe their jobs. Urban and rural principals significantly more than suburban principals responded that dealing with issues of student interaction and social control (e.g., attendance, discipline) is important to their job. With fewer student problems to attend to, suburban principals are allowed more time for planning and action and keeping up to date, both areas that would encourage implementation of change. A survey completed by teachers in all schools in a diverse school district (Gottfredson and Gottfredson, 1989) showed that teachers' perceptions of smooth administration in the school varied with a measure of average student economic status in the expected direction, although not significantly in the small sample: teachers in schools having a larger percentage of students receiving free or reduced lunch saw more problems with the school administration. A large qualitative study of urban high school principals explained some of the difficulties in leadership for innovation as a mismatch of expectations for managing change and the skills of building principals. Beleaguered principals faced expectations for dealing with improving instructional and behavioral outcomes for students without having enough authority to affect change – and expectations for handling complex reforms without necessary supervisory or instructional leadership skills (Louis and Miles, 1990).

School Climate. In addition to a burdened principal, another barrier to change in the urban school may be pervasive climate problems. Teacher morale and orderliness are lower for urban than suburban schools (Gottfredson and Gottfredson, 1989). A large study of the effectiveness of teams involved in innovations in eighty-nine schools (of which 48% comprised large cities and 67% high schools) found several climate differences by location on questionnaires given to students, teachers, and principals (Social Action Research Center, 1979). They found a relationship between location of school and school crime and disruption. In neighborhoods described by respondents as deteriorated and having problems with drugs, youth gangs, and crime, there was a significantly higher perception of danger. Large city schools had a significantly higher student-to-teacher ratio and a greater security orientation than did suburban schools. These factors affected implementation. A study of working conditions in schools in two large cities found teachers stressed by problems of security, governance, control, and participation (Ginsberg, Schwartz, Olson, and Bennett, 1987). Bryk and Driscoll (1988) showed that in schools with higher proportions of disadvantaged students, schools were less likely to include a system of shared values, a clear mission, high expectations, meaningful social interactions, collegial relations among adults, and extended teacher roles. Finally, Witte and Walsh (1990), in a study of 204 schools in the Milwaukee metropolitan area, noted that school effectiveness measures are highly dependent on the location of the school and the demographic characteristics of its students. Their measure of teacher control over decision making had large inverse correlations with a measure of city versus suburban school location.

Resources. Gottfredson and Gottfredson (1989) found teachers in schools serving more advantaged and white students reported having more resources available for teaching and learning than teachers in schools serving more disadvantaged and black students. Ostroff (1992) also found that the ratio of students to teachers and the per-pupil expenditure were significantly higher in schools serving lower-SES populations.

Teacher Characteristics. Differences in teacher skills by urban and suburban locations have not been the subject of much research. Teacher skills and mastery of new techniques and technologies facilitate change both directly by increasing the likelihood of strong implementation of a particular technology and indirectly by producing a history of successful innovation in the school that fuels morale and commitment to future attempts. Ostroff (1992) showed that teachers' satisfaction with and commitment to their jobs was lower in schools serving lower SES populations. Two additional studies provide indirect evidence that teachers in urban schools are overburdened and underskilled, at least when faced with innovations. Weiner (1990) studied eight teachers in training and found prospective city teachers discouraged by their student teaching experiences, more so than those who chose to teach in suburban schools. A study in Milwaukee looked at why teachers leave urban schools (Haberman and Rickards, 1990). Most of the fifty teachers surveyed left for "other employment," "the residence requirement," or "personal reasons" but still choose to teach. Lack of discipline and inadequate support from administration were the two top reasons cited, not diverse or underachieving students as the teachers anticipated before they began teaching. Comparative studies should clearly address the issue of teacher ability, but the evidence summarized here suggests that urban schools may not attract or keep the skilled teachers needed.

The foregoing discussion implies that school characteristics are related to the level of implementation, and that some of these school characteristics vary by the urban or suburban location of the school. Only one study provides direct evidence that differences in teacher skills, resources, leadership, and environment *explain* urban-suburban differences in the level of implementation. The Social Action Research Center (1979) quantified the level of implementation of programs initiated by school teams. They found that implementation strength was significantly related to school location (r = .42). Large urban schools in poor, crime-ridden neighborhoods also implemented different *types* of programs. The urban schools, when given a choice about what to implement, concentrated their efforts on discipline, security, and traditional options. Teams in these schools also chose interventions aimed at improving teacher morale rather than more technological and sophisticated innovations. Urban schools planned differently with more administrative participation on planning teams. The researchers noted that participation in planning decreased teachers' sense of alienation.

Although more definitive research is needed to understand better the distribution of implementation strength and fidelity implementation across different types of schools, it is precisely those schools whose populations are most in need of prevention and intervention services that seem least able to provide those services. The studies summarized here found that leadership, teacher morale, teacher mastery, school climate, and resources are different on average in urban and other schools. This "Matthew effect" (Matthew 13:12) in education was alluded to in Chapter 3: "To those schools that have [advantaged populations] more will be given. To those that have not, even what they have will be taken away. The schools serving the most disadvantaged populations lack the resources that make their schools effective. These are mostly human resources capable of managing schools in such a way as to create cohesive social organizations."

We now have a clearer picture of the school characteristics that contribute to this Matthew effect. Schools in urban areas are burdened in a number of unique ways. They serve more difficult student populations and receive less support from the community. The heterogeneity of the population and the extreme behaviors the students bring to the school place strains on the school staff to monitor and deal with the behaviors and to create discipline structures capable of handling these behaviors. The teaching task itself is also made more complex by greater heterogeneity of students. Shortages of high-quality staff, both teachers and administrators, compound these problems. The job of the educator in an urban school is more challenging than in other areas. Although data are not available on the nature of educational reforms required in urban settings, we can expect that a greater number of programs are required to meet the need, and that the "fixes" are more complex by nature. More training and better communication should be required to ensure high-quality implementation in these settings, yet the evidence suggests that urban teachers receive no more training, and that the quality of technical assistance is low. Perhaps most important, we now have evidence that the two most critical factors determining implementation quality – principal support and a climate of collegiality – are less likely to exist in urban settings.

These facts paint a dreary picture of the feasibility of major school reform to reduce crime and related problem behaviors in urban areas. As Huberman and Miles (1984, described earlier) pointed out, attempts to change schools for the better may make things worse. Change can be disruptive and wasteful of resources, particularly when the school staff is prone to infighting and has a low probability of successfully implementing the change. It may be better for some schools to continue to function at the status quo than to disrupt the routine.

Social and Economic Context of Urban Education Problems

The relatively poor performance in terms of educational as well as problem behavior outcomes of urban schools must be understood in the context of larger social and economic changes that have occurred in the United States since World War II. Kantor and Brenzel (1992) and Wilson (1997) chronicle these changes and show how they have shaped urban education.

The main factor influencing the development of urban school systems since the end of World War II was the rapid out-migration from the cities that occurred after the war. Public policies favoring home ownership encouraged people to move out of the inner cities, and this "suburbanization" of the American population occurred disproportionately for whites. As the most affluent families left the cities, cities became increasingly poorer. Poverty rates dropped in suburban and nonmetropolitan areas while they climbed in the cities. White flight from the cities resulted in high concentrations of poor black people in the urban areas. This stressed the schools serving these areas because poor people have more needs, both educational and social, than do more advantaged populations.

City schools became more and more associated with low educational achievement as the most advantaged families, both black and white, left. Inner-city public schools increasingly served low-income city children, as the remaining whites in the city resorted to private schools. Although nationwide the academic achievement of African Americans and Hispanics was increasing, educational outcomes for students in city schools consistently lagged behind outcomes for the suburbs. Although some have attributed the poor outcomes for students attending these schools to ability deficits, it seems clear that the families living in these areas are generally more stressed and have fewer resources to prepare their children to succeed in school in the first place and to continue to encourage their success in school. Because childrens' academic achievement is mostly determined by the educational levels of their families of origin, students who live in inner-city areas would be expected to perform less well than students of equivalent ability from more advantaged areas. Inner-city schools are clearly more challenged than other schools in terms of the input characteristics of their populations.

Evidence summarized here, however, also implies that the poor outcomes for students in urban areas are not solely due to their relatively poor standing at school entry. Rather, students in urban areas appear to receive lower-quality educations than their suburban counterparts. The physical facilities are less conducive to learning, and resources (both material and people) are more scarce. The erosion of the tax base in cities explains why, without additional state or federal monies, inner-city schools must operate on slimmer budgets. Taxes raise fewer total revenues in poor areas, and cities have greater demands than suburban areas for other public services and therefore cannot devote as much of their total budgets to education. Although city schools receive billions of dollars in federal assistance to reduce the differential funding of urban and suburban schools, this additional funding brings with it administrative burden and, at least in the past, has prescribed educational practices (such as pullout programs that identify slow learners and remove them from the regular education program for special programs) that were probably harmful.

On top of this differential funding of education in different areas, urban schools systems have not adapted well to their changing demographics. Some of the efforts of urban school systems to improve matters may have actually made things worse. For example, one response has been to create "magnet schools" in urban areas to try to retain more affluent families. These schools have further segregated schools within cities by creating yet another layer of segregation and siphoning off the most talented students, leaving neighborhood schools to educate the poorest of the poor. While these schools may increase the chance for success for those who attend, they almost certainly hurt the neighborhood schools.

The organizational structure of the typical urban school system has also made it difficult for the system to respond to the changing needs of its clientele. Urban school systems have been organized centrally since the early twentieth century. School board members have typically been elected at-large rather than by ward. The rationale for this was to free school matters from the influence of local political machines, but the effect was to separate the operation of the schools from the lay community. Urban school systems are generally large and bureaucratic. Over time they have grown larger, more specialized and differentiated, with increasingly more power in the hands of the superintendent. Until recently, the superintendent and professional staff were often majority white, serving nearly all-black communities.

This situation slowly began to change in the 1960s and 1970s, as several writers exposed the failures of urban education. Stimulated by the civil rights movement, local black school movements began to fight for more community control over the schools. These movements did succeed in getting more black representation on city school boards and in the large central administrative offices and in establishing parent councils and positions for school-home liaisons in some schools during the latter 1970s and 1980s. But by the end of the 1980s, this movement toward decentralization had weakened and gains were diminished. The movement, then, succeeded in changing the color of the people running the large bureaucracy but did not result in a system more responsive to the clientele in the large cities. Black administrators, it appears, are also out of touch with the needs of the urban poor.

Also during the 1980s, many books and articles were written about characteristics of effective schools, and particularly effective urban schools. Various studies documented the characteristics of "resilient" urban schools – schools that appear to beat the odds by producing well-educated students. This shifted attention to local school building characteristics such as high educational expectations, academic missions, strong leadership, and high academic standards that were found to be related to superior school outcomes. After several largely unsuccessful attempts to legislate "effective schools" from the state level during the 1980s, attention has once again shifted to decentralizing control. This latest movement – often called the "School Restructuring" reform – insists that meaningful reform must be generated at the local school level with input from the local community. Teams of teachers, principals, and parents are encouraged to work together to reshape their schools.

Some argue that efforts to reform schools will be unsuccessful unless they are able to attack the social and economic effects of inner-city isolation and expand educational and economic opportunities for poor minority youths once they finish school. They point out that a sense of hopelessness so pervades urban life that the very meaning of education has been drastically altered. Wilson's (1997) latest work, *When Work Disappears*, documents the devastating effect deindustrialization has had on America's urban areas. Beginning in the 1950s, factories began to relocate from city centers to suburban areas (due in part to cheaper costs of transportation made possible by interstate highways), and the economy shifted to favor financial, administrative, and social services over manufacturing. These economic shifts, on top of the white flight out of inner cities, caused a major economic downturn for cities. Large numbers of city dwellers lost their jobs, and the relatively higher educational credentials needed for jobs in the expanding sectors of the economy kept them out of work. These economic shifts hit black urban dwellers the hardest. Among eighteen- to twenty-four-year-olds not in school, 89% of white males participated in the labor market in 1983. For black males, this figure drifted downward beginning in the 1960s until 1983, when only 72% participated in the labor market.

Wilson (1997) shows that these national figures underestimate the seriousness of the problem in the most hard-hit areas. In ghetto census tracts in the nation's one hundred largest cities, there were only 65.5 employed persons for every 100 unemployed persons in a typical week in 1990. Also, along with the increase in joblessness has come a decline in wages for those minorities who are employed because they are often placed in relatively low-level positions in the newer sectors of the economy.

These economic realities weaken the link between education and economic prosperity for urban dwellers and make it more difficult for urban schools to maintain commitment to education among students. Faced with a future of low-wage work and little opportunity for advancement, it is no surprise that many urban youth choose to stay away from school, thus diminishing their chances for success even more.

Wilson (1997) documents the wide-ranging effects of the "suburbanization" of employment on the black urban poor. Drug trafficking and other lucrative crime become attractive options to young persons who see little future in conventional work. Parents, fearful for themselves and their children, attempt to isolate their families from negative influences by preventing their children from interacting with others in the neighborhood.

Although this strategy may shield children from involvement in crime, Wilson shows that it also cuts off their access to resources provided by the stable working residents, such as informal job networking and conventional role models. Moreover, areas in which joblessness is high transmit certain attitudes and beliefs that work against integration into the mainstream work culture. Working communities introduce structure, discipline, and regularity to life. Nonworking communities do not. Children growing up in communities in which work has "disappeared" do not learn self-discipline, rational planning, and other organizational skills necessary for adaptation to the world of work. A state of apathy ensues when people are left with nothing but free time on their hands. Idleness becomes a way of life.

Wilson discusses what joblessness does to the perceived self-efficacy of community residents. Low self-efficacy expectations may come not only from people questioning their own capabilities or preparedness but also from perceptions that their opportunities are severely restricted by discriminatory practices. Feelings of bitterness and distrust of the white middle class are common. These feelings work against integration of black workers into many workplaces but also create a normative climate in which continued reliance on welfare is legitimate and appropriate.

According to Wilson, when people from these communities do find work, they are often lacking in the attitudes and organizational skills necessary to succeed. He documents tendencies among employers to avoid hiring youths from the known ghetto areas because of their perceptions of deficiencies not only in academic training but also in necessary attitudes and social skills. Wilson quotes one employer saying "there just doesn't seem to be a work ethic involved in these people" (1997, p. 135).

Although no systematic study of city teachers' perceptions of their students has been conducted, it is a safe bet that these perceptions parallel employers' perceptions of their potential workers. Teachers expect with respect to school work the same "work ethic" employers expect of their employees and are often disappointed in the attitudes of their students. In Corcoran et al.'s (1988, pp. 59–60) interviews with teachers and administrators in five urban school systems, student motivation, attitudes, and attendance were cited as major problems in city schools:

> Many [students] believe that because their parents aren't making money, they have no chance to do better, no hope.

> Attendance is an overwhelming problem – high volume. Parents don't give priority to school; they keep kids home. Usually just a lack of self-discipline, but sometimes watching siblings.

> There is an attitude among the kids that school is not a serious activity; there are serious attendance and truancy problems here.

These quotes are reminiscent of Cohen's (1955) "middle class measuring rod" problem. Describing the problem lower-class boys face in school, Cohen stated that teachers apply a common set of standards for behavior to all students, regardless of their backgrounds. Cohen's theory suggested that teachers' lower opinions of lower-class boys created a "problem of adjustment" for these boys, one that they solved through delinquent involvement. Although the mechanism linking teacher evaluations of students to delinquency in Cohen's theory has not been supported, the discrepancy between middle-class teacher expectations and lower-class students' behavior was and is real. Ethnographic studies of inner-city schools also find that students believe that teachers do not understand them (E. Anderson, personal communication, 1999). This culture clash is an important obstacle to school reform in inner-city areas.

This historical and contextual account of inner-city education suggests that inner-city areas are special cases and that attempts to reduce problem behavior through school-based prevention and intervention activities will almost certainly face major challenges. What works in schools in other places may not work in inner-city schools without more substantial efforts to build school and community infrastructures to support innovation.

Potential Solutions

It has taken decades to destroy inner-city education. It will take decades to fix it. Wilson's agenda to reverse the downward slide of inner cities includes non-school-related actions to achieve better integration of and cooperation between suburban and urban areas, legislation (such as the earned income tax credit and universal health care) to make work more attractive to low-wage earners; better systems to transport inner-city residents to distant places of employment; and the creation of jobs. He also recommends increasing support of families by providing universal preschool, child support, and parental leave programs. In the longer run, however, the schools must be changed so that they provide a work force that is competitive in the new economy. Among the school-related solutions offered by Wilson are raising academic standards, building school's capacity for self-improvement, and teaming with the private sector to enhance computer competency training.

Holding schools and students to higher academic standards should provide structure and incentives for students and teachers. Measuring these standards regularly and publicizing schools' performance should provide educational administrators and parents with important information about the quality of the school. Wilson sees such a commitment to a system of national standards as a first step in upgrading the quality of education. Such a program, of course, would target all schools in the nation.

Critics counter that some schools will have greater difficulties in meeting these national standards because of the deficits cited here (e.g., they have fewer resources to deal with a more needy student population). They expect that under a system of national standards, these schools will be further punished. For this reason, higher standards must be introduced along with efforts to build schools' capacity to meet the standards, including teacher and administrator development, school development, and equalization of resources. One of the most important issues Wilson discusses is the difference in the talent of the school staff between wealthier suburban and city schools. Resource differentials affect both the material resources and the quality of the school staff as the best teachers avoid high-poverty schools. Some inner-city schools have difficulty recruiting teachers at all. In these schools, students are taught by a continuous flow of substitute teachers. Teachers and administrators are the main resources schools have for improvement. City schools need the best, not the worst, school staff to meet the challenges they face.

Programs to improve the quality of the teaching staff in inner-city schools might include incentives to draw higher-quality teachers to inner-city areas (such as scholarships and forgivable loans) and teacher evaluation systems to identify and displace poorly performing teachers. Systems could also be put in place to ensure more equitable distribution of teaching talent across schools in a given system. Schools in need of extra assistance could be targeted by state and local education agencies for additional school and staff development.

Data from performance assessments could be the basis for targeting schools for improvement resources. Wilson also favors a public school choice program in which data on school effectiveness would be made available (in an easily understandable form) to parents for use in choosing their childrens' schools.

Several of Wilson's recommendations for school reform resemble those included in the Clinton administration's "Goals 2000: Educate America Act" passed by the U.S. Congress in 1994. This legislation attempted to balance the need to create a more competitive work force with the desire to maintain local control over educational matters. It included funds to states and school districts to develop content and performance standards in core academic subjects. Although states were not required to align their standards with model national standards, they were required to develop *some* standards, and to assess their students on those standards. The new legislation also included a School-to-Work Opportunities Act, which sought to bring together employers and educators at the local level to develop systems to better prepare high school graduates for jobs requiring technical skill or for further education and training. The legislation funded local and voluntary demonstration projects to develop and implement innovative programs to integrate school and work. The legislation also recognized that the reforms included in the legislation would require upgrading teacher competencies. Under the Goals 2000: Educate America Act, local education authorities are able to apply for competitive grants to implement local plans for "continuing and sustained" professional development opportunities for school staff, recognizing that the typical one-shot workshops traditionally used for staff development activities are largely ineffective.

The Goals 2000 legislation also recognized that the communities in which schools are located have everything to do with schools' ability to educate children. The legislation embraced the "it takes a village" philosophy by suggesting that local partnerships between schools, families, and communities be formed to promote the social, emotional, and academic growth of children. Under the legislation, states were expected to "develop policies to assist local schools and local education agencies to establish programs for increasing partnerships that respond to the varying needs of parents and the home, including parents of children who are bilingual, or parents of children with disabilities. Every school is expected to engage parents and families actively in a partnership that supports the academic work of children at home and shared educational decision making at the school. Finally, families are expected to help ensure that schools are adequately supported and that the schools and their teachers are held to high standards of accountability" (Schneider, 1996, p. 198). Of all of the legislation included in the 1990s reform package, this piece was the most vaguely worded and least well defined in terms of strategies for accomplishing the partnerships.

Critics of the community partnership legislation argue that effective partnerships between educators and community members are not likely to be formed under current conditions in many communities. They point out that even local schoolteachers and administrators are out of touch with the people in the communities they serve. A cultural gulf separates school professionals from their students and their students' parents. Teachers often blame parents for ill-preparing their children for school and failing to be more supportive of the school and their children. Poor relations, or no relations, between teachers and parents may diminish the feasibility of true collaborative planning and action in many schools. However, the inclusion of the language in the legislation at least recognized that the disjunction between the school and the community contributes to the school's inability to meet its goals.

The 1994 legislation was far-reaching and unprecedented in establishing guidelines consistent with scientific literature on what should work. As Wilson points out, however, the voluntary nature and relatively meager federal expenditure for the reform will probably not be sufficient to solve the massive problems faced by urban school systems. The tone of the legislation made clear that the role of the federal government should be to "encourage experimentation" with these reforms at the local level rather than mandating change. Although the Goals 2000 legislation was an important first step toward improving urban education, a stronger federal commitment will be necessary to effect real change.

Summary

The optimistic outlook on the potential for school-based prevention to reduce problem behavior presented in the preceding chapters must be tempered on the basis of literature reviewed in this chapter. School-based prevention *can* work. But school-based prevention *may not* work in many settings. Unfortunately, it is the settings experiencing the most severe problems that will likely have the most difficulty implementing prevention programs.

How can the strength and integrity of school-based prevention programs be improved? Although research on the "technology" of prevention has advanced in the past decade, we know little about the conditions necessary to apply these advances under real-world conditions. The literature on school innovation reviewed earlier hardly provides a theory of implementation, but it at least provides hints about the organizational barriers to strong implementation. We need more precise information about the causal factors that determine level of implementation, and we need to develop a theory to guide attempts to strengthen intervention practices.

The available evidence identifies certain features that should be incorporated into prevention programs at the design stage in order to increase the likelihood of high-quality implementation. Teaching manuals and other program guides should be clearly written and easy to follow. Materials needed should be provided. Guidelines for training should be well organized and clear. Materials for training (e.g., videotapes, etc.) should be available. Follow-up training and on-site coaching should be provided.

Most of the suggestions from prior research are more difficult to realize. They involve changes in school staffing and organization. Some schools already have capable staff and an organizational structure that encourages teacher input into the development and management of school change. In some schools, the culture supports innovation, and resources are not a problem. In other schools, these conditions do not exist. Sometimes schools lack capable leaders. Sometimes they lack a core of high-quality teachers who are willing to take responsibility for implementing change. Such schools will require substantial capacity-building before they can be expected to innovate successfully. In these schools it will be necessary to shore up the organization to support change and establish problem-solving processes before new practices are attempted. Sometimes this will require changes in the staff. Other times it might be accomplished through an organization development process, essential features of which are a realistic needs assessment, selection of programs and practices that might be expected to solve the problems identified, clear implementation standards, and open analysis and resolution of obstacles that prevent the standards from being met. Most important, school staff must participate in this process and must be provided an environment that supports this kind of problem-solving approach. Although mere staff training may be translated into beneficial change in some schools, it will be a drop in the bucket, or even a hindrance, or perceived as a waste of precious time, in others.

Developing a theory of implementation and providing the necessary support for implementation in different types of schools requires a better understanding than we now have about the factors related to high-quality implementation and the development of valid assessment instruments to test schools' readiness for change so that differentiated organization development and technical assistance strategies can be targeted appropriately. A study now underway – the National Study of Delinquency Prevention in Schools, supported by the U.S. National Institute of Justice and Department of Education and in collaboration with Westat, Inc. – should pave the way for advances in the quality of program implementation (Gottfredson and Gottfredson, 1996).

Where Do We Go From Here?

TWENTY YEARS AGO, an extensive review of delinquency prevention and treatment programs (Wright and Dixon, 1977) concluded that *little evidence* of positive effects for prevention programs could be found in the available research, but that implementation quality and quantity helped to explain the success of the relatively few programs that produced positive results. Today we can conclude that *considerable evidence* of positive effects for prevention programs can be found in the available research, but that implementation quality and quantity qualify the positive findings. Schools can be a site for effective intervention, or a site for nonintervention or ineffective intervention. Schools have the potential to contribute to the positive socialization of youth. But the range of conditions under which they have been demonstrated to realize this potential is narrow.

This chapters summarizes the conclusions of earlier chapters and offers recommendations for the practice of school-based prevention and for additional research to advance the field.

The Practice of School-Based Prevention

Policy Recommendations

The research summarized in this book suggests four broad policy recommendations for the practice of school-based prevention:

Appropriate more dollars for school-based prevention.
Shift monies away from approaches with less research support and toward approaches with more research support.
Build in systems to monitor program implementation and provide tech-

nical assistance and organization development assistance where needed to strengthen programs.

Target urban areas.

Appropriations. The research summarized in Chapters 5 and 6 indicates that several school-based prevention strategies are effective for reducing crime and related problem behaviors. An influential report by the RAND corporation (Greenwood et al., 1996) showed that compared with home visits by child-care professionals, parent training, monitoring and supervising of already delinquent youths, and imprisoning felony offenders at a higher rate (e.g., "three strikes" legislation), a prevention intervention targeting high-school-age youths to provide educational and social development was more cost effective. Greenwood et al. estimated that the number of serious crimes prevented per million program dollars spent ranged from 11 (for home visits) to 258 (for the program targeting high-school-age youths). Two of the prevention strategies examined were far more cost effective than the three-strikes legislation. Yet, relative to federal expenditures on control strategies such as policing and prison construction, expenditures on school-based substance abuse and crime prevention efforts are modest. D. Gottfredson (1997) reported that the U.S. Office of Justice Program's total expenditures on school-based prevention are less than $25 million per year, compared with $1.4 billion for the extra police programs and $617 million for prison construction.

The single largest federal expenditure on school-based prevention in the U.S. is the Department of Education's Safe and Drug-Free Schools and Communities monies of approximately $500 million per year. Though several times larger than the Justice Department's expenditures, even this amounts to a pittance when it is distributed across all school districts in the United States. Silvia and Thorne (1997) estimate that Safe and Drug-Free Schools funds for implementing drug prevention programs averaged $6 to $8 per pupil per year. This limited investment is a major oversight because school-based crime prevention has more scientific evidence of effectiveness than do many other programs supported more generously by the federal government.

More Research Support. Not only is too little money allocated to school-based prevention, but the meager federal expenditures on school-based prevention are not well spent. Safe and Drug-Free Schools and Communities monies administered by the U.S. Department of Education fund a relatively narrow range of intervention strategies, many of which have been shown either not to work (e.g., counseling) or to have only small effects (e.g., drug instruction). The new Principles of Effectiveness put in place in 1997 to guide local expenditures of these funds call for limiting programs to those for which research and evaluation activities have demonstrated a preventive effect on drug use, violence, or disruptive behavior. This is a step in the right direction. However, state and local interpretations of research and evaluation may be faulty, especially in the absence of user-friendly, correct summaries of what works and what doesn't.

Several noteworthy attempts to provide quality information about promising prevention approaches are ongoing. These include the Center for the Study and Prevention of Violence's "Blueprints" project, the University of Maryland's Crime Prevention Program activities, and Drug Strategies' school-based prevention program reviews. All three of these efforts apply clear criteria to identify programs and practices that "work" or hold promise for reducing problem behavior, and all three publish user-friendly descriptions of the programs and practices identified. In addition to providing detailed "blueprints," Elliott's program also arranges for technical assistance and monitoring in selected communities to increase the probability that local realizations of the programs included in the Blueprints series are implemented as intended. These resources, and many more high-quality reviews, serve as a starting point to identify prevention strategies that work.

Monitoring and Assistance. As we have seen, *the quality of program implementation* is at least as important in determining the success of a prevention activity as the *type of program* selected. Policy makers must therefore establish mechanisms to monitor the quality of implementation of funded activities and to develop systems to provide necessary technical assistance and organization development assistance. Templates for programs known to work should be developed to provide a standard against which features of proposed programs can be compared. Programs could be funded on the basis of their apparent similarity to programs that have been shown to work. As programs are implemented, data on the strength and integrity of each program could be collected and again compared with the template. This comparison could provide the basis not only for decisions about continued funding but also for the provision of technical assistance and organization development assistance to the implementing organization.

Of course, work must be done to establish and regularly update "essential features" of prevention programs. Available research can be used to narrow the categories of prevention (e.g., social competency development training programs, normative change) that seem most promising. Within each category, the existing research can be combed to describe the features (e.g., duration, intensity, organization) of those models shown to work in previous research. These features would become the standard against which funded programs could be compared. Data collection systems could be established so that funded programs generate information on their level of implementation relative to the standard.

Knowledge about essential features is rudimentary at present. But it is possible to glean from the existing literature, as was accomplished in the Drug Strategies, Inc., projects described earlier, some standards of effectiveness. As future evaluations collect more systematic data on level of implementation, the knowledge base would grow and more precise understandings of the essential features of different program models would evolve.

Targeting Urban Areas. Crime and related problem behaviors occur disproportionately in urban areas, and urban areas have the least capacity for solving these problems. It is not wise, from a public policy point of view, to continue the use of funding formulas that distribute tax dollars for prevention efforts evenly across geographic areas. A concerted effort is required to reinvigorate inner-city communities so that they have the infrastructure necessary to make use of the available technology for preventing crime. The policy implication is that funds should be funneled disproportionately to these areas.

Recommendations for Practice

Environmental Change Interventions. Chapters 3 and 5 address characteristics of school environments related to levels of problem behavior and attempts to manipulate those characteristics. The nonexperimental research summarized in Chapter 3 suggested that schools control behavior by setting rules, communicating clear expectations for behavior, consistently enforcing rules, and providing rewards for rule compliance and punishments for rule infractions. Schools experiencing less problem behavior also run more smoothly: general management functions (such as coordination and resource allocation and communication) are working well, and goals for the organization are in place. In these schools, instruction is delivered in ways that promote maximal learning and that encourage a sense of community. An extended network of caring adults interacts regularly with the students and shares norms and expectations about its students.

Several of the features of effective schools identified in nonexperimental research summarized in Chapter 3 are corroborated in the quasi-experimental studies reviewed in Chapter 5. Both types of studies support the effectiveness of interventions aimed at setting rules, communicating clear expectations for behavior, consistently enforcing rules, and providing rewards for rule compliance and punishments for rule infractions. Also, both types of studies recommend improving general management functions (such as coordination and resource allocation and communication, establishing and maintaining clear goals) for the organization. Projects all showing positive results in support of discipline management interventions included the Good Behavior Game, Behavioral Consultation to Reduce Violence/Vandalism, and Bullying Prevention. PATHE and the Effective Schools Project supported both discipline and more general school management. Comer's School Development Project and the School Safety Project supported general school management.

The evidence supporting the organization of instructional delivery is mixed. The nonexperimental studies supported them, but results of attempts to manipulate these features produce mixed results. Efforts to alter instructional delivery mechanisms that are diffuse and not driven by a credible theory connecting the intervention to problem behavior outcomes (e.g., mastery learning, cooperative learning, classroom discussions) do not work. Relatively diffuse in-service teacher training on classroom processes do not work. But instructional and classroom management strategies that incorporate behavioral principles are successful, and broader programs that also incorporate social competency skill instruction (e.g., the Seattle Social Development model) show some evidence of effectiveness.

Finally, interventions to increase social control through an extended network of caring adults who interact regularly with the students and who share norms and expectations about their students – "communal social organizations" – were highly recommended by studies using survey research methodology. This type of environmental change strategy has not been the focus of much experimental or quasi-experimental research. Comer's School Development Program did produce positive results on problem behavior outcomes in one reasonably rigorous study. Some of the other more effective studies reviewed in Chapter 5 *may* have worked by creating smaller, more communally organized units. The research simply is not up to the task of isolating the mechanism through which these programs worked. Specifically, studies found that grouping students into smaller units for instruction, especially when these units include drastic changes to instructional and classroom management strategies, reduces problem behavior. This evidence comes from the STEP studies of reorganizations of high school freshman classes (although one replication did not support that efficacy of the program) and the STATUS program in both junior and senior high schools.

Organization Development Methods to Strengthen and Sustain Implementation. The school change literature discussed in Chapter 7 ties in with the environmental change literature to suggest that certain features of the organization might be manipulated to increase the probability that the innovation will be implemented in a strong fashion. High-quality implementation is more likely when sufficient training is offered, when teachers perceive that the innovation meets a need, and when teachers have participated in the planning for the innovation. The evidence also implies that greater integrity can be expected in schools that have cultural norms that do not reject the innovation, strong leadership, and a climate supporting change (e.g., problem-solving focus, high staff morale and commitment to change, no history of failed implementation, and a relatively low level of turbulence). The literature also made clear that a process of local adaptation is a necessary part of the implementation process.

How can these conditions be established in schools? Rowan (1990) describes a model of school organization that appears conducive to these facilitating conditions. The *commitment* strategy of organization design seeks to develop innovative working arrangements that support teachers' decision making and increase teachers' engagement in the tasks of teaching. This strategy assumes that collaborative and participatory management practices will "unleash" the energy and expertise of committed teachers. This strategy contrasts with the more hierarchical, bureaucratic school organization that focuses on regulation and standardization – the *control strategy*.

Four characteristics of schools organized around the commitment strategy are:

Teachers participate in decision making.
Teacher roles are expanded to facilitate the development of a network
     structure to support teacher decision making.
Teachers collaborate and "team."
Communal (rather than hierarchical) forms of organization are used.

Research (summarized in Rowan, 1990) generally supports the wisdom of including teachers in decision making. Schools with higher teacher influence in school decisions have better staff morale, teacher efficacy, and sense of community. Teacher satisfaction increases with the extent of teacher participation in school decision making. Redesigning teacher jobs by creating "lead" or "mentor" teacher positions is also related to higher levels of teacher commitment and satisfaction. Some schools rotate qualified staff through these positions to distribute them more broadly. Networks of professionals are developed in schools that use these expanded teacher roles. Teacher leaders are involved in formulating and implementing new initiatives, and they interact frequently with their colleagues to strengthen the quality of implementation of the new practice. Faculty interaction and cohesiveness results.

Collegiality among teachers can also be enhanced when teacher participation in teaming arrangements is intensive and sustained. Several studies have shown, however, that when only small amounts of time are allocated to these efforts, and when limited teacher interaction results, positive outcomes are not observed. Instead, the efforts must be substantial and sustained over long periods of time (e.g., five years). The effort must be of sufficient intensity to reinforce norms of continuous improvement.

The final element of the commitment strategy is the development of community in schools. Scant research has been conducted on how this sense of community can be developed in schools in which it does not already exist. The process would have to include the development of shared values that unify members of the school staff and orient them to a common purpose. Rowan warns that the positive outcomes associated with communal organization may depend largely on the content of the values and not only the extent to which they are shared. He cites case studies of alternative schools in which teachers shared values and beliefs about their students that were counterproductive. He also warns that schools can become too communal. When teachers, for example, must rely on personal bonds with students to maintain order and motivate learning, they may become burned out. Some hierarchical organization is required to reinforce the traditional authority relations in the school.

This process of developing communal social organizations seems particularly challenging for schools located in disorganized communities. Clinical observation suggests that a major source of tension in these schools is the low level of shared norms for behavior. It is not uncommon for teachers and principals in these schools to disagree on even the most basic of rules for behavior, such as the time school begins. Students straggle into the school at various times, and adults have no clear expectation for when students *should* arrive and, consequently, how to treat latecomers. Ethnographic studies of schools in inner-city areas (E. Anderson, personal communication, 1998) suggest that students encounter two types of teachers: those who understand students' motives and behaviors, and those who rigidly enforce rules without understanding the conditions that produce the students' behaviors. This intersection between students and teachers in inner-city schools is likely to be at the crux of the failure of inner-city schools to promote good socialization outcomes. This intersection, and the influence of school and community organization on it, is an important area for extended research.

Rowan concludes that several of the factors related to higher-quality program implementation can be achieved by increasing teacher influence in school decision making, raising levels of collegiality, and extending their roles to make them more responsible for each others' behaviors and increase their collaboration and interaction. This model of school organization has not been rigorously studied, however. We know little about the effectiveness of such an organization development intervention or about the generalizability of this model across different types of schools and communities.

Rowan's model of the commitment model of school organization has been *approximated* in studies of manipulations of organization development (OD) in schools. These include tests of Gottfredson's Program Development Evaluation (PDE; G. Gottfredson, 1984; Gottfredson et al. 1984) summarized in Chapter 5. Program Development Evaluation is an OD method developed to help organizations plan, initiate, and sustain needed changes. Researchers collaborate with school teams of teachers, administrators, counselors, and other school staff, using specific steps spelled out in the program materials, to develop and implement programs. An important part of the process involves continuous data feedback during the implementation phase to the school team.

As described in Chapter 5, PDE has been tested and replicated in urban school settings. The method tested provided a structure for prolonged interaction and collaboration among school staff. It created new roles for the team members as they took responsibility for fostering change among their colleagues. Team members planned and implemented staff development activities for the school, provided feedback to their colleagues, and often took on the role of coach or mentor to other teachers who were trying new strategies. When the teams were well integrated into the school organization, they became a mechanism through which teachers increased their decision-making capacities in the school. Measures of communal organization per se were not collected in these studies, but the OD activities did involve frequent discussions and reinforcement of values and attitudes. It is not clear, though, to what extent these discussions were successful for solidifying norms in the school. These activities improved the school's general management functions in both studies, as well as indicators of organizational health such as teacher morale and teacher involvement in planning and action to improve the school.

Several models of school improvement similar to PDE have been developed and disseminated. Several are described and critiqued in *A Consumer's Guide to School Improvement* (Mills, 1990).

Individual-Change Interventions. Chapter 2 summarized individual characteristics likely to be causes of problem behavior. Chapter 6 summarized experimental and quasi-experimental studies that attempted to manipulate one or more of these characteristics. Results from these studies correspond reasonably well with the results from the nonexperimental studies.

The superiority of programs targeting social competency skills and self-control is consistent with the finding that "conscientiousness" predicts problem behavior. This personality trait reflects many of the same traits targeted in the most successful programs. Such programs teach students how to slow down, consider the problem, weigh alternatives, and be cautious. They teach students how to think ahead, stay on top of things, and focus

on long-term goals rather than immediate gratification. Self-control is at
the heart of "conscientiousness." The studies of direct service provision to
school students to teach the cognitive and behavioral skills necessary for
self-control provide strong confirming evidence that the "conscientiousness" personality factor is central to the development of delinquent behavior and (more important) that it can be manipulated during the school
years. Consistent with findings that this factor has an enduring effect on
problem behavior across the entire school career, social competency development programs were found to be effective at all educational levels and
for both general populations and high-risk populations.

Nonexperimental research also suggested the importance of a second
set of characteristics – "agreeableness" – in preventing problem behavior.
Results from the intervention studies are consistent with this, but they do
not disentangle the effects of becoming more agreeable from the effects
of becoming more conscientious.

Field studies that manipulated these characteristics included:

Elementary
General population: PATHS curriculum.
High-risk population: Interpersonal Cognitive Problem Solving (ICPS);
    FAST Track; Anger Coping Program (but correspondence between
    measures of self-control and behavior is not always as anticipated);
    Assertiveness/Social Skills Training.

Middle or Junior High
General population: Positive Youth Development.
High-risk population: Anger Control Training; Moral Reasoning Devel-
    opment and Decision-Making Intervention.

Senior High
General population: Cognitive/Social Skills Training.

The FAST Track study also found evidence that some combination of
program elements increased peer acceptance, and regression analyses suggested that this increased popularity reduced subsequent problem behavior. It is not possible to disentangle the effects of the program elements to
determine which element or combination of elements was responsible for
the positive change. Some combination of program features increased both
self-control and peer acceptance, which decreased subsequent problem
behavior. Measures of program effects on agreeableness are extremely rare
in studies of middle school and nonexistent in studies of high school
populations.

Nonexperimental studies showed that indicators of the extent and intensity of social control (e.g., attachments to school and others, commitment to education and work, and beliefs in rules) and the kinds of influences (especially peer) to which the individual is exposed, although shaped in part by individual personality, have a causal effect on subsequent problem behavior above and beyond the enduring effects of individual characteristics. The studies hinted that the potency of the effects of these social control factors may increase over the age span. These intermediate outcomes are not often assessed in experimental and quasi-experimental studies, but the available studies provide some support for a causal effect.

Measures of social bonding and negative peer influence among elementary school students are very rare, probably because most of the elementary interventions address social problem-solving skills. But among studies of older students, the evidence is generally consistent with a mediating effect of social bonding and negative peer influence; that is, effects on these intermediate outcomes co-occur with effects on problem behaviors. For example, studies at the middle or junior high school level showed that when the intervention produces mixed effects on drug attitudies (a measure of prosocial beliefs), mixed effects on drug use are observed (Positive Youth Development). When the intervention produces no effect on prosocial attitudes or social bonding or negative peer influence, no effect on problem behavior is observed (Youth Development Project, PATHE high-risk youth component, Malvin et al. [1985] alternatives to drug use interventions, Magic Me, Multimodel School Based Prevention Demonstration). At the senior high level, when positive effects are observed on school bonding, a measure of drug control problems also improves (Personal Growth Class). But other evidence is not as consistent. For example, the Dropout Prevention Program improves attitudes toward school but has no effect on problem behavior. And several of the reports from the Seattle Social Development Project show consistent positive effects on attachment and commitment to school, but null or inconsistent effects on measures of problem behaviors. Clearly, more research is needed on the causal effect of these factors.

Finally, Chapter 2 suggested that the correlation between academic performance, at least prior to high school, and delinquency was due mostly to their common reliance on early behavior problems. Evidence from the experimental and quasi-experimental studies is mixed on this point. The Coie and Krehbiel (1984) study showed that the provision of intensive academic skills training to elementary school children increases academic performance and peer acceptance and decreases conduct problems. The FAST Track study showed that increases in cognitive development resulting from a variety of interventions mediated the positive effects of the program on later problem behavior. At the middle and high school levels, Project PATHE and the Multimodel School-Based Prevention Demonstration found that tutoring interventions that are successful for increasing academic performance and educational persistence do not reduce problem behavior. On the other hand, behavioral interventions that track and provide consequences for academic performance (e.g., the Bry work and Project PREP) both increase academic performance and reduce problem behavior. The relationship between academic performance and problem behavior is not straightforward. It is likely that improved performance alone (e.g., as would be expected in an isolated tutoring experience in which bonding to the tutor does not develop) has no effect on problem behavior. But when improved academic performance results in other changes (such as increased commitment to school or greater acceptance by prosocial peers), problem behavior declines. If borne out in future research, these speculations would have implications for the design of interventions focusing on increasing academic performance.

The research summarized in Chapter 6 also provided important evidence about what *does not* work to reduce problem behavior. Whereas programs targeting the most likely causal factors for problem behavior *do* reduce problem behavior, programs targeting other factors such as self-esteem, other forms of psychological health or adjustment, and knowledge about drugs, laws, etc. *do not* reduce problem behavior. Examples include the Reckless and Dinitz (1972) study of a special class for high-risk boys in which no attempt was made to teach social competency skills. Instead, the emphasis was on raising the boys' self-esteem and avoiding potentially stigmatizing experiences. No effects were found on any measures of problem behavior for this year-long class. Similarly, several studies of the provision of social casework and counseling showed that these strategies were at best ineffective (e.g., Rose and Marshall, 1974; Gottfredson, 1986) and at worse harmful (D. Gottfredson, 1987) in terms of their effects on problem behavior. School-based programs that provide advocacy, mentoring, alternative activities, and work apprenticeship also proved ineffective for the most part. The evidence is clear: the only programs targeting individual skills, attitudes, or beliefs that can be regarded as effective are those that target social competency skills. These programs increase youths' ability to control their own behaviors. The jury is still out on the extent to which academically oriented strategies such as tutoring (important in their own right because they clearly improve academic performance) can add to the positive outcomes observed with social competency development strategies.

Summary. Research on school-based prevention suggests that schools do contribute to the level of problem behavior exhibited by their students. Schools can decrease problem behavior by organizing and managing themselves effectively, creating environments supporting prosocial behavior, providing specific instruction, training, and coaching in the development of social competency skills necessary for self-control, and by implementing programs and practices in a high-quality fashion. Research does not recommend any particular program or practice, as several have been shown to be effective for reducing problem behavior. Rather, it points to a small number of principles on which effective prevention strategies should be based. The literature suggests that it is unrealistic to expect that schools will simply adopt strategies exactly as they were developed. Instead, school staff will adapt these strategies to fit their particular settings. One challenge for prevention is to increase the number of models for prevention that incorporate the principles elaborated here, ensure that they reach schools, and develop training and technical assistance programs that stress the essential features of these programs that should be maintained during local implementation. Another challenge is to find ways to provide ongoing organization development assistance to help schools create infrastructures that support change.

Table 8.1 provides a starting point for identifying effective strategies. It shows examples corresponding to each principle of effectiveness of programs that have demonstrated some effectiveness for reducing problem behavior. These "effective" program models might be studied by teams of educators in school districts and in local schools to identify building blocks for locally developed programs. But the decision about *what* to implement is only half the battle.

Conditions have to be established in schools to promote high-quality implementation of these new practices. These conditions should include teacher influence in school decision making, raising levels of collegiality, and extending teacher roles to make them more responsible for each others' behaviors and increase their collaboration and interaction. In some schools, these conditions are present or could be developed readily through establishment of teams and provision of time for planning and other collaborative activities. In other schools, more basic organization development will be necessary first. Staffing changes may be required. Conflict resolution and team-building interventions may be necessary. In such schools, it is not advisable to plow ahead with new initiatives before a sound organizational structure is in place.

Future Research

Knowledge about what works in school-based delinquency prevention is uneven. Effects of some school-based strategies on reducing problem behavior (e.g., elementary-level social competency development strategies) have been well studied; effects of others (e.g., efforts to create "communally organized" schools) have not. Some important areas, such as the relative importance of high-quality implementation and type of intervention

Table 8.1. *Effective Models for School-Based Prevention*

1. Setting rules, communicating clear expectations for behavior, consistently enforcing rules, and providing rewards for rule compliance and punishments for rule infractions.

Elementary: (Dolan et al., 1993; Kellam et al., 1994); Bullying Prevention (Olweus, 1991); Behavioral Consultation to Reduce Violence/Vandalism (Mayer and Butterworth, 1979; Mayer et al., 1983)

Middle/Junior High: Bullying Prevention (Olweus, 1991)

Senior High: PATHE (Gottfredson, 1986)

2. Organizing the delivery of instruction in ways that promote maximal learning and that encourage a sense of community.

Elementary: ClassWide Peer Tutoring (Greenwood et al., 1993)

Middle/Junior High: STATUS (Gottfredson, 1990)

3. Improving general management functions (such as coordination and resource allocation and communication, establishing and maintaining clear goals for the organization).

Elementary: School Development Program (Comer Process; Cook et al., 1998)

Senior High: PATHE (Gottfredson, 1986); School Safety Project (Kenney and Watson, 1996)

4. Increasing social control through an extended network of caring adults who interact regularly with the students and who share norms and expectations about their students – "communal social organizations."

Middle/Junior High: STATUS (Gottfredson, 1990)

Senior High: School Transitional Environment Project (Felner and Adan, 1988)

5. Providing behavior management interventions

Elementary: Playground Aggression Prevention (Murphy et al., 1983); Improving Attendance (Barber and Kagey, 1977).

Middle/Junior High: Behavior Modification Intervention (Bry and George, 1979, 1980; Bry, 1982); Behavior Modification and Parent Training (Patterson, 1974)

Senior High: Contingency Management for Truancy (Brooks, 1975)

6. Providing instruction, training, and coaching in the development of social competency skills – general population

Elementary: PATHS curriculum (Greenberg and Kusché, 1993; Greenberg et al., 1995; Conduct Problems Prevention Group, 1997)

Middle/Junior High: Positive Youth Development (Caplan et al., 1992; Weissberg and Caplan 1994); Life Skills Training (Botvin, Baker, Renick, et al., 1984; Botvin, Baker, Filazzola et al., 1990; Botvin, Baker, Dusenbusy, et al., 1995)

Senior High: Cognitive-Social Skills Training (Sarason and Sarason, 1981)

7. Providing instruction, training, and coaching in the development of social competency skills – high-risk populations

Elementary: Interpersonal Cognitive Problem Solving (ICPS; Shure and Spivack, 1979, 1980, 1982); FAST Track (Conduct Problems Prevention Research Group, 1992, 1997), Anger Coping Program (Lochman, 1992; Lochman et al., 1984, 1985, 1986, 1989); Social Skills Training (Rotheram, 1982; Rotheram et al., 1982)

Middle/Junior High: Anger Control Training (Feindler et al., 1984); Moral Reasoning Development and Decision Making (Arbuthnot and Gordon, 1986; Arbuthnot, 1992)

Senior High: Personal Growth Class (Eggert et al., 1994, 1995)

on problem behavior reduction, have not been studied at all. This final section discusses changes in policy regarding the study of school-based prevention that would facilitate the generation of new knowledge and makes some specific recommendations for needed research.

Policy Recommendations

Three changes in policy at the federal and state levels would foster better research. These policy recommendations parallel the general recommendations put forth in a recent Report to Congress (Sherman et al., 1997):

> Fund process rather than impact evaluations for most projects or demonstrations.
> Increase funding for replication studies to establish generalizability of effects in different settings.
> Fund only scientifically rigorous impact evaluations in carefully selected sites.

Process versus Impact Evaluations. Stop funding impact evaluations for most projects or demonstrations. High-quality impact evaluation is expensive. Funding agencies, in order to increase accountability for tax dollars spent, often require evaluation for each and every prevention activity funded. They sometimes require that a certain percentage of the total project budget be allocated to evaluation. This often results in a few thousand dollars being spent on something that might be called "evaluation," but such activities probably do more harm than good because they do not produce knowledge that can be used by any of the interested parties, and they perpetuate the perception that evaluation is useless.

A more sensible strategy is one in which grantees are required to select from a menu of possible programs that have already been shown to work (if well implemented) in other settings. Grantees could then be required to conduct a process evaluation to demonstrate that the specific realization of the program resembles that which was shown to work in prior evaluation. This plan would satisfy the need for accountability for the funding agent, provide useful information for the local project managers on what was and was not being implemented faithfully, and would have the side benefit of creating a data base that could be used to study the distribution of community and organizational features related to the quality of implementation. To make this happen, it would be necessary to identify the programs or practices to be included in the "menu," to establish implementation standards based on previous evaluation, and to develop useful and user-friendly measures of implementation that could be administered across sites.

Funding for Replication Studies. Rarely are replication studies to establish generalizability of effects in different settings funded. When a reasonably rigorous study produces evidence of effectiveness, the federal response is often to move directly to wide dissemination of the practice rather than to attempt to replicate the findings. A case in point is the Juvenile Mentoring Program (JUMP) currently supported by the Office of Juvenile Justice and Delinquency Prevention. On the basis of one solid evaluation of a highly structured community-based mentoring model (the Big Brother/Big Sister model evaluated by Tierney, Grossman, and Resch, 1995) which found evidence of a positive effect on initiation of substance use and selected self-reported delinquent behaviors, OJJDP recently invested $19 million in juvenile mentoring programs, as mandated by the U.S. Congress. The relative dearth of high-quality evaluations producing clear-cut positive results makes this response on the part of funding agents a reasonable one. But positive results are not always replicated, as, for example, the Reyes and Jason (1991) study of reorganizing ninth grade classrooms and the Jones et al. (1997) attempt to replicate the Success for All elementary school restructuring model have shown.

Replication studies would also serve to expand the pool of potentially useful program models. Chapters 5 and 6 identify numerous potentially effective models that are not being used widely. These include programs that group youths into smaller "schools within schools" to create smaller units, more supportive interactions, or greater flexibility in instruction. This type of program appears promising on the basis of nonexperimental research summarized in Chapter 2, but the only attempts to create more communal organizations have produced mixed results. The STATUS model (Gottfredson, 1990) is an example of a program that produced strikingly positive results. The program has not been replicated, and it is not clear which of the several features of the program produced the positive outcomes. Programs aimed at improving general classroom management and instructional strategies, such as the Seattle Social Development Model, also require replication because results have been mixed.

Scientifically Rigorous Impact Evaluations. Studies of school-based prevention strategies share some common weaknesses. The typical study of school-based prevention exceeds the standard for methodological rigor used in the University of Maryland Report to the U.S. Congress. In that report, a scientific method score of 3 was accepted. Among school-based studies, the typical rigor ratings were 3.4 for environmental studies and 3.7 for individual-level studies. A reasonable goal for future evaluations would be to boost the rigor of evaluation studies to at least level 4. The rigor of evaluations of school-based prevention programs can be greatly improved by:

Using more equivalent comparison groups.
Increasing the number of schools in the typical study.
Conforming the unit of analysis to the unit of assignment.
Reporting effect sizes along with tests of statistical significance.
Allowing for longer-term follow-up.
Measuring program implementation.

Random assignment of subjects to treatment and control conditions was achieved in fewer than 25% of the studies reviewed and in only three of the studies of environmental change strategies. In another 26% of the studies, a fairly equivalent (although nonrandomly assigned) comparison group was used. This leaves approximately half of the studies in which comparisons were between a group that received the intervention and another group that was known to be nonequivalent or whose equivalence was unknown. In these cases, the credibility of the conclusions rests on the ability to control statistically for initial group differences that might have affected the outcomes. Confidence in the conclusions of these studies is always compromised. Randomized studies or studies in which the selection processes through which subjects were placed in one of the other groups are to be preferred.

As noted in Chapter 6, the typical study contains too few cases, resulting in weakened statistical power. Studies of school-level interventions always involve too few schools (the average is twelve). More than half of all studies involve fewer than two hundred cases. Underpowered evaluations do more harm than good because they are unlikely to detect a meaningful difference between the treatment and the comparison condition even if one exists. Funding agencies should insist on larger-scale evaluation. Generally, power analyses conducted during the design phase of a study should guide decisions about the appropriate number of cases.

The scientific rigor of evaluations can also be improved by conforming the units of analysis to the units of allocation to treatment and control conditions. This is particularly a problem in studies of environmental interventions in which schools are typically assigned to conditions, but individuals are analyzed. As explained in Chapter 5, such studies are prone to overestimate program effects – especially as the similarity of the individuals within each group increases. Funding agents should require school- or classroom-level analyses or appropriate multilevel modeling techniques for studies of school- and classroom-level interventions.

Sole reliance on statistical significance rather than a more meaningful measure of the magnitude of program effects is another weakness found in the studies of school-based prevention. This issue is related to the issue of sample size because tests of statistical significance generally result in more findings of significance for larger studies than for smaller studies.

Comparisons across studies are misleading because the conclusions depend in part on the sample size. For example, Botvin's LST program generally shows significant results, when many other programs do not. But effect size calculations show that LST is only slightly more efficacious than the typical instructional program. Overreliance on statistical significance gives an advantage to the few programs whose studies have involved large numbers of cases and a disadvantage for programs studied with small numbers of cases. This problem would be solved by using effect size calculations, or confidence intervals around means, and by using the correct units of analysis.

Yet another weakness is the dearth of studies of the long-term effectiveness of programs. Only 43 (39%) of studies had any measurement of effects after the immediate post-test, and only six of these were studies of environmental interventions. About half of these studies followed students for as long as one year after the end of the intervention. Longer-term follow-up studies should be encouraged, particularly with interventions that demonstrate immediate effects.

A final problem in evaluation is that null results are often not interpretable because the independent variable is not measured with any precision – that is, program implementation is often treated as a binary (yes/no) variable when it is in fact a continuous variable. Failure to measure strength and integrity of program implementation leads to the erroneous conclusion that a program or strategy "does not work" when actually it has not been tested because it was not implemented with sufficient rigor.

More rigorous evaluations will be costly in terms of the personnel time needed to coordinate with the school organizations and the number of schools needed to evaluate school- and classroom-level interventions, but in the long run far more will be learned by upgrading a small number of evaluations of key programs and practices than continuing to fund a large number of relatively weak evaluations.

A Research Agenda

Most of the research on school-based prevention has been directed at programs and practices intended to reduce potential offenders' dispositions to engage in problem behaviors, enhance social control, and manage schools. Little research has been focused on the alternative strategies of reducing target attractiveness or guarding potential crime targets (e.g., security and surveillance strategies), and making the physical school building less conducive to crime (e.g., by requiring uniforms so that intruders can be easily identified, or making physical alterations such as closing off stairwells and widening passages). Although these strategies have not been discussed at length, they are plausible school-based prevention strategies that deserve closer scrutiny than they have received. The first recommendation for research is therefore:

Develop and test environmental change security-oriented strategies (e.g., aimed at reducing target attractiveness and improving the effectiveness of target guardians) and strategies that alter the physical school building to make it less conducive to crime.

Basic and applied research is needed to answer the following specific questions:

How do the magnitude and duration of effects of school-based prevention strategies compare with those from prevention attempts in other domains?

Meta-analytic studies should be conducted to increase understanding of the magnitude and durability of program effects across different domains. Such studies will be limited by the relatively small numbers of environmentally focused school-based intervention whose long-term effects have been studied.

Which of the multiple risk factors identified in the literature are causal factors?

The prevention focus on risk and protective factors is enormously popular among practitioners and has succeeded in pushing practice away from strategies with no basis in research and toward strategies with plausibility. At the same time, accumulated evidence has raised questions about the relative potency of different risk and protective factors and their possible differential effects on various problem behaviors. As Chapter 2 shows, evidence for a causal effect of academic performance and school attitudes on delinquent behavior is mixed. Some studies find support, others do not, and the effects seem to differ depending on the age of the population. Chapter 5 also shows that the mechanisms through which schools effect problem behavior are often unclear. Consistent effects on attachment and commitment to school and on achievement do not always translate into reductions in problem behavior. But because multiple risk factors are often targeted in a given study and because the targeted factors are not always measured, study results are ambiguous. These questions about causality can be most effectively addressed through experimentation. A series of small-scale studies might be conducted, each targeting a particular risk factor. Effects on problem behavior can be examined. For example, a relatively straightforward study could test the effects of tutoring on delinquent behavior. Such a study would have to measure academic performance to ensure that the targeted characteristic was actually altered.

What is the optimal dosage, timing, delivery agent, and targeting of effective prevention practices?

Although effective programs have been identified for all school-age populations, little is known about the relative advantages of earlier versus later intervention. Results summarized in Chapter 2 suggest that early intervention should target social behavior, but later intervention might target peer association, academic performance, and school attitudes as well. Chapter 6 shows that studies of programs targeting elementary school students more often report positive results, but that it was unclear why. Perhaps the intervention strategies used with younger children are more effective, perhaps early forms of problem behavior are more malleable than later (more serious) forms; or perhaps the measures of problem behavior employed in these studies (e.g., teacher ratings; observations) are more reliable than the measures used in studies of older populations (e.g., police contacts).

We also know that interventions are effective both for the general population and for selected high-risk populations, but we have little knowledge about the relative advantages of these two strategies. Many effective programs are delivered by "outsiders" – for example, university community agency personnel. Could these programs be delivered as effectively by classroom teachers? Finally, some effective programs are extremely brief (e.g., ALERT consists of seven sessions) and some are long (e.g., PATHS consists of sixty sessions). How important is the duration of the program relative to its content? Can the more effective long programs be shortened without substantial loss in effectiveness? These are questions that can easily be answered with additional research.

What are the relative contributions of program content and scope to program effectiveness?

Chapter 5 concludes that broader schoolwide approaches appear effective for reducing problem behavior, but notes that this generalization depended on the content of the program. It shows that programs with a narrow focus also appear effective when they use behavioral and cognitive-behavioral approaches, and that broader programs are unsuccessful when they lack this focus. Understanding the relative importance of scope and content is important in light of the increased emphasis in recent years on multicomponent programs. Several influential reviews have concluded that more comprehensive approaches to prevention are more likely to be effective than programs targeting single domains. Yet more easily implemented, narrower programs with a very specific focus and content may prove more potent. More research is needed to understand the relative contributions of scope and content to program effectiveness.

Do effective environmental and individual change strategies interact to alter student outcomes?

We have seen that strategies that change features of the school and classroom environment work to reduce problem behavior, as do programs targeting individuals. Are the effects of these types of programs additive in nature, or does a supportive environment boost the effectiveness of the individual-level intervention? Perhaps a violence prevention curriculum is far more effective for reducing violence if it is implemented in a school whose norms clearly support prosocial behavior than in one in which the norms for behavior are ambiguous.

How can schools become more "communal," and does this type of reorganization result in a reduction in problem behavior?

Interventions to increase social control through an extended network of caring adults who interact regularly with the students and who share norms and expectations about their students – "communal social organizations" – were highly recommended by the nonexperimental studies summarized in Chapter 2. We know very little about how, and if, such organizations can be created. One study of organizational change at the elementary school level demonstrated positive effects. Two of three studies of secondary schools summarized in Chapter 5 that attempted to alter the school environment to make it more responsive to students' needs were successful, but the mechanism through which they produced positive outcomes is not clear. Careful work must be done to catalog the features of communal organizations, translate them into specific program components, and develop training or organization strategies to encourage such behaviors. Of course, such attempts must be rigorously studied so that we learn what does and does not work.

Can the community and school conditions conducive to high-quality implementation be manipulated?

The school improvement literature implies that higher-quality program implementation can be achieved by increasing teacher influence in school decision making, raising levels of collegiality, and extending their roles to make them more responsible for each others' behaviors and increase their collaboration and interaction. But we know little about how to create these conditions in schools and how much of a difference they will make. Interventions need to be designed and tested in different types of schools and communities.

What types and levels of training, technical assistance, and organization development strategies are necessary to produce beneficial change in the most difficult, urban settings?

Chapter 7 argued that urban settings are a special case. Urban schools face a greater challenge than do other schools because their populations are more stressed and needy. Rather than meeting this challenge by fortifying the schools, we have systematically weakened schools in many urban areas by allowing valuable personnel resources to be lost to more comfortable places. It is time now to mount a concerted effort to study the effects of the most promising strategies for rebuilding urban schools. These strategies include personnel selection and allocation, organization development, training, and technical assistance. Specific strategies must be designed, and systematic attempts to implement these strategies under controlled conditions must be studied so that we may learn what it will take to restore our urban schools.

References

Ahlstrom, W. M., and Havighurst, R. J. (1971). *400 losers: Delinquent boys in high school.* San Francisco: Jossey-Bass.

    (1982). The Kansas City work/study experiment. In D. J. Safer (Ed.), *School programs for disruptive adolescents* (pp. 259–275). Baltimore: University Park Press.

Akers, R. L. (1996). *Criminological theories: Introduction and evaluation* (2nd ed.). Los Angeles: Roxbury Publishing.

Allen, J. P., Philliber, S., and Hoggson, N. (1990). School-based prevention of teen-age pregnancy and school dropout: Process evaluation of the national replication of the Teen Outreach Program. *American Journal of Community Psychology, 18,* 505–524.

Allison, K. R. (1992). Academic stream and tobacco, alcohol, and cannabis use among Ontario high school students. *International Journal of Addictions, 27,* 561–570.

American Psychiatric Association. (1994). *Diagnostic and statistical manual of mental disorders* (4th ed., rev.). Washington, DC: Author.

Arbuthnot, J. (1992). Sociomoral reasoning in behavior-disordered adolescents: Cognitive and behavioral change. In J. McCord and R. E. Tremblay (Eds.), *Preventing antisocial behavior: Interventions from birth through adolescence* (pp. 283–310). New York: Guilford Press.

Arbuthnot, J., and Gordon, D. A. (1986). Behavioral and cognitive effects of a moral reasoning development intervention for high-risk behavior-disordered adolescents. *Journal of Consulting and Clinical Psychology, 54,* 208–216.

Arneklev, B. J., Grasmick, H. G., Tittle, C. R., and Bursik, R. J., Jr. (1993). Low self-control and imprudent behavior. *Journal of Quantitative Criminology, 9,* 225–239.

Bachman, J. G. (1975). *Youth in transition: Documentation manual* (Vol. 2). Ann Arbor: University of Michigan Institute for Social Research.

Bachman, J. G., Green, S., and Wirtanen, I. D. (1971). *Youth in transition: Vol. 3. Dropping out – Problem or symptom?* Ann Arbor: University of Michigan Institute for Social Research.

Bachman, J. G., Johnston, L. D., and O'Malley, P. M. (1993). *Monitoring the future.* Ann Arbor: University of Michigan Institute for Social Research.

Bachman, J. G., O'Malley, P. M., and Johnston, J. (1978). *Youth in transition: Vol. 6. Adolescence to adulthood – Change in stability in the lives of young men.* Ann Arbor: University of Michigan Institute for Social Research.

Baerveldt, C. (1992). Schools and the prevention of petty crime: Search for a missing link. *Journal of Quantitative Criminology, 8,* 79–94.

Barber, R. M., and Kagey, J. R. (1977). Modification of school attendance for an elementary population. *Journal of Applied Behavior Analysis, 10,* 41–48.

Bartusch, D. R. J., Lynam, D. R., Moffitt, T. E., and Silva, P. A. (1997). Is age important? Testing a general versus a developmental theory of antisocial behavior. *Criminology, 35,* 13–48.

Bastian, L. D., and Taylor, B. M. (1991). *School crime: A national crime victimization survey report* (NCJ-131645). Washington, DC: Bureau of Justice Statistics.

Battistich, V., Schaps, E., Watson, M., and Solomon, D. (1996). Prevention effects of the Child Development Project: Early findings from an on-going multi-site demonstration trial. *Journal of Adolescent Research, 11,* 12–35.

Battistich, V., Solomon, D., Watson, M., Solomon, J., and Schaps, E. (1989). Effects of an elementary school program to enhance prosocial behavior on children's cognitive-social problem-solving skills and strategies. *Journal of Applied Developmental Psychology, 10,* 147–169.

Becker, H. J. (1987). *Addressing the needs of different groups of early adolescents: Effects of varying school and classroom organizational practices from different social backgrounds and abilities* (Report No. 16). Baltimore: Johns Hopkins University.

Berman, P., and McLaughlin, M. W. (1978). *Federal programs supporting educational change: Vol. 8. Implementing and sustaining innovations* (R-1589/8-HEW). Santa Monica, CA: Rand.

Bidwell, C. E., and Kasarda, J. D. (1980). Conceptualizing and measuring the effects of school and schooling. *American Journal of Education, 88,* 401–430.

Biglan, A., Metzler, C. W., Wirt, R., Ary, D., Noell, J., Ochs, L., French, C., and Hood, D. (1990). Social and behavioral factors associated with high-risk sexual behaviors among adolescents. *Journal of Behavioral Medicine, 13,* 245–261.

Block, J., Block, J., and Keyes, S. (1988). Longitudinally foretelling drug usage in adolescence: Early childhood personality and environmental precursors. *Child Development, 59,* 336–355.

Block, R. (1979). Community, environment, and violent crime. *Criminology, 17,* 46–57.

Blumstein, A., Cohen, J., Roth, J., and Visher, C. (1986). *Criminal careers and career criminals.* Washington, DC: National Academy Press.

Boruch, R., and Foley, E. (in press). Large scale controlled experiments: Sites and other entities as the unit of allocation and analysis. In L. Bickman (Ed.), *Validity and social experimentation: Donald T. Campbell's legacy.* Thousand Oaks, CA: Sage.

Botvin, G. J. (1990). Substance abuse prevention: Theory, practice, and effectiveness. In M. Tonry and J. Q. Wilson (Eds.), *Drugs and Crime* (pp. 461–520). Chicago: University of Chicago Press.

Botvin, G. J., Baker, E., Botvin, E. M., Filazzola, A. D., and Millman, R. B. (1984). Prevention of alcohol misuse through the development of personal and social competence: A pilot study. *Journal of Studies on Alcohol, 45*, 550–552.

Botvin, G. J., Baker, E., Dusenbury, L., Botvin, E. M., and Diaz, T. (1995). Long-term follow-up results of a randomized drug abuse prevention trial in a white middle-class population. *Journal of the American Medical Association, 273*, 1106–1112.

Botvin, G. J., Baker, E., Dusenbury, L., Tortu, S., and Botvin, E. M. (1990). Preventing adolescent drug abuse through a multi-modal cognitive-behavioral approach: Results of a 3-year study. *Journal of Consulting and Clinical Psychology, 58*, 437–446.

Botvin, G. J., Baker, E., Filazzola, A. D., and Botvin, E. M. (1990). A cognitive-behavioral approach to substance abuse prevention: One-year follow-up. *Addictive Behaviors, 15*, 47–63.

Botvin, G. J., Baker, E., Renick, N. L., Filazzola, A. D., and Botvin, E. M. (1984). A cognitive behavioral approach to substance abuse prevention. *Addictive Behaviors, 9*, 137–147.

Botvin, G. J., Batson, H. W., Witss-Vitale, S., Bess, V., Baker, E., and Dusenbury, L. (1989). A psychosocial approach to smoking prevention for urban black youth. *Public Health Reports, 12*, 279–296.

Botvin, G. J., Dusenbury, L., James-Ortiz, S., and Kerner, J. (1989). A skills training approach to smoking prevention among Hispanic youth. *Journal of Behavioral Medicine, 12*, 279–296.

Botvin, G. J., and Eng, A. (1982). The efficacy of a multicomponent approach to the prevention of cigarette smoking. *Preventive Medicine, 11*, 199–211.

Bowles, S., and Gintis, H. (1976). *Schooling in capitalist America.* New York: Basic Books.

Bretherton, D., Collins, L., and Ferretti, C. (1993). Dealing with conflict: Assessment of a course for secondary school students. *Australian Psychologist, 28*, 105–111.

Brewer, D. D., Hawkins, J. D., Catalano, R. F., and Neckerman, H. J. (1995). Preventing serious, violent, and chronic juvenile offending: A review of evaluations of selected strategies in childhood, adolescence, and the community. In J. C. Howell, B. Krisberg, J. J. Wilson, and J. D. Hawkins (Eds.), *A sourcebook on serious, violent, and chronic juvenile offenders* (pp. 61–141). Newbury Park, CA: Sage.

Brook, J. S., Whiteman, M., Finch, S. J., and Cohen, P. (1996). Young adult drug use and delinquency: Childhood antecedents and adolescent mediators. *Journal of the American Academy of Child Adolescence Psychiatry, 35*, 1584–1592.

Brooks, B. D. (1975). Contingency management as a means of reducing school truancy. *Education, 95*, 206–211.

Brooks-Gunn, J., Duncan, G. J., Klebanov, P. K., and Sealand, N. (1993). Do neighborhoods influence child and adolescent development? *American Journal of Sociology, 99*, 353–395.

Brophy, J. (1986). Teacher influences on student achievement. *American Psychologist, 41*, 1069–1077.

Bry, B. H. (1982). Reducing the incidence of adolescent problems through preventive intervention: One- and five-year follow-up. *American Journal of Community Psychology, 10*, 265–276.

Bry, B. H., and George, F. E. (1979). Evaluating and improving prevention programs: A strategy from drug abuse. *Evaluation and Program Planning, 2*, 127–136.

——— (1980). The preventive effects of early intervention on the attendance and grades of urban adolescents. *Professional Psychology, 11*, 252–260.

Bryk, A. S., and Driscoll, M. E. (1988). *The school as community: Theoretical foundations, contextual influences, and consequences for students and teachers.* Madison: University of Wisconsin, National Center on Effective Secondary Schools.

Bryk, A. S., and Lee, V. E., with Holland, P. B. (1993). *Catholic schools and the common good.* Cambridge, MA: Harvard University Press.

Bryk, A. S., and Thum, Y. M. (1989). The effects of high school organization on dropping out: An exploratory investigation. *American Educational Research Journal, 26*, 353–383.

Burgess, R. L., and Akers, R. L. (1966). A differential association-reinforcement theory of criminal behavior. *Social Problems, 14*, 128–147.

Bursik, R. J., Jr., and Grasmick, H. G. (1993). *Neighborhoods and crime: The dimensions of effective community control.* New York: Lexington Books.

Burton, V. S., Jr., Cullen, F. T., Evans, T. D., and Dunaway, R. G. (1994). Reconsidering strain theory: Operationalization, rival theories, and adult criminality. *Journal of Quantitative Criminology, 10*, 213–239.

Cairns, R. B., Cairns, B. D., Neckerman, H. J., Gest, S. D., and Gariépy, J.-L. (1988). Social networks and aggressive behavior: Peer support or peer rejection? *Developmental Psychology, 24*, 815–823.

Callahan, C. M., and Rivara, F. P. (1992). Urban high school youth and handguns: A school-based survey. *Journal of the American Medical Association, 267*, 3038–3042.

Cannan, C. (1970, December). Schools for delinquency. *New Society, 3*, 1004.

Caplan, M., Weissberg, R. P., Grober, J. S., Sivo, P. J., Grady, K., and Jacoby, C. (1992). Social competence promotion with inner-city and suburban young adolescents: Effects on social adjustment and alcohol use. *Journal of Consulting and Clinical Psychology, 60*, 56–63.

Caspi, A., and Bem, D. J. (1990). Personality continuity and change across the life course. In L. A. Pervin (Ed.), *Handbook of personality: Theory and research* (pp. 549–575). New York: Guilford Press.

Caspi, A., Lynam, D., Moffitt, T. E., and Silva, P. A. (1993). Unraveling girls' delinquency: Biological, dispositional, and contextual contributions to adolescent misbehavior. *Developmental Psychology, 29*, 19–30.

Caspi, A., Moffitt, T. E., Silva, P. A., Stouthamer-Loeber, M., Krueger, R. F., and Schmutte, P. S. (1994). Are some people crime-prone? Replications of the personality-crime relationship across countries, genders, races, and methods. *Criminology, 32*, 163–196.

Center for Substance Abuse Prevention. (1995). *The national structured evaluation of alcohol and other drug abuse prevention.* Rockville, MD: Substance Abuse and Mental Health Services Administration.

Centers for Disease Control and Prevention. (1993). Violence-related attitudes and behaviors of high school students – New York City, 1992. *Morbidity and Mortality Weekly Report, 42,* 773–777.

———(1995). CDC surveillance summaries, March 24, 1995. *Morbidity and Mortality Weekly Report, 44* (No. SS-1).

Cernkovich, S. A., and Giordano, P. C. (1992). School bonding, race, and delinquency. *Criminology, 30,* 261–291.

Chandler, K. A., Chapman, C. D., Rand, M. R., and Taylor, B. M. (1998). *Students' reports of school crime: 1989 and 1995* (NCES 98-241/NCJ-169607). Washington, DC: U.S. Departments of Education and Justice.

Clark, D. L., Lotto, L. S., and McCarthy, M. M. (1980). Factors associated with success in urban elementary schools. *Phi Delta Kappan, 61,* 467–470.

Cohen, A. K. (1955). *Delinquent boys: The culture of the gang.* New York: Free Press.

Cohen, J. (1994). The earth is round (p < .05). *American Psychologist, 49,* 997–1003.

Cohen, L. E., and Felson, M. (1979). Social change and crime rate trends: A routine activity approach. *American Sociological Review, 44,* 588–608.

Cohen, L. E., and Vila, B. J. (1996). Self-control and social control: An exposition of the Gottfredson-Hirschi/Sampson-Laub debate. *Studies on Crime and Crime Prevention, 5,* 125–150.

Coie, J. D. (1997, August). *Testing developmental theory of antisocial behavior with outcomes from the Fast Track Prevention Project.* Paper presented at the annual meeting of the American Psychological Association, Chicago.

Coie, J. D., Dodge, K. A., and Coppotelli, H. (1982). Dimensions and types of social status: A cross-age perspective. *Developmental Psychology, 18,* 557–571.

Coie, J. D., Dodge, K. A., and Kupersmidt, J. B. (1990). Peer group behavior and social status. In S. R. Asher and J. D. Coie (Eds.), *Peer rejection in childhood* (pp. 17–59). Cambridge: Cambridge University Press.

Coie, J. D., and Krehbiel, G. (1984). Effects of academic tutoring on the social status of low-achieving, socially rejected children. *Child Development, 55,* 1465–1478.

Coie, J. D., Lochman, J. E., Terry, R., and Hyman, C. (1992). Predicting early adolescent disorder from childhood aggression and peer relations. *Journal of Consulting and Clinical Psychology, 60,* 783–792.

Coie, J. D., Underwood, M., and Lochman, J. E. (1991). Programmatic intervention with aggressive children in the school setting. In D. J. Pepler and K. H. Rubin (Eds.), *The development and treatment of childhood aggression* (pp. 389–410). Hillsdale, NJ: Lawrence Erlbaum.

Coie, J. D., Watt, N. F., West, S. G., Hawkins, J. D., Asarnow, J. R., Markman, H. J., Ramey, S. L., Shure, M. B., and Long, B. (1993). The science of prevention: A conceptual framework and some directions for a national research program. *American Psychologist, 48,* 1013–1022.

Coleman, J. S., Campbell, E. Q., Hobson, C. J., McPartland, J., Mood, A. M., Weinfeld, F. D., and York, R. L. (1966). *Equality of educational opportunity* (2 vols.). Washington, DC: Office of Education, U.S. Department of Health, Education, and Welfare, U.S. Government Printing Office.

Comer, J. P. (1985). The Yale-New Haven Primary Prevention Project: A follow-up study. *Journal of the American Academy of Child Psychiatry, 24,* 154–160.

Comer, J. P., Haynes, N. M., and Hamilton-Lee, M. (1989). School power: A model for improving black student achievement. In W. D. Smith and E. W. Chunn (Eds.), *Black education: A quest for equity and excellence* (pp. 187–200). New Brunswick, NJ: Transaction Publishers.

Committee for Children. (1988). *Second Step, grades 1–3, pilot project 1987–88, summary report.* Seattle, WA: Author.

(1989). *Second Step, grades 4–5, pilot project 1988–89, summary report.* Seattle, WA: Author.

(1990). *Second Step, grades 6–8, pilot project 1989–90, summary report.* Seattle, WA: Author.

(1992). *Evaluation of Second Step, preschool-kindergarten, a violence-prevention curriculum kit.* Seattle, WA: Author.

Conduct Problems Prevention Research Group. (1992). A developmental and clinical model for the prevention of conduct disorder: The Fast Track Program. *Development and Psychopathology, 4,* 509–527.

(1997, April). *Prevention of antisocial behavior: Initial findings from the Fast Track Project.* Symposium presented at the biennial meeting of the Society for Research in Child Development, Washington, DC.

Connell, D. B., Turner, R. R., and Mason, E. F. (1985). Summary of the findings of the School Health Education Evaluation: Health promotion effectiveness, implementation, and costs. *Journal of School Health, 55,* 316–323.

Cooley, W. W., Bond, L., and Mao, B.-J. (1981). Analyzing multilevel data. In R. A. Berk (Ed.), *Educational evaluation methodology: The state of the art* (pp. 64–83). Baltimore: Johns Hopkins University Press.

Cook, T. D., and Campbell, D. T. (1979). *Quasi-experimentation: Design and analysis issues for field settings.* Chicago: Rand McNally.

Cook, T. D., Hunt, H. D., and Murphy, R. F. (1998). *Comer's School Development Program in Chicago: A theory-based evaluation.* Working papers. Evanston, IL: Northwestern University Institute for Policy Research.

Corcoran, T. B., Walker, L. J., and White, J. L. (1988). *Working in urban schools* (Rep. No. 143). Washington, DC: Institute for Educational Leadership.

Costa, P. T., and McCrae, R. R. (1992). *Revised NEO Personality Inventory (NEO PI-R) and NEO Five-Factor Inventory (NEO-FFI) professional manual.* Odessa, FL: Psychological Assessment Resources.

Cronin, J. (1996). *An evaluation of a school-based community service program: The effects of Magic Me.* Technical report available from Gottfredson Associates, Ellicott City, MD.

Cuttance, P. (1992). Evaluating the effectiveness of schools. In D. Reynolds and P. Cuttance (Eds.), *School effectiveness: Research, policy, and practice* (pp. 71–95). New York: Cassell.

Derr, C. B. (1976). "OD" won't work in schools. *Educational and Urban Society, 8,* 227–241.

Digman, J. M. (1990). Personality structure: Emergence of the five-factor model. *Annual Review of Psychology, 41,* 417–440.

Digman, J. M., and Inouye, J. (1986). Further specification of the five robust factors of personality. *Journal of Personality and Social Psychology, 50,* 116–123.

Dinitz, S. (1982). A school-based prevention program to reduce delinquency vulnerability. In D. J. Safer (Ed.), *School programs for disruptive adolescents* (pp. 279–296). Baltimore: University Park Press.

Dishion, T. J. (1988). *A developmental model of peer relations: Middle childhood correlates and one-year sequelae.* Unpublished doctoral dissertation, University of Oregon, Eugene.

———— (1990). The peer context of troublesome child and adolescent behavior. In P. E. Leone (Ed.), *Understanding troubled and troubling youth* (pp. 128–153). Newbury Park, CA: Sage.

Dishion, T. J., Patterson, G. R., Stoolmiller, M., and Skinner, M. L. (1991). Family, school, and behavioral antecedents to early adolescent involvement with antisocial peers. *Developmental Psychology, 27,* 172–180.

Dodge, K. A., and the Conduct Problems Prevention Research Group. (1993, March). *Effects of intervention on children at high risk for conduct problems.* Paper presented at the biennial meeting of the Society for Research in Child Development, New Orleans.

Dodge, K. A., Pettit, G. S., McClaskey, C. L., and Brown, M. M. (1986). Social competence in children. *Monographs of the Society for Research in Child Development, 51* (2, Serial No. 213).

Dolan, L. J., Kellam, S. G., Brown, C. H., Werthamer-Larsson, L., Rebok, G. W., Mayer, L. S., Laudolff, J., Turkkan, J. S., Ford, C., and Wheeler, L. (1993). The short-term impact of two classroom-based preventive interventions on aggressive and shy behaviors and poor achievement. *Journal of Applied Developmental Psychology, 14,* 317–345.

Dryfoos, J. G. (1990). *Adolescents at risk: Prevalence and prevention.* New York: Oxford University Press.

Durlak, J. A. (1995). *School-based prevention programs for children and adolescents.* Thousand Oaks, CA: Sage.

Eder, R. A., and Mangelsdorf, S. C. (1997). The emotional basis of early personality development: Implications for the emergent self-concept. In R. Hogan, J. Johnson, and S. Briggs (Eds.), *Handbook of personality psychology* (pp. 209–240). San Diego, CA: Academic Press.

Eggert, L. L., Thompson, E. A., Herting, J. R., and Nicholas, L. J. (1995). Reducing suicide potential among high-risk youth: Tests of a school-based prevention program. *Suicide and Life-Threatening Behavior, 25,* 276–296.

Eggert. L. L., Thompson, E. A., Herting, J. R., Nicholas, L. J., and Dicker, B. G. (1994). Preventing adolescent drug abuse and high school dropout through an intensive school-based social network development program. *American Journal of Health Promotion, 8,* 202–215.

Elias, M. J., Gara, M. A., Schuyler, T. F., Branden-Muller, L. R., and Sayette, M. A. (1991). The promotion of social competence: Longitudinal study of a preventive school-based program. *American Journal of Orthopsychiatry, 61,* 409–417.

Elias, M. J., Weissberg, R. P., Hawkins, J. D., Perry, C. A., Zins, J. E., Dodge, K. C., Kendall, P. C., Gottfredson, D. C., Rotheram-Borus, M., Jason, L. A., and Wilson-Brewer, R. (1994). The school-based promotion of social competence: Theory, practice, and policy. In R. J. Haggerty, N. Garmezy, M. Rutter, and L. Sherrod (Eds.), *Risk and resilience in children: Developmental approaches* (pp. 268–316). Cambridge: Cambridge University Press.

Elliott, D. S. (1966). Delinquency, school attendance, and school dropout. *Social Problems, 13,* 307–314.

(1994). Serious violent offenders: Onset, developmental course, and termination – The American Society of Criminology 1993 presidential address. *Criminology, 32,* 1–22.

Elliott, D. S., Huizinga, D., and Ageton, S. S. (1985). *Explaining delinquency and drug use.* Beverly Hills, CA: Sage Publications.

Elliott, D. S., Huizinga, D., and Menard, S. (1989). *Multiple problem youth: Delinquency, substance use, and mental health problems.* New York: Springer-Verlang.

Elliott, D. S., and Voss, H. L. (1974). *Delinquency and dropout.* Lexington, MA: Lexington Books.

Elliott, D. S., Wilson, W. J., Huizinga, D., Sampson, R. J., Elliott, A., and Rankin, B. (1996). The effects of neighborhood disadvantage on adolescent development. *Journal of Research in Crime and Delinquency, 33,* 389–426.

Epstein, S., and O'Brien, E. J. (1985). The person-situation debate in historical and current perspective. *Psychological Bulletin, 98,* 513–537.

Esbensen, F.-A., and Osgood, D. W. (1996, August). *G.R.E.A.T. program effectiveness: Results from the 1995 cross-sectional survey of eighth-grade students.* Unpublished technical report available from author.

Farrington, D. P. (1986a). Age and crime. In M. Tonry and N. Morris (Eds.), *Crime and justice: An annual review of research* (pp. 189–250). Chicago: University of Chicago Press.

(1986b). Stepping stones to adult criminal careers. In D. Olweus, J. Block, and M. R. Yarrow (Eds.), *Development of antisocial and prosocial behavior* (pp. 359–384). New York: Academic Press.

(1991). Childhood aggression and adult violence: Early precursors and later life outcomes. In D. J. Pepler and K. H. Rubin (Eds.), *The development and treatment of childhood aggression* (pp. 5–29). Hillsdale, NJ: Lawrence Erlbaum.

(1995). The challenge of teenage antisocial behavior. In M. Rutter (Ed.), *Psychosocial disturbances in young people: Challenges for prevention* (pp. 83–130). Cambridge: Cambridge University Press.

Farrington, D. P., Gallagher, B., Morley, L., St. Ledger, R. J., and West, D. J. (1986). Unemployment, school leaving, and crime. *British Journal of Criminology, 26,* 335–356.

Farrington, D. P., Loeber, R., and Van Kammen, W. B. (1990). Long-term criminal outcomes of hyperactivity-impulsivity-attention deficit and conduct problems in childhood. In L. N. Robins and M. Rutter (Eds.), *Straight and devious pathways from childhood to adulthood* (pp. 62–81). Cambridge: Cambridge University Press.

Feindler, E. L., Marriott, S. A., and Iwata, M. (1984). Group anger control training for junior high school delinquents. *Cognitive Therapy and Research, 8,* 299–311.

Feldhusen, J. F., Thurston, J. R., and Benning, J. J. (1973). A longitudinal study of delinquency and other aspects of children's behaviour. *International Journal of Criminology and Penology, 1,* 341–351.

Feldman, R. A., Caplinger, T. E., and Wodarski, J. S. (1983). *The St. Louis conundrum.* Englewood Cliffs, NJ: Prentice-Hall.

Felner, R. D., and Adan, A. M. (1988). The School Transitional Environment Project: An ecological intervention and evaluation. In R. H. Price, E. L. Cowen, R. P. Lorion, and J. Ramos-McKay (Eds.), *14 ounces of prevention: A casebook for practitioners* (pp. 111–122). Washington, DC: American Psychological Association.

Felner, R. D., Ginter, M., and Primavera, J. (1982). Primary prevention during school transitions: Social support and environmental structure. *American Journal of Community Psychology, 10,* 277–290.

Felson, M., and Cohen, L. (1980). Human ecology and crime: A routine activity approach. *Human Ecology, 8,* 389–406.

Felson, R. B., Liska, A. E., South, S. J., and McNulty, T. L. (1994). The subculture of violence and delinquency: Individual vs. school context effects. *Social Forces, 73,* 155–173.

Filipczak, J., and Wodarski, J. S. (1982). Behavioral intervention in public schools: Short-term results. In D. J. Safer (Ed.), *School programs for disruptive adolescents* (pp. 195–199). Baltimore: University Park Press.

Fitz-Gibbon, C. T. (1992). School effects at A Level: Genesis of an information system? In D. Reynolds and P. Cuttance (Eds.), *School effectiveness: Research, policy, and practice* (pp. 96–120). New York: Cassell.

Forman, S. G. (1980). A comparison of cognitive training and response cost procedures in modifying aggressive behavior of elementary school children. *Behavior Therapy, 11,* 594–600.

Fuchs, D., and Fuchs, L. S. (1989). Exploring effective and efficient prereferral interventions: A component analysis of behavioral consultation. *School Psychology Review, 18,* 260–283.

Fullan, M. G., Miles, M. B., and Taylor, G. (1980). Organization development in schools: The state of the art. *Review of Educational Research, 50,* 121–183.

Fullan, M. G., and Pomfret, A. (1977). Research on curriculum and instruction implementation. *Review of Educational Research, 47,* 335–397.

Fullan, M. G., with Stiegelbauer, S. (1991). *The new meaning of educational change.* New York: Teachers College Press.

Gainer, P. S., Webster, D. W., and Champion, H. R. (1993). A youth violence prevention program: Description and preliminary evaluation. *Archives of Surgery, 128,* 303–308.

Galloway, D., Martin, R., and Wilcox, B. (1985). Persistent absence from school and exclusion from school: The predictive power of school and community variables. *British Educational Research Journal, 11,* 51–61.

Garmezy, N. (1983). Stressors of childhood. In N. Garmezy and N. Rutter (Eds.), *Stress, coping and development in children* (pp. 43–84). New York: McGraw-Hill.

Garnier, H. E., Stein, J. A., and Jacobs, J. K. (1997). The process of dropping out of high school: A 19-year perspective. *American Educational Research Journal, 34,* 395–419.

Garrett, C. J. (1985). Effects of residential treatment on adjudicated delinquents: A meta-analysis. *Journal of Research in Crime and Delinquency, 22,* 287–308.

Ginsberg, R., Schwartz, H., Olson, G., and Bennett, A. (1987). Working conditions in urban schools. *Urban Review, 19,* 3–23.

Glueck, S., and Glueck, E. T. (1950). *Unraveling juvenile delinquency.* Cambridge, MA: Harvard University Press.

Gold, M. (1978). Scholastic experiences, self-esteem, and delinquent behavior: A theory for alternative school. *Crime and Delinquency, 24,* 290–308.

Gold, M., and Mann, D. W. (1984). *Expelled to a friendlier place: A study of effective alternative schools.* Ann Arbor: University of Michigan Press.

Goldberg, L. R. (1992). The development of markers for the Big-Five factor structure. *Psychological Assessment, 4,* 26–42.

Goldberg, L. R., and Rosolack, T. K. (1994). The Big-Five factor structure as an integrative framework: An empirical comparison with Eysenck's P-E-N model. In C. F. Halverson Jr., G. A. Kohnstamm, and R. P. Martin (Eds.), *The developing structure of temperament and personality from infancy to adulthood* (pp. 7–36). Hillsdale, NJ: Lawrence Erlbaum.

Good, T. L., and Brophy, T. E. (1987). *Looking in classrooms.* New York: Harper and Row.

Gorman, D. M. (1995). Are school-based resistance skills training programs effective in preventing alcohol misuse? *Journal of Alcohol and Drug Education, 41,* 74–98.

Gottfredson, D. C. (1986). An empirical test of school-based environmental and individual interventions to reduce the risk of delinquent behavior. *Criminology, 24,* 705–731.

(1987). An evaluation of an organization development approach to reducing school disorder. *Evaluation Review, 11,* 739–763.

(1990). Changing school structures to benefit high-risk youths. In P. E. Leone (Ed.), *Understanding troubled and troubling youth* (pp. 246–271). Newbury Park, CA: Sage.

(1997). School-based crime prevention. In L. W. Sherman, D. C. Gottfredson, D. MacKenzie, J. Eck, P. Reuter, and S. Bushway, *Preventing crime: What works, what doesn't, what's promising: A report to the United States Congress.* Washington, DC: U.S. Department of Justice, Office of Justice Programs.

Gottfredson, D. C., Fink, C. M., and Graham, N. (1994). Grade retention practices and problem behavior. *American Educational Research Journal, 31,* 4.

Gottfredson, D. C., Fink, C. M., Skroban, S., and Gottfredson, G. D. (1997). Making prevention work. In R. P. Weissberg, T. P. Gullotta, R. L. Hampton, and G. R. Adams (Eds.), *Healthy children 2010: Establishing preventive services* (pp. 219–252). Thousand Oaks, CA: Sage.

Gottfredson, D. C., Gottfredson, G. D., and Hybl, L. G. (1993). Managing adolescent behavior: A multiyear, multischool study. *American Educational Research Journal, 30,* 179–215.

Gottfredson, D. C., Gottfredson, G. D., and Skroban, S. (1998). Can prevention work where it is needed most? *Evaluation Review, 22,* 315–340.

Gottfredson, D. C., Harmon, M. A., Gottfredson, G. D., Jones, E. M., and Celestin, J. A. (1996). *Compendium of prevention program outcomes and instrument locator.* Ellicott City, MD: Gottfredson Associates.

Gottfredson, D. C., and Koper, C. (1996). Race and sex differences in the prediction of drug use. *Journal of Consulting and Clinical Psychology, 64,* 305–313.

Gottfredson, D. C., McNeil, R. J., III, and Gottfredson, G. D. (1991). Social area influences on delinquency: A multilevel analysis. *Journal of Research in Crime and Delinquency, 28*, 197–226.

Gottfredson, G. D. (1979, July). Models and muddles: An ecological examination of high school crime rates. *Journal of Research in Crime and Delinquency,* 307–331.

———(1981). Schooling and delinquency. In S. E. Martin, L. B. Sechrest, and R. Redner (Eds.), *New directions in the rehabilitation of criminal offenders* (pp. 424–469). Washington, DC: National Academy Press.

———(1984). A theory-ridden approach to program evaluation: A method for stimulating researcher-implementer collaboration. *American Psychologist, 39*, 1101–1112.

———(1987a). American education: American delinquency. *Today's Delinquent, 6*, 5–70.

———(1987b). Peer group interventions to reduce the risk of delinquent behavior: A selective review and a new evaluation. *Criminology, 25*, 671–714.

———(1988). *Issues in adolescent drug use.* Unpublished final report to the U.S. Department of Justice. Baltimore: Johns Hopkins University, Center for Research on Elementary and Middle Schools.

Gottfredson, G. D., and Gottfredson, D. C. (1985). *Victimization in schools.* New York: Plenum Press.

———(1987). *Using organization development to improve school climate* (Report No. 17). Baltimore: Johns Hopkins University, Center for Research on Elementary and Middle Schools.

———(1989). *School climate, academic performance, attendance, and dropout* (Report No. 43). Baltimore: Johns Hopkins University, Center for Research on Elementary and Middle Schools.

———(1992, November). *Development and applications of theoretical measures for evaluating drug and delinquency prevention programs.* Paper presented at the annual meeting of the American Society of Criminology, New Orleans.

———(1996, October). *A national study of delinquency prevention in schools: Rationale for a study to describe the extensiveness and implementation of programs to prevent adolescent problem behavior in schools.* Unpublished manuscript, Gottfredson Associates, Ellicott City, MD.

Gottfredson, G. D., and Hybl, L. G. (1989). *Some biographical correlates of outstanding performance among school principals* (Report No. 35). Baltimore: Johns Hopkins University, Center for Research on Elementary and Middle Schools.

Gottfredson, G. D., Rickert, D. E., Gottfredson, D. C., and Advani, N. (1984). Standards for program development evaluation plans. *Psychological Documents, 14*, 32 (Ms. No. 2668).

Gottfredson, M. R., and Hirschi, T. (1990). *A general theory of crime.* Stanford, CA: Stanford University Press.

Grasmick, H. G., Tittle, C. R., Bursik, R. J., Jr., and Arneklev, B. J. (1993). Testing the core empirical implications of Gottfredson and Hirshi's general theory of crime. *Journal of Research in Crime and Delinquency, 30*, 5–29.

Gray, J., McPherson, A., and Raffe, D. (1983). *Reconstructions of secondary education.* London: Routledge and Kegan Paul.

Graziano, W. G. (1994). The development of agreeableness as a dimension of personality. In C. F. Halverson Jr., G. A. Kohnstamm, and R. P. Martin (Eds.), *The developing structure of temperament and personality from infancy to adulthood* (pp. 267–292). Hillsdale, NJ: Lawrence Erlbaum.

Graziano, W. G., and Ward, D. (1992). Probing the Big Five in adolescence: Personality and adjustment during a developmental transition. *Journal of Personality, 60,* 425–439.

Greenberg, D. F. (1977). Delinquency and the age structure of society. *Contemporary Crisis, 1,* 189–223.

Greenberg, M. T. (1996). *The PATHS Project: Preventive Intervention for Children: Final Report to NIMH* (Grant Number R01MH42131). Technical report available from author. University of Washington, Seattle.

Greenberg, M. T., and Kushé, C. A. (1993). *Promoting social and emotional development in deaf children: The PATHS Project.* Seattle: University of Washington Press.

Greenberg, M. T., Kusché, C. A., Cook, E. T., and Quamma, J. P. (1995). Promoting emotional competence in school-aged children: The effects of the PATHS curriculum. *Development and Psychopathology, 7,* 117–136.

Greenwood, C. R., Terry, B., Utley, C. A., Montagna, D., and Walker, D. (1993). Achievement, placement, and services: Middle school benefits of Class-Wide Peer Tutoring used at the elementary school. *School Psychology Review, 22,* 497–516.

Greenwood, P. W., Model, K. E., Rydell, C. P., and Chiesa, J. (1996). *Diverting children from a life of crime: Measuring costs and benefits.* Santa Monica, CA: Rand.

Grossman, D. C., Neckerman, H. J., Koepsell, T. D., Liu, P.-Y., Asher, K. N., Beland, K., Frey, K., and Rivara, F. P. (1997). Effectiveness of a violence prevention curriculum among children in elementary school: A randomized controlled trial. *Journal of the American Medical Association, 277,* 1605–1611.

Haberman, M., and Rickards, W. H. (1990). Urban teachers who quit: Why they leave and what they do. *Urban Education, 25,* 297–303.

Hahn, A., Leavitt, T., and Aaron, P. (1994, June). *Evaluation of the Quantum Opportunities Program (QOP): Did the program work?: A report on the post secondary outcomes and cost-effectiveness of the QOP Program (1989–1993).* Unpublished manuscript, Brandeis University.

Hall, G. E. (1987, April). *The principal's role in setting school climate (for school improvement).* Paper presented at the meeting of the American Educational Research Association, Washington, DC.

Hall, G. E., Hord, S. M., Huling, L. L., Rutherford, W. L., and Stiegelbauer, S. M. (1983, April). *Leadership variables associated with successful school improvement* (Report No. 3164). Paper presented at the annual meeting of the American Educational Research Association, Montreal.

Hall, G. E., Rutherford, W. L., Hord, S. M., and Huling, L. L. (1984). Effects of three principal styles on school improvement. *Educational Leadership, 42,* 22–29.

Halverson, C. F., Jr., Kohnstamm, G. A., and Martin, R. P. (1994). *The develop-ing structure of temperament and personality from infancy to adulthood.* Hillside, NJ: Lawrence Erlbaum.

Hammond, W. R., and Yung, B. R. (1991). Preventing violence in at-risk African-American youth. *Journal of Health Care for the Poor and Underserved, 2,* 359–373.

Hansen, W. B. (1992). School-based substance abuse prevention: A review of the state of the art of curriculum: 1980–1990. *Health Education Research, 7,* 403–430.

Hansen, W. B., and Graham, J. W. (1991). Preventing alcohol, marijuana, and cigarette use among adolescents: Peer pressure resistance training versus establishing conservative norms. *Preventive Medicine, 20,* 414–430.

Hansen, W. B., and O'Malley, P. M. (1996). Drug abuse. In R. J. DiClemente, W. B. Hansen, and E. L. Ponton (Eds.), *Handbook of adolescent health risk behavior* (pp. 161–192). New York: Plenum Press.

Hauser, R. M., Sewell, W. H., and Alwin, D. F. (1976). High school effects on achievement. In W. H. Sewell, R. M. Hauser, and D. L. Featherman (Eds.), *Schooling and achievement in American society* (pp. 309–342). New York: Academic Press.

Hawkins, J. D., Arthur, M. W., and Catalano, R. F. (1995). Preventing substance abuse. In M. Tonry and D. P. Farrington (Eds.), *Building a safer society: Strategic approaches to crime prevention* (pp. 343–428). Chicago: University of Chicago Press.

Hawkins, D. J., Catalano, R. F., Kosterman, R., Abbott, R., and Hill, K. G. (1999). Preventing adolescent health-risk behaviors by strengthening protection during childhood. *Archives of Pediatrics and Adolescent Medicine, 153* (3), 226–234.

Hawkins, J. D., Catalano, R. F., and Miller, J. L. (1992). Risk and protective factors for alcohol and other drug problems in early adulthood: Impli-cations for substance abuse prevention. *Psychological Bulletin, 112,* 64–105.

Hawkins, J. D., Catalano, R. F., Morrison, D. M., O'Donnell, J., Abbott, R. D., and Day, L. E. (1992). The Seattle Social Developmental Project: Effects of the first four years on protective factors and problem behaviors. In J. McCord and R. E. Tremblay (Eds.), *Preventing antisocial behavior: Interventions from birth through adolescence* (pp. 141–161). New York: Guilford Press.

Hawkins, J. D., Doueck, H. J., and Lishner, D. M. (1988). Changing teaching practices in mainstream classrooms to improve bonding and behavior of low achievers. *American Educational Research Journal, 25,* 31–50.

Hawkins, J. D., and Lam, T. (1983, June). *Teacher practices, social development, and delinquency.* Paper presented at the Vermont Conference on the Primary Prevention of Psychopathology, Bolton, Vt.

Hawkins, J. D., Von Cleve, E., and Catalano, R. F. (1991). Reducing early child-hood aggression: Results of a primary prevention program. *Journal of the American Academy of Child and Adolescent Psychiatry, 30,* 208–217.

Haynes, N. M. (1994, May). School development effect: Two follow-up studies. In N. M. Haynes (Ed.), *School Development Program research monograph* (Chapter 8). New Haven: Yale University, Yale Child Study Center.

Haynes, N. M., Emmons, C. L., Gebreyesus, S., and Ben-Avie, M. (1996). The School Development Program evaluation process. In J. P. Comer, N. M. Haynes, E. T. Joyner, and M. Ben-Avie (Eds.), *Rallying the whole village: The Comer process for reforming education.* New York: Teachers College Press.

Heal, K. (1978). Misbehaviour among school children: The role of the school in strategies for prevention. *Policy and Politics, 6,* 321–332.

Heaton, R. C., Safer, D. J., and Allen, R. P. (1982). A contingency management program for disruptive junior high school students: A detailed description. In D. J. Safer (Ed.), *School programs for disruptive adolescents* (pp. 217–239). Baltimore: University Park Press.

Hellman, D. A., and Beaton, S. (1986). The pattern of violence in urban public schools: The influence of school and community. *Journal of Research in Crime and Delinquency, 23,* 102–127.

Hernandez, D. J. (1994). Children's changing access to resources: A historical perspective. *Social Policy Report: Society for Research in Child Development, 8,* 2–23.

Higgins, P. S. (1978). Evaluation and case study of a school-based delinquency prevention program: Minnesota Youth Advocate Program. *Evaluation Quarterly, 2,* 215–234.

Hindelang, M. J. (1973). Causes of delinquency: A partial replication and extension. *Social Problems, 20,* 471–487.

Hirschi, T. (1969). *Causes of delinquency.* Berkeley: University of California Press.

Hirschi, T., and Gottfredson, M. (1983). Age and the explanation of crime. *American Journal of Sociology, 89,* 552–584.

Hirschi, T., and Hindelang, M. J. (1977). Intelligence and delinquency: A revisionist review. *American Sociological Review, 42,* 571–587.

Holmes, A. B., Gottfredson, G. D., and Miller, J. (1992). Resources and strategies for findings. In G. D. Hawkins and R. F. Catalano (Eds.), *Communities that care* (pp. 191–210). San Francisco: Jossey-Bass.

Huberman, A. M. (1983). School improvement strategies that work: Some scenarios. *Educational Leadership, 41,* 23–27.

Huberman, A. M., and Miles, M. B. (1984). *Innovation up close: How school improvement works.* New York: Plenum Press.

Institute of Medicine, Committee on Prevention of Mental Disorders. (1994). *Reducing risks for mental disorders: Frontiers for prevention intervention research.* Washington, DC: National Academy Press.

Izzo, R. L., and Ross, R. R. (1990). Meta-analysis of rehabilitation programs for juvenile delinquents. *Criminal Justice and Behavior, 17,* 134–142.

Jackson, S. E. (1983). Participation in decision-makings as a strategy for reducing job-related strains. *Journal of Applied Psychology, 68,* 3–19.

Jarjoura, G. R. (1993). Does dropping out of school enhance delinquent involvement? Results from a large-scale national probability sample. *Criminology, 31,* 149–172.

Javetz, R., and Shuval, J. T. (1982). Vulnerability to drugs among Israeli adolescents. *Israeli Journal of Psychiatry and Related Sciences, 19,* 97–119.

Jencks, C. S., Smith, M., Acland, H., Bane, M. J., Cohen, D., Gintis, H., Heyns, B., and Michelson, S. (1972). *Inequality: A reassessment of the effect of family and schooling in America.* New York: Basic Books.

Jessor, R., Chase, J. A., and Donovan, J. E. (1980). Psychosocial correlates of marijuana use and problem drinking in a national sample of adolescents. *American Journal of Public Health, 70,* 604–613.

Jessor, R., and Jessor, S. L. (1977). *Problem behavior and psychosocial development: A longitudinal study of youth.* San Diego, CA: Academic Press.

Johnson, D. W., and Johnson, R. T. (1996). Conflict resolution and peer mediation programs in elementary and secondary schools: A review of the research. *Review of Educational Research, 66,* 459–506.

Johnson, G. (1984). *When law-related education is a deterrent to delinquency: Evaluation methods and findings.* Paper presented at the Rocky Mountain Regional Conference of the National Council for the Social Studies.

Johnson, G., and Hunter, R. (1985, October). *Law-related education as a delinquency prevention strategy: A three-year evaluation of the impact of LRE on students.* Paper adapted from a report submitted to the National Institute for Juvenile Justice and Delinquency Prevention, June 6, 1984. Boulder, CO: Institute for Social Research.

Johnston, L. D., O'Malley, P. M., and Bachman, J. G. (1994). *National survey results on drug use from the Monitoring the Future Study, 1975–1993.* Washington, DC: U.S. Department of Health and Human Services, National Institute on Drug Abuse.

Jones, E. M., Gottfredson, G. D., and Gottfredson, D. C. (1997). Success for some: An evaluation of a Success for All Program. *Evaluation Review, 21,* 643–670.

Kachur, S. P., Stennies, G. M., Powell, K. E., Modzeleski, W., Stephens, R., Murphy, R., Kresnow, M., Sleet, D., and Lowry, R. (1996). School-associated violent deaths in the United States, 1992 to 1994. *Journal of the American Medical Association, 275,* 1729–1733.

Kandel, D. B., Kessler, R. C., and Margulies, R. Z. (1978). Antecedents of adolescent initiation into stages of drug use: A developmental analysis. In D. Kandel (Ed.), *Longitudinal research on drug use: Empirical findings and methodological issues* (pp. 73–99). New York: John Wiley and Sons.

Kantor, H., and Brenzel, B. (1992). Urban education and the "truly disadvantaged": The historical roots of the contemporary crisis, 1945–1990. *Teachers College Record, 94,* 279–314.

Kasen, S., Johnson, J., and Cohen, P. (1990). The impact of school emotional climate on student psychopathology. *Journal of Abnormal Child Psychology, 18,* 165–177.

Kaufman, P., Chen, X., Choy, S. P., Chandler, K. A., Chapman, C. D., Rand, M. R., and Ringel, C. (1998). *Indicators of school crime and safety, 1998* (NCES 98-251/NCJ-172215). Washington, D.C.: U.S. Departments of Education and Justice.

Kellam, S. G., Ensminger, M. E., and Simon, M. B. (1980). Mental health in first grade and teenage drug, alcohol, and cigarette use. *Drug and Alcohol Dependence, 5,* 273–304.

Kellam, S. G., and Rebok, G. W. (1992). Building developmental and etiological theory through epidemiologically based preventive intervention trials. In J. McCord and R. E. Tremblay (Eds.), *Preventing antisocial behavior:*

Interventions from birth through adolescence (pp. 162–195). New York: Guilford Press.

Kellam, S. G., Rebok, G. W., Ialongo, N., and Mayer, L. S. (1994). The course and malleability of aggressive behavior from early first grade into middle school: Results of a developmental epidemiologically-based preventive trial. *Journal of Child Psychology and Psychiatry, 35*, 259–281.

Kelly, D. H. (1978). Track position, peer affiliation, and youth crime. *Urban Education, 13*, 397–406.

Kennedy, M. M. (1978). Findings from the follow through planned variation study. *Educational Researcher, 7*, 3–11.

Kenney, D. J., and Watson, T. S. (1996). Reducing fear in the schools: Managing conflict through student problem solving. *Education and Urban Society, 28*, 436–455.

Kornhauser, R. (1978). *Social sources of delinquency*. Chicago: University of Chicago Press.

Kozol, J. (1992). *Savage inequalities: Children in America's schools*. New York: Harper Perennial.

Krohn, M. D., Huizinga, D., and Van Kammen, W. B. (1993). Peers and delinquency. In D. Huizinga, R. Loeber, and T. P. Thornberry (Eds.), *Urban delinquency and substance abuse* (technical report, pp. 13/1–13/25). Washington, DC: U.S. Department of Justice, Office of Juvenile Justice and Delinquency Prevention.

Kupersmidt, J. B., Coie, J. D., and Dodge, K. A. (1990). The role of poor peer relationships in the development of disorder. In S. R. Asher and J. D. Coie (Eds.), *Peer rejection in childhood* (pp. 274–308). Cambridge: Cambridge University Press.

Kvaraceus, W. C. (1945). *Juvenile delinquency and the school*. New York: World Book.

LaGrange, Teresa C. (1999). The impact of neighborhoods, schools, and malls on the spatial distribution of property damage. *Journal of Research in Crime and Delinquency, 36* (4), 393–422.

Larson, J. D. (1992). Anger and aggression management techniques through the Think First curriculum. *Journal of Offender Rehabilitation, 18*, 101–117.

LeBlanc, M. (1994). Family, school, delinquency and criminality, the predictive power of an elaborated social control theory for males. *Criminal Behaviour and Mental Health, 4*, 101–117.

LeBlanc, M., Vallières, É., and McDuff, P. (1993, October). The prediction on males' adolescent and adult offending from school experience. *Canadian Journal of Criminology*, 459–478.

Lee, V. E., Bryk, A. S., and Smith, J. B. (1993). The organization of effective secondary schools. In L. Darling-Hammond (Ed.), *Review of research in education* (Vol. 19, pp. 171–267). Washington, DC: American Educational Research Association.

Lee, V. E., and Croninger, R. G. (1996). The social organization of safe high schools. In K. M. Borman, P. W. Cookson Jr., and J. Z. Spade (Eds.), *Implementing educational reform: Sociological perspectives on educational policy* (pp. 359–392). Norwood, NJ: Ablex.

Liazos, A. (1978). School, alienation, and delinquency. *Crime and Delinquency*, *24*, 355–370.

Liberman, A., and Miller, L. (1981). Synthesis of research on improving schools. *Educational Leadership*, *39*, 583–586.

——— (1984). School improvement: Themes and variations. *Teacher's College Record*, *86*, 5–18.

Lipsey, M. W. (1992). Juvenile delinquency treatment: A meta-analytic inquiry into the variability of effects. In T. D. Cook, H. Cooper, D. S. Cordray, H. Hartman, L. V. Hedges, R. V. Light, T. A. Louis, and F. Mosteller (Eds.), *Meta-analysis for explanation: A casebook* (pp. 83–128). New York: Sage.

Lipsey, M. W., and Derzon, J. H. (1997, April). *Predictors of violent or serious delinquency in adolescence and early adulthood: A synthesis of longitudinal research.* Unpublished manuscript, Vanderbilt University.

Lipsey, M. W., and Wilson, D. B. (1993). The efficacy of psychological, educational, and behavioral treatment: Confirmation from meta-analysis. *American Psychologist*, *48*, 1181–1209.

Liska, A. E., and Reed, M. D. (1985). Ties to conventional institutions and delinquency: Estimating reciprocal effects. *American Sociological Review*, *50*, 547–560.

Little, J. W. (1981, April). *The power of organizational setting: School norms and staff development.* Paper presented at the annual meeting of the American Educational Research Association, Los Angeles.

Lochman, J. E. (1985). Effects of different treatment lengths in cognitive behavioral interventions with aggressive boys. *Child Psychiatry and Human Development*, *16*, 45–56.

——— (1992). Cognitive-behavioral intervention with aggressive boys: Three-year follow-up and preventive effects. *Journal of Consulting and Clinical Psychology*, *60*, 426–432.

Lochman, J. E., Burch, P. R., Curry, J. F., and Lampron, L. B. (1984). Treatment and generalization effects of cognitive-behavioral and goal-setting interventions with aggressive boys. *Journal of Consulting and Clinical Psychology*, *52*, 915–916.

Lochman, J. E., and Curry, J. F. (1986). Effects of social problem-solving training and self-instruction training with aggressive boys. *Journal of Clinical Child Psychology*, *15*, 159–164.

Lochman, J. E., Lampron, L. B., Burch, P. R., and Curry, J. F. (1985). Client characteristics associated with behavior change for treated and untreated aggressive boys. *Journal of Abnormal Child Psychology*, *13*, 527–538.

Lochman, J. E., Lampron, L. B., Gemmer, T. C., Harris, S. R., and Wyckoff, G. M. (1989). Teacher consultation and cognitive-behavioral interventions with aggressive boys. *Psychology in the Schools*, *26*, 179–188.

Loeber, R., and Dishion, T. (1983). Early predictors of male delinquency: A review. *Psychological Bulletin*, *94*, 68–99.

Loeber, R., and Maguin, E. (1993). The relationship between reading achievement and delinquency. In D. Huizinga, R. Loeber, and T. P. Thornberry (Eds.), *Urban delinquency and substance abuse* (technical report, pp. 11/1–11/43). Washington, DC: U.S. Department of Justice, Office of Juvenile Justice and Delinquency Prevention.

Loeber, R., and Stouthamer-Loeber, M. (1987). Prediction. In H. C. Quay (Ed.), *Handbook of juvenile delinquency* (pp. 325–382). New York: Wiley.

Longstreth, L. E., Shanley, F. J., and Rice, R. E. (1964). Experimental evaluation of a high-school program for potential dropouts. *Journal of Educational Psychology, 55*, 228–236.

LoSciuto, L., Rajala, A. K., Townsend, T. N., and Taylor, A. S. (1996). An outcome evaluation of Across Ages: An intergenerational mentoring approach to drug prevention. *Journal of Adolescent Research, 11*, 116–129.

Loucks, S. F. (1983). At Last: Some good news from a study of school improvement. *Educational Leadership, 41*, 34–35.

Louis, K. S. (1986, April). *A survey of effective school programs in urban high schools.* Paper presented at the annual meeting of the American Educational Research Association, San Francisco.

Louis, K. S., and Miles, M. B. (1990). *Improving the urban high school: What works and why.* New York: Teachers College Press.

Louis Harris and Associates. (1993). *The Metropolitan Life survey of the American teacher (1993): Violence in America's public schools.* New York: Author.

Madden, N. A., Slavin, R. E., Karweit, N. L., Dolan, L. J., and Wasik, B. A. (1993). Success for All: Longitudinal effects of a restructuring program for inner-city elementary schools. *American Educational Research Journal, 30*, 123–148.

Malvin, J. H., Moskowitz, J. M., Schaeffer, G. A., and Schaps, E. (1984). Teacher training in affective education for the primary prevention of adolescent drug abuse. *American Journal of Drug and Alcohol Abuse, 10*, 223–235.

Malvin, J. H., Moskowitz, J. M., Schaps, E., and Schaeffer, G. A. (1985). Evaluation of two school-based alternative programs. *Journal of Alcohol and Drug Education, 30*, 98–108.

Mann, D. (1978). The politics of training teachers in schools. In D. Mann (Ed.), *Making change happen?* (pp. 3–18). New York: Teachers College Press.

Mayer, G. R., and Butterworth T. W. (1979). A preventive approach to school violence and vandalism: An experimental study. *Personnel and Guidance Journal, 57*, 436–441.

Mayer, G. R., Butterworth, T., Nafpaktitis, M., and Sulzer-Azaroff, B. (1983). Preventing school vandalism and improving discipline: A three-year study. *Journal of Applied Behavior Analysis, 16*, 355–369.

McCord, J. (1979). Some child-rearing antecedents of criminal behavior in adult men. *Journal of Personality and Social Psychology, 37*, 1477–1486.

McCrae, R. R., and Costa, P. T., Jr. (1990). *Personality in adulthood.* New York: Guilford Press.

McDermott, J. (1983). Crime in the school and in the community: Offenders, victims, and fearful youths. *Crime and Delinquency, 29*, 270–282.

McFall, R. M. (1982). A review and reformulation of the concept of social skills. *Behavioral Assessment, 4*, 1–35.

McKissack, I. J. (1973). Property offending and the school leaving age. *International Journal of Criminology and Penology, 1*, 353–362.

McLaughlin, M. W. (1990). The Rand change agent study revisited: Macro perspectives and micro realities. *Educational Researcher, 19*, 11–16.

McPartland, J. M., Coldiron, J. R., and Braddock, J. H., II. (1987). *School structures and classroom practices in elementary, middle, and secondary schools* (Report No. 14). Baltimore: Johns Hopkins University.

McPartland, J. M., and Nettles, S. M. (1991). Using community adults as advocates or mentors for at-risk middle school students: A two-year evaluation of Project RAISE. *American Journal of Education, 99,* 568–586.

Mensch, B. S., and Kandel, D. B. (1988). Dropping out of high school and drug involvement. *Sociology of Education, 61,* 95–113.

Meyer, H. J., Borgatta, E. F., and Jones, W. C. (1965). *Girls at vocational high: An experiment in social work intervention.* New York: Russell Sage Foundation.

Miles, M. B. (1986, April). *Improving the urban high school: Some preliminary news from 5 cases.* Paper presented at the American Educational Research Association meeting, San Francisco.

Mills, G. E. (1990). *A Consumer's Guide to School Improvement.* Eugene, OR: ERIC Clearinghouse on Educational Management.

Mischel, W., Shoda, Y., and Rodriguez, M. L. (1989). Delay of gratification in children. *Science, 244,* 933–938.

Moffitt, T. E. (1993). Adolescence-limited and life-course persistent antisocial behavior: A developmental taxonomy. *Psychological Review, 100,* 674–701.

Mortimore, P., Sammons, P., Ecob, R., Stoll, L., and Lewis, D. (1988). *School matters: The junior years.* Salisbury: Open Books.

Moskowitz, J. M., Malvin, J. H., Schaeffer, G. A., and Schaps, E. (1983). Evaluation of a cooperative learning strategy. *American Educational Research Journal, 20,* 687–696.

(1984a). Evaluation of an affective development teacher training program. *Journal of Primary Prevention, 4,* 150–162.

(1984b). An experimental evaluation of a drug education course. *Journal of Drug Education, 14,* 9–22.

Moskowitz, J. M., Schaps, E., and Malvin, J. H. (1982). Process and outcome evaluation in primary prevention: The Magic Circle Program. *Evaluation Review, 6,* 775–788.

Murphy, H. A., Hutchison, J. M., and Bailey, J. S. (1983). Behavioral school psychology goes outdoors: The effect of organized games on playground aggression. *Journal of Applied Behavior Analysis, 16,* 29–35.

Nagin, D. S., and Farrington, D. P. (1992a). The onset and persistence of offending. *Criminology, 30,* 501–523.

(1992b). The stability of criminal potential from childhood to adulthood. *Criminology, 30,* 235–260.

Nagin, D. S., and Paternoster, R. (1991). On the relationship of past to future participation in delinquency. *Criminology, 29,* 163–189.

National Center for Educational Statistics. (1991). *Teacher survey on safe, disciplined, and drug-free schools.* Washington, DC: U.S. Department of Education.

(1994). *Digest of education statistics, 1994.* Washington, DC: U.S. Government Printing Office.

National Commission on Excellence in Education. (1983). *A nation at risk.* Washington, DC: U.S. Department of Education.

National Institute of Education. (1978). *Violent schools – safe school: The safe school study report to the congress.* Washington, DC: U.S. Government Printing Office.

Nolin, M. J., Davies, E., and Chandler, K. (1995). *Statistics in brief: Student victimization at school.* Washington, DC: U.S. Department of Education, National Center for Education Statistics.

Nuttall, D. L., Goldstein, H., Prosser, R., and Rasbash, J. (1989). Differential school effectiveness. *International Journal of Educational Research, 13,* 769–776.

O'Donnell, J., Hawkins, J. D., Catalano, R. F., Abbott, R. D., and Day, L. E. (1995). Preventing school failure, drug use, and delinquency among low-income children: Long-term intervention in elementary schools. *American Journal of Orthopsychiatry, 65,* 87–100.

Oetting, E. R., Beauvais, F., and Edwards, R. W. (1988). Alcohol and Indian youth: Social and psychological correlates and prevention. *Journal of Drug Issues, 18,* 87–101.

Oetting, E. R., Swaim, R. C., Edwards, R. W., and Beauvais, F. (1989). Indian and Anglo adolescent alcohol use and emotional distress: Path models. *American Journal of Drug and Alcohol Abuse, 15,* 153–172.

Offord, D. R., Boyle, M. C., and Racine, Y. A. (1991). The epidemiology of antisocial behavior in childhood and adolescence. In D. J. Pepler and K. H. Rubin (Eds.), *The development and treatment of childhood aggression* (pp. 31–54). Hillsdale, NJ: Lawrence Erlbaum.

Offord, D. R., and Lipman, E. L. (1996). Emotional and behavioural problems. In Human Resources Development Canada, *Growing up in Canada: National longitudinal survey of children and youth* (pp. 119–126). Ottawa: Statistics Canada.

Ollendick, T. H., Oswald, D. P., and Francis, G. (1989). Validity of teacher nominations in identifying aggressive, withdrawn, and popular children. *Journal of Clinical Child Psychology, 18,* 221–229.

Olweus, D. (1983). Low school achievement and aggressive behavior in adolescent boys. In D. Magnusson and V. L. Allen (Eds.), *Human development: An interactional perspective* (pp. 353–365). New York: Academic Press.

(1991). Bully/victim problems among schoolchildren: Basic facts and effects of a school based intervention program. In D. J. Pepler and K. H. Rubin (Eds.), *The development and treatment of childhood aggression* (pp. 411–448). Hillsdale, NJ: Lawrence Erlbaum.

(1992). Bullying among schoolchildren: Intervention and prevention. In R. DeV. Peters, R. J. McMahon, and V. L. Quinsey (Eds.), *Aggression and violence throughout the life span* (pp. 100–125). Newbury Park, CA: Sage.

Olweus, D., and Alsaker, F. D. (1991). Assessing change in a cohort-longitudinal study with hierarchical data. In D. Magnusson, L. R. Bergman, G. Rudinger, and B. Törestad (Eds.), *Problems and methods in longitudinal research: Stability and change* (pp. 107–132). Cambridge: Cambridge University Press.

O'Malley, P. M. (1975). *Correlates and consequences of illicit drug use.* Unpublished doctoral dissertation, University of Michigan.

Ostroff, C. (1992). The relationship between satisfaction, attitudes, and performance: An organizational level analysis. *Journal of Applied Psychology, 77,* 963–974.

(1993). Comparing correlations based on individual-level and aggregated data. *Journal of Applied Psychology, 78,* 569–582.

Parker, J. G., and Asher, S. R. (1987). Peer relations and later personal adjustment: Are low-accepted children at risk? *Psychological Bulletin, 102,* 357–389.

Paternoster, R., and Brame, R. (1997). Multiple routes to delinquency? A test of developmental and general theories of crime. *Criminology, 35,* 49–84.

Paternoster, R., Dean, C. W., Piquero, A., Mazerolle, P., and Brame, R. (1997). Generality, continuity, and change in offending. *Journal of Quantitative Criminology, 13,* 231–266.

Patterson, G. R. (1974). Interventions for boys with conduct problems: Multiple settings, treatments, and criteria. *Journal of Consulting and Clinical Psychology, 42,* 471–481.

(1982). *Coercive family process.* Eugene, OR: Castalia Publishing.

Patterson, G. R., DeBaryshe, B. D., and Ramsey, E. (1989). A developmental perspective on antisocial behavior. *American Psychologist, 44,* 329–335.

Patterson, G. R., Reid, J. B., and Dishion, T. J. (1992). *Antisocial boys: A social interactional approach* (Vol. 4). Eugene, OR: Castalia Publishing.

Pedro-Carroll, J. L., Cowen, E. L., Hightower, A. D., and Guare, J. C. (1986). Preventive intervention with latency-aged children of divorce: A replication study. *American Journal of Community Psychology, 14,* 277–290.

Peeples, F., and Loeber, R. (1994). Do individual factors and neighborhood context explain ethnic differences in juvenile delinquency? *Journal of Quantitative Criminology, 10,* 141–157.

Pepler, D. J., King, G., and Byrd, W. (1991). A social-cognitively based social skills training program for aggressive children. In D. J. Pepler and K. H. Rubin (Eds.), *The development and treatment of childhood aggression* (pp. 361–379). Hillsdale, NJ: Lawrence Erlbaum.

Perry, D. J., Perry, L. C., and Rasmussen, P. (1986). Cognitive social learning mediators of aggression. *Child Development, 57,* 700–711.

Polakowski, M. (1994). Linking self- and social control with deviance: Illuminating the structure underlying a general theory of crime and its relation to deviant activity. *Journal of Quantitative Criminology, 10,* 41–78.

Polk, K., and Halferty, D. (1972). School cultures, adolescent commitments, and delinquency. In K. Polk and W. E. Schafer (Eds.), *Schools and delinquency* (pp. 70–90). Englewood Cliffs, NJ: Prentice-Hall.

Porter, J. N. (1974). Race, socialization, and mobility in educational and early occupational attainment. *American Sociological Review, 39,* 303–316.

Power, M. J., Benn, R. T., and Morris, J. N. (1972). Neighbourhood, school and juveniles before the courts. *British Journal of Criminology, 12,* 111–132.

Purkey, S. C., and Smith, M. S. (1983). Effective schools: A review. *Elementary School Journal, 83,* 427–452.

Ramsey, E., Patterson, G. R., and Walker, H. M. (1990). Generalization of the antisocial trait from home to school settings. *Journal of Applied Developmental Psychology, 11,* 209–223.

Rand, M., Klaus, P. L., and Taylor, B. (1983). The criminal event. *Report to the nation on crime and justice.* Washington, DC: U.S. Government Printing Office.

Raudenbush, S. W., and Bryk, A. S. (1986). A hierarchical model for studying school effects. *Sociology of Education, 59,* 1–17.

Reckless, W. C., and Dinitz, S. (1972). *The prevention of juvenile delinquency: An experiment.* Columbus: Ohio State University Press.

Reiss, A. J., Jr., and Roth, J. A. (Eds.). (1993). *Understanding and preventing violence.* Washington, DC: National Academy Press.

Reyes, O., and Jason, L. A. (1991). An evaluation of a high school dropout prevention program. *Journal of Community Psychology, 19,* 221–230.

Reynolds, D., and Cuttance, P. (Eds.). (1992). *School effectiveness: Research, policy and practice.* New York: Cassell.

Reynolds, D., Jones, D., and St. Leger, S. (1976, July). Schools do make a difference. *New Society, 29,* 223–225.

Rhodes, A. L., and Reiss, A. J., Jr. (1969). Apathy, truancy and delinquency as adaptations to school failure. *Social Forces, 48,* 12–22.

Richardson, J. L., Dwyer, K., McGuigan, K., Hansen, W. B., Dent, C., Johnson, C. A., Sussman, S. Y., Brannon, B., and Flay, B. (1989). Substance use among eighth-grade students who take care of themselves after school. *Pediatrics, 84,* 556–566.

Ringwalt, C., Greene, J., Ennett, S., Iachan, R., Clayton, R. R., and Leukefeld, C. G. (1994). *Past and future directions of the DARE Program: An evaluation review: Draft final report* (Award # 91-DD-CX-K053). Washington, DC: National Institute of Justice.

Robins, L. N. (1978). Sturdy childhood predictors of adult antisocial behaviour: Replications from longitudinal studies. *Psychological Medicine, 8,* 611–622.

Robins, L. N., and Przybeck, T. R. (1985). Age of onset of drug use as a factor in drug and other disorders. In C. L. Jones and R. J. Battjes (Eds.), *Etiology of drug abuse: Implications for prevention* (NIDA Research Monograph No. 56, DHHS Publication No. ADM 85-1335, pp. 178–192). Washington, DC: U.S. Government Printing Office.

Robins, R. W., John, O. P., and Caspi, A. (1994). Major dimensions of personality in early adolescence: The Big Five and beyond. In C. F. Halverson Jr., G. A. Kohnstamm, and R. P. Martin (Eds.), *The developing structure of temperament and personality from infancy to adulthood* (pp. 267–292). Hillsdale, NJ: Lawrence Erlbaum.

Robinson, W. S. (1950). Ecological correlations and the behavior of individuals. *American Sociological Review, 15,* 351–357.

Roff, M., and Sells, S. B. (1968). Juvenile delinquency in relation to peer acceptance-rejection and socio-economic status. *Psychology in Schools, 5,* 3–18.

Roncek, D. W., and Faggiani, D. (1985). High schools and crime: A replication. *Sociological Quarterly, 26,* 491–505.

Roncek, D. W., and Lobosco, A. (1983). The effect of high schools on crime in their neighborhoods. *Social Science Quarterly, 64,* 598–613.

Rose, G., and Marshall, T. F. (1974). *Counselling and school social work: An experimental study.* London: John Wiley and Sons.

Rosenblum, S., and Louis, K. (1979). *Stability and change: Innovation in an educational context.* Cambridge, MA: ABT Associates.

Rosenthal, R., and Rubin, D. B. (1982). A simple, general purpose display of magnitude of experimental effect. *Journal of Educational Psychology, 74,* 166–169.

Ross, J. G., Saavedra, P. J., Shur, G. H., Winters, F., and Felner, R. D. (1992). The effectiveness of an after-school program for primary grade latchkey students on precursors of substance abuse. *Journal of Community Psychology, OSAP* special issue, 22–38.

Rossman, G. B., Corbett, H. D., and Firestone, W. A. (1988). *Change and effectiveness in schools: A cultural perspective.* Albany: State University of New York Press.

Rotheram, M. J. (1982). Social skills training with underachievers, disruptive, and exceptional children. *Psychology in the Schools, 19,* 532–539.

Rotheram, M. J., Armstrong, M., and Booraem, C. (1982). Assertiveness training in fourth- and fifth-grade children. *American Journal of Community Psychology, 10,* 567–582.

Rowan, B. (1990). Commitment and control: Alternative strategies for the organizational design of schools. In C. B. Cazden (Ed.), *Review of research in education* (Vol. 16, pp. 353–392). Washington, DC: American Educational Research Association.

Rubin, K. H., and Krasnor, L. R. (1986). Social cognitive and social behavioral perspectives on problem solving. In M. Perlmutter (Ed.), *Cognitive perspectives on children's social and behavioral development: The Minnesota Symposia on child psychology* (Vol. 18, pp. 1–68). Hillsdale, NJ: Lawrence Erlbaum.

Runkel, P. J., and Bell, W. E. (1976). Some conditions affecting a school's readiness to profit from OD training. *Education and Urban Society, 8,* 127–144.

Rutter, M., Maughan, B., Mortimore, P., and Ouston, J. with Smith, A. (1979). *Fifteen thousand hours: Secondary schools and their effects on children.* Wells: Open Books.

Safer, D. J., Heaton, R. C., and Parker, F. C. (1982). A contingency management program for disruptive junior high school students: Results and follow-up. In D. J. Safer (Ed.), *School programs for disruptive adolescents* (pp. 241–253). Baltimore: University Park Press.

Sampson, R. J. (1987). Communities and crime. In M. R. Gottfredson and T. Hirschi (Eds.), *Positive criminology* (pp. 91–114). Newbury Park, CA: Sage.

——— (1995). The community. In J. Q. Wilson and J. Petersilia (Eds.), *Crime* (pp. 193–216). San Francisco: ICS Press.

Sampson, R. J., and Laub, J. H. (1993). *Crime in the making: Pathways and turning points through life.* Cambridge, MA: Harvard University Press.

Sampson, R. J., Raudenbush, S. W., and Earls, F. (1997). Neighborhoods and violent crime: A multilevel study of collective efficacy. *Science, 277,* 918–924.

Sarason, I. G., and Sarason, B. R. (1981). Teaching cognitive and social skills to high school students. *Journal of Consulting and Clinical Psychology, 49,* 908–918.

Sarvela, P. D., and McClendon, E. J. (1987). An impact evaluation of a rural youth drug education program. *Journal of Drug Education, 17*, 213–231.

Schafer, W., and Polk, K. (1972). *Schools and delinquency.* Englewood Cliffs, NJ: Prentice-Hall.

Schaps, E., Bartolo, R. D., Moskowitz, J., Palley, C. S., and Churgin, S. (1981). A review of 127 drug abuse prevention evaluations. *Journal of Drug Issues, 11*, 17–43.

Schaps, E., Moskowitz, J. M., Condon, J. W., and Malvin, J. (1984). A process and outcome evaluation of an affective teacher training primary prevention program. *Journal of Alcohol and Drug Education, 29*, 35–64.

Schinke, S. P., Botvin, G. J., and Orlandi, M. A. (1991). *Substance abuse in children and adolescents: Evaluation and interventions.* Newbury Park, CA: Sage.

Schmidt, F. L. (1996). Statistical significance testing and cumulative knowledge in psychology: Implications for training of researchers. *Psychological Methods, 1*, 115–129.

Schneider, B. (1996). School, parent, and community involvement: The federal government invests in social capital. In K. M. Borman, P. W. Cookson Jr., A. R. Sadovnik, and J. Z. Spade (Eds.), *Implementing educational reform: Sociological perspectives on educational policy* (pp. 193–214). Norwood, NJ: Ablex.

Shaw, C. R., and McKay, H. D. (1969). *Juvenile delinquency and urban areas: A study of rates of delinquency in relation to differential characteristics of local communities in American cities* (rev. ed.). Chicago: University of Chicago Press.

Shedler, J., and Block, J. (1990). Adolescent drug use and psychological health: A longitudinal inquiry. *American Psychologist, 45*, 612–630.

Sheley, J. F., McGee, Z. T., and Wright, J. D. (1995). *Weapon-related victimization in selected inner-city high school samples.* Washington, DC: National Institute of Justice.

Sherman, L. W., Gottfredson, D. C., MacKenzie, D., Eck, J., Reuter, P., and Bushway, S. (1997). *Preventing crime: What works, what doesn't, what's promising: A report to the United States Congress.* Washington, D.C.: U.S. Department of Justice, Office of Justice Programs.

Shichor, D. (1975). Perceived "school-experience" of "continuing" and "non-continuing" delinquents in Israel. *Dritte Welt, 4*, 143–156.

Shure, M. B., and Spivack, G. (1979). Interpersonal cognitive problem solving and primary prevention: Programming for preschool and kindergarten children. *Journal of Clinical Child Psychology, 8*, 89–94.

 (1980). Interpersonal problem solving as a mediator of behavioral adjustment in preschool and kindergarten children. *Journal of Applied Developmental Psychology, 1*, 29–44.

 (1982). Interpersonal problem-solving in young children: A cognitive approach to prevention. *American Journal of Community Psychology, 10*, 341–356.

Sickmund, M. H., Snyder, H., and Poe-Yamagata, E. (1997). *Juvenile offenders and victims: 1997 update on violence – statistics summary.* Washington, DC: U.S. Department of Justice, Office of Juvenile Justice and Delinquency Prevention.

Silvia, E. S., and Thorne, J. (1997). *School-based drug prevention programs: A longitudinal study in selected school districts.* Research Triangle Park, NC: Research Triangle Institute.

Simcha-Fagan, O., and Schwartz, J. E. (1986). Neighborhood and delinquency: An assessment of contextual effects. *Criminology, 24,* 667–703.

Skager, R., and Fisher, D. G. (1989). Substance use among high school students in relation to school characteristics. *Addictive Behavior, 14,* 129–138.

Skroban, S. B., Gottfredson, D. C., and Gottfredson, G. D. (1999). A school-based social competency development promotion demonstration. *Evaluation Review, 23*(1), 3–27.

Slicker, E. K., and Palmer, D. J. (1993). Mentoring at-risk high school students: Evaluation of a school-based program. *School Counselor, 40,* 327–334.

Smith, D., and Tomlinson, S. (1989). *The school effect.* London: Policy Studies Institute.

Smith, G. W., and Fogg, C. P. (1978). Psychological predictors of early use, late use, and nonuse of marijuana among teenage students. In D. Kandel (Ed.), *Longitudinal research on drug use: Empirical findings and methodological issues* (pp. 101–113). Washington, DC: Hemisphere-Wiley.

Smith, L., Ross, S., and Nunnery, J. (1997, April). *Increasing the chances of Success for All: The relationship between program implementation quality and student achievement at eight inner-city schools.* Paper presented at the annual meeting of the American Educational Research Association, Chicago.

Smith, P. K., and Sharp, S. (1994). *School bullying: Insights and perspectives.* London: Routledge.

Snyder, H. N. (1997, November). *Juvenile Justice Bulletin: Juvenile arrests, 1996.* Washington, DC: U.S. Department of Justice, Office of Justice Programs.

Snyder, J., Dishion, T. J., and Patterson, G. R. (1986). Determinants and consequences of associating with deviant peers during preadolescence and adolescence. *Journal of Early Adolescence, 6,* 29–43.

Social Action Research Center. (1979). *The school team approach Phase I evaluation* (Grant Nos. 77-NI-99-0012 and 78-JN-AX-0016). San Rafael, CA: Author.

Solomon, D., Watson, M. S., Delucchi, K. L., Schaps, E., and Battistich, V. (1988). Enhancing children's prosocial behavior in the classroom. *American Educational Research Journal, 25,* 527–554.

Spivack, G., and Cianci, N. (1987). High-risk early behavior pattern and later delinquency. In J. D. Burchard and S. N. Burchard (Eds.), *Prevention of delinquent behavior* (pp. 44–74). Beverly Hills, CA: Sage.

Stage, S. A., and Quiroz, D. R. (1997). A meta-analysis of interventions to decrease disruptive classroom behavior in public education settings. *School Psychology Review, 26,* 333–368.

Stallings, J. (1985). A study of implementation of Madeline Hunter's model and its effects on students. *Journal of Educational Research, 78,* 325–337.

Steffensmeier, D. J., Allan, E. A., Harer, M. D., and Streifel, C. (1989). Age and distribution of crime. *American Journal of Sociology, 94,* 803–831.

Stuart, R. B. (1974). Teaching facts about drugs: Pushing or preventing? *Journal of Educational Psychology, 66,* 189–201.

Tanioka, I., and Glaser, D. (1991). School uniforms, routine activities, and the social control of delinquency in Japan. *Youth and Society, 23,* 50–75.

Tellegen, A. (1982). *Brief manual for the Multidimensional Personality Question-naire.* Minneapolis: University of Minnesota Press.

Thompson, D. W., and Jason, L. A. (1988). Street gangs and preventive interventions. *Criminal Justice and Behavior, 15,* 323–333.

Thornberry, T. P., Esbensen, F.-A., and Van Kammen, W. B. (1993). Commitment to school and delinquency. In D. Huizinga, R. Loeber, and T. P. Thornberry (Eds.), *Urban delinquency and substance abuse* (technical report, pp. 10/1–10/26). Washington, DC: U.S. Department of Justice, Office of Juvenile Justice and Delinquency Prevention.

Thornberry, T. P., Lizotte, A. J., Krohn, M. D., Farnworth, M., and Jang, S. J. (1991). Testing interactional theory: An examination of reciprocal causal relationships among family, school, and delinquency. *Journal of Criminal Law and Criminology, 82,* 3–35.

—— (1994). Delinquent peers, beliefs, and delinquent behavior: A longitudinal test of interactional theory. *Criminology, 32,* 47–84.

Thornberry, T. P., Moore, M., and Christenson, R. L. (1985). Dropping out of high school on subsequent criminal behavior. *Criminology, 23,* 3–18.

Tierney, J. P., Grossman, J. B., and Resch, N. L. (1995). *Making a difference: An impact study of Big Brothers/Big Sisters.* Philadelphia: Public/Private Ventures.

Timmer, S. G., Eccles, J., and O'Brien, I. (1985). How children use time. In F. T. Juster and F. B. Stafford (Eds.), *Time, goods, and wellbeing* (pp. 353–382). Ann Arbor: University of Michigan Institute for Social Research.

Tobler, N. S. (1986). Meta-analysis of 143 adolescent drug prevention programs: Quantitative outcome results of program participants compared to a control or comparison group. *Journal of Drug Issues, 16,* 537–567.

—— (1992). Drug prevention programs can work: Research findings. *Journal of Addictive Diseases, 11,* 1–28.

Tobler, N. S., and Stratton, H. H. (1997). Effectiveness of school-based drug prevention programs: A meta-analysis of the research. *Journal of Primary Prevention, 18,* 71–128.

Toby, J. (1980). Crime in American public schools. *Public Interest, 58,* 29–32.

—— (1983). Crime in the schools. In J. Q. Wilson (Ed.), *Crime and public policy* (pp. 69–88). San Francisco: ICS Press.

—— (1995). The schools. In J. Q. Wilson and J. Petersilia (Eds.), *Crime* (pp. 141–170). San Francisco: ICS Press.

Tolson, E. R., McDonald, S., and Moriarty, A. R. (1992). Peer mediation among high school students: A test of effectiveness. *Social Work in Education, 14,* 86–93.

Torstensson, M. (1990). Female delinquents in a birth cohort: Tests of some aspects of control theory. *Journal of Quantitative Criminology, 6,* 101–115.

Tremblay, R. E., Boulerice, B., Harden, P. W., McDuff, P., Pérusse, D., Pihl, R. O., and Zoccolillo, M. (1996). Do children in Canada become more aggressive as they approach adolescence? In Human Resources Development Canada, *Growing up in Canada: National longitudinal survey of children and youth* (pp. 127–138). Ottawa: Statistics Canada.

Tremblay, R. E., Kurtz, L., Mâsse, L. C., Vitaro, F., and Pihl, R. O. (1994). *A bimodal preventive intervention for disruptive kindergarten boys: Its impact*

REFERENCES **305**

through mid-adolescence. Montreal: University of Montreal, Research Unit on Children's Psycho-Social Maladjustment.

Tremblay, R. E., LeBlanc, M., and Schwartzman, A. E. (1988). The predictive power of first-grade peer and teacher ratings of behavior: Sex differences in antisocial behavior and personality at adolescence. *Journal of Abnormal Child Psychology, 16,* 571–583.

Tremblay, R. E., and Mâsse, L. C. (1993, November). *Cognitive defects, school achievement, disruptive behavior, and juvenile delinquency: A longitudinal look at their developmental sequence.* Paper presented at the annual meeting at the American Society of Criminology, Phoenix, AZ.

Tremblay, R. E., Mâsse, B., Perron, D., LeBlanc, M., Schwartzman, A. E., and Ledingham, J. E. (1992). Early disruptive behavior, poor school achievement, delinquent behavior, and delinquent personality: Longitudinal analyses. *Journal of Consulting and Clinical Psychology, 60,* 64–72.

Tremblay, R. E., McCord, J., Boileau, H., Charlebois, P., Gagnon, C., LeBlanc, M., and Larivée, S. (1991). Can disruptive boys be helped to become competent? *Psychiatry, 54,* 148–161.

Tremblay, R. E., Vitaro, F., Bertrand, L., LeBlanc, M., Beauchesne, H., Boileau, H., and David, L. (1992). Parent and child training to prevent early onset of delinquency: The Montreal Longitudinal-Experimental Study. In J. McCord and R. E. Tremblay (Eds.), *Preventing antisocial behavior: Interventions from birth through adolescence* (pp. 117–138). New York: Guilford Press.

Trice, A. D., Parker, F. C., and Safer, D. J. (1982). A comparison of senior high school interventions for disruptive students. In D. J. Safer (Ed.), *School programs for disruptive adolescents* (pp. 333–340). Baltimore: University Park Press.

Ullmann, C. A. (1957). Teachers, peers, and tests as predictors of adjustment. *Journal of Educational Psychology, 48,* 257–267.

U.S. Department of Justice, Federal Bureau of Investigation. (1993). *Age-specific arrest rates and race-specific arrest rates for selected offenses, 1965–1992.* Washington, DC: U.S. Government Printing Office.

Victor, J. B. (1994). The five-factor model applied to individual differences in school behavior. In C. F. Halverson Jr., G. A. Kohnstamm, and R. P. Martin (Eds.), *The developing structure of temperament and personality from infancy to adulthood* (pp. 355–366). Hillsdale, NJ: Lawrence Erlbaum.

Vroom, V. H., and Yetton, P. W. (1975). *Leadership and decision-making.* Pittsburgh: University of Pittsburgh Press.

Walker, H. M., Horner, R. H., Sugai, G., Bullis, M., Sprague, J. R., Bricker, D., and Kaufman, M. J. (1996). Integrated approaches to preventing antisocial behavior patterns among school-age children and youth. *Journal of Emotional and Behavioral Disorders, 4,* 194–209.

Ward, D. A., and Tittle, C. R. (1994). IQ and delinquency: A test of two competing explanations. *Journal of Quantitative Criminology, 10,* 189–212.

Weiner, L. (1990). Preparing the brightest for urban schools. *Urban Education, 25,* 258–273.

Weissberg, R. P., and Caplan, M. (1994, February). *Promoting social competence and preventing antisocial behavior in young urban adolescents.* Manuscript submitted for publication.

Weissberg, R. P., Gesten, E. L., Carnrike, C. L., Toro, P. A., Rapkin, B. D., Davidson, E., and Cowen, E. L. (1981). Social problem-solving skills training: A competence-building intervention with second- to fourth-grade children. *American Journal of Community Psychology, 9*, 411–423.

Weissberg, R. P., Gesten, E. L., Rapkin, B. D., Cowen, E. L., Davidson, E., Flores de Apodaca, R. F., and McKim, B. J. (1981). Evaluation of a social-problem-solving training program for suburban and inner-city third-grade children. *Journal of Consulting and Clinical Psychology, 49*, 251–261.

Weissberg, R. P., and Greenberg, M. T. (1997). School and community competence-enhancement and prevention programs. In W. Damon (Series Ed.), I. E. Sigel and K. A. Renniger (Vol. Eds.), *Handbook of child psychology: Vol 4. Child psychology in practice* (5th ed., pp. 877–954). New York: John Wiley and Sons.

West, D. J., and Farrington, D. P. (1973). *Who becomes delinquent?* London: Heinemann Educational Books.

Whitaker, C. J., and Bastian, L. D. (1991). *Teenage victims: A national crime survey report* (NCJ-128129). Washington, DC: Bureau of Justice Statistics.

Wiatrowski, M. D., Hansell, S., Massey, C. R., and Wilson, D. L. (1982). Curriculum tracking and delinquency. *American Sociological Review, 47*, 151–160.

Wilson, W. J. (1997). *When work disappears: The world of the new urban poor.* New York: Alfred A. Knopf.

Witte, J. F., and Walsh, D. J. (1990). A systematic test of the effective schools model. *Educational Evaluation and Policy Analysis, 12*, 188–212.

Wodarski, J. S., and Filipczak, J. (1982). Behavioral intervention in public schools: Long-term follow-up. In D. J. Safer (Ed.), *School programs for disruptive adolescents* (pp. 201–214). Baltimore: University Park Press.

Wolfgang, M. E., Figlio, R. M., and Sellin, T. (1972). *Delinquency in a birth cohort.* Chicago: University of Chicago Press.

Wright, W. E., and Dixon, M. C. (1977). Community prevention and treatment of juvenile delinquency: A review of evaluation studies. *Journal of Research in Crime and Delinquency, 14*, 35–67.

Wyant, S. H. (1974). Effects of organization development training on intra-staff communication in elementary schools (Doctoral dissertation, University of Oregon, 1974). *Dissertation Abstracts International, 35*, 3537-A.

Yoshikawa, H. (1994). Prevention as cumulative protection: Effects of early family support and education on chronic delinquency and its risks. *Psychological Bulletin, 115*, 28–54.

Zelie, K., Stone, C. I., and Lehr, E. (1980). Cognitive-behavioral intervention in school discipline: A preliminary study. *Personnel and Guidance Journal, 59*, 80–83.

Author Index

Aaron, P., 223, 232
Abbott, R. D., 124, 125
Acland, H., 68
Adan, A. M., 147, 151
Advani, N., 141, 265
Ageton, S. S., 28, 33
Ahlstrom, W., 214
Akers, R. L., 56
Alasaker, F. D., 128
Allan, E. A., 14
Allen, J. P., 217, 233
Allison, K. R., 89
Alwin, D. F., 68
American Psychiatric Association, 27
Arbuthnot, J., 202, 232
Armstrong, M., 182, 232
Arneklev, B. J., 48
Arthur, M. W., 26, 28
Ary, D., 25
Asarnow, J. R., 26
Asher, K. N., 175, 179
Asher, S. R., 32, 3

Bachman, J. G., 7, 16, 18, 28, 32
Baerveldt, C., 77, 78, 81
Bailey, J. S., 175
Baker, E., 104, 194, 197, 198, 233, 236
Bane, M. J., 68
Barber, R. M., 174
Bartolo, R. D., 215
Bartusch, D. R. J., 51
Bastian, L. D., 19, 20
Batson, H. W., 197, 198
Battistich, V., 126, 127, 233
Beaton, S., 69
Beauchesne, H., 173
Beauvais, F., 35, 36

Becker, H. J., 89
Beland, K., 175, 179
Bell, W. E., 239, 240
Bem, D. J., 38, 45
Ben-Avie, M., 130
Benn, R. T., 69
Bennett, A., 246
Benning, J. J., 28, 53
Berman, P., 236, 237, 238, 239, 240, 241
Bertrand, L., 173
Bess, V., 197, 198
Bidwell, C. E., 81
Biglan, A., 25
Block, J., 28, 29, 35, 64
Blumstein, A., 6
Boileau, H., 173
Bond, L., 73
Booraem, C., 182, 232
Borgatta, E. F., 22
Botvin, E. M., 104, 194, 109, 215, 233, 236
Boulerice, B., 13
Bowles, S., 2, 53
Boyle, M. C., 11
Braddock, J. H., II., 89
Brame, R., 51, 52, 56
Brannon, B., 22
Brenzel, B., 64, 65, 248
Brewer, D. D., 152
Bricker, D., 230
Brook, J. S., 28
Brooks, B. D., 217
Brooks-Gunn, J., 66
Brophy, T. E., 236
Brown, C. H., 121
Brown, M. M., 30
Bry, B. H., 192, 226
Bryk, A. S., 73, 74, 75, 82, 84, 87, 88, 246

307

AUTHOR INDEX

Subject Index